WORLD WITHOUT CANCER

The Story of Vitamin B_{17}

By G. Edward Griffin

This book is available also in a paperback edition from American Media

First Printing:	Dec.	1974
Second Printing:	Mar.	1975
Third Printing:	June	1975
Fourth Printing:	Jan.	1976
Fifth Printing:	May	1976
Sixth Printing:	June	1976

Library of Congress Catalog Card Number
74-83649

International Standard Book Number
(ISBN): 0-912986-08-5
Printed in The United States of America

American Media
P.O. Box 4646
Westlake Village
California 91359

Dedicated to the millions of cancer victims and their loved ones whose suffering has been the tragic cost of scientific arrogance and political vested interest. May the story presented in this book help to arouse an indignant public awareness which, alone, can break the hold of these deadly forces.

A NOTE OF APPRECIATION AND GRATITUDE

The material in this volume could not have been assembled without the help and guidance of many others. First of all, I am indebted to Dr. John Richardson for his persistent hammering away on the significance of vitamin therapy until it finally began to penetrate into this thick skull. And to my wife, Pat, who, for months prior, had attempted unsuccessfully to arouse my curiosity on the subject. I will always be indebted to Dr. Ernst T. Krebs, Jr., for his unbelievable patience and thoroughness in explaining and re-explaining so many scientific matters. I am grateful to Bruce Buchbinder, Ralph Bowman, Bob Bradford, Malvina Cassese, Frank Cortese, Jim Foley, Grace Hamilton, Mac and Idell Hays, Dr. J. Milton Hoffman, Pokie Korsgaard, Sanford Kraemer, Maurice LeCover, Bob Lee, Betty Lee Morales, Beverly Newkirk, John Pursely, Julie Richardson, Bob Riddel, Lorraine Rosenthal, Frank Salaman, Alice Tucker, Lloyd Wallace, Kimo Welch, Ann Yalian, and others too numerous to mention for their strong encouragement, endless patience, and tangible support.

TABLE OF CONTENTS

PART ONE:
THE SCIENCE OF CANCER THERAPY

TABLE OF CONTENTS

PART TWO: THE POLITICS OF CANCER THERAPY

FOREWORD

At the time of this writing, the FDA has banned the use of Laetrile in the treatment of cancer. Anyone who manufactures it, transports it across state lines, sells it, administers it, or even recommends it for such use is subject to legal harrassment, penalties, or imprisonment. Therefore, even though this entire volume is in defense of Laetrile, it must be clearly understood at the outset that I am a researcher, not a physician; I am not qualified to practice medicine in any way; and I am not recommending Laetrile in the treatment of cancer. If the reader is favorably impressed by the facts and opinions presented in the following pages, and if he decides to seek out Laetrile for his own use, he must do so entirely on his own evaluation of those facts and opinions, and not as a result of any "recommendation" on my part.

It was during the summer of 1971 that I first remember hearing the word Laetrile. Dr. John Richardson and I were sharing a short vacation in Oregon attempting to enjoy the natural beauties of that state. I say *attempting* because the good doctor, who is an extremely intense person, had brought his briefcase with him. It was not loaded with fishing gear. In fact, it yielded an almost endless supply of correspondence, research papers, and books all on the unlikely subject of "L-mandelonitrile-beta-glucuroniside in the Treatment of Human Cancer."

At first I had about as much interest in this topic as in learning about internal stresses in the construction of girder bridges. Undoubtedly, these are fascinating subjects to the physician and the engineer whose professions are wrapped around the minutiae of related theory and formula. But to me, the lush green forest and the babbling stream were objects infinitely more worthy of my attention, and I'm sure that my impatience had begun to show. But my determined companion continued with all the persistence of a bulldog with a fresh hold on a seat of pants. And he insisted that I read the first draft of a manuscript he had prepared with the possibility of submitting it for magazine publication.

In the course of reading that manuscript, I became aware for the first time that, although there was overwhelming evidence that vitamin therapy *is* effective in the treatment of cancer, apparently there were powerful forces at work to prevent this fact from being known. Reacting as most people do when they first hear this assertion, I remember asking skeptically, "Who are *they,* John? Why would anyone want to hold back a cure for cancer?"

With the asking of that question, my interest finally had been aroused and, even though I wouldn't have believed it at the time, I was already embarked upon a course of inquiry that was to lead to the uncovering of one of the most amazing stories of the Twentieth Century.

The ambitious purpose of this book is to present at least the highlights of that story and to answer the question "Who are *they* , John?"

G. Edward Griffin
September 10, 1974

PART ONE

The Science of Cancer Therapy

I

THE WATERGATE SYNDROME

Examples of FDA dishonesty and corruption; a close look at the primary scientific study which declared Laetrile (vitamin B_{17}) "of no value;" the proof that such study was fraudulent; the FDA's ruling against the use of Laetrile because it had not been tested; and its refusal then to allow anyone to test it.

This year 350,000 Americans will die from cancer. One out of four of us will develop cancer in our lifetime. That is over fifty million people in the United States alone.

The purpose of the following study is to show that this great human tragedy can be stopped *now* entirely on the basis of existing scientific knowledge.

We will explore the theory that cancer, like scurvy or pellagra, is a deficiency disease aggravated by the lack of an essential food compound in modern man's diet, and that its ultimate control is to be found simply in restoring this substance to our daily intake.

What you are about to read does not carry the approval of organized medicine. The Food and Drug Administration, the American Cancer Society, and the American Medical Association have labelled it fraud and quackery. In fact, the FDA and other agencies of government have used every means at their disposal to prevent this story from being told. They have arrested citizens for holding public meetings to tell others of their convictions on this subject. They have confiscated films and books. They even now are prosecuting doctors who apply these theories in an effort to save the lives of their own patients.

The attitude of Big Brother, expressed bluntly in 1971 by Grant Leake, Chief of the fraud section of California's food and drug bureau, is this: "We're going to protect them even if some of them don't want to be protected."[1]

Early in 1974, the California medical board brought formal charges against Stewart M. Jones, M.D., for using Laetrile in the treatment of cancer patients. It was learned later, however, that Dr. Julius Levine, one of the members of that board, *himself* had been using Laetrile in the treatment of his own cancer. When Dr. Jones' case came up for review, the political pressures were so great that Dr. Levine felt compelled to resign from his post rather than come out openly in support of Dr. Jones and his patients.[2]

All of this is happening in a land which boasts

[1] "Debate Over Laetrile," *Time*, April 12, 1971.

[2] "Laetrile Tiff, State Medic Out," *San Jose Mercury* (Calif.), April 10, 1974.

of freedom and whose symbol is the Statue of Liberty. For the first time in our history, people are being forced to flee *from* our shores as medical emigrants seeking freedom of choice and sovereignty over their own bodies. Laetrile has been available in Australia, Brazil, Belgium, Costa Rica, England, Germany, Greece, India, Israel, Italy, Japan, Lebanon, Mexico, Peru, the Philippines, Spain, Switzerland, the U.S.S.R., Venezuela, and Vietnam—but government authorities do not permit it in the land of the free.

In spite of all this, however, an increasing number of doctors are beginning to defy the bureaucracy, and are testing and proving in their own clinics that the vitamin concept of cancer is true.

With billions of dollars spent each year in research, with additional billions taken in from the cancer-related sale of drugs, and with vote-hungry politicians promising ever-increasing government programs, we find that, today, there are far more people making a living from cancer than are dying from it. If the riddle were to be solved by a simple vitamin, this gigantic commercial and political industry could be wiped out overnight. The result is that the *science* of cancer therapy is not nearly as complicated as the *politics* of cancer therapy.

If there was one beneficial aspect of the much-publicized Watergate scandals of the Seventies, it was in the awakening of even the most trustingly naive citizen to the reality that not all government officials tell the truth. And when caught in such "mendacities," they invariably claim that they did so only to protect the national security, the public health, or to promote some other equally noble objective.

This Watergate syndrome is not new. Several years ago, an FDA agent who had testified in court against a Kansas City businessman was forced to admit under cross-examination that he had lied under oath no less than twenty-eight times. When the defense attorney asked him if he regretted what he had done, his reply was, "No. I don't have any regrets. I wouldn't hesitate to tell a lie if it would help the American consumer."[1]

During this same trial it was learned that the FDA had used wire taps to make secret tape recordings of the defendant's phone conversations. Reminiscent of Watergate, when the judge ordered these recordings to be handed over, the FDA officer replied: "We don't have any tapes; we don't have them. They've been erased!"

The FDA is not squeamish over its tactics to "help the American consumer." When a businessman falls into disfavor with the bureaucracy, then there are no holds barred, and the law is used, not as a *reason* for attack, but as a *weapon* of attack. In other words, the FDA does not take action because the law says it should. It does so because it *wants* to, and then searches through the law for a legal excuse.

In the celebrated case of U.S. *vs* Dextra Fortified Sugar, for instance, the FDA had ruled that it was "misbranding" to fortify sugar with vi-

---

[1]As quoted by Omar Garrison, *The Dictocrats,* (Books for Today, Ltd., 1970, Chicago-London-Melbourne), p. 130.

tamins and minerals and still call it sugar. But the court ruled otherwise, pointing out:

> The basic flaw in the government's case is that it is seeking, under the guise of misbranding charges, to prohibit the sale of a food in the market place simply because it is not in sympathy with its use.

The controversy surrounding Dr. Andrew Ivy's anti-cancer drug known as Krebiozen is well-known. It should be remembered, though, that, prior to crossing swords with the FDA, Dr. Ivy had been widely acknowledged as one of the nation's foremost medical specialists. As head of the University of Illinois clinical sciences department, he had prepared 350 candidates for the graduate degrees of Doctor of Philosophy (Ph.D.) and Master of Science (M.S.). He was an American representative at the Nuremberg trials after World War II in Germany. The American Medical Association had awarded him bronze, silver, and gold medals in recognition of his outstanding work in the field of medicine. He had written over a thousand articles published in scientific and medical journals. In fact, the FDA itself often had called upon him as an expert to offer medical testimony in court. But when he began to use an unorthodox approach to cancer therapy, overnight he was branded as a "quack."

During the course of Dr. Ivy's trial, a letter was read into the court record written by a doctor from Indianapolis. The doctor stated in his letter that he was treating a patient who had multiple tumors, and that a biopsy of the tissue had shown these tumors to be cancerous. The doctor said that he had obtained Krebiozen from Dr. Ivy's laboratories, and had administered it, but that it had done absolutely no good whatsoever. When called to the witness stand, however, the doctor's answers were vague and evasive. Under the pressure of close cross-examination, he finally broke down and admitted that he never had treated such a patient, never had ordered the biopsy in question, and never had used Krebiozen even once. The whole story had been a lie. Why did he give false testimony? His reply was that one of the FDA agents had written the letter and asked him to sign it. He did so because he wanted to help the agency put an end to quackery.[1]

In September of 1963, the FDA released a report to the effect that Krebiozen was, for all practical purposes, the same as creatine, a common substance that was found in every hamburger. To prove this point, they also released a photographic overlay supposedly showing the spectrograms of Krebiozen and creatine superimposed one over the other. These were dutifully published in *Life* magazine and in other prominent segments of the mass communications media as "unimpeachable proof" that Krebiozen was useless.

When Senator Paul Douglas saw the spectrograms, he was suspicious. So he asked Dr. Scott Anderson, one of the nation's foremost authorities

---

[1] *Ibid.*, pp. 134, 135.

on spectrograms, to make his own study. Using completely standard techniques of spectrogram analysis, Dr. Anderson identified twenty-nine differences between spectrograms of the two substances. Furthermore, there were sixteen chemical and color differences. The version released to the press by the FDA had been carefully moved off center until there was a maximum *appearance* of similarity, but when restored to the true axis, the two were as different as night and day.[1]

On December 5, 1971, *The Indianapolis Star* published a lengthy letter condemning Dr. Ivy and his Krebiozen. It was the typical FDA line about quackery, and fraud, and the false hopes that allegedly lead poor cancer victims to delay "really effective" therapy until it is too late. It was signed by a John T. Walden, Deputy Assistant Commissioner for Public Affairs, Krebs Laboratories, San Francisco.

Krebs Laboratories of San Francisco is owned by Dr. E. T. Krebs, Jr., co-discoverer of vitamin B_{17} and pioneer in the development of Laetrile. A letter from *his* organization, not only condemning Dr. Ivy but praising orthodox cancer therapy —well, *that* was news! Upon investigation, however, it was shown that: (1) Krebs Laboratories did not have a Commissioner of Public Affairs, (2) it had never heard of John T. Walden, (3) it had never presumed to make any tests of Krebiozen, and (4) it held Dr. Ivy "in the highest esteem as one of the great physiologists of our generation."

---

[1]*Ibid.*, pp. 278-280.

No one knows, of course, who sent the bogus letter. But several questions are worth considering. First of all, who would *want* to? Second, who would have enough details of events and places to write such a letter? Third, who would be able to repeat the FDA line so faithfully and completely? Fourth, who would be sufficiently familiar with large government bureaucracies as even to *invent* such a title as "Commissioner of Public Affairs?" And fifth, since the whole thing was obviously a lie, who would go out of his way to tell such a lie even "in the public interest?"

The tactics used against Laetrile have been even more dishonest than those against Krebiozen. Perhaps the most damaging of them has been a pseudo-scientific report released in 1953 by the Cancer Commission of the California Medical Association. Published in the April issue of *California Medicine,* the report presented an impressive collection of charts and technical data indicating that exhaustive research had been carried out into every aspect of Laetrile. Its molecular composition had been analysed, its chemical action studied, its effect on tumor-bearing rats observed, and its effectiveness on human cancer patients determined. The stern conclusion of all this supposedly objective research was stated: "No satisfactory evidence has been produced to indicate any significant cytotoxic effect of Laetrile on the cancer cell."

The conclusions of this California Report are sufficient for most physicians and researchers. Not one in ten thousand has ever even seen Laetrile, much less used it. Yet, they all *know* that Laetrile does not work because the California AMA Cancer Commission *said* so, and they have had no reason to question the reliability of those who did the work.

Reporter Tom Valentine interviewed many leading cancer specialists to determine what they thought about Laetrile. Here he describes a typical reaction:

> Dr. Edwin Mirand of Roswell Memorial Hospital in Buffalo, N.Y., said: "We've looked into it and found it has no value." When asked if the renowned little hospital, which deals only with cancer, actually tested Laetrile, Dr. Mirand said, "No, we didn't feel it was necessary after others of good reputation had tested it and found it had no effectiveness in the treatment of cancer." He referred, as all authorities do, to the California Report.[1]

Others have run up against the same stone wall. Professional researcher, David Martin, reported this experience:

> The cancer expert in question, as I had anticipated, told me that Laetrile was "sugar pills." Had he told me that he had used Laetrile experimentally on X number of patients and found it completely ineffective, I might have been impressed. But when I asked him whether

---

[1] "Government Is Suppressing Cancer Control," *The National Tattler*, March 11, 1973, p. 2.

> he had ever used it himself, he said that he had not. When I asked him whether he had ever travelled abroad to study the experience with Laetrile therapy in Germany, Italy, Mexico, the Philippines, or other countries, he replied that he had not. And when I asked him if he had ever made a first-hand study of the pros and cons of the subject, again he conceded that he had not. He was simply repeating what he had heard from others who, in turn, were probably repeating what they had heard from others, going all the way back to the antiquated 1953 report of the California Cancer Commission.[1]

It is important, therefore, to know something of the nature of the California Report and of the scientific integrity of those who drafted it.

Although the report as published in *California Medicine* was unsigned, it was written by two men: Dr. Ian MacDonald, Chairman, and Dr. Henry Garland, Secretary. Dr. MacDonald was a prominent cancer surgeon, and Dr. Garland was an internationally famous radiologist. Both are listed in *Who's Who*.

There were seven other prominent physicians on the commission—including four more surgeons, another radiologist, and a pathologist — but they played no major part in the preparation of the report. None of these men—*not even MacDonald or*

[1]*Cancer News Journal,* January/April, 1971, p. 22.

Garland—had ever used Laetrile in first-hand experiments of their own. All they had done was to make *evaluations* and *summaries* of the written records of others.

Before examining those evaluations and summaries, let us first recall that MacDonald and Garland were the two physicians who had made national headlines claiming that there was no connection between cigarette smoking and lung cancer. In an address before the Public Health Section of the Commonwealth Club of San Francisco on July 9, 1964, Dr. Garland had said:

> A current widely held hypothesis is that cigarette smoking is causally related to a vast number of different diseases, ranging from cancer to coronary arteriosclerosis. After studying the question for several years, notably in its reported relationship to primary bronchial cancer, it is my considered opinion that the hypothesis is not proven . . . .
>
> Cigarettes in moderation are regarded by many as one of the better tranquilizers . . . . It is likely that obesity is a greater hazard to American health than cigarettes.

Dr. MacDonald was even more emphatic. In a feature article in *U.S. News & World Report,* he is shown, smiling, with a cigarette in his hand, and is quoted as saying that smoking is "a harmless pastime up to twenty-four cigarettes per day." And then he added:

> One could modify an old slogan: A pack a day keeps lung cancer away.[1]

It is a curious fact that it was precisely at this time that cigarette manufacturers were fighting to recover their loss of sales that resulted from growing public concern over lung cancer. In fact, the tobacco industry had already pledged the first ten million dollars out of a total of eighteen million to the AMA for "research" into the question of smoking and health.

The effect of this veritable flood of money from a source with, shall we say, "a vested interest" in the outcome of the research, was incredible and did *not* speak well for the AMA. The result was the conversion of a relatively simple, straight-forward project into a monstrous boondoggle of confusion and waste.

In the report of the AMA's Committee for Research on Tobacco and Health, it says:

> To date, approximately $14 million has been awarded [from the tobacco industry] to 203 individual research projects at 90 universities and institutions. As a direct result of these grants, 450

[1]"Here's Another View: Tobacco May be Harmless," *U.S. News & World Report,* Aug. 2, 1957, pp. 85, 86.

> reports have been published in scientific journals and periodicals.[1]

The report then listed the research projects and described their purposes. Here are just a few:

> *Nicotine Receptors in Identified Cells of the Snail Brain.*
>
> *The Effects of Nicotine on Behavior of Mice.*
>
> *Angina Pectoris and Bronchitis in Relation to Smoking – A Study in American and Swedish Twin Roosters.*
>
> *Post-Maturity Syndrome in the Pregnant Rat After Nicotine Absorption During Pregnancy.*
>
> *Interactions of Nicotine, Caffeine and Alcohol in Squirrel Monkeys.*
>
> *The Effect of Smoking in Placental Oxygen Transfer in Gravid Ewes.*
>
> *Urinary Excretion, Tissue Distribution and Destruction of Nicotine in Monkey and Dog.*

---

[1]*Third Research Conference*, Committee for Research on Tobacco and Health, AMA Education and Research Foundation, May 7-9, 1972, p. 4.

Body Build and Mortality in 105,000 World War II Army Veterans.

Upon going through the back reports of the AMA's Committee for Research on Tobacco and Health, one is able to count but five research projects that are primarily concerned with cancer. One of those dealt with laboratory testing procedures only, and another was an experiment to see if tobacco smoke could be used to *cure* cancer of the skin! So only *three* of these projects really dealt with the area of major public concern. Three out of two hundred and three is only about one-and-a-half percent—which tells us something about the AMA's scientific integrity on the subject of smoking and cancer.

With the expenditure of a mere eighteen million dollars—which is small, indeed, compared to the tobacco industry's advertising budget over the same period—it was possible to direct the AMA's medical research away from the important question of cancer and into a hundred giddy questions that served only to confuse and delay the ultimate truth.

Dazzled by the meteor shower of thousand dollar bills, the AMA, in its December 1959 issue of the *American Medical Association Journal,* dutifully published an editorial stating flatly that there was insufficient evidence "to warrant the assumption" that cigarette smoking was the principal factor in the increase of lung cancer. Furthermore, through its gargantuan research program, the AMA was making it increasingly difficult to obtain that evidence.

Was there any connection between the eighteen million dollars given to the AMA from the tobacco industry and the public pronouncements of MacDonald and Garland, two of its most prominent members in California? Perhaps not, although it has been rumored that these gentlemen of science actually did receive $50,000 for their "testimonials."[1]

Whether or not this is true, of course, is not important now. What *is* important is the fact that their medical opinion, if it had been widely followed, clearly would have resulted in the suffering and death of untold additional millions. Also important is the fact that these are the same "experts" whose medical opinion *is* being widely quoted and followed today in the question of Laetrile.

An interesting footnote to this subject is the fact that Dr. MacDonald was burned to death in bed a few years later in a fire started by his own cigarette. Dr. Garland, who had boasted of chain-smoking since early childhood and who had claimed to be living proof that cigarettes were harmless, a few years later died of lung cancer.

In 1963, ten years after the publication of the original California Report, the California State Department of Health officially decreed that the findings of the antiquated study were "true," and adopted them as its own. When it did so, however, it performed an unexpected favor for the public, because it published for the first time all the original

---

[1]See *The Immoral Banning of Vitamin* B_{17}, by Stewart M. Jones, M.S., M.D., Ph.D., Palo Alto, Calif., Jan., 1974, p. 1. Also *Cancer News Journal*, Jan./April, 1971, p. 3.

experiments and studies upon which the report had been based and, in doing so, it made available the documentary evidence proving that MacDonald and Garland had *falsified* their summary of those experiments.

In the 1953 report, the authors published the conclusions of John W. Mehl, M.D., to the effect that cyanide could not be released from Laetrile. As will be explained in a later chapter, the release of cyanide at the cancer cell is part of the reason that Laetrile works. Implying that cyanide *cannot* be produced, therefore, was a severe blow to the credibility of Laetrile theory. Dr. Mehl was quoted as saying: "These results are inconclusive, and will be extended, but they do not support the claims made for Laetrile."

With the publication of the original experiments ten years later, however, quite a different story emerged. Buried in a maze of statistics, tables, and charts, can be found an item labeled "Laetrile Report Appendix 4." It is a laboratory report signed by G. Schroetenboer and W. Wolman. It states:

> After refluxing for three hours, the odor of hydrogen cyanide could be detected . . . . The hydrogen cyanide was distilled into sodium hydroxide and determined by the Prussian Blue technique.[1]

---

[1]*Report by Cancer Advisory Council on Treatment of Cancer with Beta-Cyanogenic Glucosides ("Laetriles")*, California Department of Public Health, 1963, Appendix 4, pp. 1,2.

This report was dated January 14, 1953—two months *before* Dr. Mehl claimed that cyanide could not be released from Laetrile. It is significant, therefore, that MacDonald and Garland completely ignored the positive report while giving prominence to the negative one.

Since that time, of course, the release of cyanide from Laetrile has been confirmed by the AMA's chemical lab, by the cytochemistry section of the National Cancer Institute, and even by the California Department of Public Health. This is the same California Department of Public Health that then officially pronounced the original report to be "true" and adopted it as its own.

Another claim made by Drs. MacDonald and Garland was that microscopic examinations of tumors from patients who had been treated with Laetrile showed absolutely no indication of favorable chemical effect. Ten years later, however, this assertion was shown to be a bald-faced lie. Appendix Three contains the findings of two pathologists who stated in plain English that they *did* observe anti-tumor effects which, indeed, could have been caused by the Laetrile. In a statement dated December 15, 1952, for instance, John W. Budd, M.D., reported:

> Case 1M . . . . Hemorrhagic necrosis of tumor is extensive . . . . An interpretation of chemotherapeutic effect might be entertained.

Also an autopsy report by J.L. Zundell,

dated September 10, 1952, discusses two clear cases of observed anti-tumor effect. It states:

> M-1 . . . . This might represent a chemical effect since the cells affected show coagulation necrosis and pyknosis . . . .
>
> M-3 . . . . There appears to be more degeneration in the tumor cells in the lymph node. I would consider this as a possible result of chemical agent . . . .
>
> Two cases . . . showed moderate changes . . . which might be considered as chemotherapeutic toxic cellular changes.[1]

What could be more plain than that? Nevertheless, MacDonald and Garland stated flatly in the California Report: *"No evidence of cytotoxic changes was observed by any of the consultants."*[2]

That statement, of course, was a lie of gigantic proportions.

Even if the findings of these independent researchers had not been falsely summarized by MacDonald and Garland, the 1953 California Report still would have been totally useless as a scientific verdict against Laetrile because the strength of the doses used on cancer patients was much too weak to prove anything. In fact, it was

---

[1]*Ibid.*, Appendix 3, pp. 1, 2.

[2]*Op. cit.*, p. 324.

about one-fiftieth of what generally is used now to obtain optimum results.

In the earlier days of Laetrile research, clinicians were cautiously administering only fifty to one-hundred milligrams at a time. Gaining confidence with experience, these levels gradually were raised until, by 1974, Laetrile was being used intravenously at levels of six to nine thousand milligrams daily. Generally, it takes an accumulation of fifty to seventy thousand milligrams over a period of about a week or ten days before the patient can report tangible indications of improvement. But in the experiments used for the California Report, the typical dose given was only about fifty milligrams per injection. The maximum single dose was less than two hundred milligrams, and the maximum accumulative dose was only two thousand milligrams spread over twelve injections. Five patients received only two injections, and five received only one.

It is not surprising, therefore, that the California experiments failed to produce conclusive evidence that Laetrile was effective against cancer. As Dr. Krebs observed at the time, "There is nothing quite so easy to accomplish as failure."

In spite of all the incredible distortions of fact and the perversions of scientific truth, Drs. MacDonald and Garland were forced to admit on page three of their California Report:

> All of the physicians whose patients were reviewed spoke of increase in the sense of well-being and appetite, gain in weight, and decrease in pain . . . .

Then, attempting to belittle these important results, they added:

> . . . as though these observations constituted evidence of definite therapeutic effect.

That statement, alone, should have disqualified the California Report, for these observations *are*, indeed, among the very things which indicate to a physician whether or not his drug therapy is effective.[1] Most doctors would be ecstatically happy if they could cause their cancer patients to experience an increase in a sense of well-being and appetite, a gain in weight, and especially a decrease in pain.

The California Report has remained for over two decades as the primary authority cited by cancer "experts" *ad nauseum* and as the basis of legal restraints against Laetrile. Yet, it was the product of bias, not objectivity. It was calculated to deceive, not to clarify. It was fiat, not science.

In addition to the California Report, there have been several other less publicized studies of Laetrile supposedly by qualified and reputable organizations. These include a 1953 project at Stanford University, a series of tests in 1960 at the National Cancer Institute, a 1961 study at the University of California at Berkeley, one in 1962 at the Diablo Labs at Berkeley, and a 1965 study on behalf of the Canadian Medical Association at McGill University in Montreal. Incredible as it may seem, every

[1]Lang, *Current Diagnosis and Treatment*, 1972, p. 902.

one of these has been tarnished by exactly the same kind of scientific ineptitude, bias, and outright deception as found in the 1953 California Report. Some of these studies openly admitted evidence of anti-cancer effect but hastened to attribute this effect to other causes. Some were toxicity studies only, which means that they weren't even trying to see if Laetrile was effective, but merely to determine how much of it was required to kill the patient. In every case, these studies dealt either with tumors transplanted into mice or with tumors *in vitro,* which means in a laboratory incubation dish not connected to living tissue in any way. Human beings with genuine spontaneous tumors were never observed.

It is obvious that transplanted tumors do not necessarily respond the same as spontaneous tumors, and that the metabolism of rodents is not necessarily the same as that of man, and certainly that tissue in a dish is not the same as that connected to and nourished by a living organism.

In most of these experiments, the only criterion used to measure the success of Laetrile was reduction in tumor size. This may sound reasonable at first, but one must realize that most tumors are a mixture of malignant and benign cells, and that the transplanted tumors used on laboratory mice contain only about three or four percent outright cancer tissue. The more malignant tissues generally are rejected by the healthy mouse and cannot be successfully transplanted. It can be seen, therefore, that even if Laetrile eliminated one hundred percent of the cancer, these tumors would be reduced only three or four percent *at the most.* Life extension, not tumor size, is the only meaningful test of therapeutic success.

In the 1963 update of the California Report, the Cancer Advisory Council attempted to defend its previous use of inadequate doses of Laetrile by claiming that subsequent experiments were based upon up to 170 times the original levels, and *still* there was no "evidence of tumor control." These experiments, however, were performed on mice, not people. Transplanted tumors were used, not spontaneous ones; tumor reduction in size was the criterion of success, not life extension. And there is no record of how many injections were given or over what period of time—which means that, conceivably, only one injection was administered. And to make matters even worse, it is quite likely that, in some of the more recent experiments, a substance was used that wasn't even Laetrile.

Dr. Dean Burk, head of the Cytochemistry section of the National Cancer Institute, confirmed this when he said:

> I have been given to understand by Dr. Jonathan Hartwell of the Drug Development Branch of NCI that the amygdalin [Laetrile] material employed was of questionable origin and chemical authenticity.[1]

Dr. Bayard Morrison, assistant director of the Na-

[1] "*High Politics Blamed for Refusal to Test Anti-Cancer Agent,*" by Don C. Matchan, Alameda *Times-Star,* July 14, 1970, p. 2.

tional Cancer Institute, is unconvinced that Laetrile has value. Nevertheless, he agrees with Dr. Burk, and has said:

> We can't say that Laetrile is no good without further proof.[1]

In 1973, after many months of extensive Laetrile studies on mice, the Southern Research Institute in Birmington, Alabama released an extensive report of it's findings to the National Cancer Institute in Washington. The NCI, in turn, announced to the world that these studies once again proved that Laetrile had no significant effect in the treatment of cancer. Upon further investigation, however, all was not as it appeared to be. Digging into the raw data contained in the reports, tables, and charts, Dr. Burk discovered that there were three general groups of mice identified in the experiment: (1) A large group that received too little Laetrile, (2) another large group that received too much, and (3) a very small group that received an optimum dose. Those that received too little died just as quickly as those in the control group which received none at all. Those that received too much died sooner than those in the control group. But those that received the proper dosage survived significantly longer than those that received none at all!

In view of these amazing and highly significant results, one may wonder at how the National Cancer Institute could have said that Laetrile was

[1] "Laetrile's Value as Cancer Cure Still Unsubstantiated," *Biomedical News*, July, 1971.

of no value. Here is how it was done. All *three* groups were lumped into the same statistics—including those which received too little and those that received too much. When these large groups were added to the small group that survived significantly longer, they brought down the *average* of the total to the point where they honestly could say that these mice, *as a total group,* did not survive significantly longer than those which had received no Laetrile at all. The statistics didn't lie. But liars had used statistics.[1]

This, then, is the background on the so-called scientific evidence that Laetrile is a fraud. Based upon this perversion of truth, laws have been passed making it illegal to prescribe, administer, sell, or distribute Laetrile, or to "make any representation that said agents have any value in arresting, alleviating, or curing cancer."[2]

Yet, leading medical authorities—even among those who are not convinced that Laetrile works, admit openly that they cannot honestly say "that Laetrile is no good without further proof."

And they are not going to seek that proof, either. In fact, every time the proponents of Laetrile attempt to obtain permission to conduct official tests in U.S. hospitals, they are turned down cold. On April 6, 1970, for example, the McNaughton Foundation, under the sponsorship of Mr. Andrew McNaughton, submitted an application to the FDA

[1] Dr. Dean Burk presented a devastating expose of this manipulation of statistics in a fourteen page open letter to Dr. Seymour Perry of the NCI dated March 22, 1974.

[2] This wording is taken from Section 10400.1, Title 17, of the California Administrative Code.

for permission to engage in what is called IND (Investigation of New Drug) Phase One studies. Permission was granted on April 27. Then, in the words of one reporter, "All hell broke loose."[1] The FDA apparently received a phone call from an irate and politically influential figure who passed the word: "Stop the tests!"

The next day, April 28, the FDA sent another letter to the McNaughton Foundation advising that, upon reviewing the records, certain "deficiences" had been found in the IND application, and demanding extensive additional data *within ten days*. Curiously, the letter was not delivered to the McNaughton Foundation until May 6, nine days after it supposedly had been written, and it is suspected that the letter may actually have been written much later but back-dated so as to make it impossible to comply with the already ridiculous ten day deadline. On May 12, six days after receipt of the "deficiency letter," McNaughton received a telegram from the FDA advising him that the approval for Investigation of New Drug had been revoked.

Nevertheless, hoping that the FDA would reinstate its IND approval upon receipt of the additional data, McNaughton proceeded with the paperwork and, on May 15, just nine days after receipt of the FDA's initial order, sent off to Washington everything that had been requested. By now, however, the FDA was firm. Laetrile would *not* be tested.

---

[1]Don C. Matchan, "Why Won't They Test Laetrile?", *Prevention*, Jan., 1971, pp. 149-150.

A former high official of the FDA told Dr. Dean Burk of the National Cancer Institute that he could not recall in over thirty years of service any instance in which just ten short days were demanded for a fifty page reply to alleged deficiencies. And, on October 1, 1970, there was nothing in the FDA procedural manual requiring termination notices after only ten days for compliance.[1]

Clearly, the entire action was contrived in response to political pressures as an excuse to stop the testing of Laetrile.

One of the reasons given for revoking approval for IND was that Laetrile might be toxic. The FDA said solemnly:

> Although it is often stated in the IND that amygdalin is non-toxic, data to demonstrate this lack of toxicity are absent . . . .It is considered to be dangerous to base the starting dose for a chronic (6 + weeks) study in man on a single dose study in mice. It is also dangerous to initiate human studies while the nature of the toxicity has not been elucidated in large animal species.[2]

This is an incredible statement. First of all, as will be illustrated in a later chapter, the non-toxicity of amygdalin (Laetrile) has been a well-known,

---

[1] Letter from Dr. Dean Burk to Elliot Richardson, Secretary of HEW, dated Oct. 19, 1971.

[2] *The Ad Hoc Committee of Oncology Consultants For Review and Evaluation of Amygdalin (Laetrile)*, FDA, Aug. 12, 1961, pp. 3,4.

fully accepted and non-controversial fact for a hundred years. Second, the human case histories submitted as part of the IND application were further proof of Laetrile's safety. And third, the very question of toxicity is absurd inasmuch as *all* of the drugs approved by the FDA and currently used in orthodox cancer therapy are *extremely* toxic. To deny the testing of Laetrile on the grounds that it *might* be toxic is the height of sophistry.

Another reason given by the FDA for refusing to permit the testing of Laetrile was that the doctors who had treated their patients with it had not kept sufficiently detailed clinical records. This, too, is an incredible excuse in view of the fact that Phase One studies do not require any clinical records at all!

In righteous indignation, the courageous Dr. Burk of the National Cancer Institute, wrote to Elliot Richardson, then Secretary of HEW (which administered the FDA), and said:

> As you should well know, the granting of FDA permission for Phase One studies of IND has no absolute or invariable requirements for any clinical studies at all, although the sponsor is requested to supply any type of indication that he may possess, which the McNaughton Foundation has complied with to the limit of current feasibility. Dr. Contreras [of Mexico] and Dr. Nieper [of Germany] have been primarily preoccupied, quite justifiably, with treating cancer patients with Laetrile and related adjunctive

> therapies, and not with carrying out a clinical evaluation of Laetrile in the precise and complete schedule of FDA protocols. For you to indicate that their records are inadequate for such a purpose is clearly a red herring, since there is no such IND Phase One requirement involved, nor corresponding claim made.[1]

But the "fix" was on, and it was on at the top. Laetrile would *not* be tested, regardless of the facts. On September 1, 1971, the FDA announced that the Ad Hoc Committee of Consultants for Review and Evaluation of Laetrile had found "no acceptable evidence of therapeutic effect to justify clinical trials." And then it announced that, because of their findings, Laetrile could no longer be promoted, sold, or *even tested* in the United States.[2]

Why would anyone, in or out of government, deliberately falsify the clinical results of past Laetrile experiments and then make it impossible for anyone else to do tests of their own? We shall have more to say about that in Part Two of this study when we examine the politics of cancer therapy. Part of the answer, however, was provided by the unsinkable Dr. Burk in a letter to the Honorable Robert A. Roe, dated July 3, 1973. He said:

> You may wonder, Congressman Roe, why anyone should go to such pains and mendacity to avoid conceding what hap-

---

[1] *Op. cit.*, Oct. 19, 1971.

[2] Press release, HEW/FDA, Sept. 1, 1971.

pened in the NCI-directed experiment. Such an admission and concession is crucially central. Once any of the FDA-NCI-AMA-ACS hierarchy so much as concedes that Laetrile anti-tumor efficacy was indeed even once observed in NCI experimentation, a permanent crack in bureaucratic armor has taken place that can widen indefinitely by further appropriate experimentation. For this reason, I rather doubt that that experimentation . . . will be continued or initiated. On the contrary, efforts probably will be made, as they already have, to "explain away" the already observed positive efficacy by vague and unscientific modalities intended to mislead, along early Watergate lines of corruption, including eventually futile arrogance . . . .

There are now several thousand persons in the United States taking Laetrile daily. M.D.s by the hundreds are studying or even taking it themselves, and certain hospitals are now undertaking its study. FDA or no FDA, NCI or no NCI, obfuscations or no obfuscations. The day may not be far off when face-saving on the part of the NCI-FDA spokesmen of the type just indicated will have lagged beyond possibility, as is already now the case for some Watergate casualties of Courts and Hearings, as a result of per-

> sons placing personal integrity secondary to other considerations.[1]

Now, that takes *guts*. For a man who is employed by the federal government, especially as head of the Cytochemistry section of the National Cancer Institute, to charge openly that his superiors are corrupt—well, such a man is, unfortunately, a rare specimen in Washington today. Concluding his testimony on Laetrile before a Congressional committee in 1972, Dr. Burk explained:

> I don't think of myself as a maverick. I am just telling you what I honestly think, and when I think something is true, I am quite willing to say so and let the chips fall where they may . . . .
>
> And now, I will get back to my laboratory where truth is distilled.[2]

Let us, figuratively speaking, follow Dr. Burk to his laboratory. Let us put aside, for the moment, the question of politics and corruption, and turn now to the distillation of scientific truth.

---

[1] Letter reprinted in *Cancer Control Journal*, Sept./Oct., 1973, pp. 8, 9.

[2] From *Hearings*, Subcommittee on Public Health and Environment of the Committee on Interstate and Foreign Commerce, House of Representatives, Ninety-Second Congress.

II

AN APPLE A DAY

A review of entrenched scientific error in history; a statement of the basic vitamin deficiency concept of cancer as advanced in 1952 by Dr. Ernst T. Krebs, Jr.; and a survey of the supportive evidence both in nature and in recent history to reinforce this concept.

The history of science is the history of struggle against entrenched error. Many of the world's greatest discoveries initially were rejected by the scientific community. And those who pioneered those discoveries often were ridiculed and condemned as quacks or charlatans.

Columbus was bitterly attacked for believing the Earth was round. Bruno was burned at the stake for claiming the earth was not the center of the Universe. Galileo was imprisoned for teaching that the Earth moved around the Sun. Even the Wright Brothers were ridiculed and condemned for claiming that a machine could fly above the earth.

In the field of medicine, in the year 130 A.D., the physician Galen announced certain anatomic theories that later proved to be correct, but at the time he was bitterly opposed and actually forced to flee from Rome to escape the frenzy of the mob. In the Sixteenth Century, the physician Andreas Vesalius was denounced as an imposter and heretic because of his discoveries in the field of human anatomy. His theories were accepted after his death but, at the time, his career was ruined, and he was forced to flee from Italy. William Harvey was disgraced as a physician for believing that blood was pumped by the heart and actually moved around the body through arteries. William Roentgen, the discoverer of X-rays, at first was called a quack and then condemned out of fear that his "ray" would invade the privacy of the bedroom. William Jenner, when he first developed a vaccine against smallpox, also was called a quack and was strongly criticized as a physician for his supposedly cruel and inhuman experiments on children. And Ignaz Semmelweis was fired from his Vienna hospital post for requiring his maternity staff to wash their hands.

Centuries ago it was not unusual for entire naval expeditions to be wiped out by scurvy. Between 1600 and 1800 the casualty list of the British Navy alone was over one million sailors. Medical experts of the time were baffled as they searched in vain for some kind of strange bacterium, virus, or toxin that supposedly lurked in the dark holds of ships. And yet, for hundreds of years, the cure was already known and written in the record.

In the winter of 1535, when the French explorer Jacques Cartier found his ships frozen in the ice off the St. Lawrence River, scurvy began to take its deadly toll. Out of a crew of one hundred and ten, twenty-five already had died, and most of the others were so ill they weren't expected to recover.

And then a friendly Indian showed them the simple remedy. Tree bark and needles from the white pine — both rich in ascorbic acid, or vitamin C — were stirred into a drink which produced immediate improvement and swift recovery.

Upon returning to Europe, Cartier reported this incident to the medical authorities. But they were amused by such "witch-doctor cures of ignorant savages" and did nothing to follow it up.[1]

Yes, the cure for scurvy was known. But, because of scientific arrogance, it took over two hundred years and cost hundreds of thousands of lives before the medical experts began to accept and apply this knowledge.

Finally, in 1747, John Lind, a young surgeon's mate in the British Navy discovered that oranges and lemons produced relief from scurvy, and recommended that the Royal Navy include citrus fruits in the stores of all its ships. And yet, it still took forty-eight *more* years before his recommendation was put into effect. When it was, of course, the British were able to surpass all other sea-faring nations, and the "Limeys" (so-called because they carried limes aboard ship) soon became the rulers of the Seven Seas. It is no exaggeration to say that the greatness of the British Empire in large measure was the direct result of overcoming scientific prejudice against vitamin therapy.

---

[1]See Virgil J. Vogel's *American Indian Medicine* (University of Oklahoma Press, 1970).

The Twentieth Century has proven to be no exception to this pattern. Only a generation ago large portions of the American Southeast were decimated by the dread disease of pellagra. The well-known physician Sir William Osler, in his *Principles and Practice of Medicine*, explained that in one institution for the insane in Leonard, North Carolina, one-third of the inmates died of this disease during the winter months. This proved, he said, that pellagra was contagious and caused probably by an as yet undiscovered virus. As far back as 1914, however, Dr. Joseph Goldberger had proven that this condition was related to diet, and later showed that it could be prevented simply by eating liver or yeast. But it wasn't until the 1940's—almost thirty years later—that the "modern" medical world fully accepted pellagra as a vitamin B deficiency.[1]

The story behind pernicious anemia is almost exactly the same. The reason why all these diseases were so reluctantly accepted as vitamin deficiencies is because men tend to look for positive cause-and-effect relationships in which something clearly *causes* something else. They find it more difficult to comprehend the negative relationship in which *nothing* or the *lack* of something can cause an effect. But perhaps of even more importance is the reality of intellectual pride. A man who has spent his life acquiring scientific knowledge far beyond the grasp of his fellow human beings is not usually inclined to

---

[1]See *History and Geography of the Most Important Diseases,* by Edwin H. Ackerknecht, (Hafner Publishing Co., Inc., N.Y. 1972) pp. 148-149.

listen with patience to someone who lacks that knowledge—especially if that person suggests that the solution to the scientist's most puzzling medical problem is to be found in a simple back-woods or near-primitive concoction of herbs and foods. The scientist is trained to search for *complex* answers and tends to look with smug amusement upon solutions that are not dependent upon his hard-earned skills.

To bring this a little closer to home, the average M.D. today has spent over ten years of intensive training to learn about health and disease. This educational process continues for as long as he practices his art. The greatest challenge to the medical profession today is cancer. If the solution to the cancer puzzle were to be found in the simple foods we eat (or *don't* eat), then what other diseases might also be traced to this cause? The implications are explosive. As one doctor put it so aptly, "Most of my medical training has been wasted. I've learned the wrong things!" And nobody wants to discover that they have learned—or taught—the wrong things. Hence, there is an unconscious but quite natural tendency among many scientists and physicians to reject the vitamin deficiency concept of all such diseases until it is proven, and proven, and proven again.

By 1952, Dr. Ernst T. Krebs, Jr., a biochemist in San Francisco, had advanced the theory that cancer, like scurvy and pellagra, is not caused by some kind of mysterious bacterium, virus, or toxin, but is merely a deficiency disease aggravated by the lack of an essential food compound in modern man's diet. He identified this compound as part of the nitriloside family which occurs abundantly in nature in over twelve hundred edible plants and found virtually in every part of the world. It is particularly prevalent in the seeds of those fruits in the *Prunus Rosacea* family (bitter almond, apricot, blackthorn, cherry, nectarine, peach, and plum), but also contained in grasses, maize, sorghum, millet, cassava, linseed, apple seeds, and many other foods that, generally, have been deleted from the menus of modern civilization.

It is difficult to establish a clear-cut classification for a nitriloside. Since it does not occur entirely by itself but rather is found in foods, it probably should not be classified as a *food*. Like sugar, it is a food component or a food factor. Nor can it be classified as a drug, inasmuch as it is a natural, non-toxic, water-soluble substance entirely normal to and compatible with human metabolism. The proper name for a food factor that contains these properties is a *vitamin*. Since this vitamin normally is found with the B-complex, and since it was the seventeenth such substance to be isolated within this complex, Dr. Krebs identified it as *vitamin* B_{17}.

Emphasizing the point that this substance is not a drug, Dr. Krebs said:

> Can the water-soluble non-toxic nitrilosides properly be described as food? Probably not in the strict sense of the word. They are certainly not drugs *per se*. . . . Since the nitrilosides are neither

> food nor drug, they may be considered as accessory food factors. Another term for water-soluble, non-toxic accessory food factors is vitamins.[1]

A chronic disease is one which usually does not pass away of its own accord. A metabolic disease is one which occurs within the body and is not transmittable to another person. Cancer, therefore, is defined as a chronic metabolic disease.

There are many of these diseases that plague modern man, such as muscular dystrophy, heart disease, multiple sclerosis, and sickle-cell anemia. Modern science has spent many millions of dollars searching for a prevention to these cripplers and killers, but they are little closer to the answers today than they were when they first started. Perhaps the reason is that they are still looking for that *something* which causes these diseases instead of the *lack* of something.

Dr. Krebs has pointed out that, in the entire history of medical science, there has not been one chronic metabolic disease that was ever cured or prevented by drugs, surgery, or mechanical manipulation of the body. In every case—whether it be scurvy, pellagra, rickets, beri-beri, night blindness, pernicious anemia, or any of the others—the ultimate solution was found only in factors relating to adequate nutrition. And he thinks that this is an important clue as to where to concentrate our scientific curiosity in the search for a better understanding of today's diseases, particularly cancer.

---

[1]Krebs, *The Laetriles/Nitrilosides in the Prevention and Control of Cancer* (The McNaughton Foundation, Montreal, Canada), p. 16.

But there are other clues as well. Before looking at the more technical aspects of Dr. Krebs' theory, it is well that we examine some of them. For example, as almost everyone who owns a dog or cat has observed, these domesticated pets often seek out certain grasses to eat even though they are adequately filled by other foods. This is particularly likely to happen if the animals are not well. It is interesting to note that the grasses selected by instinct are Johnson grass, Tunis grass, Sudan grass, and others that are especially rich in nitrilosides or vitamin B_{17}.

Monkeys and other primates at the zoo when given a fresh peach or apricot will carefully pull away the sweet fleshy part, crack open the hard pit, and devour the small seed that remains. Instinct compels them to do this even though they have never seen that kind of fruit before. These seeds are one of the most concentrated sources of nitrilosides to be found anywhere in nature.

Wild bears are great consumers of nitrilosides in their natural diet. Not only do they seek out berries that are rich in this substance, but when they kill small grazing animals for their own food, instinctively they pass over the muscle portions and consume first the viscera and rumen which are filled with nitriloside grasses.[1]

In captivity, animals seldom are allowed to eat all the foods of their instinctive choice. In the San Diego Zoo, for example, the routine diet for bears, although adequate in volume and nutritious in many

---

[1]See *Bears in The Family*, by Peter Krott, Ph.D. (E.P. Dutton & Co., Inc., N.Y., 1962).

other respects, is almost totally devoid of nitrilosides. In one grotto alone, over a six-year period, five bears died of cancer. It was generally speculated by the experts that a virus had been the cause.

It is highly significant that one never finds cancer in the carcasses of wild animals killed in the hunt. These creatures contract the disease only when they are domesticated by man and forced to eat the foods he provides or the scraps from his table.

It is amazing how cancer researchers can come face-to-face with this evidence and still fail to realize its significance. For instance, Dr. Dennis P. Burkitt, the man who first identified the form of cancer known as Burkitt Lymphoma, recently delivered a lecture at the College of Medicine at the University of Iowa. After two decades of experience and research in Uganda and similar parts of the world, Dr. Burkitt observed that non-infectious (chronic metabolic) diseases such as cancer of the colon, diverticular disease, ulcerative colitis, polyps, and appendicitis, all seem to be related in some way. "They all go together," he said, "and I'm going to go so far as to suggest that they all have a common cause." He went on to say that all of these diseases are unknown in primitive societies and "always have their maximum incidence in the more economically developed nations."

Then Dr. Burkitt turned his attention to cancer specifically and observed:

> This is a disease caused by the way we live. This form of cancer is almost un-

> known in the animal kingdom. The only animals who get cancer or polyps of the large bowel are those that live closest to our way of life—our domestic dogs eating our leftovers.[1]

These, of course, are all excellent observations. But apparently neither Dr. Burkitt nor anyone in his esteemed audience could find any meaning in these facts. The lecture closed with the conclusion that colon cancer probably is related to bacteria in the large bowel and that we should all eat more bran and other cereal fibers to increase the roughage content of our intestines and the size of our stools!

But at least Dr. Burkitt is looking at the foods we eat, which is a huge step forward. He may be heading in the wrong direction, but at least he is on the right track. If more cancer researchers would begin to think in terms of foods and vitamins rather than bacteria and viruses it wouldn't take them long to see why the cancer rate in America is steadily climbing.

Measured in terms of taste, volume, and variety, Americans eat very well, indeed. But expensive or tasty food is not necessarily good food. Most Americans assume that it makes little difference what they put into their stomachs as long as they are full. Magically, everything that goes in somehow will be converted into perfect health. They scoff at the thought of proper diet. Yet, many of these same

[1] "The Evidence Leavens: We Invite Colon Cancer," *Medical World News,* Aug. 11, 1972, pp. 33, 34.

people are fastidious about what they feed their pedigreed dogs and cats or their registered cattle and horses.

Dr. George M. Briggs, professor of nutrition at the University of California, and member of the Research Advisory Committee of the National Livestock and Meat Board, has said: "The typical American diet is a national disaster. . . . If I fed it to pigs or cows, without adding vitamins and other supplements, I could wipe out the livestock industry."[1]

A brief look at the American diet tells the story. Grocery shelves are now lined with high-carbohydrate foods that have been processed refined, synthesized, artificially flavored, and loaded with chemical preservatives.[2] Some manufacturers, aiming their advertisements at the diet-conscious consumer, even boast of how little real food there is in their product.

Everyone knows that modern processing removes many of the original vitamins from our foods, but we are told not to worry about it because they have been put back before sending to market. And so we see the word "enriched" printed cheerfully across our bread, milk, and other foods. But make no mistake about it, these are *not* the same as

---

[1]"University of California Nutrition Professor, A Health Advisor to the U.S. Government . . . Charges the Typical American Diet is a National Disaster," *National Enquirer,* Dec. 5, 1971, p. 2.

[2]According to the March 1972 issue of *Scientific American* (p.20) there are approximately 2500 additives currently used in U.S. food products for flavoring, coloring, preservation, and similar purposes. The safety factor of most of these chemicals has not been determined, except to the negative. Nevertheless, they are still being used with FDA approval.

the original. As the June 1971 *Journal of the American Geriatric Society* reported:

> Vitamins removed from food and returned as "enrichment" are not a safe substitute, as witnessed by the study in which Roger J. Williams, Ph.D., reported that rats fed enriched bread died or were severely stunted due to malnutrition. Rats fed a more whole bread flourished, for the most part, by comparison.
>
> Much illness, we are learning, may be due to vitamin-mineral deficiencies. Even senility has been proven to be caused by a deficiency of Vitamins B and C.

Indeed, here is a worthy experiment that can and should be carried out in every grade-school science class. Rodents fed only "enriched" bread very soon become anti-social. Some even become cannibalistic, apparently responding to an instinctive drive to obtain the vital food elements they are lacking. Most will die within a month or two. Once children have witnessed this, they seldom retain the same appetite for white bread that they may have had prior to the experiment.

"Enriched" bread is just one small part of the larger picture. Millet once was the world's staple grain. It is high in nitriloside content. But now it has been replaced by wheat which has practically none at all—even the whole wheat. Sorghum cane has been replaced by sugar cane with the same result. Even our cattle are fed increasingly on quick-growing, low nitriloside grasses so there is less vitamin B_{17} residue in the meat we eat. In some places, livestock now are being fed a diet containing fifteen percent *paper* to fatten them quicker for market.[1]

In retrospect, there were many customs of our grandparents that, although lacking in scientific rationale at the time, were based upon centuries of accumulated experience through trial and error, and have since been proven to be infinitely wise. "An apple a day keeps the doctor away" could well have been more than an idle slogan, especially in an era when it was customary for everyone to eat the seeds of those apples as well. It is a fact that the whole fruit—including the seeds—of an apple contains an amazingly high concentration of vitamins, minerals, fats, and proteins that are essential for health. Apple seeds are especially rich in nitrilosides or vitamin B_{17}. The distasteful "spring tonic" or sorghum molasses and sulphur also was a rich source of nitriloside. And grandma's apricot and peach preserves almost always contained the kernels of these canned fruits for winter eating. She probably didn't know what they contained or why they were good for you. But she knew that they *were* good for you simply because her mother had told her so.

And so we see that, in the past fifty years, the foods that once provided the American people with ample amounts of natural vitamin B_{17} gradually have been pushed aside or replaced altogether by foods almost devoid of this factor. Significantly, it is during this same time span that the cancer rate has moved steadily upward to the point where,

[1] "Paper Fattens Cattle," (UPI) *Oakland Tribune*, Nov. 22, 1971.

today, one out of every four persons in the United States is destined to contract this disease.

It cannot be argued that the cancer rate is up merely because other causes of death are down and people are living longer. First of all, they are *not* living that much longer—only a year or two more, on the average, over the past fifty years. In fact, in 1972, a year in which the average age of the American population was headed *downward,* a year in which the population growth rate had shrunk practically to *zero,* the death rate from cancer rose to its highest level in history: *three times* the annual average since 1950.[1] Secondly, in those countries where, statistically, people live *longer* than in the United States, the cancer rate for them is *lower* than for us.

So there is no escape from the significance of these facts. While the medical world, the federal government, and the American Cancer Society are spending billions of dollars and millions of man-hours searching for an exotic cancer virus against which they plan to spend an equal amount to create an effective man-made immunization, the answer lies right under their noses. In fact, it has existed in the written and spoken record for thousands of years:

> And God said: Behold I have given you every herb bearing seed upon the earth, and all trees that have in themselves seed of their own kind, to be your meat. (*Genesis* 1:29)

---

[1]"Cancer Cure Still Eludes Scientists," (NEA) *News Chronicle* (Calif.) Aug. 29, 1973, p. A-9.

III

THE ULTIMATE TEST

A look at the many cultures around the world that are, or have been, free from cancer; and also an analysis of their native foods.

The best way to prove or disprove the vitamin theory of cancer would be to take a great many people numbering in the thousands and, over a period of many years, expose them to a consistent diet of rich nitriloside foods, and then check the results. This, surely, would be the ultimate test.

Fortunately, it already has been done.

In the remote recesses of the Himalaya Mountains, between West Pakistan, India, and China, there is a tiny kingdom called Hunza. These people are known world over for their amazing longevity and good health. It is not uncommon for Hunzakuts to live beyond a hundred years, and some even to a hundred and twenty, or more. Visiting medical teams from the outside world report that there never has been a case of cancer in Hunza.

Although presently accepted science is unable to explain *why* these people should be free of cancer, it is interesting to note that the average Hunza diet contains over two hundred times more nitriloside than the average American diet. In fact, in that land where there is no such thing as money, a man's wealth is measured by the number of apricot trees he owns. And the most prized of all foods is considered to be the apricot seed.

One of the first medical teams to gain access to the remote kingdom of Hunza was headed by the world-renowned British surgeon and physician Dr. Robert McCarrison. Writing in the January 7, 1922, issue of the *Journal of The American Medical Association,* Dr. McCarrison reported:

> The Hunza has no known incidence of cancer. They have . . . an abundant crop of apricots. These they dry in the sun and use very largely in their food.

Visitors to Hunza, when offered a fresh apricot or peach to eat, usually drop the hard pit to the ground when they are through. Invariably, this brings looks of dismay and disbelief to the faces of their guides, for, to them, the seed inside is the delicacy of the fruit.

Dr. Allen E. Banik, an optometrist from Kearney, Nebraska, was one such visitor. In his book, *Hunza Land,* he describes what happened:

> My first experience with Hunza apricots, fresh from the tree, came when my guide picked several, washed them in a mountain stream, and handed them to me. I ate the luscious fruit and casually tossed the seeds to the ground. After an incredulous

> glance at me, one of the older men stooped and picked up the seeds. He cracked them between two stones, and handed them to me. The guide said with a smile: "Eat them. It is the best part of the fruit."
>
> My curiosity aroused, I asked, "What do you do with the seeds you do not eat?"
>
> The guide informed me that many are stored but most of them are ground very fine and then squeezed under pressure to produce a very rich oil. "This oil," my guide claimed, "looks much like olive oil. Sometimes we swallow a spoonful of it when we need it. On special days, we deep-fry our *chappatis* [bread] in it. On festival nights, our women use the oil to shine their hair. It makes a good rubbing compound for body bruises.[1]

In 1973, Prince Mohammed Ameen Khan, son of the Mir of Hunza, told Charles Hillinger of the *Los Angeles Times* that the average life expectancy of his people is about eighty-five years. He added: "Many members of the Council of Elders who help my father govern the state have been over one hundred."[2]

With a scientific distrust for both hearsay and

---

[1]*Hunza Land*, (Whitehorn Publishing Co., Long Beach, Ca.) pp. 123, 124.

[2]*Los Angeles Times*, May 7, 1973, Part 1-A.

the printed word, Dr. Ernst T. Krebs, Jr. met Prince Khan for dinner where he queried him on the accuracy of the *L.A. Times* report. The prince happily confirmed it and then described how it was not uncommon to eat thirty to fifty apricot seeds as an after-lunch snack. All of this is in addition to a diet of fresh and dried apricots. These often account for an excess of 75,000 International Units of vitamin A per day as well as for over 150 mg. of vitamin B_{17}. Despite all of this, or possibly because of it, the life expectancy in Hunza, the Prince affirmed, is about eighty-five years. This is in puzzling contrast to the United States where male life expectancy is 66.6 years.

It will be noted that the Hunzakut intake of vitamin A may run seven-and-a-half times the maximum amount the FDA allows to be used in a tablet or capsule while this agency has tried to outlaw entirely the eating of apricot seeds.

The women of Hunza are renowned for their strikingly smooth skin even into advanced age. Generally, their faces appear fifteen to twenty years younger than their counterparts in other areas of the world. They claim that their beauty secret is merely the apricot oil which they apply to their skins almost daily.

In 1974 Senator Charles Percy, a member of the Senate Special Committee on Aging, visited Hunza. When he returned to the United States he wrote:

> We began curiously to observe the life style of the Hunzakuts. Could their eating habits be a source of longevity? . . .

> Some Hunzakuts believe their long lives are due in part to the apricot. Eaten fresh in the summer, dried in the sun for the long winter, the apricot is a staple in Hunza, much as rice is in other parts of the world. Apricot seeds are ground fine and squeezed for their rich oil, used for both frying and lighting.[1]

And so, the Hunzakuts use the apricot, its seed, and the oil from its seed for practically everything. They share with most western scientists an ignorance of the chemistry and physiology of the nitriloside content of this fruit, but they have learned empirically that their life is enhanced by its generous use.

Five or six excellent volumes similar to Dr. Banik's have been written by those who have risked their lives over the treacherous Himalaya Mountain passes to gain entrance to Hunza. Also, there have been scores of magazine and newspaper articles published over the years. They all present the identical picture of the average Hunza diet. In addition to the ever-present apricot, the Hunzakuts eat mainly grain and fresh vegetables. These include buckwheat, millet, alfalfa, peas, broad beans, turnips, lettuce, sprouting pulse or gram, and berries of various sorts. All of these, with the exception of lettuce and turnips, contain nitriloside or vitamin B_{17}.

In 1927 Dr. McCarrison was appointed Director of Nutrition Research in India. Part of his work consisted of experiments on albino rats to see what

---

[1] "You Live To Be 100 in Hunza," *Parade,* Feb. 17, 1974, p. 11.

effect the Hunza diet had on them compared to the diets of other countries. Over a thousand rats were involved in the experiment and carefully observed from birth to twenty-seven months, which corresponds to about fifty years of age in man. At this point the Hunza-fed rats were killed and autopsied. Here is what McCarrison reported:

> During the past two and a quarter years there has been no case of illness in the "universe" of albino rats, no death from natural causes in the adult stock, and, but for a few accidental deaths, no infantile mortality. Both clinically and at post-mortem, examination of this stock has been shown to be remarkably free from disease. It may be that some of them have cryptic disease of one kind or another, but if so, I have failed to find either clinical or microscopic evidence of it.[1]

By comparison, over two thousand rats fed on typical Indian and Pakistani diets soon developed eye ailments, ulcers, boils, bad teeth, crooked spines, loss of hair, anemia, skin disorders, heart, kidney and glandular weaknesses, and a wide variety of gastrointestinal disorders.

In follow-up experiments, McCarrison gave a group of rats the diet of the lower classes of England. It consisted of white bread, margarine, sweetened tea, boiled vegetables, canned meat, and

---

[1]See *Hunza Health Secrets* by Renee Taylor (Award Books, N.Y., 1964), pp. 96, 97.

inexpensive jams and jellies—a diet not too far removed from that of many Americans. Not only did the rats develop all kinds of chronic metabolic diseases, but they also became nervous wrecks. McCarrison wrote:

> They were nervous and apt to bite their attendants; they lived unhappily together, and by the sixteenth day of the experiment they began to kill and eat the weaker ones amongst them.[1]

It is not surprising, therefore, to learn that westernized man is victimized by the chronic metabolic disease of cancer while his counterpart in Hunza is not. And lest anyone suspect that this difference is due to hereditary factors, it is important to know that when the Hunzakuts leave their secluded land and adopt the menus of other countries, they soon succumb to the same diseases and infirmities—*including cancer*—as the rest of mankind.

The Eskimos are another people that have been observed by medical teams for many decades and found to be totally free of cancer. In Vilhjalmur Stefanson's book, *Cancer: Disease of Civilization? An Anthropological and Historical Study,*[2] it is revealed that the traditional Eskimo diet is amazingly rich in nitrilosides that come from the residue of the meat of caribou and other grazing animals, and also from the salmon berry which grows abundantly in

[1]*Ibid.* p. 97.

[2]Hill and Wang, N.Y., 1960.

the Arctic areas. Another Eskimo delicacy is a green salad made out of the stomach contents of caribou and reindeer which are full of fresh tundra grasses. Among these grasses, Arrow grass (*Triglochin Maritima*) is very common. Studies made by the U.S. Department of Agriculture have shown that Arrow grass is probably richer in nitriloside content than any other grass.

What happens when the Eskimo abandons his traditional way of life and begins to rely on westernized foods? He becomes even more cancer-prone than the average American.

Dr. Otto Schaefer, M.D., who has extensively studied the diets and health patterns of the Eskimos, reports that these people have undergone an extremely rapid change in their eating habits. This has been caused indirectly as a result of the construction of a string of military and civilian airports built across the Canadian Arctic in the mid-50's. These attracted the Eskimos to new jobs, new homes, new schools—and new menus. Just a little over one generation ago, their diet consisted almost entirely of game and fish, along with seasonal berries, roots, leafy greens and seaweed. Carbohydrates were almost completely lacking.

Now all of this has changed. Dr. Schaefer reports:

> When the Eskimo gives up his nomadic life and moves into the settlement, he and his family undergo remarkable changes. His children grow faster and taller, and reach puberty sooner. Their teeth rot, his

> wife comes down with gallbladder disease and, likely as not, a member of his family will suffer one of the degenerative diseases for which the white man is well known.[1]

There are many other peoples in the world that could be cited with the same characteristics. The Abkhasians deep in the Caucasus Mountains on the Northeast side of the Black Sea are a people with almost exactly the same record of health and longevity as the Hunzakuts. The parallels between the two are striking. First, Abkhasia is a *hard* land which does not yield up a harvest easily. The inhabitants are accustomed to daily hard work throughout their lives. Consequently, their bodies and minds are strong right up until death, which comes swiftly with little or no preliminary illness. Like the Hunzakuts, the Abkhasians expect to live well beyond eighty years of age. Many are over a hundred. The oldest person in the world is Mrs. Shirali Mislimov of Abkhasia who, in 1972, was estimated to be 165 years old.[2]

The other common factor, of course, is the food, which, typically, is low in carbohydrates, high in vegetable proteins, and rich in minerals and vitamins, especially vitamin B_{17}.

The Indians of North America, while they re-

---

[1]*Nutrition Today,* Nov./Dec., 1971, as quoted in "Modern Refined Foods Finally Reach The Eskimos," *Kaysers Health Research,* May, 1972, pp. 11, 46, 48.

[2]"The Secret of Long Life" by Sula Benet, (N.Y. Times News Service), *L.A. Herald Examiner,* Jan. 2, 1972, p. A-12, also "Soviet Study Finds Recipe for Long Life," *National Enquirer,* Aug. 27, 1972, p. 13.

mained true to their native customs and foods, also were remarkably free from cancer. At one time the American Medical Association urged the federal government to conduct a study in an effort to discover why there was so little cancer among the Hopi and Navajo Indians. The February 5, 1949, issue of the *Journal* of the AMA declared:

> The Indian's diet seems to be low in quality and quantity and wanting in variety, and the doctors wondered if this had anything to do with the fact that only 36 cases of malignant cancer were found out of 30,000 admissions to the Ganado Arizona Mission Hospital. In the same population of white persons, the doctors said there would have been about 1,800.

Thirty-six cases compared to eighteen hundred represents only two percent of the expected number. Obviously, *something* is responsible.

Dr. Krebs, who has done exhaustive research on this subject, has written:

> I have analyzed from historical and anthropological records the nitrilosidic content of the diets of these various North American tribes. The evidence should put to rest forever the notion of toxicity in nitrilosidic foods. Some of these tribes would ingest over 8,000 milligrams of vitamin B_{17} (nitriloside) a day. My data on

> the Modoc Indians are particularly complete.[1]

A quick glance at the cancer-free native populations in tropical areas, such as South America and Africa, reveals a great abundance and variety of nitriloside-rich foods. In fact, over one-third of all plants native to these areas contain vitamin B_{17}. One of the most common is cassava, sometimes described as "the bread of the tropic." But this is not the same as the sweet cassava preferred in the cities of western civilization. The native fruit is more bitter, but it is rich in nitriloside. The sweet cassava has much less of this vital substance, and even that is so processed as to eliminate practically all nitrile ions.[2]

As far back as 1913, Dr. Albert Schweitzer, the world-famous medical missionary to Africa, had put his finger on the basic cause of cancer. He had not isolated the specific substance, but he was convinced from his observations that a difference in food was the key. In his preface to Alexander Berglas' *Cancer: Cause and Cure* (Pasteur Institute, Paris, 1957), he wrote:

> On my arrival in Gabon in 1913, I was astonished to encounter no cases of cancer. I saw none among the natives two hundred miles from the coast. . . . I can

[1]Letter from Dr. E.T. Krebs, Jr. to Dr. Dean Burk of the National Cancer Institute, dated March 14, 1972.

[2]*The Laetriles, op. cit.*, pp. 9, 10.

> not, of course, say positively that there was no cancer at all, but, like other frontier doctors, I can only say that, if any cases existed, they must have been quite rare. This absence of cancer seemed to be due to the difference in nutrition of the natives compared to the Europeans. . . .

The missionary and medical journals have recorded many such cancer-free populations all over the world. Some are in tropic regions, some in the Arctic. Some are hunters who eat great quantities of meat, some are vegetarians who eat almost no meat at all. From all continents and all races, the *one* thing they have in common is that the degree to which they are free from cancer is in direct proportion to the amount of nitriloside or vitamin B_{17} found in their natural diet.

In answer to this, the skeptic may argue that these primitive groups are not exposed to the same cancer-producing elements that modern man is, and perhaps *that* is why they are immune. Let them breathe the same smog-filled air, smoke the same cigarettes, swallow the same chemicals added to their food or drinking water, use the same soaps or deodorants, and *then* see how they fare.

This, of course, is a valid argument. But, fortunately, even that question now has been resolved by experience.

In the highly populated and often air-polluted State of California, for example, there are over 100,000 people comprising a population that shows a cancer incidence of less than fifty per cent of that for the remaining population. This unique group has the same sex, age, socio-economic, educational, occupational, ethnic and cultural profile as the remainder of the State's population that suffers twice as high an incidence of cancer. This is the Seventh Day Adventist population of the State.

There is only one detectable material difference that sets this population apart from that of the rest of the State. This population is predominantly vegetarian. By increasing greatly the quantity of vegetables in their diet to compensate for the absence of meat they increase proportionately their dietary intake of vitamin B_{17} (nitriloside). Probably the reason why this population is not totally free from cancer—as are the Hunzakuts, the aboriginal eskimos, and other such populations—is that (1) many members of this sect have joined it after almost a lifetime on a general or standard dietary pattern; (2) the fruits and vegetables ingested are not consciously chosen for vitamin B_{17} content nor are fruit seeds generally eaten by them; and (3) not *all* Seventh Day Adventists adhere to the vegetarian diet.

Another group that, because of religious doctrine, eats very little meat and, thus, a greater quantity of grains, vegetables, and fruits which contain B_{17}, is the Mormon population. In Utah, which is seventy-three percent Mormon, the cancer rate is twenty-five percent below the national average. In Utah county, which includes the city of Provo and is ninety percent Mormon, the cancer rate is below the national average by twenty-eight percent for women and thirty-five percent for men.[1]

In the summer of 1940 the Netherlands became occupied by the military forces of Nazi Germany. Under a dictatorial regime the entire nation of about nine million people gradually was compelled to change its eating habits drastically. Dr. C. Moerman, a physician in Vlaardingen, the Netherlands, described what happened:

> White bread was replaced by whole-meal bread and rye bread. The supply of sugar was drastically cut down and soon entirely stopped. Honey was used, if available. The oil supply from abroad was stopped and, as a result, no margarine was produced any more, causing the people to try and get butter. Add to this that the consumer received as much fruit and as many vegetables as possible, hoarding and buying from the farmers what they could. In short: people satisfied their hunger with large quantities of natural elements rich in vitamins.
>
> Now think of what happened later: in 1945 this forced nutrition suddenly came to an end. What was the result? People started eating again white bread, margarine, skimmed milk, much sugar, much meat, and only few vegetables and little

[1] "Cancer Rate for Mormons Among Lowest," *Los Angeles Times*, Aug. 22, 1974, Part II, p. 1.

> fruit. . . . In short: people ate too much unnatural and too little natural food, and therefore got too few vitamins.[1]

Dr. Moerman then proceeded to show that the statistical "cancer rate" published by the Netherlands Department of Welfare and Health dropped almost straight down from a peak in 1942 to its lowest point in 1945. But after 1945, with the resumption of processed foods, the cancer rate began to climb again and has shown a steady rise ever since.

Of course the experience in the Netherlands or among the Seventh Day Adventists or Mormons is not conclusive for it still leaves open the question of the *specific* food factor or factors that were responsible. So let us narrow the field.

For over two decades there has been a steadily-growing group of people who have accepted the vitamin theory of cancer and who have altered their diets accordingly. They represent all walks of life, all ages, both sexes, and reside in almost every advanced nation in the world. It is estimated that there are many thousands in the United States alone.[2] It is true that there is no way to determine their exact number or to conduct clini-

---

[1]*The Solution of the Cancer Problem* (unpublished manuscript, 1962) p. 31.

[2]Dr. Dean Burk, in a letter to Congressman Lou Frey, Jr., dated May 30, 1972, stated that, in just the previous twelve month period, he personally had been contacted by at least seven hundred and fifty persons, "including many M.D. physicians," most of whom were "using it merely with prevention of development of cancer in view." This experience has been duplicated by many other people, including the author, who have been exposed to the field of nutritional therapy.

cal examinations on each of them. But they do constitute a rather well-defined group that is both vocal and conspicuous.

It is significant, therefore, that, after starting and maintaining a diet rich in vitamin B_{17}, *none* of these people has ever been known to contract cancer.

In the summer of 1973, news spread through the health-food grapevine that Adelle Davis, one of the nation's best-known nutritionists, a woman who was considered to be an expert on the relationship between diet and cancer—herself was stricken with one of its most virulent forms, and in May of the following year it was learned that she passed away. It seemed that this was to be the first exception to the foregoing statement. But, upon closer investigation, in none of her many books or lectures did she ever treat nitrilosides as a vitamin or even as an essential food substance. She did mention that Laetrile was, in her opinion, an effective treatment for cancer *after* it was contracted, but she apparently failed to consider it, in its less concentrated and more natural form, as vital to one's daily nutrition. Even after her cancer had been diagnosed, she apparently still did not see the full connection. The author corresponded with her on this very question, and her reply was, in part, as follows:

> Since carcinogens surround us by the hundreds in food preservatives, additives, poison sprays, chemical fertilizers, pollutants and contaminants of air and

> water, the statement that cancer is a deficiency disease is certainly inaccurate and over-simplified.

It should be stated for the record that this lady was an excellent nutritionist. She had helped thousands of people regain their health through better diet and more healthful cooking. But it is plain that she did not agree with those mentioned previously who have altered their menus to include rich nitriloside foods; and so the unfortunate fact that she had contracted cancer is *not* an exception to the blunt statement made a moment ago.

So let us repeat it.

While their fellow citizens are suffering from cancer at the rate of at least one out of every four, not *one* of these thousands has ever been known to contract this dread disease.[1]

For many persons, the logic of all these facts put together is so great that it would be easy to close the case right here. But, in view of the powerful opposition against this concept, let us not content ourselves only with the *logic* of the theory. Let us reinforce our convictions with the *science* of the theory also, that we may understand *why* it works the way our logic tells us that it must.

---

[1]As will be seen in the following chapters, there *are* other factors involved in the body's natural resistance to cancer—certain pancreatic enzymes in particular. It is conceivable, therefore, that one *could* contract cancer in spite of a good nitriloside diet, and, I suppose, eventually we will learn of one or two cases. But these certainly will be exceptions, and likely will exist in the presence of severe pancreatic deficiencies, if, indeed, they occur at all.

IV

CANCER: THE ONRUSH OF LIFE

An explanation of the trophoblastic thesis of cancer; a description of a simple urine test for cancer; an appraisal of BCG vaccine as an anti-cancer agent; and a review of the vital role played by the pancreas in the control of cancer.

In 1902, John Beard, a professor of embryology at the University of Edinburgh in Scotland, authored a paper published in the British medical journal *Lancet* in which he stated that there were no discernible differences between highly-malignant cancer cells and certain pre-embryonic cells that were quite normal to the early stages of pregnancy. In technical terms these normal cells are called *trophoblasts*. Extensive research had led Professor Beard to the conclusion that cancer and trophoblast are, in fact, one and the same. His theory, therefore, is known as the trophoblastic thesis of cancer.[1]

The trophoblast in pregnancy indeed does exhibit all the classical characteristics of cancer. It

[1]Sometimes referred to also as the unitarian thesis of cancer on the basis that all cancers are, fundamentally, the same.

spreads and multiplies rapidly as it eats its way into the uterus wall preparing a place where the embryo can attach itself for maternal protection and nourishment.

The trophoblast is formed as a result of a chain reaction starting with another cell identified as the *diploid totipotent*. For our purposes let us call this simply the "total life" cell because it contains within it all the separate characteristics of the complete organism and has the total capacity to evolve into any organ or tissue or, for that matter, into the complete embryo itself.[1]

About eighty percent of these total life cells are located in the ovaries or testes serving as a genetic reservoir for future offspring. The rest of them are distributed elsewhere in the body for a purpose not yet fully understood but which may involve the regenerative or healing process of damaged or aging tissue.

The hormone estrogen is well known for its ability to effect changes in living tissue. Although it is generally thought of as a female hormone, it is found in both sexes and performs many vital functions. Wherever the body is damaged, either by physical trauma, chemical action, or illness, es-

---

[1]There is no need to go into all the details surrounding the formation of these cells, for they only tend to confuse us with facts that are not essential to an understanding of the basic theory. Anyone interested in this background can readily obtain it at the public library from any standard reference book on embryology. Of particular value are John Beard's *The Enzyme Treatment of Cancer and Its Scientific Basis* (Chatto & Windus, London, 1911) and Charles Gurchot's *The Biology of Cancer* (Friedman, San Francisco, 1948).

trogen and other steroid hormones always appear in great concentration, possibly serving as stimulators or catalysts for cellular growth and body repair.

It is now known that the total life cell is triggered into producing trophoblast when it comes into contact with these steroid hormones acting as "organizer stimuli." When this happens to those total life cells that have evolved from the fertilized egg, the result is a placenta and umbilical cord, a means of nourishing the embryo. But when it occurs non-sexually as a part of the general healing process, the result is cancer. To be more accurate, we should say that it is cancer *if* the healing process is not terminated upon completion of its task.

Hardin B. Jones, Ph.D., in his highly revealing "A Report on Cancer,"[1] touched upon this phenomenon as follows:

> A second important consideration about cancer is that all forms of overt cancer are associated with a random chance of survival which does not lessen with the duration of cancer. This strongly implies that there is some natural physiological restraint against progress of the disease and that the cause of the commonly observed rapid development of cancer in the terminal stages is the failure of the natural restraining influence.

---

[1]Paper delivered before the American Cancer Society's Eleventh Annual Science Writer's Conference, New Orleans, March 7, 1969.

We shall discuss shortly why this natural restraining influence on the healing process should fail, but, for now, at the risk of greatly oversimplifying the process, we may say that cancer is the result of *over-healing*.

We can readily see, therefore, why it has been said that smoking, or excessive exposure to the sun, or any number of harmful chemicals seem to cause cancer. *Anything* that causes damage to the body can lead to cancer *if* the body's healing processes are not functioning properly—as we shall see.

Dr. Stewart M. Jones of Palo Alto, California, has described the process this way:

> Whenever a trophoblast cell appears in the body outside of pregnancy, the natural forces that control it in a normal pregnancy may be absent and, in this case, it begins uncontrolled proliferation, invasion, extension, and metastasis. When this happens, it is initiated by an organizer substance, usually estrogen, the presence of which further promotes the trophoblast activity. This is the beginning of cancer.[1]

If it is true that the trophoblast cell is brought into being by a chain reaction which involves estrogen or other steroid hormones, then it would follow logically that an unnaturally high exposure to

---

[1]"Nutrition Rudiments in Cancer," by S.M. Jones, M.S., B.A., Ph.D., M.D., (Palo Alto, California., 1972) p. 6.

these substances would be a factor that favored the onset of cancer. And, indeed, this has been proven to be true. The use of diethylstilbestrol as a fattening agent for cattle was halted in 1972 because it was proven that this steroid, which was present in trace amounts in the beef at our grocery stores, had caused stomach cancer in experimental rats.

It also has been demonstrated that women taking contraceptive pills—especially those which are predominantly estrogen—not only undergo irreversible breast changes, but become almost three times more cancer-prone than women who do not. This fact was stressed by Dr. Otto Sartorius, Director of the Cancer Control Clinic at Santa Barbara General Hospital in California, who then added:

> Estrogen is the fodder on which carcinoma [cancer] grows. To produce cancer in lower animals, you first introduce an estrogen base.[1]

There is a slight confusion factor in all this due to the fact that, occasionally, *some* cancers appear to respond to hormone therapy—the deliberate administration of estrogen or testosterone to the cancer patient. But the only cases in which this kind of therapy is rewarded with favorable results are those involving cancer of the sexual glands, such as the breasts or prostate, or those organs that are

---

[1]As quoted in "Birth Control Pills Endanger Your Breasts," by Ida Honorof, *Prevention,* July, 1972, p. 89. Also see "Pill Linked to Cancer Risk," *L.A. Times,* Nov. 21, 1972, p. A-21.

heavily affected by sexual hormones. Female patients are given male hormones and male patients are given female hormones. The apparent favorable action is the result of the hormones' attempt to oppose or neuter those glands. If the cancer is retarded, it is because the *organ* is retarded.

The side-effects of this kind of therapy, of course, are the altering of the sexual physiology of the patient. Also, the beneficial results it produces, if any, are usually described by physicians as palliative, which means that the cancer is not cured, only retarded temporarily. But the worst part is that—especially in the case of men using estrogen—the presence of unnaturally high levels of steroids throughout the system could well be a factor favorable to the production of new cancer tissue other than at the primary site.

When cancer begins to form, the body reacts by attempting to seal it off and surrounding it with cells that are similar to those in the location where it occurs. A bump or lump is the initial result. Dr. Jones continues:

> In order to counteract the estrogenic action on the trophoblast, the body floods the areas of the trophoblast in a sea of beta-glucuronidase (BG) which inactivates all estrogen on contact. At the same time the cells of the tissues being invaded by the trophoblasts defensively multiply in an effort at local containment.

> Usually the efforts of the body to control the nidus of trophoblast are successful, the trophoblast dies, and a benign polyp or other benign tumor remains as a monument to the victory of the body over cancer.[1]

Under microscopic examination, many of these tumors are found to resemble a mixture or hybrid of both trophoblast and surrounding cells; a fact which has led some researchers to the premature conclusion that there are many different types of cancer. But the degree to which various tumors appear to be different is the same degree to which they are benign; which means that it is the degree to which there are *non*-cancerous cells within it. The greater the malignancy, the more these tumors begin to resemble each other, and the more clearly they begin to take on the classic characteristics of pregnancy trophoblast. And the most malignant of all cancers—the chorionepitheliomas—are almost indistinguishable from trophoblast cells. For, as Dr. Beard pointed out over seven decades ago, they are one and the same.

An interesting sidelight to these facts is that trophoblast cells produce a distinct hormone that readily can be detected in the urine. This is known as the chorionic gonadotrophic hormone (CGH). If it is true that cancer is trophoblast, then it is logical to expect that cancer cells also would secrete this hormone. And, indeed, they do. It is also true that

---

[1]*Ibid.*, p. 7.

no other cell is known to produce CGH.[1] This means that, if CGH is detected in the urine, it indicates that there is present either normal pregnancy trophoblast or abnormal malignant cancer. If the patient is a woman, she either is pregnant or has cancer. If he is a man, cancer can be the only cause.

The significance of this fact is far-reaching. A simple urine test similar to the well-known rabbit test for pregnancy can detect the presence of cancer long before it manifests itself as illness or a lump, and it throws serious doubt upon the rationale behind surgical biopsies. In fact, many physicians are convinced that any cutting into a malignant tumor, even for a biopsy, actually increases the likelihood that the tumor will spread. (More on that in a later chapter.) But, in any event, there is questionable need for such procedures in view of the fact that the CGH urine test is available and proven to be highly accurate. In fact, Dr. Manuel Navarro, Professor of Medicine and Surgery at the University of Santo Tomas in Manilla, has offered this test to American physicians for over a decade and reports better than 95% accuracy with both cancer and non-cancer patients. Almost all of the so-called errors have been in showing cancer activity within patients who presumably did not have cancer. But in a large percentage of these, those same patients later developed clinical manifestations of cancer, suggesting that the CGH test was accurate after all. Doctors who have had extensive experience with this test have

[1]A similar substance is produced in the anterior pituitary gland.

learned never to assume it is in error when it indicates the presence of trophoblast.[1]

Let us turn now to the question of defense mechanisms. Before we can hope to conquer cancer, first we must understand how *nature* conquers cancer—how *nature* protects the body and controls the growth of trophoblast cells.

One would suppose that this would be the primary question that determines the direction of all cancer research today. Unfortunately, it is not. Most contemporary research projects are wrapped up in the production of exotic and highly-poisonous drugs or high-voltage machines that deliver death rays to selected parts of the body. There is no counterpart for any of this in nature, and it is small wonder that progress has been so disappointing. But, recently, a small group of researchers has begun to look back to nature, and, if they persist in this course, they cannot help but succeed eventually. The most promising of all this work lies in the field of the body's natural mechanism for developing immunity against disease.

All animals contain billions of white blood cells. There are different types of white cells including lymphocytes, leukocytes, and monocytes, but they all apparently serve the same function which is to attack and destroy anything that is foreign and harmful to our bodies. Persons who develop a low white cell blood count become extremely suscepti-

[1]This is a modified, more sensitive micro-Aschheim Zondek test and is not to be confused with the Anthrone test which is based upon a similar principle but, due to technical problems connected with the test itself, so far has not been as reliable as the CGH test.

ble to infections of all kinds and, in fact, if the condition is sufficiently severe, they can die from a simple infected cut or a common cold.

Since the destruction of foreign bodies is the function of the white cells, it might seem logical, therefore, that they would attack cancer cells also. As one medical journal stated the problem recently:

> One crucial property our bodies have is the ability to distinguish between self and non-self. In other words, we can recognize (biologically) foreign material that finds its way into our bodies. This ability enables us to fight infections and to build up resistance to future infection. It also means that organ transplantation is not just a simple matter of intricate surgery. As far as the body's defense systems—the immunological apparatus—are concerned, bacteria, viruses, and transplanted organs are all foreign invaders and have to be repelled.
>
> What has puzzled immunologists for a very long time is that, although cancer cells are undoubtedly foreign, they seem to escape the lethal attentions of immunological systems. The crucial question is, how?[1]

---

[1]"New Assaults on Cancer," by Roger Lewin, *World of Research*, Jan. 13, 1973, p. 32.

In this otherwise excellent article, we find one of the great false assumptions that plagues almost all orthodox cancer research today: the assumption that cancer cells are foreign to the body. Quite to the contrary, they are a vital part of the life cycle (pregnancy and healing). Consequently, nature has provided them with a highly effective means of avoiding the white blood cells.

One of the characteristics of the trophoblast is that it is surrounded by a thin protein coating that carries a negative electrostatic charge. In technical terms this is called the *pericellular sialomucin* coat. The white blood cells also carry a negative charge. And, since similar polarities repel each other, the trophoblast is well protected. The blocking factor, so-called, is nothing more than a cellular electromagnetic field.

Commenting on the significance of these facts, Dr. Krebs wrote:

> For three-quarters of a century classical immunology has, in effect, been pounding its head against a stone wall in the vain quest for "cancer antigens," the production of cancer antibodies, etc., etc. The cancer or trophoblast cell is non-antigenic because of the pericellular sialomucin coat. . . .[1]

Part of nature's solution to this problem, as pointed out by Professor Beard in 1905, is found in

---

[1]Letter from Dr. Krebs to Andrew McNaughton, the McNaughton Foundation, San Francisco, Calif., dated Aug. 2, 1971.

the ten or more pancreatic enzymes, of which trypsin and chymotrypsin are especially important in trophoblast destruction. These enzymes exist in their *inactive* form (as zymogens) in the pancreas gland. Only after they reach the small intestine are they converted to their active form. When these, in turn, are absorbed into the blood stream and reach the trophoblast in sufficient quantity, they eat away or digest the negatively-charged protein coat. The cancer then is exposed to the attack of the white cells and it dies.[1]

In most discussions of this subject, it is assumed that the lymphocytes are the most active counterpart of all the various white blood cells. But opinions on this, also, currently are in the state of flux. In one recent study, for example, it was reported that the real aggressor was the monocyte. Although monocytes compose only two or three percent of the total, they were found to be far more destructive of cancer tissue than the lymphocytes which were more numerous. Either way, of course, the end result is still the same.[2]

---

[1]The operation of this mechanism is, of course, considerably more complex than this simplified description would indicate, and there is much that is not yet fully understood. For instance, investigators have not yet solved the puzzle of how the pregnancy trophoblast is protected from chymotrypsin during the initial phase of pregnancy. Obviously they have *some* kind of extra blocking factor that non-pregnancy trophoblast cells do not enjoy. It is possible that it is an increased local level of cobalomine that converts the hydro-cyanic acid into thiocyanate (vitamin B_{12}), plus a temporarily high level of rhodanese (protecting enzyme). But this is not at all certain, and it represents an interesting area for future research.

[2]See "Cancer Killing Cells Found to Eat Tumors," by Harry Nelson, Times Medical Writer, *L.A. Times,* April 4, 1973, p. 32.

Starting in 1972 there was a great flurry of publicity given to the "promising" experimental work done with BCG (the anti-tuberculosis vaccine known as Bacillus Calmette Guerin). The theory behind it is that the BCG, which actually is a TB virus which has been weakened so as to pose no serious threat to the patient, stimulates the body's production of white blood cells as part of its natural defense mechanism. When the vaccine enters the blood stream, the body does not know that the TB virus is weak or dead and it begins to produce specific combinations of white cells to repel the invader. These, then, remain as a barrier to any real TB virus that may come along in the future. These cells not only act as a future barrier against TB but, theoretically at least, they also are presumed to be effective against cancer cells. And there have been cautious reports of some highly-qualified progress in this direction. But, as we have seen, the presence of white cells *by themselves* is but one part of the solution to the cancer problem. Without consideration of the pancreatic and nutrition factors, real progress along these lines will be highly limited.

Interestingly, many of the reports of success with BCG, upon closer examination, may have been due as much to nutritional factors as anything else. For example, one such report appearing in the press described the treatment for cancer of one physician, Dr. Owen W. Wheeler, by another physician, Dr. Virginia Livingston. Dr. Wheeler had decided from his own experience that, since the conventional methods of cancer therapy were so unproductive of results, he would try BCG instead. So he approached Dr. Livingston who, at the time, was one of the few physicians who knew very much about this approach to cancer therapy. The article then explained the treatment:

> Dr. Wheeler was injected with BCG and put on a strict low-cholesterol diet and given antibiotics. The diet, he said, banned refined sugar, poultry and eggs, and called for raw vegetables, plenty of fish and multiple vitamin supplements.
>
> Within two months, the swelling was down, Dr. Wheeler said.
>
> Recent laboratory tests showed a remission of cancerous cells—that is, a return to a normal healthy state—and the presence of new, healthy tissue, he said.[1]

Let us analyze. The diet given to Dr. Wheeler consists of foods that do *not* consume pancreatic enzymes for their digestion. This is similar to the kind of diet prescribed by doctors using vitamin B_{17} therapy because it releases almost all of the pancreatic enzymes for absorption into the blood stream where they can do their work on the cancer cell. In addition to this, Dr. Wheeler was given "multiple vitamin supplements." It is quite possible, therefore, that these two factors were just as

[1] "Vaccine BCG Used With Amazing Success — Brings Complete Reversal Of Cancer in Patient With Malignant Neck Tumor," *National Enquirer,* Nov. 26, 1972.

important, if not more so, than the administration of BCG.

Returning to the subject of pancreatic enzymes, we find that the trophoblast cells in the normal embryo continue to grow and spread right up to the eighth week. Then suddenly, with no apparent reason, they stop growing and are destroyed. Dr. Beard had the general answer to why this happens as long ago as 1905. But recent research has provided the specific explanation. It is in the eighth week that the baby's pancreas begins to function.

It is significant that the small intestine, near the point where the pancreas empties into it, is one of the few places in the human body where cancer is almost never found. The pancreas itself often *is* involved with primary malignancy, but this is because the all-important enzymes do not become activated until they leave the pancreas and enter the intestines or the blood stream. Thus, the small intestine is bathed in these substances whereas the pancreas itself may receive very little. As one clinician has observed:

> One of the most striking features about the pathology of malignant disease is the almost complete absence of carcinoma [cancer] in the duodenum [first segment of the small intestine] and its increasing frequency throughout the gastrointestinal tract in direct proportion to the distance from this exempt segment.[1]

---

[1]Raab, W.: *Klin. Wchnschr.* 14:1633, as quoted in *The Laetriles, op. cit.,* p. 35.

We note, also, that diabetics—those who suffer from a pancreas malfunction—are three times more likely to contract cancer than non-diabetics.[1]

These facts, which have puzzled medical investigators for years, at last can be explained in light of the trophoblastic thesis of cancer. This thesis, as Dr. Krebs has asserted, "is not a dogma inflexibly held by its proponents; it is merely the only explanation that finds total congruence with all established facts on cancer."

To which Dr. Stewart M. Jones adds:

> This theory is the oldest, strongest, and most plausible theory of cancer now extant. It has stood the test of seventy years of confrontation with new information about cancer without ever being disproved by any new fact. . . . The voluminous, heterogenous science of cancer developed since then is coherent only in the light of this theory.[2]

Actually, it is the height of restraint to continue to call this a *thesis* or a *theory*. There comes a time when prudent men must admit that truth is truth and that the basic search is over. For many, of course, the search is more exciting (and infinitely more profitable) than the discovery. So they will continue to clutter their minds and laboratories with dead-

---

[1]Jones, *Nutrition Rudiments in Cancer, op. cit.*, p. 8.
[2]*Ibid.*, pp. 1, 6.

end theories and projects for as long as the money holds out.

But the truth is both startling and simple. While most researchers are operating on the assumption that cancer is foreign to the body and part of a process of death and decay, it is, instead, a vital part of the life cycle and an expression of the onrush of both life and healing.

V

THE TOTAL MECHANISM

The nutritional factor as a back-up mechanism to the enzyme factor; a biographical sketch of Dr. Ernst T. Krebs, Jr. and his development of Laetrile; the beneficial secondary effects of vitamin B_{17} on a wide range of human disorders; and an appraisal of the complexity of the total natural anti-cancer mechanism.

As demonstrated in the previous chapter, cancer can be thought of as a kind of over-healing process in which the body produces trophoblast cells as a part of its attempt to overcome specific damage to or aging of normal tissue. These trophoblast cells are protected by an electrostatically-charged protein coat. But in the presence of sufficient quantities of the pancreatic enzymes, this protective coating is digested away, exposing the trophoblast to the destructive force of the body's white blood cells. Thus, nature has assigned to the pancreas the vital job of preventing cancer by keeping trophoblast cells under control.

But what happens if, due to age or hereditary

factors, the pancreas is weak, or if the kinds of foods we eat consume almost all of the pancreatic enzymes for their digestion leaving very little for the blood stream, or if, due to surgery or radiation, there is scar tissue around the cancer which inhibits circulation and prevents the enzymes from reaching it, or if the rate of cancer growth is so high due to massive tissue damage that the pancreatic enzymes can't keep up with it? Then what?

The answer is that nature has provided a back-up mechanism, a second line of defense, that has an excellent chance of doing the job even if the first line should fail. It involves a unique chemical compound that literally poisons the malignant cell while nourishing all the rest. And this is where the vitamin concept of cancer finally comes back into the picture.

The chemical compound in question, of course, is vitamin B_{17}, which is found in those natural foods containing nitriloside. It is known also as amygdalin and, as such, has been used and studied extensively for well over a hundred years. But, in its concentrated and purified form developed by Dr. Krebs specifically for cancer therapy, it is known as Laetrile. For the sake of clarity in this volume, however, we shall favor the more simple name: vitamin B_{17}.

Professor John Beard, the man who first advanced the trophoblastic thesis of cancer, had suspected that there was a nutritional factor in addition to the enzyme factor but was never able to identify it. It wasn't until 1952 that this "extrinsic" factor was discovered by Dr. Ernst T. Krebs, Jr., and his famous father of the same name.

During the great flu epidemic of 1918 which took the lives of over ten million Americans, Dr. Krebs, Sr., was able to save almost 100% of the hundreds of patients who came under his care. As both a graduate pharmacist and an accredited physician practicing in Nevada, he had taken a keen interest in the fact that the Washoe Indians of that area enjoyed almost complete freedom from the respiratory diseases of the white man. He discovered that their native remedy for such ailments was called "Dortza Water," a decoction of the root of a wild parsley-like plant, known botanically as *Leptotaenia Dissecta*. He experimented with this herb, devised more efficient methods to extract the active ingredients, and discovered that it possessed amazing antiseptic and healing properties. It was this extract that was used to save the lives of his patients during the epidemic of 1918.

Thus Dr. Krebs, Sr., in 1918 was the first to introduce and use an antibiotic in scientific medicine. At that time, however, even the claim for the possibility of an antibiotic or "internal germicide" that would kill bacteria without harming the body was considered preposterous. The *Journal of the American Medical Association* on June 5, 1920, dismissed these claims out of hand. Thirty years passed before Carlson and Douglas of the Western Reserve University in Cleveland, Ohio, rediscovered leptonin—the antibiotic in the roots of Leptotaenia—and published their findings in the *Journal of Bacteriology* in May of 1948. Their summary reads:

> The antibiotic activity of oil fractions from the root of *Leptotaenia dissecta* was determined on 62 strains and species of bacteria, molds and fungi. The . . . agent was bactericidal for gram-positive bacteria . . . and gram-negative bacteria.

In 1953 scientists at the University of Utah School of Medicine published a number of papers on "Studies on Antibiotic Extract of Leptotaenia".[1] Even the effect Dr. Krebs, Sr. claimed for leptonin against flu viruses was confirmed in the case of the Pr-8 flu virus in embryonated eggs. The reality of leptonin as a broad spectrum antibiotic had now become so well established that the Department of Bacteriology at the University of Southern California School of Medicine granted a student a master's degree in microbiology for its study. The same student, Daniel Everett Johnson, later obtained his doctorate in microbiology at the University of California at Los Angeles in 1953 on the basis of his thesis showing the antibiotic action of leptonin against hundreds of different microorganisms.

Dr. Krebs, Sr., also had taken an early interest in cancer. He noticed that here, too, this appeared to be primarily a white man's disease. Remembering the lesson of "Dortza Water," he suspected

[1]*Antibiotics and Chemotherapy* (3 (4) 393), 1953.

that the key probably was hidden either in an herb or in the food itself. The final discovery, however, was made, not by him, but by his son who, by that time, had become totally wrapped up in the search for an answer to the cancer riddle.

Dr. Ernst T. Krebs, Jr., initially had wanted to follow in his father's footsteps and practice medicine. At one time he even had enrolled in medical school, but the deeper he became involved with science the more convinced he was that his primary interest lay, not in the treatment of patients, but in the world of medical chemistry. So after three years of anatomy and medicine at Hahnemann Medical College in Philadelphia, he changed his direction and became, not a medical doctor, but a Doctor of Biochemistry.

He pursued much of his undergraduate work at the University of Illinois between 1938 and 1941. Specializing in bacteriology, he received his Bachelor's Degree at the University of Illinois in 1942. He did graduate work at the University of California from 1943 to 1945, and later at the University of Mississippi, researching mostly in pharmacology during that period. He is the author of many scientific papers including "The Unitarian or Trophoblastic Thesis of Cancer," and "The Nitrilosides in Plants and Animals." He is the recipient of numerous honors and doctorates both at home and abroad. He is the science director of the John Beard Memorial Foundation. He is the discoverer of vitamin B_{15} (pangamic acid–*not* the same as B_{17}), which has proven to be an important adjunctive therapy in the treatment of many illnesses related to impaired circulation.

Early in his student work, Dr. Krebs became familiar with the trophoblastic thesis of cancer advanced by Professor John Beard. Working within the context of this theory, and encouraged by Dr. Charles Gurchot, a professor of pharmacology at the University of California Medical School, he began a search for the nutritional factor hinted at by Beard.

By 1950 he had identified the specific composition of this substance, had isolated it into crystalline form, and given it the name Laetrile,[1] and had tested it on animals to make sure it was not toxic. The next step was to prove that it was not harmful to humans. There was only one way to do that, of course. So he rolled up his sleeve and injected it into his own bloodstream!

Just as he had predicted, there were absolutely no harmful or distressing side effects. He was now ready for the final state of experiments—cancer patients themselves.

The B_{17} molecule contains two units of glucose (sugar), one of benzaldehyde, and one of cyanide, all tightly locked together within it. As everyone knows, cyanide can be highly toxic and even fatal if taken in sufficient quantity. However, locked as it is in this natural state, it is completely inert chemically and has absolutely no effect on living tissue.

[1]The material was derived from apricot kernels. Because it was *lae*vorotatory (left-handed) to polarized light, and because chemically it was a "Mandelo-ni*trile*," the first and last syllables were united to produce the word *Laetrile*.

By way of analogy, chlorine gas also is known to be deadly. But when the chlorine is chemically bound together with sodium forming sodium chloride, it is a relatively harmless compound known as common table salt.

There is only one substance that can unlock the B_{17} molecule and release the cyanide. That substance is an enzyme called *beta-glucosidase,* which we shall call the "unlocking enzyme."[1] When B_{17} comes in contact with this enzyme in the presence of water, not only is the cyanide released, but also the benzaldehyde, which is highly toxic by itself. In fact, these two working together are at least a hundred times more poisonous than either of them separately; a phenomenon known in biochemistry as synergism.[2]

Fortunately, the unlocking enzyme is not found to any dangerous degree anywhere in the body *except at the cancer cell,* where it always is present in great quantity, sometimes at levels in excess of one hundred times that of the surrounding normal cells. The result is that vitamin B_{17} is unlocked at the cancer cell, releases its poisons to the cancer cell, and *only to the cancer cell.*

---

[1]This is a generic term that can be applied to a category or grouping of enzymes that act on the vitamin in its natural state. The specific one that appears to be responsible for the unlocking action on the synthesized B_{17} known as Laetrile is *beta glucuronidase.*

[2]In passing, it is interesting to note that nature has used this same synergism as a defense mechanism for the poisonous millipede found in Louisiana and Mississippi. The creature is equipped with paired glands located on eleven of its segments. When threatened, it ejects cyanide and benzaldehyde from these glands with a deadly effectiveness that is well known. See "Secretion of Benzaldehyde and Hydrogen Cyanide by the Millipede Pachydesmus Crassicutis," *Science,* 138:513, 1962.

There is another important enzyme called *rhodanese,* which we shall identify as the "protecting enzyme."[1] The reason is that it has the ability to neutralize cyanide by converting it instantly into by-products that actually are beneficial and essential to health. This enzyme is found in great quantities in every part of the body *except the cancer cell* which, consequently, is not protected.[2]

Now let us examine what, at first, may appear to be exceptions to these rules. We have said that the unlocking enzyme is not found to any dangerous degree anywhere in the body except at the cancer cell. This is true, but please note the phrase "to any dangerous degree." The fact is that the unlocking enzyme actually is found in various concentrations *everywhere* in the human body. It is particularly prevalent in the healthy spleen, liver, and endocrine organs. In all of these instances, however, there *also* is present an even greater quantity of the protecting enzyme (rhodanese). The healthy tissue is protected, therefore, because the excess of this protecting enzyme completely neutralizes the effect of the unlocking enzyme.

The malignant cell by comparison not only has a greater concentration of the unlocking enzyme than found in most normal cells but it is totally

---

[1]Since about 1965 rhodanese has been identified in technical literature as *thiosulfate transulfurase*.

[2]Of necessity, this is a greatly condensed and simplified explanation of a rather complex biochemical chain reaction involving many intermediate stages. For those interested in a more technical evaluation, refer to *Suggested Mechanisms of Action of Vitamin B_{17},* by Charles Gurchat, Ph.D., reprinted in the Appendix of this book.

lacking in the protecting enzyme. Thus, it is singularly vulnerable to the release of cyanide and benzaldehyde.

The non-cancerous organs, therefore, are endowed by nature with the unique capacity of protecting themselves and even nourishing themselves from the digestion of the B_{17} molecule, whereas cancerous tissue converts the same vitamin substance into powerful toxins against which it has no defense.

With this in mind, it is amusing to watch the scientific "experts" who oppose Laetrile reveal their abysmal ignorance and arrogance on this subject. In the 1963 report of the California Cancer Advisory Commission, for example, we read:

> The opinion of Dr. Jesse P. Greenstein, chief of the laboratory of biochemistry at the National Cancer Institute was obtained in respect to the distribution of beta-glucuronidase in neoplastic [cancer] and non-neoplastic [healthy] tissues, and as to the implication that there was a "tumor" beta-glucuronidase [unlocking] enzyme. The fact is, reported Doctor Greenstein, that beta-glucuronidase is found in all tissues of the animal body. . . . In other words, there is much more "normal" beta-glucuronidase than "tumor" beta-glucuronidase in any animal body. In a letter dated November 10, 1952, Dr. Greenstein wrote "Such

> statement as . . . 'the malignant cell . . . is virtually an island surrounded by a sea of beta-glucuronidase' is sheer nonsense.[1]

Dr. Greenstein is perfectly correct in observing that the unlocking enzyme is found in all tissue of the animal body, but he is one hundred percent in error when he tries to scoff at its abundance within and around the malignant cell. His lack of expertise, however, is made abundantly clear by the fact that apparently he is totally unaware of the corresponding presence and counter-action of the protecting enzyme in these tissues. He is castigating as "sheer nonsense" a bio chemical mechanism of which he apparently is totally ignorant.

Dr. Otto Warburg received the Nobel Prize for proving that cancer cells obtained nourishment, not through oxidation as do other cells, but through fermentation of sugar. Warburg explained:

> From the standpoint of physics and chemistry of life, this difference between normal and cancer cells is so great that one can scarcely picture a greater difference. Oxygen gas, the donor of energy in plants and animals, is dethroned in the cancer cells and replaced by an energy-yielding reaction of the lowest living forms; namely, a fermentation of glucose.[2]

---

[1] *Op. cit.*, pp. 14, 15.

[2] As quoted in *Prevention,* May 1968.

From this it is easy to see why anything that improves normal respiratory metabolism is automatically an inhibitor to cancer growth. The important point here, however, is that any benzaldehyde that might diffuse away from the cancer cell and come into contact with normal cells, will be oxidized and converted into harmless benzoic acid. Benzoic acid is known to have certain antirheumatic, antiseptic, and analgesic properties. This could well partially account for the fact that B_{17} produces the unexpected effect of relieving the intense pain associated with terminal cancer, and does so without the aid of narcotics. Although not a pain reliever *per se*, when it comes in contact with cancer cells, it releases benzoic acid right at the inflicted location and, thus, bathes that area with a natural analgesic.[1] Meanwhile, the benzaldehyde that remains at the cancer cell will find itself in an almost total lack of oxygen causing it to linger and perform its deadly synergistic action for a prolonged period of time.

On the other hand, if a small amount of cyanide should diffuse into adjacent normal cells, it is converted by the enzyme rhodanese, in the presence of sulphur, into thiocyanate which, as stated previously, is perfectly harmless. But, more than that, thiocyanate is known as a natural regulator of blood pressure. It also serves as a metabolic pool for the body's self-production of vitamin B_{12} or

---

[1]It is the opinion of Laetrile clinicians, however, that the *primary* cause of pain reduction probably is due to the direct act of halting the tumor's invasion and destruction of healthy tissue.

cyanocobalamin, a substance essential for health. It comes as a great surprise for many to learn that cyanide is an essential and integral part of vitamin B_{12} as well as B_{17}.[1]

Another unexpected but welcome consequence of vitamin B_{17} is that it stimulates the hemoglobin or red blood cell count. As long ago as 1933 it was shown that exposure to small amounts of cyanide gas produced this effect in mice,[2] but only since the work begun by Dr. Krebs has this also been demonstrated in humans as a result of the internal chemical action of Laetrile.

Other experiments have indicated that trace amounts of cyanide and benzaldehyde released in the mouth and intestine, far from being cause for panic, actually are a part of the delicate balance of nature and serve entirely beneficial purposes. In the mouth and stomach these chemicals apparently attack the bacteria associated with tooth decay and bad breath. In the intestines they interact with the bacterial micro-flora to suppress or eliminate the flatulence long associated with westernized foods.

Perhaps the most interesting sidelight of all, however, is the probable connection between vitamin B_{17} and the modern black man's disease, *sickle-cell anemia*. In Africa, the Negro race has developed sickle cells in the blood apparently as a natural immunity factor to malaria. The develop-

---

[1]Vitamin B_{12} is not produced in plant tissue. It is the product of animal metabolism in which the cyanide radical is combined with hydrocobalamin ($B_{12}a$) to form cyanocobalamin (B_{12}).

[2]Maxwell and Bischoff, *Journal of Pharmacology and Experimental Therapy,* 49:270.

ment of this trait was dependent, in part, on the rich nitrilosidic content of the native African diet. Once the black man began to migrate into the modern cities of America and Europe, his eating habits were changed drastically and suddenly. The result is the painful hemolytic crisis caused by the clumping of the red cells. It already has been learned that this disease can be ameliorated by cyanate tablets. But cyanate also can be produced by vitamin B_{17} acting within the body, and it seems logical to assume that this is the way nature intended it to be taken.[1]

Let us pause, then, and reflect on the significance of these indicators. Is it possible that the rheumatic diseases, certain aspects of hypertension or high-blood pressure, tooth decay, much of our gastrointestinal disorders, sickle-cell anemia—*and cancer*—all are related directly or indirectly to a simple vitamin B_{17} deficiency? And if this is possible, what then of the other non-infectious diseases that plague mankind and puzzle medical research? Could their solutions also be found in the field of nutrition rather than drugs?

Having asked those reflective questions, which, unfortunately, may not be fully answered for decades, let us return to the main topic —cancer—and to the realm of those questions for which we *do* have answers. It is no longer a speculation but a fact supported by a mountain of evidence

[1]Since over 50,000 black Americans now are suffering from this disease, it is a topic of prime concern and importance. For that reason, we have included in the appendix of this volume the excellent paper entitled "Sickle-Cell Anemia and Vitamin B_{17} Metabolites" by Robert G. Houston.

that vitamin B_{17} is a vital part of an amazing biochemical process that destroys cancer cells while, at the same time, nourishing and sustaining noncancer cells.

Every person possesses trophoblast cells as a result of the continuing and normal regeneration process. These, however, are held in check by a metabolic barrier consisting of the pancreatic enzyme chymotrypsin and the nitriloside food factor vitamin B_{17}. This barrier is an intricate and perfect mechanism of nature that simply could not have been accidental.

As mentioned in the previous chapter, there is much speculation today about *carcinogens*—the things that supposedly cause cancer. We are told that smoking or extensive exposure to the sun, or chemical additives to our food, or even certain viruses all can cause cancer. But, as we have seen, the real cause is an enzyme and vitamin deficiency. These other things merely are the specific triggers that start the process.

Anything that produces prolonged stress or damage to the body can initiate the healing process. If this goes unchecked because the body lacks the necessary chemical ingredients to restore the equilibrium, then the result is cancer.

Specific carcinogens, therefore, like smoking or viruses, do not *cause* cancer, they merely determine where it is going to occur.

We must understand also that nature's defenses against cancer include more than just the pancreatic enzymes and vitamin B_{17}. For example, doctors in Europe have reported that *hyperthermy*—the deliberate raising of the patients' body temperature—has increased the effectiveness of vitamin therapy so greatly as to suggest another synergism, as between cyanide and benzaldehyde. They tell us that when the body temperature is raised from its normal thirty-seven degrees centigrade, to forty-one degrees, there is a gain in effect of from three to ten-fold. In other words, at forty-one degrees, three to ten times lower concentrations of Laetrile are required for a given anti-cancer effect in a given period of time. It is possible that the fermentive function of the cancer cell is impaired by the increased oxygenation and circulation customarily associated with fever.

Along this line, it is interesting to note also that Dr. Wilfrid Shute (the world-famous champion of vitamin E therapy for heart patients) reports that, for some reason, his patients who are on massive doses of E do not appear to contract cancer at the same rate as other patients. Nobel Prize winner Dr. Linus Pauling has suggested that vitamin C might also have value as an anti-cancer agent.[1] Dr. Umberto Saffiotti of the National Cancer Institute has blocked lung cancer in mice with vitamin A.[2] And, as reported in the October, 1971, issue of *Biochemical News,* massive oral doses of vitamin B reduced the growth of cancer in experimental mice by as much as seventy percent.

---

[1] "Linus Pauling Defends Vitamin C Claims Against 'Double Standard'," *Berkeley Gazette,* Nov. 6, 1971.

[2] "Is There An Anti-Cancer Food?" by Gena Larsen, *Prevention,* April, 1972.

So it is plain to see that there is much yet to be learned, and no one claims that vitamin B_{17} is the whole answer. In addition to hyperthermy, vitamins A, B, C, and E, it is possible that an important role also may be played by other enzymes, other vitamins, and even PH levels. Vitamin B_{17} seems to be the most vital and direct-acting of all these factors, but none of them can be ignored, for they are an interlocking part of the total natural mechanism.

Fortunately, it is not necessary for man to understand fully every minute theoretical aspect of this mechanism in order to make it work for him. The necessity of eating foods rich in *all* the vitamins and minerals—particularly vitamin B_{17}—and of minimizing prolonged damage or stress to the body is all that he really needs to know.[1]

---

[1]An excellent guide to the preparation of foods rich in vitamin B_{17} is June de Spain's *The Little Cyanide Cookbook* (American Media, Thousand Oaks, Calif., 1975).

VI

THE CYANIDE SCARE

A newspaper account of a couple who reportedly were poisoned by eating apricot kernels; a close look at the real facts in this case; an evaluation of the toxic potential of seeds containing B_{17}*; a common sense rule for eating same; and the clinical evidence that Laetrile is less toxic than sugar.*

On September 1, 1972, the California State Health Department released its Monthly Morbidity Report to the medical profession and to the press. It contained an entry about a Los Angeles couple who were treated for "cyanide poisoning" after eating thirty apricot kernels. On September 4, the *Los Angeles Examiner* ran a UPI dispatch under the heading: FRUIT PITS CAN CAUSE CYANIDE. And six days later, the *New York Times* ran a similar story: APRICOT KERNELS LINKED TO POISONINGS ON COAST.

All Americans had been warned—and scared—to stay away from those seeds! For those who were only vaguely familiar with the story of Laetrile, it was a near knock-out blow to the use of vitamin B_{17}. And, as shall be demonstrated in a following chapter, it is likely that it was *intended* to be just that.

In response to this news story, Mr. Jay Huchinson, a former cancer patient who attributes his recovery to Laetrile, dashed off the following letter, airmail special delivery, to Mohammed Jamel Khan, Mir of Hunza:

> Dear Mir and Rhani of Hunza:
>
> I am rushing this extremely urgent warning to you so that you can take immediate steps to notify your government and your people of the health hazard reported by the California State Department of Public Health during the week of September 3, 1972. I enclose articles from San Francisco newspapers . . . .
>
> Mir, you must get your people to stop eating those pits! Stop making flour out of them! Stop feeding your new-born infants the oil, and, for Mohammed's sake, stop anointing them with it! . . .
>
> Please write soon, and when you do, would you mind telling us why your people are among the healthiest in the world, and why your men and women live vigorous lives well into their 90's, and why you and your beautiful people never get cancer?[1]

---

[1]Quoted in "Of Apricot Pits and Hunzaland," by Mike Culbert, *Berkeley Daily Gazette,* August 13, 1972.

For most people, however, the sarcasm was completely lost. They took the story of the poisoned couple with *deadly* seriousness. Many who had heard that these seeds might be helpful against cancer, but who did not understand the chemistry involved, now were afraid to use them and were filled with doubts. An over-zealous health department in Hawaii confiscated all apricot seeds from the shelves of health food stores, and most of the stores on the mainland were intimidated — or confused — into dropping them from their line. The "news" story had served its purpose well.

Suspecting that there might be more to the story than met the eye, this writer attempted to get more details from the Department of Health — particularly the names of the couple in question. But it seemed that the department did not want them questioned. Dr. Ralph W. Weilerstein, the California Public Health Medical Officer, Bureau of Food and Drug, replied: "We regret that the confidentiality of morbidity reporting precludes interviewing the patients who were poisoned in Los Angeles."[1]

Dr. Dean Burk of the National Cancer Institute apparently was able to get more information. In a letter dated December 13, 1972, he explained:

> This couple from Los Angeles . . . really got sick and were treated in an emergency hospital, following ingestion by mouth of an overnight brew made from

---

[1]Letter to author, dated Sept. 20, 1972.

apricot nuts, apricot fruit, and distilled water — a concoction that probably fermented somewhat overnight, and was undoubtedly very bitter, and which brought on the illness (nausea, vomiting, etc.) after "about an hour," which is rather long for cyanide, which usually acts within minutes of being swallowed. Mr. Murray [of the Los Angeles County Health Department] was not willing to commit himself that cyanide was the chief cause of the illness, from which it would appear they promptly recovered. He said "that under the circumstances . . . you don't want to leap to conclusions and say that their illness was definitely due to the ingestion of amygdalin . . . . I don't think I could personally say that I proved that their illness was due to apricot kernels."

It is interesting, of course, that, somehow, out of the, I presume, thousands of items in the California Monthly Morbidity Reports, the Murray-Chinn material on amygdalin [the story of the Los Angeles couple] made the press throughout the country — presumably with the help and guidance of the state health authorities.

Mr. Gray has written, in an incipient article, "The health department's approach has been to discredit Laetrile without

> ever mentioning it directly. They have gotten the cooperation of the press when reporters have not gone beyond the offices of the health department in writing their stories."[1]

In another letter, dated December 20, 1972, Dr. Burk expanded his views even further:

> The facts are that a very considerable number of people eat 10-20 apricot kernels throughout a day, and after awhile, even 50-100 kernels safely, though hardly all at once as the . . . Angeleno gastronomes actually did. The same general situation holds with respect to a large number of ordinary foods that can be poisonous or allergic, etc., such as strawberries, onions, shrimps, and so on, that are never removed *en masse* or *in toto,* from food store shelves by health agencies imbued with the spirit of 1984 . . . .
>
> It is one thing for a health agency to warn people against foolish and rare actions with respect to any aspect of health, and quite another to totally deprive people of excellent food quite safe if ingested in a normal common sense way observed by 99.999% of the population.[2]

---

[1]Letter from Dr. Dean Burk to Mr. M. Standard, Attorney-at-Law, dated Dec. 13, 1972.

[2]Letter from Dr. Dean Burk to Mr. B. Stenjen, President of the Waikiki Chapter of the National Health Federation, dated December 20, 1972.

We have said that vitamin B_{17} is harmless to non-cancer cells. This is true, but perhaps it would be more accurate to say it is as harmless as any substance *can* be. After all, even life-essential water or oxygen can be fatal if taken in unnaturally large doses. And this is true also of vitamin B_{17}. For instance, there normally is a very small amount of beta-glucosidase (the "unlocking" enzyme) found within the seeds of most nitriloside fruits. This enzyme, when activated by the secretions of the mouth and stomach, causes a minute amount of cyanide and benzaldehyde to be released in these locations. As mentioned previously, the presence of limited amounts of these chemicals in the mouth, stomach, and intestines, is not dangerous and, in fact, appears to be part of an intended delicate chemical balance of nature, the absence of which can contribute to tooth decay, bad breath, and all kinds of gastrointestinal disorders. But what happens if these seeds are eaten in gigantic quantities?

There is one case of a man who, reportedly, died from devouring almost a cup of apple seeds. Incidentally, the case never has been authenticated and could well be entirely fictitious; but assuming it's true, if the man had eaten the apples also, he would have obtained enough extra rhodanese (the "protecting enzyme") from the fleshy part of the fruit to offset the effect of even that many seeds in his stomach. But that would have required that he eat several *cases* of apples which, of course, would have been impossible in the first place.

It should be noted that, in a few places in the world, there are certain strains of apricot trees that produce seeds containing ten times the concentration of nitriloside found in those trees grown in the United States. Even these seeds are not dangerous, of course, when eaten in reasonable quantity and with the whole fruit, but when eaten as seeds only, and in large quantity, they can present a danger. In Hunza, the first fruit of all new apricot trees is tested by the elders for extreme bitterness.[1] If it is found to be so — which is very rare — the tree is destroyed.

Occasionally, these unusual trees are found also in Turkey. But here, they are not destroyed because the seed is considered to be "good for health." As a result, there have been one or two cases in Turkey where little children have mistaken the seeds from the "wild apricot" to be those from the domestic variety, and they have become ill or died. But even in Turkey this is extremely rare. In the United States, of course, there is no record of such trees even having been in existence.

During a public lecture on the subject of Laetrile, Dr. E.T. Krebs, Jr., was asked by a woman in the audience if there was any danger from eating too many seeds containing the B_{17} factor. Here was his reply:

> This is an excellent question. In fact, it sometimes illustrates the indwelling cussedness of the human spirit. If we eat the seed with the whole fruit, it is impossible for us to get an excess of nitrilosides from

---

[1] All nitriloside-bearing seeds are bitter to the taste buds of westernized man. But when the Hunzakuts say a seed is bitter, it's *bitter!*

> the seeds. On the other hand, if we take apples, throw away all of the fruit, and collect half a cup of apple seeds, and decide to eat that half cup of apple seeds, there is a possibility we can suffer seriously from an overdose of cyanide . . . .
>
> You can't eat enough peaches or apricots or prunes or cherries or apples to get a sufficient amount of seeds to provide a toxic quantity of nitrilosides, but you can take a part of the plant and do so.[1]

Dr. Krebs further pointed out that roasting these seeds does not impair the vitamin B_{17} factor, but it does destroy the unlocking enzyme. So, those who are overly concerned about this matter can take the added precaution of roasting their seeds before eating.[2] It should be remembered, however, that this is not the way nature intended them to be consumed and, by so doing, we lose whatever benefit there may be from chemical activity in the mouth, stomach, and intestines.

The amount of nitriloside needed by the body is an unknown quantity. Perhaps it never can be determined for, surely, it will vary depending on the person — his age, sex, condition of pancreas, diet, weight, and hereditary factors. That is why it is absurd for anyone to try to publish or decree by law

---

[1]Text of remarks published in the *Cancer News Journal,* Sept./Dec., 1970, pp. 7, 8.

[2]For those who want to do this, Dr. Krebs suggests roasting for thirty to fifty minutes at 100° centigrade or 212° fahrenheit to de-activate the beta glucosidase.

the so-called Minimum Daily Requirements (MDR's) or Recommended Daily Allowances (RDA's), as they now are called.

Also, there is a tendency to think of deficiency diseases as either existing or not existing, with nothing in between. We either have scurvy or we don't. This can be terribly misleading. Actually, scurvy is the *extreme form* of a vitamin C deficiency. A lesser form may not reveal the classic symptoms of scurvy but could well manifest itself as fatigue, susceptibility to infection, and other non-fatal maladies.

World-famous biologist, Albert Szant-Gyorgyi, phrased it this way:

> Scurvy is not the first symptom of deficiency. It is a sign of the final collapse of the organism, a pre-mortal syndrome, and there is a very wide gap between scurvy and a completely healthy condition . . . .
>
> If, owing to inadequate food, you contract a cold and die of pneumonia, your diagnosis will be pneumonia, not malnutrition, and chances are that your doctor will have treated you only for pneumonia.[1]

Likewise, it is impossible to know what health problems, short of cancer, may be caused by a *partial* vitamin B_{17} deficiency. So, when in doubt,

[1]*The Living State; With Observations on Cancer* (Academic Press, N.Y. & London, 1972) p. 77.

most observers agree that it is best to err in the direction of surplus.

Dr. Krebs has suggested a minimum level of fifty milligrams of B_{17} per day for a normal healthy adult. Naturally, one who is pre-disposed to cancer would require more, and one who already was afflicted with the disease would need *much* more.

The average apricot seed grown in the United States contains approximately four or five milligrams of B_{17}. But this is an average figure only and can vary as much as by a factor of six, depending on the size of the kernel, the type of tree, the climate, and soil conditions. But, using the average figure, we can see that it would take ten to twelve apricot kernels per day to obtain fifty milligrams of B_{17}.

Is this a dangerous quantity? Hardly. There are cases reported in which people eat eighty-five to one hundred apricot kernels every day with no ill effects. Let us hasten to point out, however, that this is not a recommended dosage. Since it is possible for these kernels to vary in nitriloside content by as much as six to one, it is conceivable that eighty-five kernels from one tree could be the same as over *five hundred* kernels from another tree.

Nature can only do so much. It cannot anticipate excess of this kind. Therefore, it is wise to follow the simple rule that one should not eat at one time more seeds of any kind than he likely could consume if he also were eating a reasonable quantity of the whole fruit. This is a common sense rule with a *large* safety margin that can be followed with complete confidence.

There is no chemical substance in nature that

has been more misunderstood than cyanide. There has developed over the years an ignorance bordering on superstition dating back to the early days of science when it was first discovered that cyanide had a toxic potential. This ancient misapprehension has been perpetuated right up to the present time so that, to the average person, the word *cyanide* is synonymous with *poison*. As a result, we have developed a cultural antipathy toward this substance whenever it is discovered in our food. Every effort has been made to eliminate it. Local health agencies swarm over our grocery shelves to make sure that it does not reach us, and the federal Food and Drug Administration even has promulgated laws that make it illegal to sell any substance containing more of it than one four-hundreths of one percent![1] With that kind of "protection," it is small wonder that the American people are victims of the fulminating deficiency disease known as cancer.

So much for the cyanide in natural foods. What about the laboratory forms of vitamin B_{17} known as amygdalin or Laetrile? The answer is that here there is even *less* cause for concern. For over a hundred years standard pharmacology reference books have described this substance as non-toxic. After almost two centuries of use in all parts of the world, there never has been even one reported case of related death or serious illness.

Amygdalin generally is said to have been first discovered in 1830 by the German chemist Leibig. According to the *American Illustrated Medical*

---

[1]See "Requirements of the United States Food, Drug, and Cosmetic Act," FDA Publication No. 2, Revised June, 1970, p. 26.

Dictionary (1944 Edition) amygdalin means "like an almond," suggesting that the material from which the first sample was isolated was the bitter almond seed.[1] In one form or another, it has been used and studied almost constantly since that time and, according to Dr. Burk, "More is known chemically and pharmacologically about amygdalin than most drugs in general use." It was listed in pharmacopoeias by 1834. Toxicity studies were conducted with it on dogs as early as 1848. By 1907 it was listed in the Merck Index. And in 1961 it appeared in the Chinese-Korean Herbal Pharmacopoeias by Sun Chu Lee and Yung Chu Lee describing its reported use specifically for "cancer dissolution."[2]

Like many chemical compounds, amygdalin may exist in several different crystalline forms. Which form it takes depends on the number of molecules of water that are incorporated into it. Regardless of the form, however, once the crystals are dissolved, they all yield one and the same amygdalin.

The particular type of amygdalin crystal developed by Dr. Krebs, known as Laetrile, is unique because it is considerably more soluble than any of the other forms and, thus, can be administered to

---

[1]In the United States the commercial or "sweet" almonds contain no vitamin B_{17}. The "bitter" almonds, however, are very rich in this substance—even more rich than apricot kernels. But partly due to the American preference for the flavor of the sweet almond, and partly because the FDA has limited the sale of bitter almonds (see previous footnote), almost all bitter almond trees now have been destroyed.

[2]Letter from Dr. Dean Burk to Mr. M. Standard, *op. cit.*

the patient in a much greater concentration in the same volume of injectible material.

Commenting on the question of possible toxicity of Laetrile, Dr. Burk has summed it up with this emphatic statement:

> With forty-five years of study and research on the cancer problem, the last thirty-three years in the U.S. National Cancer Institute, and with files of virtually all published literature on the use of amygdalin ("Laetrile") with reference to cancer, and with innumerable files of unpublished documents and letters, I have found no statements of demonstrated pharmacological harmfulness of amygdalin to human beings at any dosages recommended or employed by medical doctors in the United States and abroad.[1]

Dr. D.M. Greenberg, Professor Emeritus of Bio-Chemistry at the University of California at Berkeley, and consultant to the Cancer Advisory Council of the California Department of Public Health added this note of concurrence:

> There is no question that pure amygdalin (Laetrile) is a non-toxic compound. This is not questioned by anyone who has

---

[1]Letter from Dr. Dean Burk to Stephen Wise and Gregory Stout, Attorneys, dated Dec. 17, 1972.

studied the reports submitted to the Cancer Advisory Council of the State of California.[1]

In the early days of experimentation with Laetrile, it was feared that the substance might be toxic if taken orally. This concern was based on the fact that, in the beginning, ways had not yet been perfected to remove the beta glucosidase (unlocking enzyme) from the apricot extract and, since Laetrile is a highly-concentrated form of B_{17}, on the basis of theory, it was feared that it might pose a problem when activated by the secretions of the stomach. Consequently, some of the early written works on Laetrile recommended injections only and cautioned against taking the substance orally. That caution, however, has long outlived its usefulness, and there is now no medical reason whatsoever to avoid the oral form.

Aspirin tablets are twenty times more toxic than the equivalent amount of Laetrile. The toxicity of aspirin is cumulative and can build up for days or even months. The chemical action of B_{17}, however, is completed usually within a few hours leaving behind absolutely no build-up. Each year in the United States, over ninety people die from aspirin poisoning. No one ever has died from B_{17}. Aspirin is a drug, alien to nature and to the body, whereas B_{17} is a vitamin found abundantly in plants that are appropriate for human consumption. Laetrile is even less toxic than sugar.

---

[1]Statement made on Oct. 13, 1969, as quoted in report attached to letter from Dr. Dean Burk, *Ibid.*

In a series of tests on adult mice, Dr. Dean Burk reported that they could live in perfect health to extreme old age when their normal diet consisted of fifty percent defatted apricot kernels. He said that this provided each mouse with a whopping one hundred and twenty-five milligrams of vitamin B_{17} per day. And he added that this was "in addition, excellent food material, rich in protein and minerals."[1]

In another series of tests, white rats were fed *seventy times* the normal human dose of Laetrile, and the only side-effects produced were greater appetite, weight gain, and superior health; just what one would expect from taking a vitamin.

---

[1]Letter from Dr. Dean Burk to Congressman Lou Frey, Jr., dated May 30, 1972.

VII

THE LAETRILE "QUACKS"

The names, professional standings, medical achievements, and clinical findings of some of the more prominent doctors who endorse Laetrile; the beneficial side-effects produced by its use; a suggested anti-cancer diet; and a brief description of vitamin B_{15}.

"Laetrile is goddamned quackery!"

Such is the pronouncement of Helene Brown, president of the American Cancer Society of California.[1]

There have been at least twenty-six published medical papers written by well-known physicians who have used Laetrile experimentally in the treatment of their own patients, and who have concluded that Laetrile is both safe and effective in the treatment of cancer.[2] In addition, there are the voluminous private records of physicians who have used it clinically but have never published their findings except in letters to their colleagues or in

---

[1]"The Pain Exploiters; The Victimizing of Desperate Cancer Patients," *Today's Health,* Nov., 1973, p. 28.

[2]A complete list of these papers is contained in *The Laetriles, op. cit.*, pp. 84, 85.

public lectures or interviews. The American Cancer Society and other spokesmen for orthodox medicine would have us believe that only quacks and crackpots have endorsed this conclusion. But the doctors who conducted these experiments and those who share their conclusions are *not* quacks. Here are just a few of the names:

In West Germany there is Hans Nieper, M.D., Director of the Department of Medicine at the Silbersee Hospital in Hanover. He is a pioneer in the medical use of cobalt and is credited with developing the anti-cancer drug, *cyclophosphamide*. He is the originator of the concept of "electrolyte carriers" in the prevention of cardiac necrosis. He was formerly the head of the Aschaffenburg Hospital Laboratory for chemical circulatory research. He is listed in *Who's Who in World Science* and is the Director of the German Society for Medical Tumor Treatment. He is one of the world's most famous and respected cancer specialists.

During a visit to the United States in 1972, Dr. Nieper told news reporters:

> After more than twenty years of such specialized work, I have found the non-toxic Nitrilosides — that is, Laetrile — far superior to any other known cancer treatment or preventative. In my opinion it is the only existing possibility for the ultimate control of cancer.

In Canada there is N.R. Bouziane, M.D., Director of Research Laboratories at St. Jeanne d'Arc Hospital in Montreal. He is a member of the hospital's tumor board in charge of chemotherapy. He graduated *magna cum laude* in medicine from the University of Montreal. He received also a doctorate in science from the University of Montreal and St. Joseph's University, an affiliate of Oxford University in New Brunswick. He is a Fellow in chemistry and a Fellow in hematology, and is certified in clinical bacteriology, hematology and biochemistry from the college. He is Dean of the American Association of Bio-Analysts.

After the first series of tests with Laetrile shortly after it was introduced, Dr. Bouziane reported:

> We always have a diagnosis based on histology [microscopic analysis of the tissue]. We have never undertaken a case without histological proof of cancer . . . .
>
> In our investigation, some terminal cases were so hopeless that they did not even receive what we consider the basic dose of thirty grams. Most cases, however, became ambulatory and some have in this short time resumed their normal activities on a maintenance dose.[1]

---

[1] "The Laetrile Story," *op. cit.* p. 3. Also *Cancer News Journal,* Jan./April, 1971, p. 20.

In the Philippines there is Manuel Navarro, M.D., Professor of Medicine and Surgery at the University of Santo Tomas in Manila. He is an Associate Member of the National Research Council of the Philippines; a Fellow of the Philippine College of Physicians, the Philippine Society of Endocrinology and Metabolism; and a member of the Philippine Medical Association, the Philippine Cancer Society, and many other medical groups. He is distinguished internationally as a cancer researcher and has over one hundred major scientific papers to his credit, some of which have been read before the International Cancer Congress. In 1971 Dr. Navarro wrote:

> I . . . have specialized in oncology [the study of tumors] for the past eighteen years. For the same number of years I have been using Laetrile-amygdalin in the treatment of my cancer patients. During this eighteen year period I have treated a total of over five hundred patients with Laetrile-amygdalin by various routes of administration, including the oral and the I.V. The majority of my patients receiving Laetrile-amygdalin have been in a terminal state when treatment with this material commenced.
>
> It is my carefully considered clinical judgment, as a practicing oncologist and researcher in this field, that I have obtained most significant and encouraging

> results with the use of Laetrile-amygdalin in the treatment of terminal cancer patients, and that these results are comparable or superior to the results I have obtained with the use of the more toxic standard cytotoxic agents.[1]

In Mexico there is Ernesto Contreras, M.D., who, for over a decade, has operated the Good Samaritan Cancer Clinic in Tijuana. He is one of Mexico's most distinguished medical figures. He received postgraduate training at Harvard's Children's Hospital in Boston. He has served as Professor of Histology and Pathology at the Mexican Army Medical School and as the chief pathologist at the Army Hospital in Mexico City.

Dr. Contreras was introduced to Laetrile in 1963 by a terminal cancer patient from the United States who brought it to his attention and urged him to treat her with it. The woman recovered, and Dr. Contreras began extensive investigation of its properties and use. Since that time he has treated thousands of cancer patients, most of whom have been American citizens who have been denied the freedom to use Laetrile in their own country.

Dr. Contreras has summarized his experiences with vitamin therapy as follows:

> The palliative action [improving the comfort and well-being of the patient] is in

---

[1]Letter from Dr. Navarro to Mr. Andrew McNaughton, The McNaughton Foundation, dated January 8, 1971, published in the *Cancer News Journal,* Jan./April, 1971, pp. 19, 20.

> about 60% of the cases. Frequently, enough to be significant, I see arrest of the disease or even regression in some 15% of the very advanced cases.[1]

In Japan there is Shigeaki Sakai, a prominent physician in Tokyo. In a paper published in the October 1963 *Asian Medical Journal,* Dr. Sakai reported:

> Administered to cancer patients, Laetrile has proven to be quite free from any harmful side-effects, and I would say that no anti-cancer drug could make a cancerous patient improve faster than Laetrile. It goes without saying that Laetrile controls cancer and is quite effective wherever it is located.

In Italy there is Professor Etore Guidetti, M.D., of the University of Turin Medical School. Dr. Guidetti spoke before the Conference of the International Union Against Cancer held in Brazil in 1954 and revealed how his use of Laetrile in terminal cancer patients had caused the destruction of a wide variety of tumors including those of the uterus, cervix, rectum, and breast. "In some cases," he said, "one has been able to observe a group of fulminating and cauliflower-like neoplastic masses resolved very rapidly." He reported also

[1]*Cancer News Journal,* Jan./April, 1971, p. 20. Again, we must bear in mind that these are *terminal* patients — people who have been given up as hopeless by orthodox medicine. Fifteen percent recovery out of *that* group is a most impressive accomplishment.

that, after administering Laetrile to patients with lung cancer, he had been "able to observe, with the aid of radiography, a regression of the neoplasm or the metastases."

After Guidetti's presentation, an American doctor rose in the audience and informed everyone present that Laetrile had been thoroughly investigated in the United States and found to be worthless. Dr. Guidetti replied, "I do not care what was determined in the United States. I am merely reporting what I saw in my own clinic."[1]

In Belgium there is Professor Joseph H. Maisin, Sr., M.D., of the University of Louvain where he is Director of the Institute of Cancer. He is President Emeritus of the International League Against Cancer which conducts the International Cancer Congress every four years.

And in the United States there are such respected names as Dr. Dean Burk of the National Cancer Institute, the late Dr. John A. Morrone of the Jersey City Medical Center, Dr. Ernst T. Krebs, Jr., who developed Laetrile,Dr. John A. Richardson, the courageous San Francisco physician who challenged the government's right to prevent Laetrile from being used in the United States, and many more from over twenty countries with equally impeccable credentials.

Most of these researchers have reported independently that patients experience several important side effects. These usually include a normalizing of blood pressure in hypertensive patients, improved appetite, an increase in the hemoglobin

---

[1]*Cancer News Journal,* Jan./April, 1971, p. 19.

and red blood cell count, the elimination of the fetor (which is the unpleasant odor often associated with terminal cancer patients), and above all, a release from pain without narcotics. Even if the patient has started Laetrile therapy too late to be saved, this last effect is a merciful blessing in itself.

In addition to the clinical results obtained by these physicians in the treatment of humans, there have been at least five carefully controlled experiments on mice that have shown definite Laetrile anti-cancer action. These include: (1) The experiments done by Scind Laboratories of San Francisco in 1968, (2) the studies completed at the Pasteur Institute (Paris) in 1971, (3) those at the Institute von Ardenne (Dresden, Germany) in 1973, (4) the experiments done by the Southern Research Institute in 1973, and (5) the first and third trials at the Sloan-Kettering Institute in 1973 and 1974. And in spite of all this, spokesmen for orthodox medicine still proclaim there is no evidence that Laetrile works. The evidence, however, is everywhere.[1]

While the use of Laetrile alone has proven to be effective in many instances, far better results usually are obtained with supplemental therapy as well. John Richardson, M.D., of San Francisco has achieved one of the highest recovery rates among Laetrile practitioners in the entire world. Here, in his own words, is the advice he gives to his patients:

> *Vegetable Kingdom:* In the vegetable kingdom eat anything and everything that

[1] "See How They Lie, See How They Lie," by Dr. Dean Burk, *Cancer News Journal,* Vol. 9, no. 3 (June, 1974), p. 5.

is edible and for which you have no idiosyncrasy. Eat everything whole. Eat all of the edible parts of the food — especially the roughage. This food is preferably eaten raw; but when you cannot tolerate it raw, cook the food just sufficiently to make it tolerable or edible.

Animal Kingdom: Eat any or all fish as fresh as possible and lightly cooked in the absence of animal fats (vegetable oils may be used). Eat the skin-free meat of poultry. Whatever does not fall within this formula, forget it. Don't eat it. The formula is all-inclusive so it's not necessary to mention: no dairy products, beef, mutton, pork, bacon, ham, etc.

The liver is to neoplastic diseases what the heart is to circulatory diseases. The liver is central.

Adequate liquid intake with fresh fruit juices plain or carbonated.

Vitamin Supplements: Vit. C, 1500 mg to 5000 mg; 800 - 1200 International Units of d alpha tocopherol (vitamin E) plus a good brand of therapeutic multi-vitamins, preferably of organic or natural derivatives.

Toxins of all kinds to be avoided includ-

> ing tobacco, alcohol. Discourage coffee, tranquilizers, sedatives, analgesics. Antibiotics OK.
>
> Rest important while exercise should spare the affected area . . . .
>
> You should include Vitamin B_{15} (pangamic acid) which detoxifies the liver as a transmethylating agent, and increases the oxygen uptake potential of the tissues, and since trophoblast lives by the fermentative process, the rationale for the B_{15} is obvious.
>
> *Pancreatic Enzyme Supplementation:* We find dessicated pancreas substances to be an effective supplement.[1]

The dietary restrictions prescribed by Dr. Richardson are, of course, for those who have cancer and are undergoing Laetrile therapy. It is not recommended for healthy persons because it is unnecessarily restrictive. For those who do not have cancer, a general diet containing foods rich in nitriloside content should be adequate.[2] As an example, here is what Dr. Krebs suggests:

> For breakfast, gruel of buckwheat, millet, and flaxseed, with elderberry jelly on millet toast. All this accompanied by stewed prunes.

---

[1]Open letter to interested doctors dated Nov. 1972, revised 1974.

[2]Again we highly recommend June de Spain's *The Little Cyanide Cookbook,* (American Media, Thousand Oaks, Calif., 1975).

> For lunch, lima beans or a succotash with chick peas; millet rolls with plum jam; elderberry wine.
>
> For dinner, a salad with bean and millet sprouts; dinner rolls of buckwheat and millet sweetened with sorghum molasses extracted from sorghum cane; rabbit which, hopefully, fed on clover; and after dinner apricot, peach, cherry, or plum brandy originally prepared from crushing the entire or whole fruit.
>
> Nibbling on any member of the raspberry family, macadamia nuts, and bamboo sprouts is also suggested.

Dr. Krebs has pointed out that in the Old Testament there is a formula for the preparation of grains for bread, and it speaks of six ingredients, five of which are rich in nitrilosides. They are barley, beans, lentils, millet and vetch (chickpea or garbanzo beans).[1]

The intended balance of nature does not require a *vast* amount of vitamin B_{17} in the daily diet any more than it is required of the other vitamins. It is possible that if one did no more than eat the seeds from an apple or two a day he could obtain an adequate supply. But that would probably be bordering on the low side, especially considering the fact that, in westernized society, B_{17} is not generally available in other foods to supplement it. So it

---

[1]*Ezekiel* IV, 9.

probably would be advisable to obtain a higher level of intake than that.

Obviously, some of the foods mentioned by Dr. Krebs are not always readily available to the average city dweller. As a substitute, many people simply have adopted the habit of eating six to twelve apricot or peach seeds each day, or have ground them in their blenders and used them as a light seasoning for cereals, salads, and the like. For those who dislike the slight bitter taste of these seeds, they can be ground up and loaded into empty capsules. Which means that no one need be deprived of this vitamin if he really wants it.

Vitamin B_{15} has been mentioned several times as an important auxiliary therapy in addition to vitamin B_{17}, and there often is quite a bit of confusion between the two. So let's take a moment to differentiate.

Vitamin B_{15} technically is called *pangamic acid. Pan* implies *everywhere* and *gami* means *seed.* It was so named because it is found in small amounts almost everywhere on earth in seeds and usually in the company of other members of the vitamin B complex.

Like B_{17} it too was discovered by Dr. E.T. Krebs, Jr., while exploring the chemical properties of apricot kernels in 1952. It could be said that it was an unexpected bonus or by-product of the search for vitamin B_{17}.

The best way to understand the effect of vitamin B_{15} is to think of it as instant oxygen. It increases the oxygen efficiency of the entire body and aids in the detoxification of waste products. Since cancer cells do not thrive in the presence of oxygen but depend rather on fermentation of glucose, it is probable that B_{15}, indirectly, is an enemy of cancer.

Vitamin B_{15} is not widely known or used in the United States. The reason is almost an exact parallel to the Laetrile story. The government officially has refused to recognize that B_{15} is of value. Meanwhile it is used extensively in many other countries. Russia in particular is far ahead of the United States in the use of this substance and has conducted extensive research into its many uses. In fact, in 1965 the U.S.S.R. Academy of Sciences released a 205-page symposium of its findings up to that date. In 1968 the Scientific Advisory Committee of the Ministry of Health unanimously ratified all the original claims in the report and authorized the Soviet drug industry to begin mass-production of B_{15} for general use.

It has been reported that the Russian athletes have been given heavy doses of B_{15} during their participation at the Olympics. If this is true, there is good reason for it. Experiments have shown that this substance, although just a natural food factor, greatly increases physical strength and stamina. When rats were put into tubs of water and forced to swim, those that had been vitaminized with B_{15} were all still swimming long after the others had fatigued and drowned. When other rats were put into glass chambers from which oxygen gradually was removed, the vitaminized rats lived considerably longer — thus on less oxygen — than the control group.

The Soviet scientists disclosed that vitamin

B_{15} is effective in such areas as circulatory problems, heart conditions, elevated blood cholesterol, various skin disorders, hardening of the arteries, bronchial asthma, diabetes mellitus, and wound healing. They were especially emphatic in their findings that B_{15} was effective in retarding the ageing process! Professor Shpirt of the City Clinical Hospital No. 60 in Moscow concluded: "I believe the time will come when there will be calcium pangamate (B_{15}) next to the salt shaker on the table of every family with people past forty."[1]

Doctors, such as John Richardson, who wish to use vitamin B_{15} in America, have been forced to operate on the fringe of the law because their government has harassed its manufacturers and blocked its movement in commerce. As Dr. Krebs observed:

> Our concern is with vitamin B_{15} — a natural constituent of natural foods, one that experimentation has shown to be of definite value in increasing resistance to disease and in maintaining healthy functioning of the body as well.
>
> Pangamic acid is giving the people of Russia, Japan, Yugoslavia, France, Spain, and Germany a tremendous health

---

[1] For a detailed analysis of these findings, see *Vitamin B_{15} (Pangamic Acid); Properties, Functions, and Use*. (Science Publishing House, Moscow, U.S.S.R., 1965) reprinted by McNaughton Foundation, Sausalito, Calif.

> and longevity advantage. But it is not available to us in the land in which it was first discovered.

Fortunately, there is some evidence that B_{15} is finally becoming recognized by several of the more prestigious medical institutions in spite of government obstacles. Let us hope that the trend rapidly continues.

It is possible that B_{15} will be recognized and accepted by orthodox medicine long before B_{17}. This is because there is less vested interest to overcome. There have been no broad derogatory pronouncements by the AMA and, hence, no reputations are at stake. But, in time, the sheer weight of the facts will force the acceptance of B_{17} as well. And the men who now bear the brunt of controversy, professional ostracism, and social scorn, will emerge, not as quacks, but as the great medical pioneers of their day.

VIII

"UNPROVEN" CANCER CURES

Clinical evidence in support of the trophoblastic thesis; laboratory experiments showing that Laetrile kills cancer cells; and case histories of a variety of terminal cancer patients who attribute their recovery to the effect of Laetrile.

The cyanide scare mentioned previously was but one small salvo in the continuing barrage of officialdom's attacks against Laetrile.The total weaponry runs the gamut from scare tactics to outright falsehoods. But mostly they take the form of scholarly pronouncements, cloaked in the cloth of apparent concern for the public welfare, that vitamin therapy may sound good in theory, but in practice, it simply does not work.

Dr. Ralph Weilerstein, Public Health Medical Officer of the California Food and Drug Administration has said flatly: "Nobody's come up with any reliable data that it is of any value."[1] The Federal

[1]"Food Additive Ban Likely," *San Jose Mercury* (Calif.), Sept. 9, 1972.

FDA has proclaimed: "The Food and Drug Administration has seen no competent, scientific evidence that Laetrile is effective for the treatment of cancer."[1] And the American Cancer Society, in an impressive volume entitled *Unproven Methods of Cancer Management,* has stated:

> After careful study of the literature and other information available to it, the American Cancer Society does not have evidence that treatment with Laetrile results in objective benefit in the treatment of cancer in human beings.[2]

Commenting on this particular statement, Dr. Dean Burk of the National Cancer Institute described it as:

> . . . a statement with close to zero scientific worth, however much sheer propaganda value. The fact is . . . there are few "proven" methods operating on a large scale anywhere, so that the word "unproved," as used by the ACS, is a highly and unjustifiedly weighted word."[3]

As far as the general public is concerned, how-

---

[1]*A Cancer Journal for Clinicians* (published by ACS) July/Aug., 1972.

[2]Published 1971, p. 139.

[3]Letter from Dr. Dean Burk to Dr. Frank Rauscher, Director of the National Cancer Institute, dated April 20, 1973.

ever, if the American Cancer Society classifies vitamin B_{17} or Laetrile as an "unproven cancer cure," that's all they need to know. Consequently, official pronouncements from prestigious organizations such as these are hard to ignore. But so are the favorable findings of those clinicians who have used Laetrile on their own patients. *Somebody* is wrong!

In a previous chapter we examined in detail the scientific integrity of the one research project upon which almost all official opposition to Laetrile is based, and we discovered that it is shockingly lacking on all counts. We discovered, also, that almost all of the cancer "experts" who have spoken out against Laetrile have done so, not out of personal experience or experimentation, but simply out of their complete faith in the scientific integrity of this one discredited report. In other words they have been quoting still other experts who, in turn, have been quoting the "findings" of *two* men. And we learned that these two men not only had never used Laetrile themselves but actually had falsified the records of what was reported to them by members of the research team.

Showing that the case against Laetrile is fraudulent, however, does not constitute a case *for* Laetrile. It is necessary, therefore, first to examine at least some of the overwhelming evidence that vitamin B_{17} actually *does* work in practice just as well as it does in theory.

The effectiveness of the trophoblastic thesis as a basis of cancer therapy has been demonstrated both in the laboratory and in the clinic beyond any doubt. In 1935, for example, long before the development of Laetrile, Dr. Isabella Perry of the Department of Pathology at the University of California Medical School conducted a series of experiments in which she subjected tumor-bearing rats to prolonged inhalation of cyanide fumes. Here is what she wrote:

> A considerable percentage of the animals so treated showed complete regression of the tumor. Both regressing and growing tumors in treated animals had little capacity for transplantation.[1]

Perry observed that these experiments were probably of little value to humans because, in order to be effective, the level of cyanide fumes had to be dangerously close to lethal — a problem that is not present when the cyanide is released only at the cancer cell, as it is in the action of vitamin B_{17}. Nevertheless, these rats showed, not only complete tumor regression, but, compared to the control group without cyanide, an average life extension in excess of three hundred percent.

When we turn to the laboratory reports on *Laetrile,* the results are even more encouraging, especially since there is none of the danger connected with the inhalation of cyanide fumes. Dr. Dean Burk, Director of the Cytochemistry Section of the federal government's National Cancer Insti-

---

[1] "The Effects of Prolonged Cyanide Treatment on The Body and Tumor Growth in Rats," *American Journal of Cancer,* 1935, 25:592.

tute, has reported that, in a series of tests on animal tissue, the B_{17} had no harmful effect on normal cells, but released so much cyanide and benzaldehyde when it came in contact with cancer cells that not one of them could survive. He said, "When we add Laetrile to a cancer culture under the microscope, providing the enzyme glucosidase also is present, we can see the cancer cells dying off like flies."[1]

While participating in the Seventh International Congress of Chemotherapy held in Prague in 1971, Dr. Burk declared:

> Laetrile appears to work against many forms of cancer including lung cancer. And it is absolutely non-toxic . . . .
>
> *In vitro* tests with Ehrlich ascites carcinoma [a particular type of cancer culture] revealed that, where cyanide alone killed one percent of the cells and benzaldehyde alone killed twenty percent, a combination of the two was effective against all the cells. Amygdalin [Laetrile] with glucosidase [the "unlocking enzyme"] added also succeeded in killing 100 percent of the ascites tumor cells, due to the freeing of the same two chemicals.[2]

---

[1] "Laetrile Ban May Be Lifted," *Twin Circle,* June 16, 1972, p. 11.

[2] "Amygdalin Claimed Nontoxic Anti-Cancer Therapeutic Agent," *Infectious Diseases,* Oct. 15, 1971, pp. 1, 23.

In another series of tests, Dr. Burk reported that Laetrile was responsible for prolonging the life of cancerous rats eighty percent longer than those in the central group not so innoculated.[1]

The man who made these findings is one of the foremost cancer specialists in the world. In 1965 he received the Gerhard Domagk Award for Cancer Research, and in 1952 and 1955, the Hillebrand Award of the American Chemical Society, and most recently the Commander Knighthood Of The Medical Order of Bethlehem (Rome) founded in 1459 by Pope Pius the Eleventh. He holds a Ph.D. in biochemistry earned at the University of California. He was a Fellow of the National Research Council at the University of London, Kaiser Wilhelm Institute for Biology, and also at Harvard. He was senior chemist at the National Cancer Institute, which he played a role in establishing, and since 1946 has been director of the Cytochemistry Section. He belongs to eleven scientific organizations, has written three books relating to chemotherapy research in cancer, and is author or co-author of more than two hundred scientific papers in the field of cell chemistry.

If Dr. Burk says Laetrile works, *it works!*

Dr. Burk, of course, is not a physician. He is a biochemist. His experiments have been with cancer cultures and with laboratory animals, not people.

---

[1]Testimony in *Hearings* before the Subcommittee on Public Health and Environment, Committee on Interstate and Foreign Commerce, House of Representatives, Ninety-Second Congress, as quoted in *Cancer News Journal*, July-October, 1972, p. 48.

As we have seen, however, the health records of the Hunzakuts, and Eskimos, and many other groups around the world are statistically conclusive that vitamin B_{17} does control cancer in human beings with an effectiveness approaching 100%. There can be little controversy over that. But what about cancer once it already has started? Can B_{17} restore a person to health after he has contracted the disease?

The answer is yes, *if* it is caught in time, and *if* the patient is not too badly damaged by prior X-ray treatment or toxic drugs. Unfortunately, most cancer victims start taking Laetrile only after their disease is so far advanced that they have been given up as hopeless by routine medical channels. Usually they have been told that they have only a few more months or weeks to live. And it is in this tragic state of near death that they turn to vitamin therapy as a last resort. If they die — and, indeed, many of them do — then they are counted as statistical failures for Laetrile. In reality, it is a victory for Laetrile that *any* of them should be saved at this stage. For once a deficiency disease has progressed so far, the damage it does simply cannot be reversed.

It is known, for example, that a severe vitamin A deficiency in a pregnant animal will result in an offspring that is completely blind. In fact, it will be born without orbits, retina, or even optical nerves. No amount of vitamin A administered at that late stage can cause the eyes to grow back.

Likewise, a child whose legs become bowed by rickets (a vitamin D deficiency disease) can never achieve a normal bone structure again no matter how much vitamin D he receives.

In cancer, of course, the process is somewhat different. Instead of normal tissue *failing* to form or becoming *mal*formed, it literally becomes destroyed. The cancerous growth invades and corrupts, leaving behind organs that cannot function simply because they are almost completely gone.

A man who has been shot with a gun can have the bullet removed but still die from the wound. Likewise, a patient can — and often does — have his cancer destroyed by vitamin B_{17} and still die from the irreversible damage already done to his vital organs.

And so, in view of this tremendous handicap, the number of terminal patients who *have* been restored to health is most impressive. In fact there literally are thousands of such case histories in the medical record. The American Cancer Society has tried to create the impression that the only ones who claim to have been saved by Laetrile are those who merely are hypochondriacs and who never really had cancer in the first place. But the record reveals quite a different story. Let's take a look at just a few examples.

Mr. David Edmunds of Pinole, California, was operated on in June of 1971 for cancer of the colon, which also had metastasized or spread to the bladder. When the surgeon opened him up, he found that the malignant tissue was so widespread it was almost impossible to remove it all. The blockage of the intestines was relieved by severing the colon and bringing the open end to the outside of his abdomen — a procedure known as a colostomy. Five months later, the cancer had worsened, and Mr. Edmunds was told that he had only a few more months to live.

Mrs. Edmunds, who is a Registered Nurse, had heard about Laetrile and decided to give it a try. Six months later, instead of lying on his deathbed, Mr. Edmunds surprised the doctors by feeling well enough to resume an almost normal routine.

An exploratory cystoscopy of the bladder revealed that the cancer there had completely disappeared. At his own insistence, he was re-admitted to the hospital to see if his colon could be put back together again.

In surgery, they found nothing even resembling cancer tissue. So they re-connected the colon and sent him home to recuperate. It was the first time in the history of the hospital that a *reverse* colostomy of this type had been performed.

Mr. Edmunds now is living a normal life of health and vigor.[1]

In 1967 in Walnut Creek, California, Mrs. Joanne Wilkinson, mother of six, had a tumor removed from her left leg just below the thigh. Four months later there was a recurrence requiring additional surgery and the removal of muscle and bone.

---

[1]See "Cancer 'Miracle-Cure' " by Mark Trantwein, *Berkeley Daily Gazette,* July 27, 1972. Story confirmed in tape-recorded personal interview by author.

A year later, a painful lump in the groin appeared and began to drain. A biopsy revealed that her cancer had returned and was spreading.

Her doctor told her that surgery would be necessary again, but this time they would have to amputate the leg, the hip, and probably the bladder and one of the kidneys as well. The plan was to open up her lungs first to see if cancer had located there. If it had, then they would not amputate, because there would be no chance of saving her anyway.

At the urging of her sister and of a mutual friend, Mrs. Wilkinson decided not to undergo surgery but to try Laetrile instead. Her doctor was greatly upset by this and told her that, if she did not have the surgery, she couldn't possibly live longer than twelve weeks. Mrs. Wilkinson describes in her own words what happened next:

> That was Saturday, November 16, 1968. I'll never forget that day! The stitches from the biopsy were still in the leg.
>
> Dr. Krebs[1] gave me an injection of Laetrile—and the tumor reacted. It got very large — from walnut size to the size of a small lemon — and there was bleeding four or five days. I went back on Monday, Wednesday, and Friday each week for five weeks to get injections, and the

[1]She is referring here to Byron Krebs, M.D., the brother of Dr. E.T. Krebs, Jr.

> tumor then started getting smaller. Five weeks later I could no longer feel it.
>
> An X-ray was taken the first Monday, and regularly after that to watch the progress. Injections were continued for six months — ten cc's three times a week — and of course the diet: No dairy products, nothing made with white flour — no eggs — but white fish, chicken, turkey.
>
> And I felt wonderful! In fact, in August, 1969, the doctor told me I needed no more injections. My X-rays were clear, showing that the tumor had shrunk, was apparently encased in scar tissue, and was not active.

Today, *years* after her doctor told her she couldn't possibly live longer than twelve weeks without surgery, Mrs. Wilkinson is living a healthy and productive life. All that is left as a grim reminder of her narrow escape is a small scar from the biopsy.[1]

Mr. Joe Botelho of San Pablo, California, underwent surgery (trans-urethral subresection) and was told by his doctor that he had a prostate tumor that simply had to come out. His reaction?

> I didn't let them take it out because I figured that would only spread it. The

[1]See "Laetrile — An Answer to Cancer?" *Prevention,* Dec. 1971, pp. 172-175. Story confirmed in personal interview by author.

> doctor told me I wouldn't last too long. He wanted to give me cobalt, and I wouldn't agree to that either.
>
> At a health food store I heard about a doctor in San Francisco who used Laetrile. I went to see him, was told that the prostate was the size of a bar of soap. I got one injection every four days for several months.[1]

Mr. Botelho, who was sixty-five at the time, also maintained a strict diet designed specifically not to use up the body's pancreatic enzyme, trypsin. He is no longer afflicted with his tumor and even reports that his hair is turning dark again. He's not sure what has caused that, but attributes it to his better eating habits.

Alicia Buttons, the wife of the famous actor-comedian Red Buttons, is among the thousands of Americans who attribute their lives to the action of Laetrile. Speaking before a cancer convention in Los Angeles, Red Buttons declared:

> Laetrile saved Alicia from cancer. Doctors here in the U.S. gave her only a few months to live last November. But now she is alive and well, a beautiful and vital

[1] "Laetrile—An Answer to Cancer?" *op cit.*, pp. 175, 176.

> wife and mother, thanks to God and to those wonderful men who have the courage to stand up for their science.[1]

Mrs. Buttons had been suffering from advanced cancer of the throat and was given up as terminal by practitioners of orthodox medicine. As a last resort, however, she went to West Germany to seek Laetrile therapy from Dr. Hans Nieper of the Silbersee Hospital in Hanover. Within a few months her cancer had completely regressed, the pain had gone, her appetite had returned, and she was as healthy and strong as ever before. Doctors in the United States verified the amazing recovery, but could not believe that a mere vitamin substance had been responsible.

The reluctance of many physicians to accept the reality of the vitamin concept of cancer was well described by Miss Carol Vencius, a former cancer victim from Marin County, California. After successful Laetrile treatment in Tijuana, Mexico, under the care of Dr. Ernesto Contreras, Miss Vencius returned home. Here is what she reported:

> I went to another doctor who had treated me. He greeted me with "Well, what do they do down there? Do you crush the apricot pit, bathe in it? Do they light incense over you?"

---

[1] "Comedian Red Buttons Says 'Laetrile Saved My Wife From Death By Cancer,' " *The National Tattler,* Aug. 19, 1973, p. 5.

> I said to him, "Okay, enough with the jokes," and asked him to read the *College of Marin Times* article [which contained information about Laetrile]. He said his mind was closed on the matter. When I pressed, he finally said, "Carol, I guess you might be able to help me after all. You see, I have insomnia and I'm sure that if I read that article it would put me to sleep."[1]

Miss Vencius' story, unfortunately, is not unique. Several years ago, she began to complain of feeling generally ill: night sweats, itching, fever, and headaches. After extensive tests in the hospital she was told that she had Hodgkin's Disease (a form of cancer initially affecting the lymph nodes), Miss Vencius continued:

> Only a couple of days after that, a friend came to visit and told me about vitamin therapy in Mexico called Laetrile. I never followed up on his advice, I was too frightened. And besides, at the time I had complete faith in my doctors . . . .
>
> The first thing they tried was cobalt radiation treatments. Soon after they began,

[1] "Laetrile Works Through C.O.M. Times," *College of Marin Times*, April 12, 1972.

> my doctor told me, "Carol, of course you know this treatment will make you sterile." Hell no, I didn't know. Naturally I became pretty upset . . . . I went through menopause at the age of 28.

Other "side effects" were indescribable pain, loss of appetite, and temporary loss of hair. Six months after the treatments, her lungs and heart cavity began to fill with fluid. They tried draining it with a hypodermic, but it continued to fill up. She was having minor heart attacks.

After six weeks and three heart cavity taps, her physicians were still debating whether or not to remove the pericardium (the membrane enclosing the heart cavity). On November 28, 1970, it was removed.

By July, general fatigue, sleeplessness, and loss of appetite had returned and for several months grew worse until it was decided to try drugs.

> The first injection left me with mild nausea. Two weeks later, I received two more injections which produced acute nausea and diarrhea followed by a week of intense pain in my jaw. It was so bad I couldn't eat. This was followed by a one-week migraine headache, followed by stomach cramps, followed by leg cramps. In all, the symptoms lasted four weeks.

> For ten days following this, however, I felt great, better than I had in years. This positive response, I was told, was a sign that the disease was still active and that the drugs had done some good. Then it was downhill again, a return of pain, sleeplessness, fatigue, and all the rest. I decided then, whatever happened, I would not undergo chemotherapy again.

At this point, Miss Vencius concluded that it was hopeless anyway so there was no reason why she should not go to Mexico and try Laetrile after all. Dr. Contreras told her that Hodgkins Disease was slower to respond to vitamin therapy than many other cancers such as those of the lung, pancreas, liver, or colon, but that it certainly was worth a try. After just the third day on Laetrile, however, she reported that her pain had gone completely and that within only a week she was feeling almost entirely normal again. She since has recovered her health and continues on a routine maintenance dose of vitamin B_{17}.

The issue of maintenance doses is important. Once a person has contracted cancer and recovered, apparently his need for vitamin B_{17} is considerably greater than for those who have not. Most physicians who have used Laetrile in cancer therapy have learned through experience that their patients, once recovered, can reduce their dosage levels of Laetrile, but if they eliminate it altogether, it is almost a certain invitation to a return of the cancer. It's for this reason that physicians using Laetrile never say that it *cures* cancer. They prefer the more accurate word *control*, implying a continuing process.

This fact was illustrated most dramatically and tragically in the case of Mrs. Margaret De Grio, wife of a County Supervisor in Sierra County, California. After undergoing surgery twice, and with her cancer continuing to spread, she was told by three physicians that her case was hopeless and that there was nothing further that modern medical science could do. But Mike De Grio had read a book about Laetrile and decided to take his wife to Mexico for treatment. It was the same old story: she began to improve immediately and, after four months of intensive treatment, she returned to her Northern California home with only minor symptoms of her original cancer. The rapid disappearance of her tumors was confirmed by her American doctor, although he could not explain why it happened.

Shortly afterward, however, Mrs. De Grio contracted a serious respiratory infection and was hospitalized in San Francisco for pneumonia. While she was there for over three weeks, her physician and the hospital staff refused to allow her the maintenance dose of Laetrile because they feared it might be against the California anti-quackery law. The denial of this dose came at a critical time in the recovery and healing stage. Mrs.

De Grio died on the night of October 17, 1963, not from pneumonia, but of cancer.[1]

In 1972, Dr. Dale Danner, a podiatrist from Santa Paula, California, developed a pain in the right leg and a severe cough. X-rays revealed a carcinoma of both lungs and what appeared to be massive secondary tumors in the leg. The cancer was inoperable and resistant to radio therapy. The prognosis was: incurable and fatal.

At the insistence of his mother, Dr. Danner agreed to try Laetrile, although he had no faith in its effectiveness. Primarily just to please her, he obtained a large supply in Mexico. But he was convinced from what he had read in medical journals that it was nothing but quackery and a fraud. Perhaps it was even dangerous, he thought, for he noticed from the literature that it contained large amounts of cyanide.

Within a few weeks the pain and the coughing had progressed to the point where no amount of medication could hold it back. Forced to crawl on his hands and knees, and unable to sleep for three days and nights, he became despondent and desperate. Groggy from the lack of sleep, from the drugs, and from the pain, finally he turned to his supply of Laetrile.

---

[1]"The Laetrile Story," by Jim Dean and Frank Martinez, *The Santa Ana Register,* Sept., 1964. For an excellent portrayal of the futility and tragedy of orthodox cancer therapy, read *See the Patients Die,* by Wynn Westover (Science Press International), Sausalito, Calif., 1974).

Giving himself one more massive dose of medication, hopefully to bring on sleep, he then proceeded to administer the Laetrile directly into an *artery*. Before losing consciousness from the medication, Dr. Danner had succeeded in taking at least an entire ten-day supply — and possibly as high as a twenty-day supply — all at once.

When he awoke thirty-six hours later, much to his amazement, not only was he still alive, but also the cough and pain were greatly reduced. His appetite had returned, and he was feeling better than he had in months. Reluctantly he had to admit that Laetrile was working. So he obtained an additional supply and began routine treatment with smaller doses. Three months later he was back at work.[1]

The use of vitamin B_{17} in the treatment of cancer is not new. The earliest recorded case was published in 1845 in the *Paris Medical Gazette*.[2] A young cancer patient was given 46,000 milligrams of amygdalin over a period of several months in 1842 and, reportedly, was still living at the time of the article three years later. A woman with extensive cancer throughout her body received varying amounts of amygdalin starting in 1834 (!) and was still surviving at the time of the report eleven years later.

From the publication of this first report up until the present, there have been literally *thousands* of

---

[1]Story confirmed in tape recorded interview by author.

[2]*Gazette Medical de Paris,* vol. 13, pp. 577-582.

similar case histories reported and documented. It is important to know this because, as demonstrated previously, official spokesmen for orthodox medicine have stated authoritatively that there simply is no evidence that Laetrile works. The truth is that the evidence is *everywhere*.

When confronted with this evidence, some doctors, because of their professional bias against nutritional medicine, seek alternate explanations. Their favorite is that the cancer had a delayed response to previous treatment such as radiation or drugs. And when it occasionally occurs that there has been no previous treatment except Laetrile, they say then that the patient probably didn't have cancer in the first place. And when it is demonstrated that the presence of cancer was proven by surgery or biopsy, then they fall back on the claim that it was a *spontaneous remission,* meaning that it just went away on its own with no outside help.

It is true, of course, that, occasionally, there are cases in which cancers either stop spreading or disappear without medical treatment.[1] But such cases, statistically, are extremely rare. With certain cancer locations — such as testicular chorionepithelioma, for instance — they are so rare as to defy statistical analysis. And when one comes up with a *series* of such cases, all of which have

[1]It would be extremely interesting to examine such cases for a possible change in eating habits to see if there were any connection between the two. My guess is that such a study would show a change in foods, either by selection or by a change in locale, that placed less of a demand upon the pancreas and/or provided a higher source of natural vitamin B_{17}.

involved proven cancers, and all of which have responded to B_{17}, it is beyond reason to speak of spontaneous regressions.

In a banquet speech in San Francisco on November 19, 1967, Dr. Ernst T. Krebs, Jr., briefly reviewed *six* such cases. Then he added:

> Now there is an advantage in not having had prior radiation, because if you have not received prior radiation that has failed, then you cannot enjoy the imagined benefits of the delayed effects of prior radiation. So this boy falls into the category of the "spontaneous regression . . . ."
>
> And when we look at this scientifically, we know that spontaneous regression occurs in fewer than one in 150,000 cases of cancer. The statistical possibility of spontaneous regression accounting for the complete resolution of six successive cases of testicular chorionepithelioma is far greater than the improbability of the sun not rising tomorrow morning.[1]

With the passage of each year and the presence of a growing stream of patients who are living proof

[1]Speech delivered before a meeting of the International Association of Cancer Victims and Friends at the Jack Tar Hotel, Nov. 19, 1967.

of their claim, it becomes increasingly difficult to ignore or dismiss these recoveries. If they *are* spontaneous remissions, then, indeed, it must be said in all fairness that Laetrile produces far more spontaneous remissions than all other forms of therapy put together!

Returning to the question of "proven" *vs.* "unproven" cancer cures, Dr. Dean Burk has said:

> It's foolish ever to talk about a cure in cancer . . . but when you compare the reports on Laetrile, they stack up very well with the conventional methods, regardless of what you might hear otherwise — such as from the California Board of Health. They simply are not telling the truth.
>
> You know how administrative organizations do have power. When you have power you don't have to tell the truth. That's a rule that's been working in this world for generations. And there are a great many people who don't tell the truth when they are in power in administrative positions.
>
> For instance, the California State Board of Health published many times that

Laetrile is worthless. Well, now, there is no scientific basis for that that I have ever seen. It . . . is just not true.[1]

---

[1]Interview on the Owen Spahn Talk Show, San Francisco, June 28, 1972.

IX

"PROVEN" CANCER CURES

The effects of surgery and radiation on prolonging the life of the cancer patient; a comparison showing that those who receive no treatment at all live just as long, if not longer, than those who are treated.

The advocates of Laetrile therapy have always gone out of their way to emphasize that there is no *cure*, as such, for cancer. Since it is essentially a deficiency disease, one can only speak of *prevention* or *control* but not *cure*. Among the advocates of orthodox therapies, however, there is no such restraint. Official spokesmen for the medical profession repeatedly tell the American public, without batting an eyelash, that they have *proven cures* for cancer, and that anyone who resorts to such nostrums as Laetrile is merely wasting valuable time in which he would be far better off availing himself of these proven cures. What are these cures? They are surgery, radiation, and drugs.

The following news report carried in a Los Angeles paper is typical:

Warnings of a mounting scale of cancer quackery activity affecting the San Fernando Valley were issued today by the American Cancer Society.

Mrs. Stanley Grushesky, Education Chairman of the Society's Valley area, said she is concerned over the possibility that some local residents have been deceived in recent weeks by propaganda issued on behalf of unorthodox practitioners with claims of unproven cancer "cures." . . .

She declared that "under the banners of freedom of speech, with the slogan of freedom of choice, advocates of unorthodox cancer remedies have been making wild claims which could easily lure unsuspecting victims into a quackery mill." . . .

Mrs. Grushesky said that surgery and radiation are the only known methods for successfully treating cancer, although some beneficial effects have been obtained in certain cases through the administration of chemicals or hormones. . . .

"Cancer quackery kills many unsuspecting patients because time wasted on

> phony devices and treatments delays effective treatment until it is too late to save the patient's life."[1]

Echoing the same theme, Dr. Ralph Weilerstein of the California Department of Public Health declared:

> The use of Laetrile in early cancer cases to the exclusion of conventional treatment might well be dangerous since treatment with acceptable, modern curative methods—surgery or radiation—would thereby be delayed potentially until such time as metastases had occurred and the cancer, therefore, might no longer be curable.[2]

Public Library reference volumes on cancer often contain bookmarks printed and distributed by the American Cancer Society. One of these depicts an ace of spades on the front along with the slogan: THE UNPROVEN CANCER CURE. DON'T BET YOUR LIFE ON IT. On the back it says: "For more information on proven cancer cures, write or phone the American Cancer Society."

In response to this bookmark, a letter was sent to the headquarters expressing surprise at the asser-

---

[1]"Amer. Cancer Soc. Warns of Valley Quacks," *The Valley News* (Van Nuys, Calif.), Dec. 10, 1972.

[2]As quoted in *College of Marin Times* (Kentfield, Calif.), April 26, 1972.

tion about there being any cancer therapy successful enough to warrant being called a proven cure. This is the reply received:

> To Mr. G. Edward Griffin:
>
> Thank you for your note. There *are* proven cures *if* detected in time—surgery and/or radiation and, more and more, chemotherapy is playing its part.[1]

This, then, is the position of orthodox medicine. For comparison, therefore, let us take a look at the results and benefits of the so-called cures obtained through surgery, radiation, and chemotherapy.

As we shall see, surgery is the least harmful of the three. In all fairness it must be said that, in some cases, it can be a life-saving stop-gap measure—particularly where intestinal blockages and adhesions must be relieved in order to prevent the patient from dying from secondary complications. Surgery also has the psychological advantage of visibly removing the tumor. And, from that point of view, it offers the patient and his family some temporary comfort and hope. However, the degree to which surgery is useful is the same degree to which the tumor is *not* malignant. The greater the proportion of cancer cells in that tumor, the less likely it is that surgery will help. And the most highly malig-

---

[1]Letter from Mabel Burnett dated Dec. 18, 1972.

nant tumors of all generally are considered inoperable.

A further complication of surgery is the fact that any cutting into the tumor—even a biopsy—does at least two things that logically should aggravate the condition. First, it causes physical trauma to the area. This triggers off the healing process which, in turn, brings more trophoblast cells into being as a by-product of that process. (See Chapter IV.) The other effect is that, if not all the malignant tissue is removed, what remains tends to be encased in scar tissue from the surgery. Scar tissue tends to act as a barrier between the cancer cell and the rest of the body. Consequently, the cancer tends to become insulated from the action of the pancreatic enzymes which, as we have seen, are so essential in exposing trophoblast cells to the surveillant action of the white blood cells.

Perhaps the greatest indictment of all against surgery is the gnawing suspicion among even many of the world's top surgeons that, statistically, there is no solid evidence that patients who submit to surgery have any greater life expectancy, on the average, than those who do not. This is an area which desperately needs intensive and unbiased study.

The first statistical analysis of this question was compiled in 1844 by Dr. Leroy d'Etoilles and published by the French Academy of Science. It is, to date, the most extensive study of its kind ever released. Over a period of thirty years, case histories of 2,781 patients were submitted by 174 physicians. The average survival after surgery was only one year and five months—not much different than the average today.

Dr. Leroy d'Etoilles separated his statistics according to whether the patient submitted to surgery or caustics, or refused such treatment. His findings were electric:

> The net value of surgery or caustics was in prolonging life two months for men and six months for women. But that was only in the first few years after the initial diagnosis. After that period, those who had not accepted treatment had the greater survival potential by about fifty percent.[1]

1844, of course, was a long time ago. But recent surveys invariably have produced nearly the same results. For instance, it long has been accepted practice for patients with breast cancer to have not only the tumor removed but the entire breast and the lymph nodes as well. In more recent years, the procedure often includes removal of the ovaries also on the theory that cancer is stimulated by their hormones. Finally, in 1961, a large-scale controlled test was begun, called the National Surgical Adjuvant Breast Project. After seven-and-a-half years of statistical analysis, the results were conclusive: There was no significant difference between the percentage of patients remaining alive who had re-

---

[1]Walshe, Walter H., *The Anatomy, Physiology, Pathology and Treatment of Cancer,* (Ticknor & Co., Boston, 1844).

ceived the smaller operation and those who had received the larger.[1]

One of the most distinguished statisticians in the medical field is Hardin B. Jones, Ph.D., professor of medical physics and physiology at the University of California at Berkeley. After years of searching published and unpublished clinical records, he appeared at an American Cancer Society convention and reported bluntly:

> In regard to surgery, no relationship between intensity of surgical treatment and duration of survival has been found in verified malignancies. On the contrary, simple excision of cancers has produced essentially the same survival as radical excision and dissection of the lymphatic drainage.[2]

All of this, of course, related only to surgery of the breast. Turning his attention to surgery in general, Dr. Jones reported:

> Although there is a dearth of untreated cases for statistical comparison with the treated, it is surprising that the death risks

---

[1]Ravdin, R.G., *et.al.*, "Results of a Clinical Trial Concerning The Worth of Prophylactic Oophorectomy for Breast Carcinoma," *Surgery, Gynecology & Obstetrics,* 131:1055, Dec., 1970. Also see "Breast Cancer Excision Less with Selection," *Medical Tribune,* Oct. 6, 1971, p. 1.

[2]A Report on Cancer," paper delivered to the ACS's 11th Annual Science Writers Conference, New Orleans, Mar. 7, 1969.

> of the two groups remain so similar. In the comparisons it has been assumed that the treated and untreated cases are independent of each other. In fact, that assumption is incorrect. Initially, all cases are untreated. With the passage of time, some receive treatment, and the likelihood of treatment increases with the length of time since origin of the disease. Thus, those cases in which the neoplastic process progresses slowly [and thus automatically favors a long-term survival] are more likely to become "treated" cases. For the same reason, however, those individuals are likely to enjoy longer survival, whether treated or not. Life tables truly representative of untreated cancer patients must be adjusted for the fact that the inherently longer-lived cases are more likely to be transferred to the "treated" category than to remain in the "untreated until death."
>
> *The apparent life expectancy of untreated cases of cancer after such adjustment in the table seems to be greater than that of the treated cases.* [Emphasis added]

What, then, *is* the statistical chance for long-term survival of five years or more after surgery? That, we are told, depends on the location of the cancer, how fast it is growing, and whether or not it has spread to a secondary point in the body. For instance, two of the most common forms of cancer requiring surgery are of the breast and the lung. In the case of breast cancer, only sixteen percent will respond in any way to either surgery or X-ray therapy. In the case of lung cancer, the percentage of patients who will survive five years after surgery is somewhere between five and ten percent.[1] And these are optimistic figures when compared to survival expectations for some other types of cancers such as testicular chorionepitheliomas.

When we turn to cancers which have metastasized to secondary locations within the body, then the picture virtually is hopeless—surgery or no surgery. As one cancer specialist summarized it bluntly:

> A patient who has clinically detectable distant metastases when first seen has virtually a hopeless prognosis, as do patients who were apparently free of distant metastases at that time but who subsequently return with distant metastases.[2]

---

[1]See "Results of Treatment of Carcinoma of the Breast Based on Pathological Staging," by F.R.C. Johnstone, M.D., *Surgery, Gynecology & Obstetrics,* 134:211, 1972. Also "Consultant's Comment," by George Crile, Jr., M.D., *Calif. Medical Digest,* Aug.,1972, p. 839. Also "Project Aims at Better Lung Cancer Survival," *Medical Tribune,* Oct. 20, 1971. Also statement by Dr. Lewis A. Leone, Director of the Department of Oncology at Rhode Island Hospital in Providence, as quoted in "Cancer Controls Still Unsuccessful," *L.A. Herald Examiner,* June 6, 1972, p. C-12.

[2]Johnstone, *op. cit.*

An objective appraisal, therefore, is that the statistical rate of long-term survival after surgery is, on the average *at best,* only ten or fifteen percent. And once the cancer has metastasized to a second location, surgery has almost *no* survival value whatsoever. The reason, of course, is that, like the other therapies approved by orthodox medicine, surgery removes only the tumor. It does not remove the cause.

The rationale behind X-ray therapy essentially is the same as with surgery. The medical objective is to remove the tumor, but to do so by burning it away rather than cutting it out. Here, also, it is primarily the non-cancer cell that is destroyed. The more malignant the tumor, the more resistant it is to radio therapy. This should be obvious for, if it were the other way around, then X-ray therapy would have a high degree of success—which, of course, it does not.

If the average tumor is composed of both cancer and non-cancer cells, and if radiation is more destructive to non-cancer cells than to cancer cells, then it would be logical to expect the results to be a *reduction* of tumor *size,* but also an *increase* in the *percentage of malignancy*. This is, in fact, exactly what happens.

Commenting on this mechanism, Dr. John Richardson has explained it this way:

> Radiation and/or radiomimetic poisons *will* reduce palpable, gross or measurable tumefaction. Often this reduction may

amount to seventy-five percent or more of the mass of the growth. These agents have a selective effect—radiation and poisons. They selectively kill everything except the definitively neoplastic [cancer] cells.

For example, a benign uterine myoma will usually melt away under radiation like snow in the sun. If there be neoplastic cells in such tumor, these will remain. The size of the tumor may thus be decreased by ninety percent while the relative concentration of definitively neoplastic cells is thereby increased by ninety percent.

As all experienced clinicians know—or at least should know—after radiation or poisons have reduced the gross tumefaction of the lesion the patient's general well-being does not substantially improve. To the contrary, there is often an explosive or fulminating increase in the biological malignancy of his lesion. This is marked by the appearance of diffuse metastasis and a rapid deterioration in general vitality followed shortly by death.[1]

---

[1]Open letter to interested doctors, Nov., 1972.

And so we see that X-ray therapy is cursed with all the same limitations and drawbacks of surgery. But it also has one more: it actually increases the likelihood that cancer will develop in other parts of the body!

Yes, it is a well-established fact that excessive exposure to radioactivity is an effective way to induce cancer. This was first demonstrated by observing the increased cancer incidence among the survivors of Hiroshima, but it has been corroborated by many independent studies since then. For example, a recent headline in a national circulation newspaper tells us: FIND 'ALARMING' NUMBER OF CANCER CASES IN PEOPLE WHO HAD X-RAY THERAPY 20 YEARS AGO.[1]

The *Textbook of Medical Surgical Nursing,* a standard reference volume for Registered Nurses, is most emphatic on this point. It says:

> This is an area of public health concern because it may involve large numbers of people who may be exposed to low levels of radiation over a long period of time. The classic example is of the women employed in the early 1920's to paint watch and clock dials with luminizing (radium-containing) paints. Years later, bone sarcomas resulted from the carcinogenic effect of the radium. Similarly, leukemia occurs more frequently in radiologists

[1]*The National Enquirer,* Oct. 7, 1973, p. 29.

> than other physicians. Another example is the Hiroshima survivors who have shown the effects of low levels of radiation. . . .
>
> Among the most serious of the late consequences of irradiation damage is the increased susceptibility to malignant metaplasia and the development of cancer at sites of earlier irradiation. Evidence cited in support of this relationship refers to the increased incidence of carcinoma of skin, bone, and lung after latent periods of 20 years and longer following irradiation of those sites. Further support has been adduced from the relatively high incidence of carcinoma of the thyroid 7 years and longer following low-dosage irradiation of the thymus in childhood, and from the increased incidence of leukemia following total body irradiation at any age.[1]

In 1971, a research team at the University of Buffalo, under the direction of Dr. Robert W. Gibson, reported that less than a dozen routine medical X-rays to the same part of the body increases the risk of leukemia in males by at least sixty percent.[2] Other scientists have become increasingly con-

---

[1](J.B. Lippincott Co., Philadelphia, Pa., 1970) 2nd Edition, p. 198.

[2]"Too Many X-Rays Increase Risk of Leukemia, Study Indicates," *National Enquirer,* Dec. 5, 1971, p. 11.

cerned about the growing American infatuation with X-rays and have urged a stop to the madness, even calling for an end to the mobile chest X-ray units for the detection of TB.[1] And these "routine" X-rays are harmlessly mild compared to the fantastically intense radiation beamed into the bodies of cancer patients today.

X-rays induce cancer because of at least two factors. First, they do physical damage to the body which triggers off the production of trophoblast cells as part of the healing process. Second, they weaken or destroy the production of white blood cells which, as we have seen, constitute the immunological defense mechanism, the body's front-line defense against cancer.

Now to the question of statistics. Again we find that, on the average, there is little or no solid evidence that radiation actually improves the patient's chances for survival. The National Surgical Adjuvant Breast Project, previously mentioned in connection with surgery, also conducted studies on the effect of irradiation, and here is a summary of their findings:

> From the data available it would seem that the use of post-operative irradiation has provided no discernible advantage to patients so treated in terms of increasing

---

[1] "Top FDA Officials Warn: Chest X-Rays in Mobile Vans Are Dangerous and Must Be Stopped," *National Enquirer*, Sept. 10, 1972, p. 8.

> the proportion who were free of disease for as long as five years.[1]

This is an embarrassingly difficult fact for a radiologist to face, for it means, quite literally, that there is little real justification for his existence in the medical fraternity. If he were to admit publicly what he knows privately from experience, a guy could talk himself right out of a job! Consequently, one does not expect to hear these facts being discussed by radiologists or those whose livelihood depends on the construction, sale, installation, use, or maintenance of the multi-million dollar linear accelerators. It comes as a pleasant surprise, therefore, to hear these truths spoken frankly and openly by three well known radiologists sharing the same platform at the same medical convention. They were William Powers, M.D., Director of the Division of Radiation Therapy at the Washington University School of Medicine, Phillip Rubin, M.D., Chief of the Division of Radiotherapy at the University of Rochester Medical School, and Vera Peters, M.D., of the Princess Margaret Hospital in Toronto, Canada. Dr. Powers stated:

> Although preoperative and postoperative radiation therapy have been used extensively and for decades, it is still not possible to prove unequivocal clinical benefit

---

[1]Fisher, B., *et.al.*, "Postoperative Radiotherapy in the Treatment of Breast Cancer; Results of the NSAPP Clinical Trial," *Annals of Surgery*, 172, No. 4, Oct. 1970.

> from this combined treatment. . . . Even if the rate of cure does improve with a combination of radiation and therapy, it is necessary to establish the *cost* in increased morbidity which may occur in patients without favorable response to the additional therapy.[1]

Dr. Rubin's statement was even more to the point. After reviewing the statistics of survival previously published in the *Journal of the American Medical Association,* he concluded:

> The clinical evidence and statistical data in numerous reviews are cited to illustrate that no increase in survival has been achieved by the addition of irradiation.

To which Dr. Peters added:

> In carcinoma of the breast, the mortality rate still parallels the incidence rate, thus proving that there has been no true improvement in the successful treatment of the disease over the past thirty years, even though there has been technical improvement in both surgery and radiotherapy during that time.

---

[1] "Preoperative and Postoperative Radiation Therapy for Cancer," speech delivered to the Sixth National Cancer Conference, sponsored by the American Cancer Society and the National Cancer Institute, Denver, Colorado, Sept. 18-20, 1968.

In spite of the almost universal experience of physicians to the contrary, the American Cancer Society still prattles to the public that *their* statistics show a higher recovery rate for treated patients as compared to untreated patients. After all, if this were not the case, why on earth would anyone spend the money or undergo the pain and disfigurement associated with these orthodox treatments? But how can they get away with such outright lies?

The answer is that they are not really lying —just bending the truth a little. In other words, they merely adjust the method of gathering and evaluating statistics so as to guarantee the desired results. In the words of Dr. Hardin Jones:

> Evaluation of the clinical response of cancer to treatment by surgery and radiation, separately or in combination, leads to the following findings:
>
> The evidence for greater survival of treated groups in comparison with untreated is biased by the method of defining the groups. All reported studies pick up cases at the time of origin of the disease and follow them to death or end of the study interval. If persons in the untreated or central group die *at any time* in the study interval, they are reported as deaths in the control group. In the treated group, however, deaths which occur be-

> fore completion of the treatment are rejected from the data, since these patients do not then meet the criteria established by definition of the term "treated." The longer it takes for completion of the treatment, as in multiple step therapy, for example, the worse the error. . . .
>
> With this effect stripped out, the common malignancies show a remarkably similar rate of demise, whether treated or untreated.[1]

But there is far more to it than that. Such statistical error is significant, but it is doubtful if it could account for the American Cancer Society's favorite claim that "there are on record a million and a half people cured of cancer through the efforts of the medical profession and the American Cancer Society with the help of the FDA."[2]

The answer lies in the fact that there are some forms of cancer, such as skin cancer, that respond very well to treatment. In fact, often they are arrested or disappear even without treatment. Seldom are they fatal. But they affect large numbers of people—enough to change the statistical tabulations *drastically*. In the beginning, skin cancers were not included in the national tabulations be-

---

[1]"A Report on Cancer," *op.cit.*

[2]Letter from Mrs. Glenn E. Baker, Executive Director, Southern District, ACS, addressed to Mr. T.G. Kent, reprinted in *Cancer News Journal,* Jan./Feb., 1972, p. 22.

cause of these considerations plus the fact that, in those days, very few people sought medical treatment for their skin disorders, preferring to treat them with home remedies, many of which, incidentally seem to have worked just as well as some of the more scientifically acceptable techniques today.

At any rate, as doctors became more plentiful, as people became more affluent and able to seek out professional medical help, and as the old-time remedies increasingly fell into disrepute or oblivion, the number of *reported* skin cancers gradually increased until it is now listed by the ACS as a "major site." So, all they had to do to produce most of those million-and-a-half "cures," was to change their statistics to include skin cancers—*presto-chango!*

As Dr. Hardin Jones revealed:

> Beginning in 1940, through redefinition of terms, various questionable grades of malignancy were classed as cancer. After that date, the proportion of "cancer" cures having "normal" life expectancy increased rapidly, corresponding to the fraction of questionable diagnosis included.[1]

When X-ray therapy is used, the body's white blood cell count is reduced which, in turn, leaves

---

[1] "A Report on Cancer," *op.cit.*

the patient far more susceptible to infections and other diseases as well. It is common for such patients to succumb to pneumonia, for instance, rather than cancer. And that is what appears on the death certificate—as well as in the statistics. As Dr. Richardson has observed:

> I have seen patients who have been paralyzed by cobalt spine radiation, and after vitamin treatment their HCG test is faintly positive. We got their cancer, but the radiogenic manipulation is such that they can't walk. . . .
>
> It's the cobalt that will kill, not the cancer.[1]

If the patient is strong enough or lucky enough to survive the radiation, then he still faces a closed door. As with all forms of currently popular treatments, once the cancer has metastasized to a second location, there is practically no chance that the patient will live. So, in addition to an almost zero survival value, radio therapy has the extra distinction of also spreading the very cancer it is supposed to combat.

It is commonly believed—because it is commonly heard—that early diagnosis and early treatment greatly increases the chance of survival. This, in fact, does not appear to be so, at least when

---

[1]Letter from John Richardson, M.D., to G. Edward Griffin, dated Dec. 2, 1972.

applied to the orthodox therapies. It is true that the American Cancer Society claims to have statistics to support this claim, but the higher "cure" rate apparently is caused by a heavy weighting in favor of the slow-growing easy-to-control cancers, such as skin cancer, and does not become true of the more serious tumors affecting the reproductive or vital organs. As Dr. Hardin Jones stated emphatically:

> In the matter of duration of malignant tumors before treatment, no studies have established the much talked about relationship between early detection and favorable survival after treatment. . . . Serious attempts to relate prompt treatment with chance of cure have been unsuccessful. In some types of cancer, the opposite of the expected association of short duration of symptoms with a high chance of being "cured" has been observed. A long duration of symptoms before treatment in a few cancers of the breast and cervix is associated with longer than usual survival. . . . Neither the timing nor the extent of treatment of the true malignancies has appreciably altered the average course of the disease. The possibility exists that treatment makes the average situation worse.[1]

---

[1] "A Report on Cancer," *op.cit.*

Or, putting it even more succinctly, Dr. Irwin H. Krakoff, of the Sloan-Kettering Institute for Cancer Research, says simply:

> We are concerned with a disease for which there is no really satisfactory treatment.[1]

In view of all this, it is exasperating to find spokesmen for orthodox medicine continually warning the public against using Laetrile on the grounds that, supposedly, that will prevent the cancer patient from benefiting from "proven" cures. The pronouncement by Dr. Ralph Weilerstein of the California Department of Public Health cited at the opening of this chapter is typical. But Dr. Weilerstein is vulnerable on two points. First of all, it is extremely rare to find any patient seeking Laetrile therapy who hasn't already been subjected to the so-called "modern curative methods" of surgery and radiation. In fact, most of them have been pronounced hopeless after these methods totally have failed, and it is only then that these people turn to vitamin therapy as a last resort. So Dr. Weilerstein has set up a straw-man objection on that score. But, far more important than that is the fact that the Weilersteinian treatments simply *do not work.*

Battling as a lone warrior within the enemy stronghold, Dr. Dean Burk of the National Cancer

---

[1]Speech delivered before the American Society of Clinical Oncology in 1968.

Institute repeatedly has laid it on the line. In a letter to his boss, Dr. Frank Rauscher, he said:

> In spite of the foregoing evidence, . . . officials of the American Cancer Society and even of the National Cancer Institute, have continued to set forth to the public that about one in every four cancer cases is now "cured" or "controlled," but seldom if ever backed up with the requisite statistical or epidemiological support for such a statement to be scientifically meaningful, however effective for fund gathering. Such a statement is highly misleading, since it hides the fact that, with systemic or metastatic cancers, the actual rate of control in terms of the conventional five-year survival is scarcely more than one in twenty. . . .
>
> One may well ask Dr. Weilerstein where are all the modern curative methods to which he, the California Cancer Advisory Council, and indeed so many administrators so glibly refer? . . .No, disseminated cancer, in its various forms and kinds remains, by and large, as "incurable" as at the time of the Kefauver Amendment ten years ago — Dr. Weilerstein or no Dr. Weilerstein, FDA or no FDA, ACS or no ACS, AMA or no AMA, NCI or no NCI.[1]

---

[1]Letter to Congressman Frey, *op. cit.*

The statistics of the ACS are fascinating to study. They constitute page after page of detailed tables and complex charts telling about percentages of cancer by location, sex, age, and geography. But when it comes to hard statistics about their so-called "proven cures," there is nothing. The only "statistic" one can get is their unsupported statement: "One out of three patients is being saved today as against one out of five a generation ago." Now, this may or may not be true, depending on one's definition of terms. But even if we do not challenge it, we must keep in mind that there also is a correspondingly *larger* gain in the number of those who are *getting* cancer. How come?

Here is the official explanation:

> Major factors are the increasing age and size of the population. Science has conquered many diseases, and the average life span of Americans has been extended to nearly seventy years. Longer life brings man to the age in which cancer most often strikes—from the fifth decade on.[1]

All of which sounds very plausible — until one compares it to the facts:

First of all, the growth in population has absolutely nothing to do with it. The statistics of "one out of three" and "one out of five" are *proportional* rather than *numerical*. They represent *ratios* that

---

[1] *Ibid.*, p. 20.

apply universally, regardless of the population size. They *cannot* explain the increasing cancer *rate*.

Second, in spite of the fact that life expectancy has increased slightly, nevertheless, the average age of the population in the last generation has increased only from 26.5 years in 1930 to 27.2 years in 1969. This could not possibly account for the drastic increase of the cancer death rate within that time.

Third, increasing age need not be a factor, anyway — as the cancer-free Hunzakuts and Abkhasians prove quite conclusively.

And fourth, the cancer rate among the very young is now rapidly climbing, even faster than among the very old.

It is clear that the American Cancer Society — or at least someone very high within it — is trying to give the American people a good old-fashioned snow job. The truth of the matter is — ACS statistics notwithstanding — that orthodox medicine simply does *not* have "proven cancer cures," and what it *does* have is pitifully inadequate considering the prestige it enjoys, the money it collects, and the snobbish scorn it heaps upon those who do not wish to subscribe to its treatments.

X

A NEW DIMENSION OF MURDER

Orthodox anti-cancer drugs shown to be ineffective and cancer-causing; FDA-approved experiments on humans resulting in death from drugs rather than from cancer.

The following news article appeared in the *Los Angeles Times* on August 18, 1973, under the heading: CANCER 'CURE' LAETRILE HIT:

> Los Angeles (UPI) — The manufacturers and distributors of the drug Laetrile were called "purveyors of deceit and outright quackery" Wednesday by the president of the California division of the American Cancer Society.
>
> Helene Brown . . . said the FDA has tested Laetrile at regular intervals, obtained negative results, and prohibited its use as a cancer remedy.

> Cancer quackery is "a new dimension of murder," according to Mrs. Brown who said . . . there are now 10 kinds of cancer which can be cured or controlled by chemotherapy — the treatment of disease by drugs.

Less than a month later, while speaking at an ACS national conference on cancer nursing, Mrs. Brown said flatly: "Present medical knowledge makes it possible to cure seventy percent of all cancers, if they are detected early." (!)[1]

Leaders of the American Cancer Society apparently never tire of perpetuating the myth of "proven cures." But they never look quite so foolish in the eyes of those who know anything about actual survival statistics as they do when they speak of cures by *chemotherapy*.

We briefly have viewed the miserable results obtained by orthodox surgery and radiation. The record of so-called anti-cancer *drugs,* however, is even worse. The primary reason for this is that most of them currently in use are highly poisonous, not just to cancer but to the rest of the body as well. In fact, generally they are *more* deadly to healthy tissue than they are to the malignant cell.

All substances, of course, can be toxic if taken in sufficient quantity. This is true of aspirin, sugar, Laetrile, or even water. But, unlike these, the anti-cancer drugs are poisonous, not as a result of an

[1] "Cancer Quacks Deadly," (AP) *The Clarion Ledger,* (Miss.), Sept. 13, 1973.

overdose, or as a *side*-effect, but as a *primary* effect. In other words, their poisonous nature is not tolerated merely as a necessary price to pay in order to achieve some desired effect, it *is* the desired effect.

In theory, these chemicals are selected because they are capable of differentiating between types of cells and, consequently, of poisoning some types more than others. But don't jump to the conclusion that they differentiate between cancer and non-cancer cells, killing only the cancer cells, because they do not.

The cellular poisons used in orthodox cancer therapy today cannot distinguish between cancer and non-cancer cells. They act instead to differentiate between cells that are fast-growing and those that are slow-growing or not growing at all. Cells that are actively dividing are the targets. Consequently, they kill, not only the cancer cells that are dividing, but also a multitude of normal cells all over the body that also are caught in the act of dividing.

In the case of those cancers that are dividing more rapidly than normal cells, theoretically, they will be killed before the patient is, but it is nip and tuck all the way. In the case of a cancer that is dividing at the same rate or even slower than normal cells, then there isn't even a *theoretical* chance of success.

In either event, the poisoning of the system is the whole objective of these drugs, and the resulting pain and illness often is a torment worse than the disease itself. The toxins catch the blood cells in the act of dividing and cause blood poisoning. The gastrointestinal system is thrown into convulsion usually causing violent nausea, diarrhea, loss of appetite, cramps, and progressive weakness. Hair cells are fast-growing, so usually the hair falls out during treatment. Reproductive organs are affected causing sterility. The brain becomes fatigued. Eyesight and hearing is impaired. In fact, every conceivable function is disrupted with such agony for the patient that many of them elect to die of the cancer rather than to continue treatment.

Most of the "accepted" drugs are described as *radiomimetic,* which means they mimic or produce the same effect as radiation. Consequently, they also suppress the immunological defense mechanism and, thus, help to spread the cancer to other areas. But whereas X-rays usually are directed to only one or two locations, these chemicals do their deadly work on every cell in the entire body. As Dr. John Richardson has pointed out:

> Both radiation therapy and attempts to "poison out" result in a profound hostal immunosuppression that greatly increases the susceptibility to metastasis. How irrational it would be to attempt to treat cancer immunologically and/or physiologically, and at the same time administer immunosuppressants in the form of radiation of any kind, methotrexate, 5-FU, Cytoxin, or similarly useless and

> dangerous *general* cellular poisons. All of these modalities, as we know, have been used to depress the rejection phenomena associated with organ transplantation. The entire physiological objective in rational cancer therapy is to *increase* the rejection phenomena.[1]

The view that toxic "anti-cancer" drugs usually accomplish just the opposite of their intent is not restricted to the advocates of Laetrile. It is a fact of life (or shall we say death?) that is becoming widely acknowledged even by those who use these drugs. Dr. John Trelford, for instance, of the Department of Obstetrics and Gynecology at Ohio State University Hospital has said:

> At the present time, chemotherapy of gynecological tumors does not appear to have increased life expectancy except in sporadic cases. . . . The problem of blind chemotherapy means not only a loss of the effect of the drugs, but *also a lowering of the patient's resistance to the cancer cells* owing to the toxicity of these agents. [Emphasis added.][2]

Nor is Dr. Trelford alone in his observation. A

---

[1]Open letter to interested doctors, Nov., 1972.

[2]"A Discussion of the Results of Chemotherapy on Gynecological Cancer and the Host's Immune Response," Sixth National Cancer Conference proceedings, *op. cit.*

report from the Southern Research Institute, dated April 13, 1972, based upon recent research conducted for the National Cancer Institute, indicated that all of the currently accepted drugs in the American Cancer Society's "proven cure" category produced cancer in laboratory animals that previously had been healthy![1]

In a courageous letter to Dr. Frank Rauscher, his boss at the National Cancer Institute, Dr. Dean Burk condemned the Institute's policy of continuing to endorse these drugs when everyone *knew* that they caused cancer. He argued:

> Ironically, virtually all of the chemotherapeutic anti-cancer agents now approved by the Food and Drug Administration for use or testing in human cancer patients are (1) highly or variously *toxic* at applied dosages; (2) markedly *immunosuppressive,* that is, destructive of the patient's native resistance to a variety of diseases, including cancer; and (3) usually highly *carcinogenic* [cancer-causing]. . . . These now well-established facts have been reported in numerous publications from the National Cancer Institute itself, as well as from throughout the United States and, indeed, the world. Furthermore, what has just been said of the FDA-approved

---

[1]NCI research contract PH-43-68-998. Information contained in letter from NCI's Dr. Dean Burk to Congressman Lou Frey, Jr., dated May 30, 1972.

anti-cancer chemotherapeutic drugs is true, though perhaps less conspicuously, of radiological and surgical treatments of human cancer. . . .

In your answer to my discussion on March 19, you readily acknowledged that the FDA-approved anti-cancer drugs were indeed toxic, immunosuppressive, and carcinogenic, as indicated. But then, even in the face of the evidence, including your own White House statement of May 5, 1972, all pointing to the pitifully small effectiveness of such drugs, you went on to say quite paradoxically it seems to me, "I think the Cancer Chemotherapy program is one of the best program components that the NCI has ever had." . . .One may ask, parenthetically, surely this does not speak well of the "other program areas?". . .

Frankly, I fail to follow you here. I submit that a program and series of the FDA-approved compounds that yield only 5-10% "effectiveness" can scarcely be described as "excellent," the more so since it represents the total production of a thirty-year effort on the part of all of us in the cancer therapy field.[1]

---

[1]Letter dated April 20, 1973, *op.cit.*

It is not surprising that, after chemotherapy, the statistical evidence for long-term survival is totally lacking. Here is just a sampling of the negative verdict handed down reluctantly but honestly by those physicians who, by the way, *still continue to prescribe it:*

Dr. B. Fisher, writing in the September 1968 issue of *Annals of Surgery,* stated:

> As a result of its severe toxicity and its lack of therapeutic effect, further use of 5-FU as an adjuvant to breast surgery in the regimen employed is unwarranted.[1]

Dr. Saul A. Rosenberg, Associate Professor of Medicine and Radiology at Stanford University School of Medicine:

> Worthwhile palliation is achieved in many patients. However, there will be the inevitable relapse of the malignant lymphoma, and, either because of drug resistance or drug intolerance, the disease will recur, requiring modifications of the chemotherapy program and eventually failure to control the disease process.[2]

---

[1] "Surgical Adjuvant Chemotherapy in Cancer of the Breast: Results of A Decade of Cooperative Investigation," *Annals of Surgery,* 168, No. 3, Sept., 1968.

[2] "The Indications for Chemotherapy in the Lymphomas," Sixth National Cancer Conference proceedings, *op. cit.*

Dr. Charles Moertal of the Mayo Clinic:

> Our most effective regimens are fraught with risks and side-effects and practical problems; and after this price is paid by all the patients we have treated, only a small fraction are rewarded with a transient period of usually incomplete tumor regressions. . . .
>
> Our accepted and traditional curative efforts, therefore, yield a failure rate of 85%. . . . Some patients with gastrointestinal cancer can have very long survival *with no treatment whatsoever.* [Emphasis added.][1]

Dr. Robert D. Sullivan, Department of Cancer Research at the Lahey Clinic Foundation:

> There has been an enormous undertaking of cancer research to develop anti-cancer drugs for use in the management of neoplastic diseases in man. However, progress has been slow, and no chemical agents capable of inducing a general curative effect on disseminated forms of cancer have yet been developed.[2]

---

[1]Speech made at the National Cancer Institute Clinical Center Auditorium, May 18, 1972.

[2]"Ambulatory Arterial Infusion in the Treatment of Primary and Secondary Skin Cancer," Sixth National Cancer Conference proceedings, *op.cit.*

If it is true that orthodox chemotherapy is (1) toxic, (2) immunosuppressant, (3) carcinogenic, and (4) futile, then why on earth would doctors continue to use it? The answer is that they simply don't know what else to do. Patients usually are not scheduled into chemotherapy unless their condition seems so hopeless that the loss of life appears to be inevitable anyway. Some doctors refer to this stage, not as *therapy,* but *experimentation,* which, frankly, is a more honest description.

Another reason for using drugs in the treatment of cancer is that the doctor does not like to tell the patient there is no hope. In his own mind he knows there is none, but he also knows that the patient does not want to hear that and will seek out another physician who will continue *some* kind of treatment, no matter how useless. So he solves the problem by continuing the treatment himself.

Dr. Victor Richards, in his book *The Wayward Cell, Cancer,*[1] made it very clear that chemotherapy today is used primarily just to keep the patient returning for treatment and to build his morale while he dies. But there is more! He said:

> Nevertheless, chemotherapy serves an extremely valuable role in keeping patients oriented toward proper medical therapy, and prevents the feeling of being abandoned by the physicians in patients with late and hopeless cancers.

---

[1] The University of Calif. Press, 1972.

> *Judicious employment and screening of potentially useful drugs may also prevent the spread of cancer quackery.* [Emphasis added.]

Heaven forbid that anyone should forsake the nauseating, pain-racking, cancer-spreading, admittedly ineffective "proven cures" for such "quackery" as Laetrile!

Here, at last, is revealed the true goal of much of the so-called "educational" programs of orthodox medicine — psychologically to condition people not to try any other forms of therapy. That is why they perpetuate the myth of "proven cures."

The American Cancer Society, in its *Unproven Methods of Cancer Management,* stated quite frankly:

> When one realizes that 1,500,000 Americans are alive today because they went to their doctors in time, and that the proven treatments of radiation and surgery are responsible for these cures, he is less likely to take a chance with a questionable practitioner or an unproven treatment.[1]

Before leaving the subject of cancer therapy and moving on to the field of cancer *research,* let

---

[1]*Op. cit.*, pp. 17, 18.

us clarify and summarize our findings so far. Here is a brief outline of the four optional modes of cancer therapy:

> SURGERY: Least harmful. Sometimes a life-saving, stop-gap measure. No evidence that patients who receive radical or extensive surgical options live any longer than those who receive the most conservative options, or, for that matter, those who receive none at all. Believed by some to increase likelihood of disseminating the cancer to other locations.
>
> When dealing with internal tumors affecting reproductive or vital organs, the statistical rate of long-term survival is, on the average, 10-15%. After metastasis, the statistical chances for long-term survival are close to zero.
>
> RADIOLOGY: Very harmful in many ways. Spreads the cancer and weakens the patient's resistance to other diseases. Serious and painful side-effects. No evidence that treated patients live any longer, on the average, than those not treated. Statistical rate of long-term survival after metastasis is close to zero.
>
> CHEMOTHERAPY: Also spreads the cancer through weakening of immunological defense mechanism plus general

toxicity. Leaves patient susceptible to other diseases and infections, often leading to death from these causes. Extremely serious side-effects. No evidence that treated patients live any longer, on the average, than untreated patients. Statistical rate of long-term survival after metastasis is close to zero.

VITAMIN THERAPY: Non-toxic. Side effects include increased appetite, weight gain, lowered blood pressure, increased hemoglobin and red blood cell count. Eliminates or sharply reduces pain without narcotics. Builds up body's resistance to other diseases. Is a natural compound found in foods and, as such, is totally compatible with human biological experience. Destroys cancer cells while nourishing non-cancer cells. Considering that most patients begin vitamin therapy only after they have been cut, burned, or poisoned by orthodox treatments and have been told that there no longer is any hope, the number of patients who have been brought back to normal health on a long-term survival basis (10-20%) is most encouraging.

Turning, at last, to the question of cancer *research,* we find that it is plagued with exactly the same frustrations and self-induced failures as cancer *therapy*. Almost all current research projects are preoccupied with the question of how to *cure* cancer rather than what *is* cancer. Consequently, the basic problem of cancer research today remains one of *fundamental* rather than *applied* science.

The 1926, Thirteenth Edition of the *Encyclopedia Britannica* says of cancer theories:

> The very number and variety of hypotheses show that none are established. Most of them attempt to explain the growth but not the origin of the disease.

Unfortunately, when applied to orthodox medicine, that statement is just as true today as it was in 1926. As a result, researchers have come up with a constantly lengthening list of things that supposedly "cause" cancer — everything from smog in the air to insecticides on our raw fruits and vegetables, to a multitude of obscure viruses. Not recognizing that all of these merely act as trigger mechanisms for the *real* cause — an enzyme and vitamin deficiency — they then run off in all directions at once trying to find a thousand separate "cures," each designed specifically to filter out the smog, to eliminate the insecticide, to destroy the virus, and so on. The more they research, the more "causes" they discover, and the more hopeless becomes their task.

In spite of this fact, almost daily we can read in

our press encouraging stories about how we are on the very brink of a tremendous cancer breakthrough. On September 23, 1972, the *Los Angeles Herald-Examiner* even announced to the world in bold front-page headlines: CANCER CURE FOUND! And respected researchers from the nation's most prestigious medical institutions parade routinely before our television cameras to tell us how their latest findings have, at last, brought the solution to the cancer problem well within their grasp. We have been "on the verge of a great breakthrough" for decades!

The reason for this is simple. These men are the beneficiaries of gigantic research grants from the federal government, tax-exempt foundations, and from the American Cancer Society. They *must* claim to be making encouraging progress or else their funding will not be continued. If they reported honestly that they have worked for years, have directed the activities of a large staff consuming many thousands of man-hours, and have spent hundreds of thousands of dollars to produce nothing of consequence — well, one can imagine what would happen to the future funding of their research project. The cancer research pie now is reaching out to the multi-billion dollar mark annually. The ones who will get the biggest slice out of that lucrative pie are the ones who claim to be "on the verge of a great breakthrough," for who would want to be responsible for cutting off funds just when the cure appeared so close?

In the meantime, researchers are busying

themselves, not in trying to understand what cancer *is*, but in finding a substance or a treatment to get rid of it. And it seems that, the more wild the theory, the better chance it has of getting federal money.

A rapid survey of recent research grants, as reported in the press, reveals a series of headlines that tell the story by themselves: SEA SQUIRTS HELP SUPPRESS MICE CANCER, *(L.A. Times);* EXPERTS HUNT MYSTERIOUS CANCER AGENT, *(L.A. Times);* RAT POISON HELPS TERMINAL CANCER PATIENTS LIVE LONGER, CLAIMS TEAM OF DOCTORS, *(National Enquirer);* WAITING IN THE WINGS? *(Medical World News).*

This last headline perhaps needs expansion. The article began:

> On an educated hunch that insects synthesize compounds that can inhibit cell growth, chemist George R. Pettit of the University of Arizona in Tempe has spent six years and some $100,000 extracting chemicals from a quarter of a million butterflies . . . part of a National Cancer Institute program. . . .
>
> To get his butterflies, Dr. Pettit enlisted the help of 500 collectors in Taiwan.

And so the search goes on — rat poison, jet fuel, butterfly wings, sea squirts — everything except the natural foods of man.

It is significant that the only time orthodox research produces really tangible and useful information is when it is in conformity with the trophoblastic thesis of cancer. Or, stated another way, there is nothing in the realm of solid scientific knowledge gained through recent research that does not conform to the trophoblastic thesis of cancer. This is true of a wide range of research projects.

For example, the recent excitement over the possibility of BCG acting as an anti-cancer agent is in conformity with the fact that the body's white blood cells are a front-line defense mechanism against cancer, as beautifully theorized by Dr. John Beard almost a century ago.

Dr. Robert Good, president of the Sloan-Kettering Institute for Cancer Research, while previously serving as chairman of the Pathology Department of the University of Minnesota, discovered that altering the protein content of the diet in mice appears to have an effect on increasing their resistance to cancer. He said: "The work raises questions about the role of diet in human cancer."

His studies were sparked after observing that the aborigines of Australia consumed a low-protein diet and showed an excellent immunity to cancer. The good Doctor Good was on the right track.[1]

Dr. J. N. Davis, Professor of Pathology at Albany Medical College, also stumbled across a

[1] "Protein Study—Diet Linked to Cancer Control," *San Francisco Chronicle*, October 21, 1971. Also, "American College of Surgeons, A New Cancer Link; Gene-Pool Pollution," *Modern Medicine*, Nov. 29, 1971, p. 13.

part of the solution when he noticed that there was a staggering increase in cancer of the esophagus in Kenya, Africa, in the last thirty years, while there was practically none in neighboring Uganda. He noticed, also, that there appears to be some kind of relationship between cancer of the colon and diet. He asked, "Why should there be a low incidence of colon cancer in poor countries where food is scanty?"

For those familiar with the traditionally high nitriloside content of unrefined foods in poor countries, the answer is obvious. If Dr. Davis keeps asking the right questions, sooner or later he is bound to find the right answers. And then he will have the whole medical establishment to fight. In the meantime, he has come to the conclusion that the reason for the difference may be found in the types of beer drunk in these two countries — which may not be too far off, for the different beers are made out of different grains such as maize, sorghum, and millet, all of which have varying concentrations of vitamin B_{17}.[1] But as long as Dr. Davis theorizes only about the beer and not the vitamin, he will retain the respect of his colleagues and probably will continue to receive funding for his research program.

And so it goes. Over and over again, the trophoblastic thesis (fact) of cancer is confirmed and strengthened by independent researchers who, unfortunately, have no inkling of the significance of

---

[1]See "Seek Clues to Dramatic Rise of Throat Cancer in Kenya," *Infectious Diseases*, July 2, 1972.

their discoveries. Some of them, of course, eventually do begin to grasp the picture. Dr. Bruce Holstead, for instance, is Director and founder of the World Life Research Institute of Colton, California, which, incidentally, is supported partly by funds from the U.N. He has travelled to the Soviet Union and discovered that scientists there are studying natural non-toxic compounds and appear to be way ahead of the United States in this field. He speaks glowingly of one such compound called Eleuterococcus which, from his description, sounds suspiciously like pangamic acid or vitamin B_{15} discovered by Dr. Krebs.

At any rate, Dr. Holstead has been unsuccessful in getting the FDA to approve experimentation with this compound. He complains:

> I've tried everywhere. I can't get any pharmaceutical company to support it because of the FDA's regulations which are for specifics. This is where the whole field of medicine is in conflict.

Dr. Holstead also is on the right track, which undoubtedly is why he is now running up against a stone wall of resistance from the Medical and Political Establishment. After noting that Congress had just authorized 1.6 billion dollars for cancer research, he said that, in his opinion, it would not produce results because it all would be spent for research into exotic and toxic artificial drugs rather than in the investigation of natural non-toxic compounds. Then he added:

> I predict that cures for cancer can be expected out of the natural products field. Someday we'll discover that some native population had the cancer cure product and was using it. They may not have been using it intentionally for this reason, but we'll find out that they were using it, and the results were bona fide.
>
> I believe that if we could really do a thorough study of all the natural occurring materials used by primitive tribes on a world scale, we (the U.S.) could become a highly-productive area of cancer research.[1]

But this is not the approach of those government agencies that now dictate to the half-free men of medicine. Instead, infatuated with their newly acquired skills in creating marvelously complex artificial chemicals, they scorn nature and plunge billions of tax dollars into their poisonous concoctions. And, as scores of these drugs are developed each year, cancer patients become the human guinea pigs upon which they are tested.

Not all testing, of course, is in an attempt to

---

[1] "Russia, U.S. Join Ranks in Cancer Battle Project," *L.A. Herald-Examiner,* Feb. 20, 1972, p. A-18.

cure cancer. Much of it is done just because the researchers have at their disposal large numbers of patients who, as they reason, are going to die anyway, so why not use their bodies while they still have some life. If that sounds like too harsh a judgment, then consider the research project funded by the federal government at the Maryland Psychiatric Research Center in Cantonsville. The project was headed by Dr. Stanislav Grof, a Czechoslovakian-born psychiatrist who specializes in the use of psychedelic drugs, particularly LSD.

The story here is so bizarre that many persons will find it hard to believe. So let us examine the eye-witness account of a special reporter to the *Washington Post* who visited the research center and observed video-tapes of some of the experiments. The reporter, by the way, was extremely sympathetic to the entire experimental program and presented it in the most favorable light possible. But even in spite of this bias, the report is a shocking exposé of the total disregard that these men have for the human "specimens" given to them for experimentation:

> On the morning of his session, the patient is given a single red rose in a vase. The center's music therapist has selected a program intended to heighten the experience — Vivaldi, Beethoven, Bach, Wagner, Simon and Garfunkel, the Balinese Ramazana monkey chant, and others. . . .

Here is an example of one session preserved on video-tape: The cancer patient, a laborer in his late forties who was depressed and afraid of his imminent death, was apprehensive as he sat on the couch talking with Grof and the nurse.

"It hurts so bad," he said in a choked voice. "I never cry, I mean I can't help it, but I've got to let it come out sooner or later." He sobbed, and Grof comforted him.

The nurse injected him intravenously with a single high dose of LSD, and he waited the ten to thirty minutes for it to start to take effect. When it did, he reacted with fear. "I don't know what to do," he cried, and he moaned and eventually vomited into a pan. . . .

The patient, wearing the customary eyeshades, finally relaxed. Grof soothed him with a few words then slipped a stereophonic headset over his ears. The patient was overcome with the mighty sound of the Morman Tabernacle Choir singing "The Lord's Prayer."

He lay motionless.

Cantonsville's therapists prefer to play an indirect role, letting the patients make their own discoveries. So Grof sat back, and after a long while the patient started uttering words:

> "Like a ball of fire. Everything was dumped into this that I can remember. Everything was destroyed in a final way. It had all disappeared. I don't remember, but whoever it was said they was set free. Somebody was free. I don't know who it was. I don't know who it was, but he was free."

> Grof asked the patient if it was he who was set free, and the man replied, "Yes, yes."[1]

The next day, the patient was convinced he had had a genuine religious experience. The staff was pleased because, as they explained it, they had helped the patient to find "meaning in his life and to enjoy his last months more fully."

Four days later, the man died from cancer.

It is shocking to learn that, under the code of ethics followed by the FDA and the medical profession it now controls, it is not necessary to advise a patient that he or she is being experimented upon. This is an ominous fact, not only in regard to the patient who is receiving the experimental drug, but also to the patient who expects medical help but

---

[1] "LSD Therapy: Quiet Revolution in Medicine," *L.A. Times,* Dec. 15, 1972, Part VII, pp. 10, 11.

who is placed into the control group and, thus, receives placebos—no help at all. Robert N. Veatch, a specialist in medical ethics, told a Senate Health Subcommittee in 1973 that, in just one typical research project, ninety-one children acting as controls in a study of treatment for asthma "received ineffective treatment for periods lasting up to fourteen years." He confirmed also that "no mother or child in the study knew any sort of study was underway."[1]

As of 1970, there were over 100,000 cancer patients who had been used in experiments without either their knowledge or consent.[2]

In a report prepared for the Chairman of a Senate Subcommittee, and published in the Congressional Record of October 5, 1966, Dr. Miles H. Robinson revealed:

> An undetermined number of cancer patients with an otherwise substantial expectation of life have died in these tests, according to reports in NCI's *Cancer Chemotherapy Reports*. The full extent of mortality and morbidity is difficult to estimate, since the journal's editor told me only the "best" investigations are published.[3]

---

[1]"Unethical Experiments Hit," *Prevention*, July, 1973, p. 97.

[2]Omar Garrison, *The Dictocrats*, (Books for Today, Ltd., Chicago, London, Melbourne, 1970), p. 271.

[3]*Ibid.*, p. 273.

The following statements are taken from just a few of these "best" official *Chemotherapy Reports:*

> An effort was made to choose patients who were well enough to withstand the anticipated toxicity. . . . Unexpectedly, early death of two of the first five patients treated caused a reduction to 8.0 mg/kg/day. No significant anti-tumor benefit of any duration was observed. . . .

> In this study, six of the eight patients [children] died. . . . No therapeutic effect was observed. Toxic clinical manifestations consisted of vomiting, hypotension, changes in oral mucus membranes, and diarrhea, in that order of frequency. Renal damage and cerebral edema were observed at postmortem examination in each of the six patients who died while receiving this drug. . . .

> The death of two patients was unequivocally caused by drug toxicity. . . . Eight of the fourteen patients who survived their initial courses of therapy showed rapid general deterioration, and died within ten weeks after therapy began. It was our opinion that drug

> toxicity contributed to the rapid demise of these patients . . . .
>
> Because of severe toxicity, which led to the death of a number of the forty patients initially treated with the full five-day "priming doses" used by the Wisconsin workers, investigators in the Eastern group voted to omit the fifth "priming" doses of each course.[1]

It is a fact that many of these experiments are carried out, *not* to see if the drug is effective against cancer, but only to determine how much of it can be administered before the patient becomes ill or dies from its toxic effect.

It is difficult for the average person to fathom the full depth of these legalized tortures and murders committed on unsuspecting victims in the name of science. And it is a sad commentary that so many people in and near the medical profession accept them without protest. In fact, it is insult added to injury when the FDA finances and encourages the wider use of these killer-drugs while at the same time, forbidding doctors to experiment with Laetrile — which is known to be at least a thousand times less toxic — on the absurd contention that it has not yet been proven to be *safe!* The fact is that *none* of the FDA-approved cancer drugs has been proven to be safe, and most of them, quite

---

[1]*Ibid.* pp. 273, 274.

to the contrary, have been proven to be extremely *unsafe*. And the American Cancer Society has the gall to label the use of Laetrile as "a new dimension of murder," when, in reality, it is they and their worthless, unproven nostrums that truly have earned this epithet.

XI

A STATISTICAL COMPARISON

The inherent weaknesses of all cancer statistics; the need for statistical comparisons in spite of these weaknesses; the methods of computing statistical values for both orthodox and nutritional therapies; and a reflection on the consequences of consensus medicine.

A major part of the total effort of the American Cancer Society and the National Cancer Institute is devoted to gathering statistics. Each year the records of thousands of physicians and hospitals are combed through to produce cancer statistics by age, sex, geography, site, extent, type of treatment, and length of survival. It is a mammoth task consuming hundreds of thousands of man-hours and millions of dollars. This activity is about as important to victory over cancer as is a body count in time of war. The experts know all about who *has* cancer but nothing about how to *cure* it.

Unlike the proponents of orthodox medicine who publish reams of statistics on just about everything, the proponents of vitamin therapy are extremely reluctant to speak in these terms. At first this may appear as a lack of confidence on their part or, even worse, as an indication that they really don't have any solid evidence to back up their claims. Upon analysis, however, their reluctance is well-founded.

First of all, in order to have statistics from which meaningful comparisons can be made, there has to be a control group. In other words, it would be necessary for those who believe in vitamin therapy to accept cancer patients but then not to treat them or to treat them with orthodox therapies. This, of course, to the physicians involved would be tantamount to murder, and they never could participate in it. These men have already witnessed the tragic results of orthodox therapies on patients who come to them as a last resort. To ask these physicians to assign some of their patients to a continuation of these treatments would be like asking them to place a hot poker on human flesh to see if it would cause burns and pain. And yet, not to set up such control groups would leave an opening for the claim that, if the patient recovers, it would be due to "spontaneous regression" or "delayed response of the orthodox treatments."

Another fact is that, even if control groups were to be set up, it would be impossible to make sure that they were meaningful. There are so many variables in such factors as location of cancer, degree of metastasis, dietary background, hereditary characteristics, emotional state, age, sex, general health, medical history, environment, and so on. Almost any of these variables could be claimed as reasons for invalidating the statistics.

Whenever the proponents of vitamin therapy have attempted to offer surveys of their clinical results, the proponents of orthodox medicine have descended on them like a swarm of locusts condemning them because their studies did not have adequate control groups, or that their results could be explained by some other factors, or that their follow-up records were inadequate. And who can argue with these objections? But exactly these same weaknesses are present in all of the statistical studies of orthodox medicine as well, and not one of them could stand up under the same kind of negative scrutiny that they apply to those they so readily condemn! The only difference is that theirs are not challenged because they are *presumed* to be accurate.

The truth of the matter is that, because of the many variables previously mentioned, there is no field of medicine in which statistics are more confusing and meaningless than in the field of cancer. In fact, there are many times when pathologists will disagree among themselves as to whether or not a particular tissue even *is* cancer. So it is not just the nutritional therapist whose statistics are open to challenge.

But it is only the nutritional therapist who, generally speaking, honestly recognizes these problems and, consequently, is reluctant to speak in terms of hard numbers or ratios. Dr. Krebs, for example, repeatedly has refused to quote statistics because he thinks they are meaningless from a scientific point of view and cannot prove the reality of his theory. Anyone who insists on numbers, he says, reveals his lack of understanding of the scientific concept involved. It would be like trying to prove the value of oxygen by collecting case histories of people who claim that breathing saved their lives. Of *course,* it saved their lives. But anyone who didn't believe it could find a hundred plausible explanations as to why something *other* than oxygen was responsible for their being alive.

Dr. Richardson also advised strongly against using statistics, and then added:

> But this is a vitamin and enzyme deficiency disease. We dare not talk about five-year survivals when we are really talking about 100% survival with prophylaxis [prevention]. When you start killing people with radiomimetic insults to their bodies — you're talking about radiation deaths, not deaths from cancer.
>
> There are several other reasons for not using their false and misleading yardsticks. One is that this yardstick is not applied to vitamin deficiency diseases. Later on when B_{17} is accepted . . . we may appear the fool by having cheapened our presentation by acquiescing in the use of the yardstick. Anyone who begins to

> see the vitamin aspect soon realizes that it is like measuring water and steel with the same clumsy apparatus.[1]

It is obvious, therefore, that the reluctance to deal in statistics on the part of proponents of vitamin therapy — a reluctance not shared by the proponents of orthodox therapy — is based upon a respect for scientific truth. In spite of this, however, the general public clamors for a statistical comparison, and it is not apt to take the trouble to study the problems deeply enough to understand why such comparisons are not to be trusted. The result is that orthodox medicine, with its mountains of statistical charts and tables, easily wins the race for public opinion, while the nutritionists are condemned to the role of quacks, charlatans, and murderers.

Let us make it an honest race. Without defending the value of such statistics, let us at least see what they tell us, such as they are. Let us acknowledge that one should view all cancer statistics with great reservation, but let us also give the nutritional therapists the same right to use them that their critics have enjoyed.

On May 5, 1972, a press conference was held at the White House by Dr. Frank J. Rauscher on the occasion of his appointment as Director of the National Cancer Institute. After speaking of plans for international cooperation in the search for a cancer cure, he then turned his attention to the current

---

[1]Letter from John Richardson, M.D., to G. Edward Griffin, dated August 2, 1972.

level of successful "cures" already being achieved by surgery, radiation, and chemotherapy. He said:

> We know, for instance, that of the one hundred cancers that afflict man, about fifteen percent of these can be treated extremely well, to the point of at least fifty percent five-year survivals.

Unscrambled, that means that, on the average, the *best* that can be claimed is a seven-and-a-half percent long-term survival. (15% x 50 % = 7½%). And that figure includes those patients who survive *without* treatment of any kind, which means that the rate for those who survive with (in spite of ?) treatment actually is even less.[1] But let us accept this figure at face value and agree that the current average "cure rate" is seven-and-a-half percent.

The statistics of the American Cancer Society are considerably more optimistic. They have said that, according to present rates, cancer will strike two out of every three families. Of every six deaths from all causes, one is from cancer. And, of every three persons who get cancer, one will be saved and two will die.[2] One out of three, therefore, represents an ACS "cure rate" of approximately thirty-three percent.

These figures, of course, are heavily weighted to present the most favorable picture possible. As

---

[1]This fact was brought to Dr. Rauscher's attention in a letter from Dr. Dean Burk, dated April 20, 1973, *op. cit.*

[2]*Cancer Facts and Figures*' ACS, 1972, pp. 3,4.

mentioned previously, they include the relatively non-fatal cancers such as skin cancer, and they do not include those patients who die from cancer before they have completed their prescribed course of treatment — which is a *substantial* number.

Of course, we cannot use *both* statistics. So, for the sake of making a stab at a comparison with nutritional therapy, let's put the two together and take an average. This produces a survival rate of approximately twenty percent for all cancers and all groups together. And then, just to make sure that we are estimating on the conservative side and giving every benefit of the doubt, let's add another five percent as a margin of error and use the figure of twenty-five percent.

Now let us attempt to break this down into three categories:

> ADVANCED OR "TERMINAL" — Those whose cancer has disseminated to two or more distant locations, who have not responded to surgery, radiation, or drugs, and who have been told by their doctor that there no longer is any hope.
>
> MODERATE SPREAD — Those whose cancer has been detected before extensive metastasis to a distant location, and which appears sufficiently limited, regional, or slow-growing to offer some hope of successful control by orthodox treatments. Skin cancer not included in this category.

PRESENTLY HEALTHY — Those who are in reasonably good health and who have no clinical cancer to begin with.

Admittedly, these categories are not absolute. They are rightly subject to all the criticisms of any such statistical categorization. The first two are especially dependent upon the subjective evaluation of the physician since no one can point out the clear dividing line between them. But, whatever errors might be generated by these problems will work randomly and equally on behalf of both orthodox and nutritional therapies. Neither will have an advantage.

The chances of a terminal cancer patient surviving five years after the point at which he has been classified as such are so small as to defy statistical statement. Most physicians will say that there isn't one chance out of ten thousand. Some will say one out of a thousand. Let's not quibble. We shall use the more favorable figure which is one-tenth of one percent.

When it comes to "moderate spread" cancers, it is difficult to know what figures to use. An unoffician poll conducted by the author in 1972 directed to a random group of Southern California doctors, produced an "opinion" of approximately fifteen percent long-term survival in this category. The American Cancer Society was unable to produce either statistics or opinion. But, more recently, a letter was received from the National Cancer Institute which claims that "regional spread" (as distinguished from "distant spread") cancer patients can anticipate a five-year survival of a whopping twenty-eight percent![1] Frankly, that is extremely difficult to believe, even allowing for all the built-in enhancement factors. But, following our practice of taking these statistics as we find them, let us accept this one also, even if it is with an extremely large grain of salt.

For those who are presently healthy with no cancer at all, we return to the American Cancer Society's statement that one out of four (25%) Americans will get cancer. We previously estimated from a synthesis of the ACS and NCI statistics that apparently twenty-five percent of those who contract cancer will survive five years. That means, of course, that seventy-five percent will die. So, if seventy-five percent out of the twenty-five percent will die, that is a net fatality rate of approximately nineteen percent, and an overall survival rate of approximately eighty-one percent.

Here, then, is a summary of our statistical conclusions regarding long-term survival:

	ORTHODOX THERAPY
ADVANCED, "TERMINAL"	$^1/_{10}$%
MODERATE SPREAD	28%
PRESENTLY HEALTHY	81%

[1] Letter from Marvin A. Schneiderman, Ph.D., Associate Scientific Director for Demography, NCI, to G. Edward Griffin, dated March 21, 1973.

Now let's turn to the record of vitamin therapy.

As mentioned several times previously, almost all of the patients who have sought out Laetrile have done so only after they have moved into the advanced or "terminal" category. The fact that most of them do not survive five years after beginning vitamin and enzyme therapy is not surprising. What is surprising is that *any* of them should be saved at this late stage. Yet, Doctor Contreras of Mexico, one of the few doctors who has been using Laetrile for a long enough period to be *able* to speak of five-year survivals, reports that approximately fifteen percent of his patients have survived this period or longer. Fifteen percent, of course, is not good. But considering that less than one-tenth of one percent survive under orthodox therapy, that record is truly amazing. Even more encouraging is the fact that the rate of survival obtained by doctors who have been using Laetrile only for three or four years promises eventually to produce a five-year rate substantially higher than fifteen percent. But, for the purposes of our comparison, let us use the lower firmly-established, and more conservative figure.

Those whose cancer has not yet metastasized to distant secondary locations and who, thus, fall into the "moderate spread" category can look forward to approximately an eighty percent long-term survival in response to vitamin therapy. Some doctors are finding the response as high as eighty-five percent, providing the vital organs have not been too badly damaged by surgical, X-ray, or chemical intervention during prior treatment.[1]

Of those who presently are healthy with no clinical cancer at all, close to one hundred percent can expect to be free from cancer as long as they routinely obtain adequate amounts of vitamin B_{17}, and, presuming, of course, that they are not subject to some rare pancreas malfunction or subjected to a totally unnatural exposure to carcinogenic agents such as massive radiation. Fortunately, the "control group" for this category already has been provided through the existence of the Hunzas, the Abkhasians, the Eskimos, the Hopi and Navajo Indians, and many other similar groups around the world.

Putting the two columns of statistics together, here is the story they tell:

LONG-TERM SURVIVAL

	ORTHODOX THERAPY	VITAMIN THERAPY
ADVANCED, "TERMINAL"	1/10%	15%
MODERATE SPREAD	28%	80%
PRESENTLY HEALTHY	81%	100%

---

[1]An 80% survival was reported by the McNaughton Foundation in the 6th volume of its data submitted to the FDA in connection with its IND-6734 application for Phase One testing of Laetrile. See *Cancer News Journal,* Vol. 6, No. 1, Jan./Apr., 1971, p. 12. Also, Dr. Richardson has stated: "The second category of early detection — say the lump and bump stage and without radiomimetic or surgical interference — will have a 75% to 85% survival (5 yr.)." Letter to G. Edward Griffin, dated Dec. 2, 1972.

It bears repeating still one more time that *all* cancer statistics are subject to a host of unseen and undefined premises and, consequently, are useful only for the most general reference purpose. These, in particular, because they attempt to present a *composite* picture, can be extremely misleading when it comes to applying them to any *particular* person with any *particular* condition. The data that goes into these figures vary widely depending on age, sex, cancer location, and degree of malignancy. Also, the categories are extremely arbitrary when it comes to separating moderately spread cancers from those that are far advanced, for often there is a grey area between the two. Nevertheless, for those who simply must have statistics, these are as accurate as any such tabulation *can* be and, especially considering that they have given the proponents of orthodox treatments every conceivable advantage, they tell an impressive story that cannot be brushed aside.

As physicians become aware of these facts and begin to experiment with the nutritional approach to cancer therapy, they soon find themselves the victims of something called *consensus medicine*. Consensus medicine is the tangible result of the belief that doctors need to be policed in order to prevent them from injuring or cheating their patients, and that the best people to police doctors are other doctors acting through professional organizations, hospital staffs, and government agencies. The result of this seemingly proper arrangement is that, no matter how useless or even harmful current practices may be, consensus medicine demands that they be used by every physician. Regardless of how many patients are lost, the doctor's professional standing is upheld because those who pass judgment through "peer review" are using the same treatments and getting the same tragic results. On the other hand, if a doctor deviates from this pattern and dares to apply nutrition as the basis of his treatment, even if he attains a high degree of success, he is condemned as a quack. He loses his hospital privileges, is denied malpractice insurance, and even becomes subject to arrest.

The result of this is that many physicians are just as afraid of cancer as their patients — afraid that they may miss a diagnosis or cause a month delay before surgery. They may know in their own mind that the extra month really makes little difference in the survival of the patient, but they know it will make a great difference in their reputations. It takes a brave man not to operate or recommend radiation, or drugs. This is especially true if he knows that, if the patient dies anyway, relatives of the deceased could easily institute a malpractice law suit against him on the grounds that he did not do all that he could have done or should have done. And, in light of the present abysmal ignorance about the true nature of cancer, it would be next to impossible for the doctor to convince either the judge or the jury that the patient would have died anyway, even without the "benefit" of surgery, radiation, or drugs. This is especially true if a spokesman for the American Cancer Society were called to the witness stand and unleashed the "statistic" of a million-and-a-half who, supposedly, are now alive only because of such treatments.

And so the physician cannot follow his own judgment or his own conscience. He gets into far more trouble by prescribing a few non-toxic vitamins than by prescribing the most radical surgery or violent chemical poisons. All but the very brave toe the line. *That* is consensus medicine.

The hard fact of life is that — consensus or no consensus, statistics or no statistics — cancer is a disease for which orthodox medicine does *not* have either a cure or control worthy of being called such. And the rate of cancer deaths continues to climb every year in spite of billions of dollars and millions of man-hours spent annually in search for even a clue. Under the circumstances it seems more than ironic that those who have failed to find the answer themselves spend so much of their time and energy condemning and harassing others who merely want the freedom to be able to choose an alternate approach.

Dr. Krebs often has commented that using a Chinese prayer wheel would produce just as good or possibly better results than orthodox treatment. And this is not said in jest, for the use of such a prayer wheel would be the same as no treatment at all which, at least, mercifully would spare the patient the deadly side-effects of radiation and chemical poisoning. One cannot expect to cure cancer by removing only the tumor, for the tumor is the *symptom* or the *result* of cancer, not the *cause*. One cannot expect to burn away or cut away a chronic deficiency disease.

"Cancer," says Dr. Krebs, "is properly described as one of the last outposts of mysticism in medical science." He is referring, of course, to the great wall of ignorance and prejudice and vested interest that still prevents large numbers of present-day scientists — men who like to fancy that they are above such traits — from objectively viewing the evidence all around them and humbly admitting that they have been wrong. And it *is* a humbling experience for a man who has spent a lifetime learning complex surgical procedures, creating elaborate man-made chemical structures, or mastering monster ray machines, to accept in the end that during all these years the answer was right under his nose — not as the product of his brilliant intelligence and technical manipulation of the cosmos — but in the form of a simple food factor found in the lowly apple seed. So he persists in his quest for the complex answer. Yet, just as we are amused today at the primitive medical practices of history — the trepanning of skulls, the bloodletting, the medicinal elixirs of dog hair, goose grease, lizard blood, or old Indian Kickapoo Juice — future generations surely will look back at our own era and cringe at the senseless cutting, burning, and poisoning that now passes for medical science.

symptom or the result of cancer, not the cause. One cannot expect to burn away or cut away a chronic deficiency disease.

"Cancer," says Dr. Krebs, "is properly described as one of the last citadels of mysticism in medical science." He is referring, of course, to the great wall of ignorance and prejudice and vested interests that still protects large numbers of present-day scientists — men who like to fancy that they are above such things — from objectively viewing the evidence all around them and humbly admitting that they have been wrong. And it is a humbling experience for a man who has spent a lifetime learning complex surgical procedures, or devising elaborate mathematical formulas for calculating the proper dosage of radiation, to find that he has been wrong all these years, and that the answer was right under his nose — not as the product of [illegible] intelligence and [illegible] sophisticated [illegible] — but in the form of a simple food factor found in the lowly apricot seed. So he persists in his quest for the complex answer. Yet, just as we are amused today at the primitive medical practices of history — the bleeding of patients to let out the evil humors, the medicinal [illegible] — future generations surely will look back at our own era and cringe at the senseless cutting, burning and poisoning that now passes for medical science.

PART TWO

The Politics of Cancer Therapy

XII

CARTELS – THE ESCAPE FROM COMPETITION

A short review of the science of cancer therapy; a thesis summary of the politics of cancer therapy; the early history of the I.G. Farben chemical and pharmaceutical cartel; a look at the cartel's early success in the United States with particular emphasis on its "marriage" with DuPont, Standard Oil, and Ford.

In Part One we presented the science of cancer therapy. Before proceeding with Part Two, the *politics* of cancer therapy, let's review briefly the major points previously covered.

As we have seen, cancer is the unnatural and unchecked growth of trophoblast cells which, themselves, are a normal and vital part of the life process.

Trophoblast cells are produced in the body as a result of a chain reaction involving the hormone estrogen. Estrogen always is present in large quantities at the site of damaged tissue, possibly serving as an organizer or catalyst for body repair.

Cancer, therefore, can be triggered by any prolonged stress or damage to the body — whether it be smoking or chemical additives to our food, or even certain viruses — for these are what cause the production of estrogen as part of the normal healing process.

Nature, fortunately, has provided a metabolic barrier — a complex mechanism to limit and control the growth of these trophoblast cells. Many factors are involved, but the most direct-acting of these appear to be the pancreatic enzymes and the food factor known as nitriloside or vitamin B_{17}, a unique compound that destroys cancer cells while nourishing and sustaining all others.

The answer to cancer, therefore, simply is to avoid excessive damage or stress to the body, to minimize foods that preempt the pancreatic enzymes for their digestion, and to maintain a diet rich in *all* minerals and vitamins — especially vitamin B_{17}.

As mentioned previously, opposition to the nutritional concept of cancer is both strong and vocal. This concept has been branded as fraud and quackery by the Food and Drug Administration, the American Cancer Society, and the American Medical Association.

It is important to stress again, however, that the average physician is not part of this opposition — except, perhaps, to the extent to which he trustingly accepts the official pronouncements of these prestigious bodies. Most doctors, however, would be more inclined to give Laetrile a try before passing final judgment. As a result, an increasing number of physicians all around the world now are testing and proving the value of vitamin therapy in their own clinics. Doctors in the United States, however, are forbidden both by law and by the pressures of peer review from experimenting with unorthodox therapies. Consequently, they are not able to find out if Laetrile works, only if it is *said* to work.

Meanwhile, with the evidence continuing to mount in favor of vitamin therapy, the opposition and the controversy also continue to grow. The reason is both simple and unpleasant. Cancer, in the United States, at least, has become a multi-billion dollar business. Not only are fortunes made in the fields of research, drugs, and X-ray, but political careers, also, are enhanced by promising ever larger tax-supported programs and government grants.

It is an ominous fact that, each year, there are more people making a living from cancer than are dying from it. If the riddle were to be solved by a simple vitamin found abundantly and inexpensively in nature, this gigantic commercial and political industry could be wiped out almost overnight. It is not unexpected, therefore, that vested interest should play an important role in clouding the scientific facts.

This does not mean that the surgeons, the radiologists, the druggists, the researchers, or the thousands of people who supply and support them would consciously withhold a control for cancer. In the first place, they are, for the most part, highly motivated and conscientious individuals who would like nothing better than to put an end to human suffering. Secondly, they and their families are inflicted with cancer just as much as the rest of the population. Obviously, they are not keeping any secret cures to themselves.

But does it necessarily follow that *all* opposition is innocent? Are we to believe that personal gain or vested interest is not a factor *anywhere* along the line? The purpose of the second half of this presentation is to provide the answers to these questions. We will demonstrate that, at the very top of the world's economic and political pyramid of power there is a grouping of financial, industrial, and political interests that, by the very nature of their goals, are the natural enemies of the nutritional approach to health. It will be shown that they have created a popular climate of bias that makes scientific objectivity almost an impossibility, and that they, themselves, often become the victims of their own bias.

It will be shown that these forces wield tremendous influence over the medical profession, the medical schools, and the medical journals; and that the average doctor is the last to suspect that much of his knowledge and outlook have been shaped subtly by these non-medical interests.

It will be shown, also, that this elite group can move long levers of political power that activate government agencies in their behalf; and that these agencies, which supposedly are the servants and protectors of the people, have become almost the total mechanism of vested interest.

All of these, of course, are serious indictments. They are not made lightly, nor should they be accepted without challenge. So let us turn now to the record to see what evidence there is to support them.

The information that follows is taken primarily from government hearings and reports published by various Senate and House committees from 1928 to 1946. Principal among these are the House Subcommittee to Investigate Nazi Propaganda in 1934, the Special Senate Committee Investigating the Munitions Industry in 1935, the report on cartels released by the House Temporary National Economic Committee in 1941, the Senate Special Committee Investigating the National Defense Program in 1942, the report of the Senate Patents Committee in 1942, and the Senate Subcommittee on War Mobilization in 1946.

Other sources include the Senate Lobby Investigating Committee, the Senate Committee on Banking and Currency, court records of the Nuremberg trials, and dozens of volumes found as standard references in any large library. In other words, although the story that follows is not widely known, it is, nevertheless, part of the public record and can be verified by anyone willing to take the time.

This is that story.

In the years prior to World War II, there came into existence an international cartel, centered in

Germany, that dominated the entire world's chemical and drug industries. It had spread its operations to ninety-three countries and was a powerful economic and political force on all continents. It was known as I.G. Farben.

I.G. stands for *Interssen Gemeinschaft*, which means "community of interests," or more simply, "cartel." Farben means "dyes," which, because the modern chemical industry had its origin in the development of dyestuffs, now is a deceptively innocent sounding category that, in reality, encompasses the entire field of chemistry, including munitions and drugs.

Munitions and drugs, of course, can be transformed into powerful human motivators. One offers the promise of health and prolonged life, while the other can be the carrier of death and destruction. There can be no greater earthly desire for men than to have the first but to avoid the second. He who controls munitions and drugs, therefore, holds the ultimate carrot and stick.

The basic ingredient for almost all chemicals—including those that wound as well as those that heal—is coal tar or crude oil. With the advent of the internal combustion engine, the value of these raw materials as the precursor of petroleum has given those who control their chemical conversions a degree of power over the affairs of the world that is frightening to contemplate. In other words, the present movement of civilization is driven by the engine of chemistry. But the fuel of chemistry is oil. Whereas gold once was the key to world power, now it is oil. And, as we shall see, it has come to pass that it is the same men who now control both.

Howard Ambruster, author of *Treason's Peace,* summarized as follows:

> I. G. Farben is usually discussed as a huge German cartel which controls chemical industries throughout the world and from which profits flow back to the headquarters in Frankfort. Farben, however, is no mere industrial enterprise conducted by Germans for the extraction of profits at home and abroad. Rather, it is and must be recognized as a cabalistic organization which, through foreign subsidiaries and by secret tie-ups, operates a far-flung and highly efficient espionage machine — the ultimate purpose being world conquest — and a world super-state directed by Farben.[1]

Much of the earlier scientific knowledge that made it possible for German industry to assume world leadership in the field of organic chemistry was the result of the pioneering genius of the well-known chemist, Justus von Leibig. It is an interesting historical aside that Leibig, shortly after he completed his university training in 1824, first attracted attention within the scientific community by publishing a paper on the chemical properties of the

---

[1] Ambruster, *Treason's Peace,* (Beechhurst Press, N.Y., 1947), p. vii.

bitter almond, a substance rich in vitamin B_{17}. He specifically identified the presence of benzaldehyde, one of the important ingredients that act specifically against cancer cells, but there is no indication that he ever followed up these studies with particular application to cancer therapy.[1]

I.G. Farben was created in 1926 primarily by the dual genius of two men: a German industrialist by the name of Hermann Schmitz and a Swiss banker by the name of Eduard Greutert.[2] Greutert's stock-in-trade was keeping "loose books" and creating financial mazes to conceal Farben ownership of specific companies. Schmitz also was a director of the great Deutsche Reichsbank and of the Bank of International Settlements headquartered in Switzerland. And so, from the very beginning, the leaders of I.G. Farben had been an integral part of the international banking structure.

By the beginning of World War II, I.G. Farben had become the largest industrial corporation in Europe, the largest chemical company in the world, and part of the most gigantic and powerful cartel of all history.[3] It would take over an hour just to read aloud the names of the companies around the world with which it had interlocking cartel agreements.

---

[1]Richard Sasuly, *I.G. Farben,* (Boni & Gaer, N.Y., 1947), p. 21.

[2]Greutert was a German national also. His bank was located in Basel and was known as Greutert & Cie.

[3]This was the opinion of the U.S. Department of Justice as expressed in *U.S.* vs. *Allied Chemical & Dye Corp. et. al.*, U.S. District Court of New Jersey, May 14, 1942.

There were, in fact, over 2,000 of them.[1] When the list is narrowed to include just those companies which it owned or controlled outright, it still would fill many pages in a book. Here are just a few of the better known:

Inside Germany, the cartel included the top six chemical firms and extended to virtually all of heavy industry as well, especially the steel industry. Hermann Schmitz was a dominant figure in the Krupp Steel Works and was on its board of directors as well as on the board of the major steel combine, Vereinigte Stahlwerke. All-in-all, more than 380 German firms were controlled by the cartel.

Elsewhere in Europe, I.G. Farben dominated such industrial giants as Imperial Chemical in Great Britain, Kuhlmann in France, and Allied Chemical in Belgium. Leslie Waller, in his *The Swiss Bank Connection,* described this network quite modestly when he wrote:

> Through the Basel connection, I.G. Farben spread out across the face of the globe widening its grasp of the chemical business by establishing thoroughly concealed interests in companies in Belgium, England, France, Greece, Holland,

[1]General Eisenhower, as Supreme Commander in the American Zone of Occupation, reported that I.G. had stock interests in 613 corporations, including 173 in foreign countries, piled up assets of 6 billion Reichsmarks, and "operated with varying degrees of power in more than 2,000 cartels." See *New York Times,* Oct. 21, 1945, Sec. I, pp. 1, 12.

Hungary, Norway, Poland, Romania, various nations of South America, Sweden and the United States.[1]

In the United States the cartel had established important agreements with a wide spectrum of American industry including Abbott Laboratories, Alcoa, Anaconda, Atlantic Oil, Bell and Howell, the Borden Company, the Carnation Company, Ciba-Geigy, Dow Chemical, DuPont, Eastman Kodak, Firestone Rubber, Ford Motor, General Drug Company, General Electric, General Mills, General Motors, General Tire, Glidden Paint, Goodyear Rubber, Gulf Oil, the M.W. Kellogg Company, Monsanto Chemical, National Lead, Nestle's, Owl Drug Company, Parke Davis and Company, Pet Milk, Pittsburgh Glass, Proctor and Gamble, Pure Oil, Remington Arms, Richfield Oil, Shell Oil, Sinclair Oil, Socony Oil, Standard Oil, Texaco, Union Oil, U.S. Rubber, and hundreds more.

The list of companies which it owned *outright* or in which it had (or eventually *would* have) a substantial financial interest is equally impressive. It includes the Bayer Co. (producers of aspirin), the American I.G. Chemical Corporation (manufacturers of photographic film and supplies), Lederle Laboratories, the Sterling Drug Company, Winthrop Chemical, Metz Laboratories, Hoffman-LaRoche Laboratories, the J.T. Baker Chemical

---

[1]Waller, *The Swiss Bank Connection,* (Signet Books, The New American Library, Inc., N.Y., 1972), p. 162.

Company, Whitehall Laboratories, Frederick Stearns and Company, the Nyal Company, Dern and Mitchell Laboratories, Chef-Boy-Ar-Dee Foods, Breck, Inc., Heyden Anti-biotics, MacGregor Instrument Company. Antrol Laboratories, the International Vitamin Corporation, Cardinal Laboratories, Van Ess Laboratories, the William S. Merrill Company, the Jensen Salsberry Laboratories, Loesser Laboratories, Taylor Chemical, the Ozalid Corporation, Alba Pharmaceutical, Bristol Meyers, Drug, Inc., Vegex, Inc., Squibb and Sons Pharmaceutical, and scores of others, many of which were large enough to be holding companies which, in turn, owned numerous smaller companies — and some not-so-small — as well.[1]

By 1929, I.G. Farben had concluded a series of limited cartel agreements with its largest American competitor, the DuPont Company. DuPont, of course, was a major power in itself and it always had been reluctant to enter into cooperative ventures with Farben which usually insisted on being the dominant partner. Consequently, the ultimate agreements were made indirectly through Farben's subsidiary, Winthrop Chemical, through Imperial

---

[1]The listing of these firms does not imply illegality or impropriety. It is merely to establish the historical facts of either cartel contractual interlock or outright control. These facts can be verified by consulting back issues of standard business references such as *Standard and Poor's Corporation Records* and *Moody's Industrial Manual*. See also the published findings of previous researchers in this field such as *Cartels in Action*, by Stocking and Watkins; *Treason's Peace*, by Ambruster; and *The Devil's Chemist*, by DuBois; all mentioned elsewhere in this study.

Chemical (its cartel partner in Great Britain), and through Mitsui, its cartel partner in Japan. By 1937, American I.G. had substantial stock holdings in both DuPont and Eastman Kodak. The Olin Corporation, a Farben holding, entered into the manufacture of cellophane under a DuPont license.

The primary reason that such an industrial giant as DuPont ultimately relented and entered into cartel agreements with I.G. is that Standard Oil of New Jersey had just done so. The combination of these two goliaths presented DuPont with a serious potential of domestic competition. DuPont might have been able to stand firmly against I.G. alone, but it could not hope to take on both I.G. *and* the great Rockefeller empire as well. Standard Oil, therefore, was the decisive factor that brought together the ultimate "community of interest"—I.G., Standard Oil, Imperial Chemical, DuPont, and as we shall see, Shell Oil.

The cartel agreement between I.G., Standard, and Shell was consummated in 1929. How it came about is a fascinating story in itself and sheds considerable light on the behind-the-scenes maneuvers of companies that, in the public eye at least, are considered to be competitors.

One of the prime causes of Germany's defeat in World War I was its lack of petroleum. German leaders resolved never again to be dependent upon the outside world for gasoline. Germany may not have had oil deposits within its territory, but it did have abundant reserves of coal. One of the first goals of German chemists after the war, therefore, was to find a way to convert coal into gasoline.

By 1920, Dr. Bergius had discovered ways to make large quantities of hydrogen and to force it, under great pressure, at high temperatures, and in the presence of specific catalysts, into liquid coal products. The final steps into refined gasoline were then assured. It was only a matter of perfecting the hydrogenation process. I.G. suddenly was in the oil business.

One might assume that the cartel would have jumped into production with both feet. But their plan, instead, was to interest existing oil producers in their process and to use their patents as leverage to gain concessions and business advantages in other areas. In particular, this was to be the bait to ensnare Standard Oil which, in turn, would bring in DuPont. And it worked exactly as planned.

Frank Howard of Standard Oil was invited to visit the great Baldische plant at Ludwigshafen in March of 1926. What he saw was astounding — gasoline from coal! In a near state of shock, he wrote to Walter Teagle, president of Standard Oil:

> Based upon my observations and discussions today, I think that this matter is the most important which has ever faced the company . . . .
>
> The Baldische can make high-grade motor oil fuel from lignite and other low-quality coals in amounts up to half the weight of the coal. This means absolutely the independence of Europe on the matter of gasoline supply. Straight price competition is all that is left . . . .

> I shall not attempt to cover any details, but I think this will be evidence of my state of mind.[1]

The following three years were devoted to intense negotiation. On November 9, 1929, the cartel agreement was signed. It accomplished several important objectives: First, it granted Standard Oil one-half of all rights to the hydrogenation process in all countries of the world except Germany. This assured Standard that it would control, or at least profit from, its own competition in this important field. In return, Standard gave I.G. 546,000 shares of its stock valued at more than $30,000,000. The two parties also agreed never to compete with each other in the fields of chemistry and petroleum products. In the future, if Standard Oil wished to enter the broad field of industrial chemicals or drugs, it would do so only as a partner of Farben. Farben, in turn, agreed never to enter the field of petroleum except as a joint venture with Standard. Each party disavowed "any plan or policy" of "so far expanding its existing business in the direction of the other party's industry as to become a serious competitor of that other party."[2]

As Frank Howard of Standard Oil phrased it several years later:

> The I.G. may be said to be our general partner in the chemical business . . .

---

[1]Sasuly, *I.G. Farben, op. cit.*, pp. 144-145.

[2]Stocking & Watkins, *Cartels in Action,* (The Twentieth Century Fund, N.Y., 1946), p. 93.

> the desire and intention of both parties is to avoid competing with one another.[1]

To facilitate the implementation of this agreement, several jointly-owned companies were formed. One of these was the International Hydrogenation Patents Company (I.H.P.). Shell Oil also became a partner in this venture. Its purpose was *not* to promote the international use of the hydrogenation process, but to keep the lid on it as much as possible. An official Standard memorandum declared:

> I.H.P. should keep in close touch with developments in all countries where it has patents, and should be fully informed with regard to the interest being shown in hydrogenation and the prospect of its introduction . . . . It should not, however, attempt to stir up interest in countries where none exists.[2]

The other jointly-owned company was created in 1930 and was known as Jasco, Inc. Its purpose was to allow each company to share in any future new chemical developments of the other. Under the agreement, whenever I.G. or Standard developed a new chemical process, it would offer to the other party an option of obtaining one-third interest in the patent. Jasco then would exploit the marketing of that process throughout the world.

---

[1] As quoted by Armbruster, *Treason's Peace, op. cit.*, p. 52.

[2] *Ibid.*, pp. 492, 493.

Here, then, was a perfect example of how two giant industrial empires came together, step at a time, until eventually, in large areas of their activity, they were moving in unison as one. The goal of each simply was to remove all marketplace competition between themselves and assure that each had a secure guarantee of future growth and profit. Dr. Carl Bosch, head of I.G. at the time, was not merely being picturesque, when he said that I.G. and Standard had "married." He was describing quite accurately the philosophical essence of all major cartel agreements.

Space does not permit a detailed chronicle of all of I.G. Farben's polygamous marriages with other major U.S. firms, but at least two more should be mentioned in passing. On October 23, 1931, I.G. and Alcoa signed an accord, known as the Alig Agreement, in which the two companies pooled all their patents and technical knowledge on the production of magnesium. The other industrial giant that became part of the international web was none other than the Ford Motor Company.

When Henry Ford established a branch of his company in Germany, I.G. Farben immediately purchased most of the forty percent of the stock which was offered for sale. The marriage was completed when Carl Bosch, I.G.'s president, and Carl Krauch, I.G.'s chairman of the board, both joined the board of directors of the German Ford Company. In the United States, Edsel Ford joined the board of directors of the American I.G. Chemical Company, as did Walter Teagle, president of Standard Oil, Charles E. Mitchell, president of Rockefeller's National City Bank of New York, and Paul M. Warburg, brother of Max Warburg who was a director of the parent company in Germany.

To the student of contemporary history, these names are highly significant. Paul Warburg comes from a family well-known in international banking circles. He generally is credited with being one of the chief architects of the Federal Reserve System which succeeded in placing control over the American monetary system into the hands of those same banking circles he represented. He not only was instrumental in introducing the Federal Reserve Act, but became the first chairman of the Federal Reserve Board. According to the memoirs of Frank A. Vanderlip, published years later, this whole scheme was hatched at a secret meeting on the remote Jekyll Island in Georgia attended by Vanderlip himself, Senator Aldrich (both representing Rockefeller), Benjamin Strong (representing J.P. Morgan), and Paul Warburg. Paul's brother, Felix, married Frieda Schiff, the daughter of Jacob Schiff who headed the banking firm of Kuhn, Loeb and Company. Years later, according to his grandson, John, Jacob Schiff had given twenty million dollars to Trotsky for use in establishing a Soviet Dictatorship in Russia.[1]

There is much more of significance known

[1]The comments by John Schiff first appeared in the Charlie Knickerbocker column of the *New York Journal American,* Feb. 3, 1949. See also the exclusive interview with Alexander Kerensky, leader of the Russian revolution, *U.S. News & World Report,* Mar. 13, 1967, p. 68.

about these men, but suffice it to say that they were far more than mere businessmen looking for a means of expanding markets and securing profits. They were part of that special breed of businessmen whose visions extend far beyond the profit-and-loss ledgers to the horizons of international intrigue and politics.

Which brings us to the question: What *are* the motives of such men? What do they hope to accomplish? And how do they operate?

To answer these questions, it is necessary first to understand fully the nature and function of cartels. A cartel is an international grouping of companies that is bound together by contracts or agreements designed to promote inter-company cooperation and, thereby, reduce competition among them. Some of these agreements may deal with such harmless subjects as industry standards and nomenclature. But most of them involve the exchange of patent rights, the dividing up of regional markets, the setting of prices, and agreements not to enter into product competition within specific categories. Generally, a cartel is a means of escaping the rigors of competition in the open free-enterprise market. The result always is higher prices and fewer products from which to choose. Cartels and monopolies, therefore, are *not* the result of free enterprise, but the escape *from* it.

The motivation that drives businessmen into cartel agreements is very similar to that which leads laborers and skilled workers into trade unions and professional associations. They reason that by lowering the price on their product or their labor they might be able to attract a greater share of the existing market. But that is only true if others do not follow their example. It is reasonable to assume, however, that the competition *will* lower its prices also in order to avoid losing patronage. A price cut by one tends to lower the prices of all. A person is encouraged, therefore, to join with other firms or other workers and draw up agreements between them, not to follow competitive policies that will impoverish all.

This does not mean, however, that the cartel members have succeeded in eliminating all conflict or competition between them. Occasionally a party to an agreement will decide that the terms of the agreement no longer are acceptable, and it will break away and attempt to go it alone. Price wars and fierce contests for markets periodically erupt with all the overtones of military war itself. But, just as in the case of war between nations, eventually it comes to an end. One party either is vanquished or, as is more often the case in business wars, one party clearly emerges with the dominant position, and then a "truce" and a new negotiated cartel agreement is worked out on the basis of the new balance of power.

Stocking and Watkins, writing in *Cartels in Action*, describe this process quite succinctly:

> "Price wars" broke out, were terminated by "armistices," recurrently flamed up again, and finally settled into a long siege . . . .

> Chemical companies usually decide who shall sell what, where, how much, and on what terms in foreign markets, by negotiation rather than by competition, because they believe that cooperation "pays." They reach their decisions by driving hard-headed bargains. Each party tries to obtain the best terms for itself. Thus these decisions reflect the relative bargaining power of the parties involved. This depends on many factors including the efficiency of their processes, strength of their patent positions, quality of their products, extent of their financial resources, and support of their governments. In the final analysis, the issue turns on the comparative readiness of the several parties for a competitive "war" if negotiations break down.
>
> This kind of business rivalry differs from effective competition in that the bulk of its benefits are likely to go to the cartel members rather than to the consumers.[1]

There can be no doubt that this is an accurate description of the hidden reality behind most of the world's major products today. Stocking and Watkins made extensive calculations of pre-war trade and proved quite convincingly that, in the United States, in the year 1939, cartels controlled eighty-seven percent of the mineral products sold, sixty

---

[1]*Op. cit.*, pp. 398, 420.

percent of the agricultural products, and forty-two percent of all manufactured products. Needless to say, the trend has greatly accelerated since 1939, so one can well imagine what the situation is like today. The chemical industry—and that includes pharmaceuticals—is, and has been from the very beginning, almost completely cartelized. Even as far back as 1937, this fact was so obvious that *Fortune* magazine editorialized:

> The chemical industry, despite its slowly lowering curve of real prices, is an "orderly" industry. It was practicing "cooperation" long before General Johnson invented it in 1933. It has seldom been bedeviled by over production, has had no private depression of its own, and has not often involved itself in long or bloody price wars . . . . By and large, the chemical industry has regulated itself in a manner that would please even a Soviet Commissar . . . . The industry . . . is . . . the practitioner of one definite sort of planned economy.[1]

This is highly reminiscent of the sentiments expressed in 1973 by the United States Tariff Commission. In its report to the Senate, it said:

> In the largest and most sophisticated multinational corporations, planning and subsequent monitoring of plan fulfillment

[1] "Chemical Industry," *Fortune*, Dec., 1937, pp. 157, 162.

> have reached a scope and level of detail that, ironically, resemble more than superficially the national planning procedures of Communist countries.[1]

The comments about resembling the planned economy of a Soviet Commissar in a Communist country are quite "on target." They shed a great deal of light on the inherent philosophy of cartels. If it is true that cartels and monopolies are not the result of free enterprise but the escape *from* it, then it follows that the best way to escape free enterprise is to destroy it altogether. This is why cartels and collectivist governments inevitably work together as a team. They have a common enemy and share a common objective: the destruction of free enterprise.

A million dollars put into politics to bring about the passage of a protective tariff law, a so-called fair-trade law, or an anti-quackery law, is a tremendous bargain for those who benefit. Even though these laws are masqueraded as for the benefit for the people, in reality they are designed as a means of putting the entire machinery of government into motion against cartel competitors, and result in a return on their original investment many times over. Big government, therefore, with its capacity to regulate every facet of economic life, is the natural friend and ally of cartels and monopolies.

Anyone who pauses to reflect on this for even a

---

[1]Report entitled *Implications of Multinational Firms for World Trade and Investment for U.S. Trade and Labor,* Feb. 1973, p. 159.

moment is bound to realize not only the truth but the profound importance of this statement. Cartels and monopolies, outside of the political environment of big government, would be hard-pressed to exist, at least at the level and size that they do now. Look at any of the major world markets — in sugar, tea, chocolate, rubber, steel, petroleum, automobiles, food — *any* of them, and one will find a mountain of government restrictions, quotas, and price supports. And behind this mountain, there is an army of lobbyists representing special interests applying endless pressures on politicians who, in turn, endorse the laws that, supposedly, are designed to protect the people.

Cartels are not alone in this racket. Organized labor sought the escape from free-market competition when it demanded government-enforced minimum wage laws and the closed shop. Farmers did the same with price supports and subsidies. It seems that, increasingly of late, almost everyone wants the government to step in and "protect" him from the rigors of open and honest competition. The cartels are no different in this except that they were ahead of most of the others, have more money to spend, and have perfected the art to its ultimate state.

It is not merely a question of prestige, therefore, but a matter of pure necessity that large multinational corporations often have prominent political figures on their boards. ITT, for example, displays on its main board in New York such significant names as Eugene Black, former head of the World Bank, and John McCone, former director of the Central Intelligence Agency. In Europe it has had such figures as Trygve Lie, first Secretary-General of the United Nations, Paul-Henri Spock of Belgium, and Lord Caccia of Britain. There was even an attempt to recruit Harold McMillan.[1]

It is no coincidence that all of the above-named individuals are self-classified either as socialists or, at the very least, political liberals. None of them would be caught dead defending the classical free enterprise system. They all know that, in the last few decades, that system quietly has been changed into one in which the road to wealth is traveled not by the carriage of industrial expertise, but by the rocket of political influence. Government is where the action is.

The consequences of this reality can be seen everywhere—especially in the world of international finance. The situation was well expressed in the January 1973 *Monthly Review* of the Bank of Hawaii:

> There appears to be no ready answer to the complex interrelated domestic and international developments. Those standing to lose the most include the individuals who seek to establish their own business, and those independent domestic firms seeking to compete in the traditional open market place. They face increasing regimentation through bureaucratic red

---

[1] Anthony Sampson, *The Sovereign State of ITT*, (Stein & Day, N.Y., 1973), pp. 113, 114.

> tape and pre-empted markets by federally subsidized competition.
>
> Virtually immune are the multi-national corporations whose massive investments abroad, and effective lobbying positions, and allegiance to a world market unobstructed by local government and competition, place them in a position to not only straddle these developments but to encourage them.

Ferdinand Lundberg, in his monster of a book, *The Rich and the Super Rich*, put aside his clichés about the "exploitation of the working class," and his outspoken apologies for the Soviet system long enough to recognize certain truths, or half-truths at least, about the American system. He wrote, almost with glee:

> The restriction of free enterprise has also come principally from businessmen who have constantly sought to increase government regulation in their own interest, as in the case of tariffs, subsidies, and prohibition of price-cutting on trademarked items.
>
> In fact, the interests of businessmen have changed to a considerable extent from efficiency in production, to efficiency in public manipulation, including manipulation of the government for attainment of preferential advantages . . . .

> As everything thus far inquired into has obviously flowed under the benign providence of government, it is evident that, government and politics have more than a little to do with the gaudy blooms of extreme wealth and poverty in the feverish American realm.[1]

All of which is true; but it is not all that is true. There are two traps that can ensnare the unwary student of these trends. The first is the hasty conclusion that cartels and monopolies are an expression of capitalism or free enterprise, and that the solution to the problem lies in the replacement of capitalism with some other kind of system. As we have emphasized, however, cartels and monopolies are just the opposite of competitive capitalism and free enterprise. The second trap is the conclusion that the solution for the abuses of cartels and monopolies is to be found in the increase of government regulations and controls. But that is precisely the problem already. It simply is not humanly possible to draw up a new law or combination of laws granting increased power to government, supposedly to regulate commerce and to *prevent* monopoly and their political puppets, without accomplishing just the opposite of its stated objective. Current anti-trust laws are a perfect example.

To understand the truth of this fact, all one needs to do is recall the recent ITT scandals involving the presidency itself. Anti-trust laws, more

---

[1]Lundberg, *The Rich and the Super-Rich,* (Bantam Books, N.Y., 1968), pp. 153, 154, 584.

often than not, end up merely being the instruments whereby one business group uses the power of government to supress or hinder its less politically influential competitors. *Bigger and stronger government is not the solution, it is the problem!*

Lundberg avoided the first trap successfully but fell total victim to the second. He recognized that monopoly was not free enterprise. He even saw that government was the inseparable partner of monopoly. But, having done so, he then turned around and opened the door for a move into bigger government, and even a "forward" step into Communism itself.

> We cannot go back to competition. We must go forward to some new system — perhaps Communism, perhaps co-operativism, perhaps much more complete governmental regulation than we now have. I don't know what lies ahead and I am not particularly concerned. . . .[1]

There, in a nutshell, is the most likely reason that Mr. Lundberg's amazingly dull and oversized book (1009 pages) has been pushed into the best-seller list by the very Establishment which, on the surface at least, he supposedly condemns. If men like Lundberg would only stop to wonder why they are hired to teach at Establishment universities, and why their books are eagerly sought by Establishment publishers, and why they are in demand for

[1]*Ibid.*, p. 154.

TV and radio appearances on Establishment networks, and why they receive generous financial grants from Establishment foundations, they just might begin to catch on. The "super-rich" do not particularly care if their vast wealth and power is exposed so long as nothing practical is done to stop them.

If anyone has to be recognized as a crusader against them, how much better it is to have someone like Lundberg, rather than an individual who also is a foe of big government. There is now a whole breed of government-worshipping intellectuals leading the American people in their struggle against the increasingly oppressive Establishment. Yet, the Establishment happily tolerates them all and even sponsors them in their heroic efforts. As long as they can view "much more complete government regulation" or even Communism as a step "forward," then they certainly are no threat, to say the least. Quite to the contrary, as the following chapters will make amply clear, the continued concentration of government power into the hands of a few — until it is *total* power — is exactly what the world's "super-rich" are determined to achieve.

XIII

THE ULTIMATE MONOPOLY

Early examples of cartel endorsement of totalitarian regimes; particular focus on I.G. Farben's role in lifting Hitler out of political oblivion and converting the Nazi state into an instrument of hidden cartel power.

At this point in our survey, the reader may wonder what on earth does all of this have to do with the politics of cancer therapy. The answer — as will become evident further along — is that it has *everything* to do with it. The politics of cartels and monopolies can be likened to a football game with specific goals and rules. If one who had never heard of football before came across two teams playing on the field, and if he knew nothing at all about the sport, he would be totally confused as to what was going on. Likewise, we can look at the actions of giant corporations and government agencies but, if we are unaware of the rules that determine the play, we will never be able to understand why things happen as they do, or even be able to tell what is happening in the first place.

As outlined in the previous chapter, cartels and monopolies result from an effort to escape the rigors of free enterprise. In the long run, the best way to do that is to enlist the aid of government, to seek the passage of laws that will put the regulatory power of the state on the side of the business venture and against its competition.

An individual or a corporation can succeed in breaking the cartels if they are determined and talented enough and can raise the necessary capital. The capital is relatively easy if the promise of profits is great — as it *will* be if the cartel's marketing and pricing policies are far out of line. If they are not out of line, then the harm they do is relatively small and there is no pressing need to disrupt them.

It follows, therefore, that cartels and monopolies could not flourish as they do if they existed in a political environment of limited government. Conversely, the more extensive the power of government, the more it is accepted by its citizens as the proper regulator and arbiter of commerce — even though this acceptance may be on the naive assumption that this will *prevent* monopolies and cartels — then the more fertile is the ground for their nourishment and growth.

It follows, also, that if *big* government is good for cartels, then *bigger* government is better, and *total* government is best. It is for this reason that, throughout their entire history, cartels have been found to be the behind-the-scenes promoters of every conceivable form of totalitarianism. They supported the Nazis of Germany, they embraced the Fascists in Italy. They financed the Bolsheviks in Russia. And they are the driving force behind that nameless totalitarianism that increasingly becomes a grim reality in the United States of America.

At first glance, many persons cannot understand why the "super rich" so often are found in support of socialism or socialist measures. To the uninitiated, it would appear that these would be the people with the most to lose. But, under socialism — or any other form of big government — there is no competition and there is no free enterprise, a goal much to be desired if one not only is operating a cartelized industry but also happens to have powerful political influence "at the top." This way, one can make larger profits and be part of the ruling class as well. These people do not fear the progressive taxation scheme that oppresses the middle class, for their political influence enables them to set up elaborate tax-exempt foundations to preserve and multiply their great wealth with virtually no tax at all. Which is why monopolists can never be true capitalists.

In the narrow sense of the word, a capitalist merely is a person who believes in the concept of private ownership of property. But this is not an adequate definition for a clear understanding of the ideological conflicts between the term capitalism, as it generally is used, and opposing concepts usually identified as socialism or communism. In many barbaric tribes there supposedly is no such thing as private property. All things are held by the chief on behalf and in the name of his followers. The net result, though, is that the property belongs to the chief, because he can do with it whatever he pleases. Freedom of use is the test of ownership. If you think you own a piece of property but cannot use it without getting permission from someone else, then you do not own it, *he* does. The extent to which you do not have control over your property is the extent to which someone else has a share of ownership in it. So the chief owns all the property, and the business about holding it in the name of his followers is just to keep them from becoming too unhappy with the situation.

Likewise, our own TVA or other public utilities are supposed to be owned by "the people." If you really think you own a part of the TVA, however, just try to sell your share and see how far you get. The TVA is owned by those who determine how it is to be used. Which means it is owned by the politicians and the bureaucrats.

In Communist countries, almost all of the property supposedly is owned by "the people" — which means, in reality, by the three percent who are members of the Communist Party and, more particularly, by the handful who comprise the Politburo.

All of this merely is to set the stage for the fact that *everyone* is a capitalist. All desirable property is owned by someone. And some of the world's greatest wealth is very privately owned by Communist commissars who are experts at condemning the "evil" doctrine of capitalism.

So just owning property does not make one a capitalist. The more classical and correct use of the word includes the additional concept of free enterprise, the open marketplace with an absence or a minimum of government intervention. It is with this connotation that the word *capitalist* is used here.

So, returning to our point of departure, monopolists never can be true capitalists. Without exception, they embrace either socialism or some other form of collectivism, for these represent the ultimate monopoly. Such government monopolies generally are tolerated by the people because they assume that, by the magic of the democratic process and the power of their vote, somehow, it is they who are the benefactors. This might be true *if* they took the trouble to become thoroughly informed on such matters, and *if* they had totally independent and honest candidates from which to choose, and *if* the political parties were not dominated by the super-rich, and *if* it were possible for men to win elections without vast sums of campaign money. In other words, government monopolies theoretically could work in the best interest of the voters only on some other planet, with some other life form responding to some other motives, and under some other system. As for us earthlings, forget it.

The reality, therefore, is that government becomes the tool of the very forces that, supposedly, it is regulating. The regulations, upon close examination, almost always turn out to be exactly what the cartels have agreed upon beforehand, except that now they have the police power of the state to enforce them. And it makes it possible for these financial and political interests to become totally secure from the threat of possible competition.

About the only time that these regulations are used to the actual detriment of any of the multi-national companies or financial institutions is when they are part of the internal struggle of one group maneuvering for position or attempting to discipline another group. The "people" are *never* the benefactors.

One of the earliest examples of cartel support for totalitarian regimes occurred in Germany even before World War I. Those cartels which, later, were to join together into the I. G. Farben, supported Bismarck because they saw in his collectivist philosophy of government an excellent opportunity to gain favoritism in the name of patriotism.

Bismarck was the first to introduce socialized medicine as we know it in the modern world. He recognized that its popular appeal among the masses would cause it to become the opening wedge for socializing — and thus controlling — the rest of the economy later on. It was his view that socialized medicine would lead the way to a socialized nation. It was a pilot operation studied and imitated by all the world's totalitarians in succeeding years.[1] And fascism certainly was no exception.

In 1916, while still under the regime of Kaiser Wilhelm, an official of I. G. Farben, named Werner Daitz, wrote an essay that was printed and widely distributed by the cartel. In it he said:

---

[1]For background on Bismarck's first government health insurance program, and its ultimate incorporation into the programs of the International Labor Organization (ILO), see Marjorie Shearon's *Wilbur J. Cohen: The Pursuit of Power,* (Shearon Legislative Service, 8801 Jones Mill Rd., Chevy Chase, Md., 20015, 1967), pp. 3-8.

> A new type of state socialism is appearing, totally different from that which any of us have dreamed or thought of. Private economic initiative and the private capitalist economy will not be crippled, but will be regimented from the points of view of state socialism in that capital will be concentrated in the national economy and will be directed outward with uniform impetus. . . . This change in capitalism demands with natural peremptoriness a reconstruction of a former counterpoise, international socialism. It breaks this up into *national socialism.*[1]

Here, indeed, is a most rare and revealing glimpse into the cartel mind. Note that, in the "new" socialism, there will be no conflict with economic initiative (for the cartels) and no threat to a "private capitalist economy" (meaning the private ownership of wealth, *not* the free enterprise system). Capital will be "regimented" and "concentrated in the national economy and directed outward with uniform impetus" (controlled by government according to cartel priorities). The change will require a "reconstruction of a former counterpoise, international socialism" (an acceptance of certain features of a system which formerly was opposed, Marxian communism). And we must not only embrace the international socialism of Marx,

---

[1]Sasuly, *I. G. Farben, op cit.*, p. 53.

but we must apply it differently to each country on the basis of "national socialism" (Nazism, fascism, or any other purely national manifestation of socialism).

Eighteen years later, the forward glimpse had become the reality. On September 30, 1934, Farben issued a report that declared: "A phase of development is now complete which conforms to the basic principles of national socialist economics."[1]

The encyclopedia reminds us that national socialism is the term used in Germany to identify the goals of the Nazi party. In fact, the party's correct name was the National Socialist German Workers' Party (NSDAP). But Nazism was also identified with the fascism of Mussolini, and the two terms have come to be interchangeable. Although the two did differ in some minor respects, they both were merely local manifestations of *national* socialism, and were, consequently, totalitarian regimes regardless of the labels.

The basic dictionary definition of fascism is government control over the means of production with ownership held in private hands. That definition may satisfy the average college exam in political science, but falls far short of squaring with the facts. In reality, the Twentieth Century fascism of Germany was private monopolist control over the government which then *did* control industry, but in such a way as to favor the monopolists and to prevent competition.

---

[1]*Scientific and Technical Mobilization,* Hearings before the Kilgore Subcommittee of the Senate Committee on Military Affairs, Pt. *XVI*, p. 1971.

The American economist, Robert Brady, described the German fascist state as "a dictatorship of monopoly capitalism. Its 'fascism' is that of business enterprise organized on a monopoly basis and in full command of all the military, police, legal and propaganda power of the state."[1]

Stocking and Watkins summed it up this way:

> The German chemical industries came as close to complete cartelization as the combined efforts and organizational talents of German business and a Nazi state could achieve — and that was close, indeed. Even before 1933, industrial syndicalization had progressed far, perhaps farthest of all in chemicals. Fascism merely completed the program and integrated the entire structure. . . . In the cartels which the Nazi state set up over German industry, it was often hard to determine where state control ended and cartel control began. Totalitarianism ultimately involved almost complete unification of business and state.[2]

This unification, of course, did not just happen. It came about as a result of long and patient efforts on the part of cartel leaders, plus the corruptibility of politicians, plus the abysmal naivete of the voters. Long before Hitler became a national

---

[1]Sasuly, *I. G. Farben, op. cit.,* p. 128.

[2]Stocking and Watkins, *Cartels in Action, op. cit.,* pp. 411, 501.

figure, the cartel had been the dominant force, behind the scenes, in a long succession of German governments. I. G.'s president Hermann Schmitz, had been a personal advisor to Chancellor Bruening. Dr. Karl Duisberg, I. G.'s first chairman, (also founder of the American Bayer Co.) and Carl Bosch, Schmitz's predecessor as president of I. G., recognizing the possibilities of controlling government officials from behind the scenes, created a secret four-man Political Committee for the purpose of forcing a controlling link with *each* of Germany's political parties. At the Nuremberg trials, Baron von Schnitzler testified that I.G. did not hesitate to use plenty of hard cash in its role of hidden political manipulator. He estimated that each election cost the cartel about 400,000 marks — which in the 1930's was a considerable expenditure. But in this way, the cartel was protected no matter who came out on top in the political arena.[1]

As early as 1925, the cartel was setting the pace of German politics. In a speech to the central organization of industry, the Reichsverband der Deutschen, Karl Duisberg explained:

> Be united, united, united! This should be the uninterrupted call to the parties in the . . . Reichstag. . . . We hope that our words of today will work, and will find the strong man who will finally bring

[1]A parallel to the hidden manipulation of American political parties is both obvious and ominous. For the author's analysis of this situation, see his *The Capitalist Conspiracy,* (American Media, Thousand Oaks, Calif., 1971).

> everyone under one umbrella . . . for he [the strong man] is always necessary for us Germans, as we have seen in the case of Bismarck.[1]

At first, the cartel was not convinced that Hitler was the "strong man" that would best serve their purposes. But his program of national socialism and his ability to motivate large crowds through oratory, singled him out for close watching. Although certain leading members of the trust had cast their lot with Hitler as early as 1928, it wasn't until 1931 that the cartel officially began to make sizable contributions to the Nazi war chest. Max Ilgner, a nephew of Hermann Schmitz, was the first to establish a close and personal contact with Hitler. Ilgner generally was referred to as I. G.'s "Director of Finance." His real function, however, was as head of the organization's international spy network. Originally conceived as a means of gathering information about competitive business ventures, it expanded rapidly into a politically oriented operation that seldom has been equalled even by the efficient intelligence agencies of modern governments. In fact, as Sasuly observed:

> So complete was the coverage of every important aspect of conditions in foreign countries, that Farben became one of the main props of both Wehrmacht and Nazi Party intelligence. ...What is remarkable

[1]Sasuly, *I. G. Farben, op. cit.* p. 65.

> is the fact that the Supreme Command of the Army, which boasted of having the most highly-developed staff in the world, should call on a private business concern to do this work for it. Even more remarkable is Ilgner's own admission that *relations with the OKW* [Army Supreme Command] *began as far back as 1928.*[1]

In the following years, even closer ties were to be established by an I. G. official named Gattineau. Gattineau had been the personal assistant of first Duisberg and then Bosch. He also acted as I. G.'s public relations director.

In the fall of 1932, the Nazi Party began to lose ground badly, yet, out of all the contesting groups, the Nazis were most suitable to Duisberg's plans. So, at the crucial moment, the entire weight of the cartel was thrown in Hitler's direction. Just the initial financial contribution alone was three million marks! And much more was to follow.

As Sasuly described it:

> Hitler received backing more powerful than he had ever dared hope for. The industrial and financial leaders of Germany, with I. G. Farben in the lead, closed ranks and gave Hitler their full support. . . . With that backing, he quickly established a blood-thirsty fascist state.[2]

[1] *Ibid.*, pp. 97, 98.

[2] *Ibid.*, pp. 63, 69.

Not only did the money come in what seemed like unlimited quantities, but many of the leading German newspapers, which were either owned by or beholden to the cartel because of its advertising accounts, also lined up behind Hitler and, thus, created that necessary image of universal popularity that, in turn, conditioned the German people to accept him as *the* great leader.

Even in the United States this heavy-handed tactic was used. If an American newspaper was unfriendly to the Nazi regime, I. G. withheld its advertising — which was a tremendous economic lever. In 1938, I. G. sent a letter to Sterling Products, one of its American subsidiaries, directing that, in the future, all advertising contracts must contain ". . . a legal clause whereby the contract is immediately cancelled if overnight the attitude of the paper toward Germany should be changed."[1]

As previously mentioned, Schmitz had been the personal advisor to Chancellor Bruening. After Hitler, he became an honorary member of the Reichstag and also a *Geheimrat,* a secret or confidential counselor. Another high-ranking Farben official, Carl Krauch, became Goering's trusted advisor in carrying out the Four Year Plan. But, as a matter of policy, the leaders of the cartel avoided taking official government positions for themselves, even though they could have had almost any post they desired. As a matter of fact, Schmitz repeatedly had declined the offer to be named as the "Commissar of German Industry."

---

[1]*Ibid.,* p. 106.

The Nazi regime was the Frankenstein monster created by Farben. But Farben was, at all times, the master, in spite of shrewd efforts on its part to make it look to outsiders as though it had become the helpless victim of its own creation. This was extremely wise, as was demonstrated later at the Nuremberg trials. Almost all of these men were deeply involved with the determination of Nazi policies throughout the war — and even had coordinated the operation of such concentration camps as Auschwitz, Bitterfeld, Walfen, Hoechst, Agfa, Ludwigshafen, and Buchenwald for the value of the slave labor they provided. They built the world's largest poison gas industry and used the product experimentally on untold thousands who perished in those camps.[1]

Also, they had used their international business operations as a cover for espionage, sabotage, and terror all around the world.

In May of 1941, Richard Krebs, who had been first a Communist and then a Nazi (and subsequently turned against both),[2] testified before the House Committee on Un-American Activities and said:

> The I. G. Farbenindustrie, I know from personal experience, was already in 1934 completely in the hands of the Gestapo.

---

[1]For an excellent account of Farben's role in administering these camps, see *The Devil's Chemists,* by Josiah E. DuBois, Jr., legal counsel and investigator for the prosecution at the trial of I. G. Farben's leaders at Nuremberg, (Beacon Press, Boston, 1952).

[2]See Krebs' own personal account, written under the pen name of Jan Valtin, entitled *Out of the Night* (Alliance Book Corporation, N.Y., 1941).

> They went so far as to have their own Gestapo prison on the factory grounds of their large works at Leuna and . . . began, particularly after Hitler's ascent to power, to branch out in the foreign field through subsidiary factories.[1]

At the Nuremberg trials, however, the leaders of Farben were dismissed by the judges, not as Nazi war criminals like their underlings who wore the uniforms, but as over-zealous businessmen merely in pursuit of profits. At the conclusion of the trials, a few were given light sentences, but most of them walked out of the courtroom scot-free. Yes, their strategy of remaining behind the scenes was wise, indeed.

One cannot help drawing parallels to political realities in the United States. More and more, we are learning that the men who wield the greatest power in America are not those whose names appear on our ballots but those whose signatures appear on the bottoms of checks — particularly when those checks are for campaign expenditures.

From time to time, the operations of these *finpols* (financier-politicians) accidentally are exposed to public view, and, for a fleeting second, we can see their hidden hands in every sphere of government activity. Time and again we have learned of some private sector wielding undue influence in foreign policy, monetary decisions, farm programs, labor laws, tariffs, tax reform, military contracts, and, yes, even cancer research. We are assured,

[1]As quoted by Ambruster, *Treason's Peace, op. cit.,* p. 273.

however, that these manipulators are just businessmen. They are not politically motivated for, otherwise, they would run for office or would accept appointments to important public posts. If they have any political ideology at all, undoubtedly, they must oppose socialism because, see, they are rich capitalists! They may be guilty of greed and a little graft, but nothing more serious than that.

Let us hope that the memory of Auschwitz and Buchenwald will dispel such nonsense while there still is time.

XIV

WAR GAMES

Germany's industrial preparations for World War II; the continued support by American industrialists given to Farben and to the Nazi regime during this period; and the profitable role played by Ford and ITT in war production for both Nazi Germany and the United States.

By 1932 it was obvious to many observers that Nazi Germany was feverishly preparing for war. It was equally obvious that I. G. Farben was both the instigator and the benefactor of these preparations. It was during these years that German industry experienced its greatest growth and its highest profits.

In the United States, however, things were not going as smoothly for the cartel subsidiaries and partners. As the war drew nearer, the American companies continued to share their latest patents and technical information on their newest processes. But Farben was returning the favor less and less — especially if the information had any potential value in war production, which, of course, much of it did. When the American companies complained, Farben replied that it was *forbidden* by the Nazi government to give out this information and, that if they did so, they would be in serious trouble with the authorities!

Meanwhile, the American companies continued to honor their end of the contracts, mostly because they were afraid not to. In almost every case Farben controlled one or more patents that were vital to their operations, and any overt confrontation could easily result in a loss of these valuable processes which would mean certain business disaster. This was particularly true in the field of rubber.

Rubber, of course, is basic to modern transportation. It is a companion product to gasoline inasmuch as it supplies the wheels which are driven by the gasoline engines. Without rubber, normal economic life would be most difficult. Modern warfare would be almost impossible.

I. G. had perfected the process for making buna rubber but did not share the technology with its American partners. Standard Oil, on the other hand, had been working on another process for butyl rubber and passed on all of its knowledge and techniques.

Sasuly summarizes the situation that resulted:

> True to their obligations to the Nazis, Standard sent the butyl information. But they did not feel any obligation to the U.S. Navy. In 1939, after the outbreak of war, a representative of the Navy's

> Bureau of Construction and Repair visited Standard's laboratories and was steered away from anything which might give clues as to the manufacture of butyl.
>
> Standard did not have the full buna rubber information. But what information it did have, it only gave to the U.S. rubber makers after much pressure by the government when war was already underway. As for butyl rubber, Standard did not give full rights to manufacture under its patents until March, 1942. . . .
>
> Because of a cartel of the natural rubber producers, the United States found itself facing an all-out war without an adequate rubber stock-pile. And because of the operation of the I. G.-Standard Oil cartel, no effective program for making synthetic rubber was underway.[1]

Aluminum is another basic product that is essential for modern warfare. But, here, too, a cartel monopoly stood in the way of American development. Even though the United States was the greatest user of aluminum in the world, and in spite of the fact that its industrial capacity was greater than any other nation, in 1942 it was Nazi Germany that was, by far, the world's greatest producer of this war-essential metal. Alcoa (the Aluminum

[1]Sasuly, *I. G. Farben, op. cit.*, pp. 151, 155.

Company of America) had a major subsidiary in Canada known as Alted, which was an integral part of the world aluminum cartel. It was the policy of this group to restrict the production of aluminum in all nations except Germany — this, probably in return for valuable patent rights and promises of non-competition in other fields. Even though Alcoa never admitted to becoming a direct participant in these agreements, nevertheless, the record speaks for itself. It *did* limit its production during those years far below the potential market demand. Consequently, here was another serious industrial handicap confronting the United States as it was drawn into war.

The production of the drug atabrine — effective in the treatment of malaria — also was hindered by the cartel. Quinine was the preferred prescription, but it was entirely controlled by a Dutch monopoly which possessed its only source in Java. The Dutch company apparently chose not to join the international cartel, however, because Farben entered into competition by marketing its own drug, atabrine, a synthetic substitute. When the Japanese captured Java, the United States was totally dependent on Nazi Germany as a source. Needless to say, the cartel did not share the manufacturing technology of atabrine with the United States, and it took many months after Pearl Harbor before American drug firms could produce an effective material. Meanwhile, the first GIs who fought in the Pacific Islands suffered immensely from malaria with no drugs to treat it — thanks, again to the cartel.

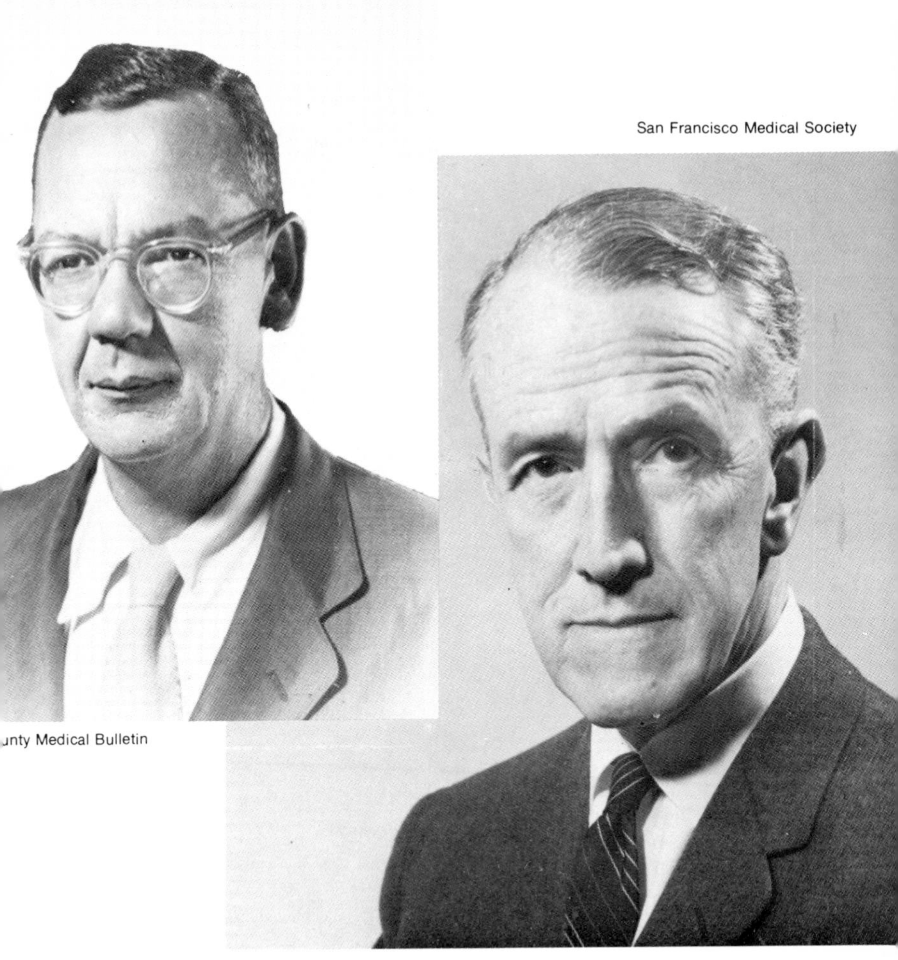

San Francisco Medical Society

...unty Medical Bulletin

Dr. Ian MacDonald (left) and Dr. Henry Garland (right) wrote the famous 1953 report of the California Medical Association that since has become the basis of almost all scientific opposition to Laetrile. It was learned later, however, that the findings in this report had been falsified. Both doctors had defended cigarette smoking as a harmless pastime unrelated to lung cancer. Dr. MacDonald had said: "A pack a day keeps lung cancer away."

The elders of Hunza, typically ninety years or older.

The Hunzakuts eat organic foods and drink mineral-rich wa

Iunza the apricot and its seed are the most prized of all foods.

The Hunzakuts are world reknowned for their amazing longevity and good health. There never has been a case of cancer in Hunza. The native diet contains over two hundred times more vitamin B_{17} than found in the average diet of industrialized societies. (Photos courtesy of Dr. J. Milton Hoffman.)

G.E.G.

Interntl. Assoc. Cancer Victims & Friends

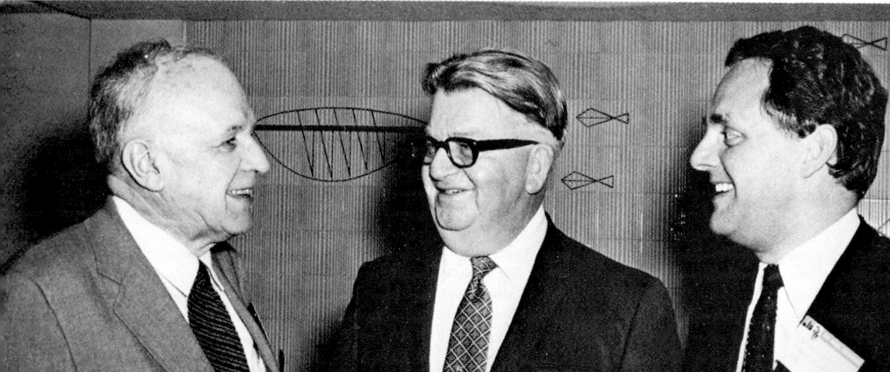

G.E.G.

Dr. Ernst T. Krebs, Jr. (above, left), the biochemist who pioneered the vitamin concept of cancer, undoubtedly will be acknowledged in history as the Louis Pasteur of our day.

Shown at left are (from left to right) Dr. Dean Burk, head of the Cytochemistry section of the National Cancer Institute, Dr. Krebs, and Dr. Hans Nieper, famous cancer specialist from Hanover, Germany. Drs. Burk and Nieper are among the many prominent supporters of Dr. Krebs and his work with Laetrile.

John Richardson, M.D. (above) is the first American physician to win the legal right to administer Laetrile to his own patients.

G.E.

G.E.G.

Dr. Dale Danner (left), a terminal cancer victim himself, at first had no faith in Laetrile. On the brink of death he self-administered a massive dose as a last resort and was amazed to experience a release from pain and a return of appetite. Just three months later he was able to return to work.

In 1967 cancer victim Joanne Wilkinson (bottom left) was told that it would be necessary to remove her leg, hip, bladder, and one of her kidneys as well. When she chose Laetrile instead, her irate physicians warned her that she could not possibly live longer than twelve weeks. Today, years afterward, Mrs. Wilkinson is living a healthy and productive life.

Alicia Buttons, wife of the famous actor-comedian Red Buttons (below), had been given up as hopeless by practitioners of orthodox medicine. After a few months of Laetrile therapy, however, her cancer had completely disappeared. The couple is shown here at the 1973 Cancer Control Convention in Los Angeles.

Tattler

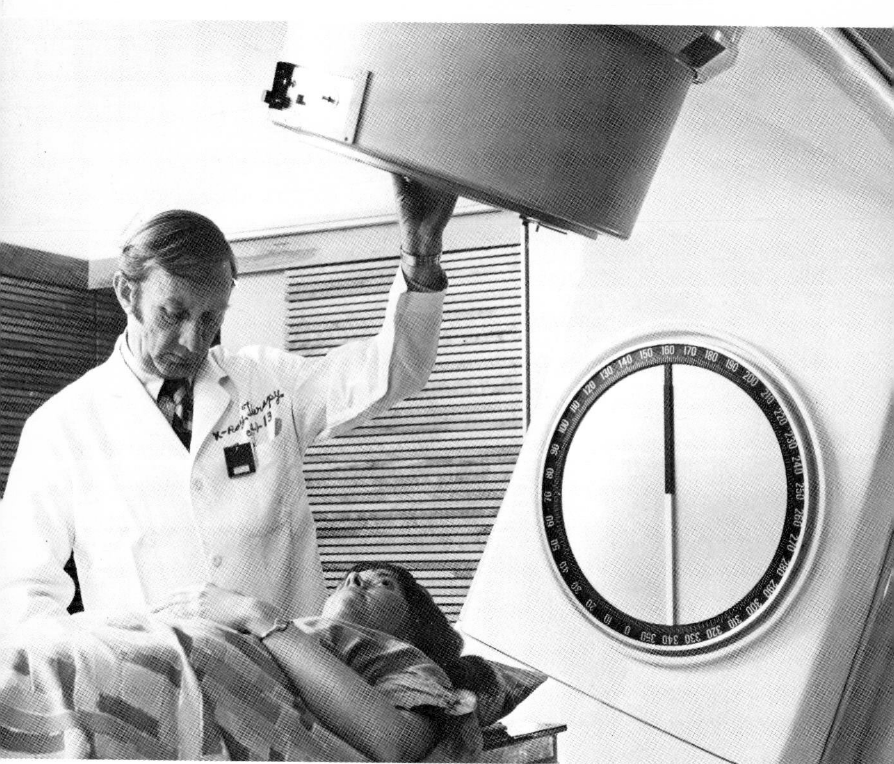

Varian

X-rays are known to cause cancer, not to cure it. Also they weaken the patient who often dies from X-ray damage rather than from cancer. Statistics show that patients who receive no treatment at all live just as long — or longer — than those who subject themselves to radiology or chemotherapy. Orthodox cancer therapies treat the symptom (the tumor) rather than the cause.

National Archives

(above) I.G. Farben, the world's largest chemical and drug cartel, was headquartered in this building in Frankfort, Germany. It became the backbone of the Nazi war machine. Yet, during the massive bombing raids on Frankfort, American bombardiers were instructed to spare this building. It survived without a scratch.

(below) During the Nuremberg trials it was learned that the business leaders of I.G. Farben actually had controlled the Nazi state. Oswald Pohl, an SS Lieutenant General who was sentenced to hang, is shown here explaining how Farben operated such concentration camps as Auschwitz and Buchenwald.

U.S. Army

U.S. Army P

U.P.I.

Adolph Hitler (above) at a 1932 meeting in Berlin. Hitler's rise to power would have been impossible without the secret financial support of I.G. Farben. The Nazi state became the means by which cartel agreements were enforced.

At left are key Farben defendents at the Nuremberg War Crimes trials. Hermann Schmitz, the mastermind of the cartel, was an integral part of the international banking structure. Carl Krauch was chairman of Farben's board of directors. Max Ilgner, Farben's "Director of Finance," in reality was in charge of espionage and propaganda. Otto Ambros (bottom right) was production chief of Farben's poison gas facilities.

U.P.I.

Photoworld

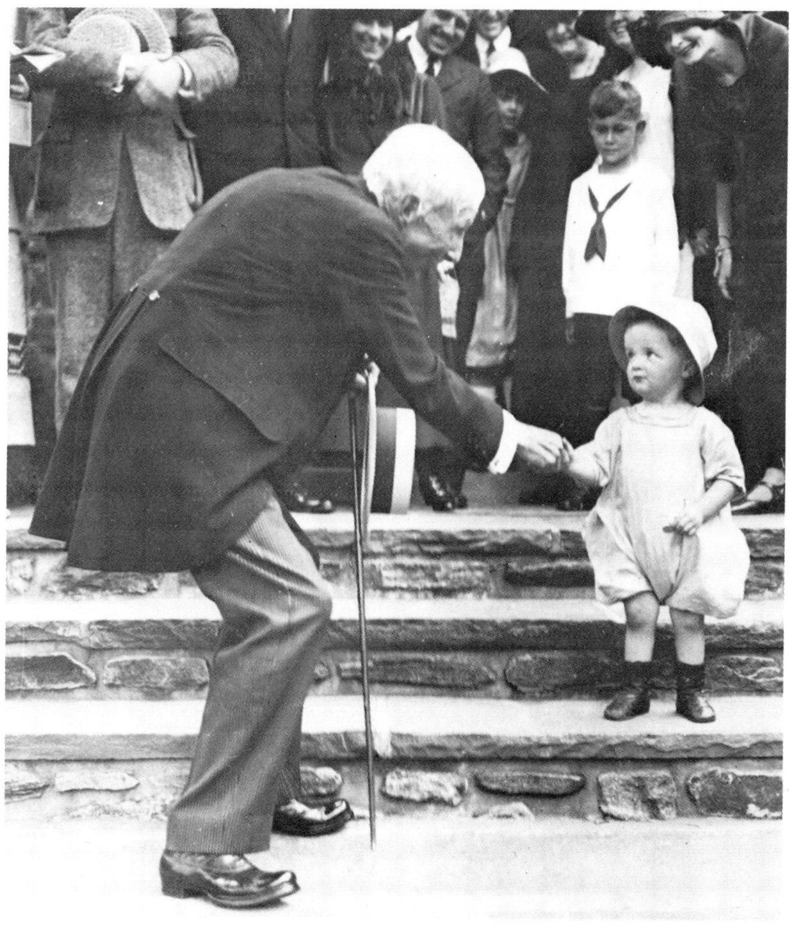

Photoworld

John D. Rockefeller, Sr. (above), often gave away shiny dimes to small children in an attempt to improve his public image. This device was suggested by Ivy Lee (left) one of the world's foremost public relations experts. Mr. Lee also had been retained by I.G. Farben to appraise the public image potential of Adolph Hitler.

Walter Teagle (above, left), while president of Standard Oil, secretly held stock in Farben enterprises on behalf of the Rockefeller family. Through such ploys the Rockefellers have attempted to conceal their financial interest in the field of drugs.

Photoworld

Pictoral Parade

Photoworld

Abraham Flexner (above), author of the famous Flexner Report of 1910, led the crusade for upgrading the medical schools of America. All the while he was in the employ of Andrew Carnegie (above, left) and John D. Rockefeller (left) who had set up gigantic tax-exempt foundations for that purpose. The end result was that all medical schools became heavily oriented toward drugs and drug research, for it was through the increased sale of these drugs that the donors realized a profit on their donations.

U.P

John D. Rockefeller, Sr., shown here at age 93, had created fantastic wealth. When he interlocked his own empire with that of I.G. Farben in 1928, there was created the largest and most powerful cartel the world has ever known. Not only has that cartel survived through the years, it has grown and prospered. Today it plays a major role in both the science and politics of cancer therapy.

The American development of optical instruments was another victim of this era. The firm of Bausch and Lomb was the largest producer of American high-quality lenses of all kinds. Most of these lenses were manufactured by the German firm of Zeiss. As was the pattern, American technology deliberately was retarded by cartel agreement.

We could go on. But these were the major products that were critically short or lacking altogether when the United States entered the war: rubber, aluminum, atabrine, and military lenses such as periscopes, rangefinders, binoculars, and bombsights. These were handicaps that, in a less productive and resourceful nation, could well have made the difference between victory and defeat.

Meanwhile, the Nazis continued to enjoy the solicitous cooperation of their American cartel partners. And they benefited immensely by American technology. A document found in the captured files of I. G. at the end of the war reveals how lop-sided was the exchange. In this report to the Gestapo, Farben was justifying its "marriage" with Standard Oil, and concluded:

> It need not be pointed out that, without lead tetraethyl, modern warfare could not be conceived. . . . In this matter we did not need to perform the difficult work of development because we could start production right away on the basis of all the experience that the Americans had had for years.[1]

[1]*New York Times,* Oct. 19, 1945, p. 9.

American ties to German industry began almost immediately after the guns were silenced in World War I. The name of Krupp has become synonymous with German arms and munitions. Yet, the Krupp enterprises literally were salvaged out of the scrap heap in December of 1924 by a loan of ten million dollars from Hallgarten and Company and Goldman Sachs and Company of New York.

Vereinigte Stahlwerk, the giant Farben-controlled steel works, likewise, received over one hundred million dollars in favorable long-term loans from financial circles in America.

The 1945 report of the United States Foreign Economic Administration concluded:

> It is doubtful that the [Farben] trust could have carried out its program of expansion and modernization without the support of the American investor.[1]

But far more than money went into Nazi Germany. Along with the loans to German enterprises, there also went American technology, American engineers, and whole American companies as well. Ford is an excellent example.

As pointed out previously, the Ford Motor Company of Germany was eagerly embraced by the cartel. Ford put forty percent of the stock on the market, and almost all of that was purchased by I. G. Both Bosch and Krauch joined the board of directors soon afterward in recognition of their

---

[1]*Ibid.*, p.82.

organization's substantial ownership interest. But well over half of the company was still owned by the Ford family.

War preparations inside Germany included the confiscation or "nationalization" of almost all foreign-owned industry. As a result, the Ford Company was a prime target. It never happened, however, primarily due to the intercession of Karl Krauch, I. G.'s chairman of the board. During questioning at the Nuremberg trials, Krauch explained:

> I myself knew Henry Ford and admired him. I went to see Goering personally about that. I told Goering that I myself knew his son Edsel, too; and I told Goering that if we took the Ford independence away from them in Germany, it would aggrieve friendly relations with American industry in the future. I counted on a lot of success for the adaptation of American methods in German industries, but that could be done only in friendly cooperation.
>
> Goering listened to me and then he said: "I agree. I shall see to it that the Deutsche Fordwerke will not be incorporated in the Hermann Goering Werke."
>
> So I participated regularly in the supervisory-board meetings to inform myself about the business processes of

> Henry Ford and, if possible, to take a stand for the Henry Ford works after the war had begun. Thus, we succeeded in keeping the Fordwerke working and operating independently.[1]

The fact that the Nazi war machine had received tremendous help from its cartel partners in the United States is one of the most uncomfortable facts that surfaced during the investigation at the end of the war. And this was not just as the result of negotiations and deals made before the war had started. It constituted direct collaboration and cooperation during those same years that Nazi troops were killing American soldiers on the field of battle.

The Ford Company, for example, not only operated "independently" supplying military hardware in Germany all through the war, but in Nazi-occupied France as well. Maurice Dollfus, chairman of the board of Ford's French subsidiary, made routine reports to Edsel Ford throughout most of the war detailing the number of trucks being made each week for the German army, what profits were being earned, and how bright were the prospects for the future. In one letter, Dollfus added:

> The attitude you have taken, together with your father, of strict neutrality, has been an invaluable asset for the production of your companies in Europe.[2]

---

[1]DuBois, *The Devil's Chemists, op. cit.*, pp. 247, 248.

[2]*Ibid.*, p. 248.

It was clear that war between the United States and Germany made little difference. Two months *after* Pearl Harbor, Dollfus reported net profits to Ford for 1941 of fifty-eight million francs. And then he said:

> Since the state of war between the U.S.A. and Germany, I am not able to correspond with you very easily. I have asked Lesto to go to Vichy and mail this. . . .
>
> We are continuing our production as before. . . . The financial results for the year are very satisfactory. . . . We have formed our African company. . . .[1]

There is no record of Edsel Ford's return communications with Dollfus after Pearl Harbor, if indeed there were any. It is likely that there were, however, in view of the continuing letters that were sent by Dollfus. It is also impossible to prove that Ford approved of his factories being used to supply the same army that was fighting against the United States. But there is no doubt about the fact that both Dollfus and the German High Command considered those factories as belonging to Ford all through the war. And that is a circumstance that could not have continued for long without some kind of friendly assurances "of strict neutrality." At any rate, it was one of the curious quirks of war that, because of cartel interlock, the Ford Motor

[1]*Ibid.*, p. 251.

Company was producing trucks for Nazis in both Germany and France, producing trucks for the Allies in the United States, and profiting handsomely from both sides of the war. And if the Axis powers had won the war, the top men of Ford (as well as of other cartel industries) undoubtedly would have been absorbed into the ruling class elite of the new Nazi order. With close friends like Bosch and Krauch they could not lose.

The Ford Company was not the exception, it was the rule. As Stocking and Watkins explained:

> When World War II broke out, I. G. and Mitsui on the one hand, and DuPont, ICI, and Standard Oil on the other, did not completely sever "diplomatic relations." Although direct communication was disrupted by the war, the companies merely "suspended" their collaboration. The general understanding was that they would take up again at the close of the war where they had left off, in an atmosphere of mutual concord and cooperation.[1]

The authors are much too cautious in their appraisal. The record is painfully clear that the heads of those financial interests did *not* suspend their collaboration. They merely made them secret and reduced them to the bare minimum. In October of 1939, Frank Howard of Standard Oil was in Europe for the specific purpose of finding ways to

---

[1]Stocking and Watkins, *Cartels in Action, op. cit.*, p. 423.

keep the Standard-I. G. cartel functioning in spite of the war. Howard himself described his mission:

> We did our best to work out complete plans for a *modus vivendi* which would operate through the term of the war, *whether or not the United States came in.* [Emphasis added.][1]

On June 26, 1940, the day after France capitulated to the Nazis, a meeting was held at the Waldorf-Astoria which brought together some of the key American business tycoons who were interested in protecting their German-based operations during the war. The meeting was called by Torkild Rieber, chairman of the board of Texaco. Among others present were James Mooney, chief of General Motors' overseas operations; Edsel Ford; executives from Eastman Kodak; and Col. Behn, head of ITT.[2]

The case of ITT is most instructive. ITT began to invest in the Nazi pre-war economy in 1930. It formed a holding company called Standard Elektrizitats and then bought another company, Lorenz, from Phillips. Seeing that war was rapidly approaching, ITT did everything possible to make its new holdings look like German companies. Then in 1938, just as the Nazi troops were preparing to march into Poland, ITT, through its subsidiary, Lorenz, purchased twenty-eight percent ownership

---

[1]Sasuly, *I. G. Farben, op. cit.*, pp. 149, 150.
[2]Ladislas Farago, *The Game of the Foxes*, (D. McKay Co., N.Y., 1972), pp. 463-479.

of the Focke-Wulf Company, which, even then, was building bombers and fighter planes. ITT could not claim either ignorance or innocence. They simply were investing in war.

During the course of that war, ITT's plants in Germany became important producers of all kinds of military communications equipment. They also installed and serviced most of the key telephone lines used by the Nazi government.

In the United States, ITT was regarded as highly patriotic. It developed the high-frequency direction finder, nicknamed Huff-Duff, which was used to detect German submarines in the Atlantic. And Colonel Behn, the head of ITT at the time, was awarded the Medal of Merit, the highest civilian honor, for providing the Army with land-line facilities.

Anthony Sampson, in his *The Sovereign State of ITT*, summarizes:

> Thus, while ITT Focke-Wulf planes were bombing Allied ships, and ITT lines were passing information to German submarines, ITT direction finders were saving other ships from torpedoes. . . .
>
> In 1967, nearly thirty years after the events, ITT actually managed to obtain twenty-seven million dollars in compensation from the American government for war damage to its factories in Germany, including five-million dollars for damage to Focke-Wulf plants — on the basis that

> they were American property bombed by Allied bombers. It was a notable reward for a company that had so deliberately invested in the German war effort, and so carefully arranged to become German.
>
> If the Nazis had won, ITT in Germany would have appeared impeccably Nazi; as they lost, it re-emerged as impeccably American.[1]

It is not within the scope of this study to analyze all of the possible motives of the men who led us into the two global wars of the Twentieth Century. The university student is exposed only to the surface of this subject and earns his degree by committing to memory such explanations as ancient rivalries, desire for natural resources, militarism, offended national or racial pride, and so forth. These factors *did* play a part, but an extremely minor one compared to the financial and political goals of the men who, from behind the scenes, deliberately set the forces of war into motion.

War has been profitable to these men in more ways than one. True, fantastic profits can be made on war production through government-enforced monopolies. But those who were the most responsible also looked upon war as a means of bringing about rapid and sweeping political changes in the system. The men behind a Hitler, a Mussolini, a

---

[1]Sampson, *The Sovereign State of ITT*, (Stein & Day, N.Y., 1973), pp. 40, 47.

Stalin, and, yes, even an FDR could recognize that, in wartime, the people would be far more willing to accept hardship, police-state tactics, the expansion of government, and the concentration of power into the hands of political leaders than they ever would have dreamed of doing in times of peace and tranquility. The concept of big government — and certainly the appeal of *world* government — could not have taken root in America except as the outgrowth of national crisis. Economic depressions were helpful, but not enough. Sporadic riots and threats of internal revolution were helpful, but not enough. War was, by far, the most effective approach. This was doubly so in Europe and Asia as one can confirm merely by comparing maps and ruling regimes before 1939 and after 1945. As Lenin had predicted, the best way to build a "new order" is not by gradual change, but by first destroying the old order completely, and then building upon the ashes.[1]

The desire for rapid political and social change, therefore, can be a powerful motivation for war on the part of the *finpols* who would be the direct benefactors of those changes — especially if they were playing their chips on both sides of the field. Yes, war can be extremely profitable for those who know how to play the game.

---

[1] It is important to know that Lenin accepted but did not favor outright war as a means of destroying the old order. He claimed that Communists should work at destruction *from within,* not from without. True to form, during World War II, Soviet troops were not conspicuous in the fighting except in defense of their own territory, or at the close of the war when, with the German army in full retreat, and the Japanese army in obvious defeat, they moved rapidly to claim as much territory as possible in Eastern Europe and Mongolia.

XV

CONSPIRACY

Efforts to camouflage Farben ownership of firms in America; the repeated assistance rendered by various Rockefeller interests; the successful penetration into the U.S. government by cartel agents; and the final disposition of the Farben case.

Once again the reader may be wondering if it is really necessary to include all of this history about cartels in a study of cancer therapy. And, once again, let us state most emphatically that it is. Not only does this history lead us to a clearer understanding later of how the pharmaceutical industry has come to be influenced by factors other than simple product development and scientific truth, but it also gives us the answer to an otherwise most perplexing question. That question, often asked at the point of first discovering that vitamin therapy is the target of organized opposition usually is stated something like this:

"Are you suggesting that people high in government, in business, or in medicine, could be so base and inhuman as to place their own financial or political interests above the health and well-being of their fellow citizens? That they actually would stoop so low as to hold back a cure for cancer?"

The answer, of course, in the light of cartel history, is obvious. If prominent citizens, highly respected in their own communities can plan and execute global wars, if they can operate slave labor camps and gas ovens for the extermination of innocent human beings, if they can scheme to reap gigantic profits from the war industry of, not only their own nation, but of their nation's enemy as well, then the answer is, "You'd better believe it!"

So let us return to the dusty historical record for further enlightenment on current events.

The American cartel partners who attempted to conceal their ownership in German industry before the war were not unique. German interests were active doing exactly the same thing in the United States. World War I had taught them a lesson. During that war, all German-owned industry in America was seized by the federal government and operated in trust by the office of the Alien Property Custodian. At the end of the war, the industries were sold under conditions which, supposedly, were to prevent them from reverting to German control. In the field of chemicals and pharmaceuticals, however, this goal was completely thwarted. Within a very few years, all of these companies were back under Farben ownership or control even more firmly than before the war.

One of the key figures in administering the disposition of this property was an attorney for the Alien Property Custodian's office by the name of

Earl McClintock. Shortly afterward, McClintock was hired (rewarded?) by one of the cartel companies, Sterling Products, at many times the salary he had earned on the government payroll.

It was during this period that Farben experienced its greatest expansion in the United States. Sterling organized Winthrop Chemical. They brought DuPont into half interest of the Bayer Semesan Company. The American I. G. Chemical Company transformed itself several times and, in the process, absorbed the Grasselli Dyestuff Company, which had been a major purchaser of former German properties. Sterling acquired numerous nationally advertised patent "remedies" such as Fletcher's Castoria and Phillip's Milk of Magnesia. With Lewis K. Liggett they formed Durg, Incorporated, a holding company for Sterling, Bayer, Winthrop, United Drug, and Rexall-Liggett Drugstores. They bought Bristol Meyers, makers of Sal Hepatica; Vick Chemical Company; Edward J. Noble's Life Savers, Incorporated; and many others. By the time the Nazis began to tool up for war in Europe, Farben had gained control over a major portion of America's pharmaceutical industry. Investment in both the arts of wounding and healing always have been a dominant feature of cartel development, for the profit potential is greater in these respective fields than in any other. When one wishes to wage a war or regain his health, he seldom questions the price.

When Farben's extensive files fell into the hands of American troops at the end of World War II, they were turned over to the Justice and Treasury Departments for investigation and analysis. One of the inter-office memorandums found in those files explained quite bluntly how the cartel had attempted to conceal its ownership of American companies prior to the war. The memorandum states:

> After the first war, we came more and more to the decision to "tarn" [camouflage] our foreign companies . . . in such a way that the participation of I. G. in these firms was not shown. In the course of time the system became more and more perfect. . . .
>
> Protective measures to be taken by I. G. for the eventuality of [another] war should not substantially interfere with the conduct of business in normal times. For a variety of reasons, it is of the utmost importance . . . that the officials heading the agent firms, which are particularly well qualified to serve as cloaks, should be citizens of the countries where they reside. . . .[1]

This memorandum shed considerable light on previous events. On October 30, 1939, the directors of American I. G. (including Walter Teagle of Rockefeller's Standard Oil, Charles Mitchell of

---

[1]Ambruster, *Treason's Peace, op. cit.*, p. 89. Also see Sasuly, *I. G. Farben, op. cit.*, p. 95, 96.

Rockefeller's National City Bank, Paul Warburg of the Federal Reserve System, Edsel Ford, William Weiss, Adolph Kuttroff, Herman Metz, Carl Bosch, Wilfried Greif, and Hermann Schmitz, who also had been president of American I. G.) announced that their company had ceased to exist. It had been absorbed by one of its subsidiaries, the General Analine Works. Furthermore, the newly dominant company was changing its name to the General Analine and Film Corporation. The dead give-away letters "IG" had vanished altogether.

Nothing had changed, of course, except the name. Exactly the same board of directors had served both companies since 1929. Later on, as the system to "tarn" became "more and more perfect," Hermann Schmitz was replaced as president of General Analine by his brother Dietrich who was an American citizen. But even that was too obvious, so, by 1941, Dietrich was replaced by easy-going Judge John E. Mack of Poughkeepsie. Mack was not qualified to lead such a giant conglomerate, but he easily could be told what to do by those on the board and by strategically-placed advisors and assistants. His prime value was in his name and reputation. Known to be an intimate friend and neighbor of President Roosevelt, he brought to GAF a brilliant aura of American respectability. The obviously German names on the board were replaced by names of similar American prestige, such as Ambassador William C. Bullitt — men who were flattered to be named, but too busy with other matters actually to serve.

As part of the general strategy of camouflage,

Schmitz turned to his banking expert in Switzerland, Edward Greutert. He formed a Swiss corporation called Internationale Gessellschaft fur Chemische Unternehmungen A.G., or more commonly referred to as I. G. Chemie.

T. R. Fehrenbach, in his *The Swiss Banks*, described the elaborate precautions in this way:

> The best North Atlantic legal firms, with offices in London, Paris, Berlin, Amsterdam, and New York, were paid to study the problem. These firms had contacts or colleagues in Basel, Lausanne, Fribourg, and Zurich. They got together. It was quite simple to plan a succession of "Swiss" corporations to inherit licenses, assets, and patents owned by certain international cartels. This was to muddy the track and to confuse all possible investigating governments.
>
> The transactions themselves were incredibly complex. . . . Some of them will probably never be known in their entirety. Edward Greutert and his bank, and a large number of "desk-drawer" corporations formed through Greutert's services, became Schmitz' agents.
>
> Schmitz, who can only be described as a financial wizard, made a weird and wonderful financial structure in Basel involving a dozen corporations and sixty-five

> accounts in the Greutert Bank. Each account was in a different name. Some were for the paper corporations, and some were in the names of corporation groups or syndicates — the European term is *consortia*. These consortia were owned by each other in a never-ending circle, and by Greutert and Farben executives.[1]

The final step in this planned deception was to go through the motions of selling its American-based companies to I. G. Chemie. Thus, in the event of war, these companies would appear to be Swiss owned (a neutral country) and with thoroughly American leadership. The phrase "going through the motions" is used because all of the money received by the American corporations as a result of the "sale" was returned almost immediately to Farben in the form of loans. But, on paper, at least, I. G. Chemie of Basel was now the official owner of eighty-nine percent of the stock in Farben's American companies.

The entire transaction was handled by Rockefeller's National City Bank of New York. This is not surprising inasmuch as the head of its investment division, Charles Mitchell, also was on the board of these I. G. holding companies. But Rockefeller was far more deeply involved than that. In 1938, the Securities and Exchange Commission began a lengthy investigation of American I. G. Walter Teagle, a member of the board, was called to

---

[1]Fehrenbach, *The Swiss Banks, (McGraw-Hill, N.Y., 1966), pp. 216, 219.*

the witness stand. Mr. Teagle, recall, was also president of Rockefeller's Standard Oil. Under questioning, Mr. Teagle claimed that he did not know who owned control of the company he served as a director. He did not know how many shares were held by I. G. Chemie, or who owned I. G. Chemie. In fact, he even had the audacity to say that he didn't have the slightest idea who owned the block of 500,000 shares — worth over a half-a-million dollars — that had been issued in *his* name!

Mr. Teagle, of course, was either lying, or suffering from a classical case of convenient amnesia. Evidence was introduced later showing that, in 1932, he had received a letter from Wilfried Greif, Farben's managing director, stating in plain English: "I.G. Chemie is, as you know, a subsidiary of I.G. Farben."[1]

Also brought out in the investigation was the fact that on May 27, 1930, while Teagle was in London, he received a cable from Mr. Frank Howard, vice-president of Standard Oil, carrying this message:

> In view of the fact that we have repeatedly denied any financial interest in American I. G., it seems to me to be unwise for us to now permit them to include us as stockholders in their original listing which is object of present transaction. It would serve their purpose to issue

---

[1]*Ambruster, Treason's Peace, op. cit.*, p. 114.

> this stock to you personally. . . . Will this be agreeable to you as a temporary measure?[1]

Finally, in June of 1941, after more than three years of intensive investigation, the Securities and Exchange Commission abandoned the cause. Either because it was utterly baffled by the cartel's camouflage (unlikely) or because it yielded to pressure from the cartel's friends high in government (likely), it issued a report to Congress and concluded:

> All attempts to ascertain the beneficial ownership of the controlling shares have been unsuccessful. . . . As a consequence, the American investors, mainly bondholders, are in the peculiar position of being creditors of a corporation under an unknown control.[2]

The evidence of cartel influence within government — especially within those agencies of government that are supposed to prevent these same cartels from acting against the best interests of the people — should not be passed over lightly. It is, unfortunately, a part of the ugly stain that mars and obscures the picture of cancer research. So let us turn our attention now to that aspect of the record.

The subject is so vast as to permit touching on

[1] *Ibid.*, p. 114.
[2] *Ibid.*, p. 121.

only a few highlights. But a good place to begin is in 1916. It was during that year that Dr. Hugo Schwitzer, of the Bayer Company, wrote a letter to the German Ambassador von Bernstorff in which he spoke of the necessity of bringing about the election of a president of the United States whose attitude and party politics were in harmony with the cause of I.G. Farben and its American partners. It was obvious, furthermore, that, at that time, the Republican Party was favored for this purpose over the Democratic Party. Shortly afterward, incidentally, Herman Metz, a Tammany leader and lifelong Democrat, suddenly switched allegiance to the Republican Party. Herman Metz also was the president of the H.A. Metz Company of New York, a large pharmaceutical house that was owned and controlled by Farben. In 1925, he had helped to organize and become president of General Dyestuff Corporation, another Farben outlet. In 1929, he had helped to organize the American I.G., and he became vice-president and treasurer of that organization. The conversion of Metz from a Democrat to a Republican, therefore, is highly significant.

In October of 1942, the Library of Congress received a sealed gift of some nine thousand letters comprising the files of the late Edward T. Clark. These files were important because Clark had been the private secretary to President Calvin Coolidge. On March 4, 1929, Mr. Clark left his position in the White House and, in an amazing switch of roles, became vice-president and Washington representative of Drug, Incorporated, which was, of course, the giant Farben combine that pulled together such important companies as Sterling and Liggett and the multitude of subsidiaries which they owned.

Mr. Clark undoubtedly earned his pay. That he continued to maintain excellent contacts and to exercise influence at the highest levels of government is beyond doubt. In fact, in August of 1929, President Herbert Hoover asked him to return to the White House as *his* personal secretary — which he did.

Nor was that all, Louis K. Liggett also was in Republican politics. As Republican National Committeeman from Massachusetts, he was no stranger to the intrigue of smoke-filled rooms. Working together with Clark and other "men of influence," he was able to secure complete approval from the Justice Department for the merger that created Drug, Incorporated, in 1928, in spite of that merger being in direct conflict with the anti-cartel policies established by Congress some years earlier.

Did President Hoover receive the support of the cartel because he was a man whose party politics were "in harmony" with its cause? It is hard to imagine otherwise. While Hoover was Secretary of Commerce, he was given the heavy responsibility of deciding what to do about the menace of I.G. Farben. To broaden the share of responsibility for this decision and to brighten the process with the aura of "democracy," he set up a Chemical Advisory Committee to study the problem and make recommendations. This, by the way, has become a standard ploy for making the voters think that all viewpoints have been melted down into a "consensus." The committee members always are carefully selected so that a clear majority can be counted on to "conclude" exactly what was wanted in the first place.

If there were ever any exceptions to this rule, they certainly did not occur on the Chemical Advisory Committee. Hoover appointed such men as Henry Howard, vice-president of the Grasselli Chemical Company, Walter Teagle, president of Standard Oil, Lammot DuPont of the DuPont Company, and Frank A. Blair, president of the Centaur Company, a subsidiary of Sterling Products. The cartel was in no danger.

The record of how the cartel succeeded in frustrating the mission of the office of the Alien Property Custodian at the end of World War I is truly amazing. There is no clearer proof that the "conspiratorial view of history" is as valid in the Twentieth Century as it was during the endless intrigue and counter-plots of the Old World. Digging into the story is like trying to separate a can of worms, but here, at least, are the visible and identifiable components.

Francis Garvan had been the Alien Property Custodian during World War I. After American entry into the war he was instrumental in having all German-owned companies taken out of the hands of enemy control and held for later sale to American business firms. After the war, any Germans who could demonstrate that, as private citizens, they had been deprived of personal property through this action, were to be fully compensated out of the proceeds of the sale. But, under no circumstances were these industries to be returned to German control. That was the firm directive given to the APC by Congress. As chronicled previously, however, within only a few years after the truce, and after Garvan had left government service, every one of these major enterprises had reverted to Farben control.

Garvan was enraged. He spoke out bitterly and publicly against the corruption in Washington that made this possible. He sent letters to Congressmen. He testified before investigating committees. He named names.

He had to be silenced.

Suddenly, in 1929, Garvan found himself as the *defendant* in a suit filed by the Justice Department charging malfeasance in the discharge of his duties as the Alien Property Custodian! It was a perfect case of the best defense being a strong offense, and of accusing one's accuser of exactly the things which one has done himself. If nothing else, it tends to discredit the first accuser and to confuse the issue so badly that the casual observer simply doesn't know whom to believe.

The prosecution against Garvan was carried mainly by two men: Merton Lewis and John Crim, both on the staff of the Attorney General's office. The most significant thing about these two men is that each of them previously had been intimately involved with the Farben cartel. Lewis had been retained as counsel by the Bosch Company in

1919. Crim had been the counsel for Hays, Kaufman and Lindheim, representing the German Embassy. (Garvan had sent two members of that law firm to jail for treasonous activity during the war.)

In spite of the carefully planned confusion of charges and counter charges, Garvan's testimony came through loud and clear. He had the documents, the dates, the inside information that could not be brushed aside. Here is what he revealed:

Herman Metz had made campaign contributions to Senator John King, former Republican National Committeeman from Connecticut.

Before running for the Senate, John King had been on the payroll of the Hamburg American line for three years, receiving an annual salary of $15,000 for mysterious, unspecified services.

King also had been appointed to the office of the Alien Property Custodian through the influence of Senator Moses.

Senator Moses had appointed Otto Kahn as treasurer of a fund for the election of new senators.

Otto Kahn was the investment partner of Paul Warburg, one of the directors of American I.G.

King and Moses together secured the appointment of Thomas Miller to the APC.

Later, Miller was convicted and sent to the Atlanta Prison for being an agent of an enemy during wartime.

Garvan spared no names. His files showed that the office of the Attorney General, itself, had long been considered as the prize of the cartel. Homer Cummings, who had been the Attorney General for six years, later was employed as counsel for General Analine and Film at an annual retainer reported to be $100,000.

Garvan testified:

> All that time, the Attorney General of the United States . . . and the Alien Property Custodian, Thomas Miller, were in the employ and pay of German people and had $50,000 worth of U.S. Government bonds handed to them and put in their pockets by whom? By John T. King, the $15,000 representative who died three days before he could be tried . . . .

> Some of you saw the other day that Senator Moses had appointed Otto Kahn as treasurer for the election of new senators. You did not associate the fact that his friend and partner, Warburg, is the head and front of the American interest in the American Interessen Gemeinschaft . . . .

> It is never a dead issue. Peace? There is no peace. Always the fight goes on for the supremacy in the chemical industry because it is the keystone to the safety of the United States or of any country in the world today.[1]

---

[1]Ambruster, *Treason's Peace,* op. cit., pp. 147, 151.

The three posts in government which naturally would be of special interest to cartels are the presidency itself, the office of Attorney General, and the office of Secretary of State. We have touched upon the first two. Now let us examine the third.

Secretary of State John Foster Dulles was the leading partner in Sullivan and Cromwell, the largest of the law firms on Wall Street. Sullivan and Cromwell specializes in representing foreign business interests, and its partners hold interlocking directorates with many leading corporations and banking houses — especially those comprising the Farben-American interlock.

John Foster Dulles represented Blyth and Company, the investment banking partner of the First National City Bank and the First Boston Corporation, two key investment enterprises of the Rockefeller group associated with the Chase Manhattan Bank. Dulles also represented Standard Oil and was made chairman of the Rockefeller Foundation, a position signifying great trust on the part of the Rockefeller family. Sullivan and Cromwell had been the principal representatives of such powerful investment houses as Goldman, Sachs, and Company, Lehman Brothers, and Lazard Freres, the firm that, together with Kuhn, Loeb, and Company, had masterminded the expansion and mergers of ITT.

As recently as 1945, Dulles had been listed as one of the directors of the International Nickel Company of Canada. This also was part of the Farben interlock and had been the prime mover behind the stockpiling of nickel in Nazi Germany before the war.[1]

Avery Rockefeller was a director of the J. Henry Schroeder Banking Corporation and the Schroeder Trust Company. He also was a partner and stockholder in its affiliate, Schroeder, Rockefeller, and Company. It is not surprising to learn, therefore, that John Foster Dulles also had been the American representative of the Schroeder trust which was Hitler's agent in the United States. Westrick had been a Sullivan and Cromwell representative in Germany where he represented such multi-nationals as ITT. And at the beginning of World War II, Dulles became a voting trustee of Farben-controlled American corporations in an attempt to prevent them from being seized as enemy property.

Instead of this man going down in American history as a tool of international monopoly, and a possible traitor in war, he was appointed as a member of a special high-level consulting committee established by the Alien Property Custodian to formulate the basic policies of that office. And then he was chosen by President Eisenhower as Secretary of State. His brother, Allen Dulles, also a partner of Sullivan and Cromwell, was equally enmeshed in the cartel web as a negotiator with Farben interests for the Office of Strategic Services in Switzerland. (It was then that Allen Dulles had

---

[1]William Hoffman, *David; Report on a Rockefeller,* (Lyle Stuart, Inc., N.Y., 1971), pp. 18, 19. Also Ambruster, *Treason's Peace, op. cit.,* p. 85.

said, "Only hysteria entertains the idea that Germany, Italy or Japan contemplates war upon us.") At the end of the war, after using his influence to protect Hitler's agent, Westrick,[1] he was placed by President Eisenhower at the head of the Central Intelligence Agency.

Such is the power of the forces we are here describing.

Perhaps the best way to judge the extent of hidden cartel power in the United States government is to observe how its German component fared during and after the war. As noted previously, its American holdings were seized by the federal government in February of 1942. Within a few months, all of the original directors and officers were compelled to resign. But whom did the government put in their places? Richard Sasuly answers:

> Operating control has passed to a group of men who are tied in with a constellation of corporate interests which is rising rapidly in American business under the leadership of an international financier, Victor Emanuel. Emanuel himself sits on the board of directors of G.A. & F. There is a liberal sprinkling of his associates among the other directors and officers.[2]

Emanuel's assumption of leadership over I.G.'s holdings in the United States is significant.

---

[1]Sampson, *The Sovereign State of ITT, op. cit.*, p. 43.
[2]Sasuly, *I.G. Farben, op. cit.*, p. 186.

Between 1927 and 1934, he had been in London as an associate of the Schroeder banking interests. This is the same organization that, in conjunction with the Rockefeller group, represented I.G. and became the financial agent of Adolph Hitler.

Sasuly continues:

> As is well known, the Schroeders of London are related to the Schroeders of Germany. Baron Bruno Schroeder is credited with having introduced Hitler to the principal industrialists of the Ruhr. Baron Kurt Schroeder held a high rank in the SS and was known as "The SS banker." The London banking house, J. Henry Schroeder and Company, was described by *Time* magazine in July, 1939, as an "economic booster of the Rome-Berlin Axis."[1]

And what of Mr. Victor Emanuel, President of Standard Gas and Electric, who dominated the "new" leadership of the Rockefeller-Farben empire? The answer was provided in one short sentence in a report of the Securities and Exchange Commission dated January 19, 1943. It said:

> The Schroeder interests in London and New York have worked with Emanuel in acquiring and maintaining a dominant position in Standard affairs.[2]

---

[1] *Ibid.*, p. 187.

[2] Ambruster, *Treason's Peace, op. cit.*, p. 366.

The much publicized shuffling of G.A.F. directors and officers was a charade. Men totally loyal to the cartel's interests continued to dominate. As usual, the American people hadn't the slightest inkling of what was really happening.

What transpired in Germany itself, however, is even more revealing of cartel influence at the very highest levels of American government. During the later stages of the war, the major industrial cities of Germany were levelled by massive bombing raids. This was the decisive factor that crippled the Nazi war machine and brought the conflict to an end. But when the Allied occupational forces moved into Frankfort, they were amazed to discover that there was one complex of buildings left standing amid the rubble and destruction around it. Somehow, these and these only had been spared. The buildings, of course, housed the international headquarters of I.G. Farben. Bombardiers had been instructed to avoid this vital target — the very backbone of Nazi war production — on the lame excuse that American forces would need an office building when they moved into town.

Parenthetically, it should be noted that the Under-Secretary of War at that time (promoted to Secretary of War in 1945) was Robert P. Patterson who, before his appointment by President Roosevelt, had been associated with Dillon-Read and Company, another Rockefeller investment banking firm. Dillon-Read had helped to finance a substantial portion of Farben's pre-war expansion — including Farben's sprawling office building that was spared in the bombing raids. James Forrestal, former *president* of Dillon-Read & Co., was Secretary of the Navy at the time but later became the first Secretary of Defense. If one were of a suspicious nature, one might conclude that men like Mr. Patterson and Mr. Forrestal might have used their influence to protect some of the assets of their company's investment.

As the Allied armies pushed into Germany, the extent of cartel power within the American government suddenly became visible — literally. Scores of investment bankers, lawyers, and industrial executives — all with personal connections with the Farben mechanism — showed up in brigadier general uniforms to direct the "de-Nazification and decartelization" of post-war Germany!

One such figure was Kenneth Stockton, the chairman of ITT's European board of directors, who, according to Anthony Sampson, appeared "alongside Westrick."[1] But the most conspicuous among these "generals" was Brigadier General William Draper, Commanding Officer of the Economics Division of the American Control Group, which was the division with the greatest responsibility for implementing the de-cartelization program. And what was Draper's civilian experience that qualified him for this post? He, too, was with the Wall Street firm of Dillon and Read, of course!

---

[1]*Op. cit.*, p. 41.

In May of 1945, Max Ilgner was arrested and held for later trial at Nuremberg. As head of I.G.'s international spy network which became the backbone of the Nazi Supreme Command, one might think that Ilgner would be concerned over the future. He was not. Shortly after being arrested, he wrote a letter to two of his assistants and instructed them to keep in close touch with each other and with all the other I.G. leaders. He stressed the importance of keeping the structure functioning because, he said, it would not be much longer before the Americans would remove all restrictions.[1]

He was correct, of course. Within six months the cartel's factories were humming with activity. I.G. shares were enjoying spectacular confidence in the German stock market, and free American money in the form of the Marshall Plan was on its way.

Meanwhile, Colonel Bernard Bernstein, chief investigator for the Finance Division of the Allied Control Council, and an outspoken critic of American coddling of cartelists, was fired by his superior officers. James Martin, the man who was head of the de-cartelization branch of the Department of Justice resigned in total disgust. One by one, the true foes of entrenched monopoly were squeezed out. In anger and frustration, Martin explained his resignation:

> We had not been stopped in Germany by German business. We had been stopped in Germany by American business. . . .

---

[1]Sasuly, *I.G. Farben, op. cit.,* p. 201.

> We have to enable the government to control economic power instead of becoming its tool.[1]

The stage now was set for the final act of the drama. With Farben rapidly returning to its pre-war position of prosperity and influence in Europe, all that was left was to release its American holdings from government control. By this time, I.G. Chemie in Switzerland had brightened its image by changing its name to French: Societe Internationale pour Participations Industrielles et Commerciales. In German, however, this translated into International Industrie und Handelsbeteiligungen A.G., or Interhandel, the name by which it became widely known. Once again, nothing had changed but the name.

On behalf of Interhandel, the Swiss banks and the Swiss government demanded that the United States government now release the "Swiss-owned" companies. They claimed that Interhandel was not owned by German nationals (although they steadfastly refused to reveal who *did* own it), and that its American properties had been illegally seized. In court, however, the Treasury Department proved — primarily from Farben's own files captured in Frankfort — that Interhandel was merely the latest name for what Treasury described as:

> . . . a conspiracy to conceal, camouflage, and cloak the ownership control, and

---

[1]Sampson, *The Sovereign State of ITT*, *op. cit.*, p. 45.

> domination by I.G. Farben of properties and interests in many countries of the world, including the United States.[1]

The impasse was finally resolved under the Kennedy Administration. Robert Kennedy, the president's brother, was the Attorney General at the time. He proposed that General Analine be put up for sale to the highest bidder among American investment and underwriting houses. The successful bidder then would be required to offer the stock for public sale. Basically, the proceeds were to be split between the United States government and the Swiss government, both of which would use the money to compensate American, Swiss, and German nationals respectively for losses due to damage during the war.

The proposal was accepted by all parties — as well it should have been. As it turned out, all of the Swiss share of the proceeds went directly to I.G. Farben, and much if not most of the American proceeds found its way into the pockets of those American firms which had invested in pre-war German industry (such as ITT, previously mentioned). It is not at all impossible that Farben's share of the "sale" found its way right back into the New York Stock Exchange, via Swiss banks, dummy accounts, and cooperative American cartel partners, to reacquire its former possessions.

The auction took place in March of 1962. It was the largest competitive transaction ever to take

---

[1]Quoted by Leslie Waller, *The Swiss Bank Connection*, (Signet Books, New American Library, Inc., N.Y., 1972), p. 164.

place on Wall Street. A 225-company underwriting syndicate won the sealed bid with a price of over $329 million dollars. The victorious bidders were represented by — you guessed it — the First Boston Corporation and Blyth and Company. Rockefeller agents, both!

Yes, Virginia, the cartel is not dead. It has grown. It has prospered. Its center of gravity may have shifted away from Frankfort as a result of the displacements of war, but it is alive and well in the United States of America.

The conclusion of this drama was well summarized by Leslie Waller when he wrote:

> Like the legendary phoenix, this colossus of business organizations was born in fire, yet survives the fiercest flames. It is an almost perfect example of corporate immortality, based on Swiss banking . . . . Schmitz and Greutert were long dead. But thanks to Swiss tenacity, the original decision to conceal his holdings under the Matterhorn had withstood the ravages of war, time, and politics.[1]

The written record of this period of history is voluminous. The serious researcher should be cautioned, however, not to accept everything he reads as fact. In the wake of war, there were two powerful groups vying with each other for dominance within the United States government. One was the international financial and industrial con-

[1]*Ibid.*, pp. 160, 166.

sortium which is the subject of these chapters. The other was the apparatus of international Communism. Their goals and methods of operation were (and are) almost identical, and there was considerable overlapping and cooperation between them. (Algier Hiss, for example, was able to operate in both groups with little difficulty.) But just as members of a cartel will cooperate with each other against the best interests of the general public, yet still maneuver in limited competition between themselves for advantage within the cartel, so, also, do we find that the Communists and their so-called anti-Communist opponents of "monopoly capitalism" routinely cooperate with each other against the best interests of the general public, yet will fight each other bitterly for dominance within the political systems of the world. Consequently, a great deal that was written about the evils of Nazi or Communist influence after the war was done so primarily for propaganda purposes. The Communists charged that the Nazis were monopoly capitalists and that they had strong ties to American industrialists and to the American government itself. In this they were correct. But they used this truth as a springboard to launch the line that monopoly capitalism was synonymous with the traditional American system, and that, therefore, the system must be overthrown and replaced with socialism and, ultimately, Communism. In other words, they proposed to replace the existing imperfect monopoly with their more perfect monopoly known to the peasants simply as Communism.

Their cartel opponents, on the other hand, publicly became outspoken "anti-Communists," and wrapped themselves in the stars and stripes of patriotism. They called for thorough investigations and promised to sweep the Reds and Pinks out of the State Department and other branches of government. They even prosecuted one or two! In time, they led the United States into a series of limited wars against Communist regimes all around the world. (Don't forget, wars *are* profitable, both economically and politically.) But they never tried to win those wars, for both sides had come to an understanding that unlimited competition would not be to their mutual advantage.

This background must be clearly understood if one is to make sense out of the flood of books and articles that have inundated the American scene since World War II. Much truth is to be found in the special pleadings of both sides, but neither side can be trusted for either solutions or leadership. If reliable national or international leadership should ever present itself, it will be recognized by a single quality that neither Communism nor Nazism, or any other totalitarianism can ever possess. *It will advocate and promote the drastic reduction of government.* To recognize this leadership, we will not have to be political scientists, or philosophers, or students of history. By this test alone, we will be able to distinguish between the genuine and the imitation. And, with this kind of leadership, political conspiracies will be doomed to oblivion.

XVI

THE ROCKEFELLER GROUP

A biographical sketch of John D. Rockefeller, Sr., including his lifelong crusade against competition; the growth of Standard Oil; the entry of the Rockefellers into the investment banking field; the Rockefeller influence in the cartelized American pharmaceutical industry; and an overview of the importance of the Rockefeller family in international politics.

It would be a serious mistake to categorize the international cartel that has been the subject of these chapters as strictly German. It is abundantly clear that the leaders of its component parts, regardless of their nationality, consider themselves as internationalists — or more accurately, supranationalists — with little or no loyalty to the country of their birth. Their patriotism is directed toward the giant multi-national industrial and financial organizations that protect and sustain them.

Robert Stevenson, vice-president of the Ford Motor Company, is an excellent specimen of these new citizens of the world. *Business Week* magazine of December 19, 1970, quotes Stevenson as saying:

> We don't consider ourselves basically an American company. We are a multi-national company. And when we approach a government that doesn't like the U.S., we always say, "Whom do you like? Britain? Germany? We carry a lot of flags."

During a television interview in the fall of 1973, a top executive of Mobil Oil was even more explicit when he said:

> I've never been faced with the situation where I'd say to myself I'm only going to be a good citizen of one country, because if I do that I'm no longer a multi-national oil company.[1]

We must keep in mind, also, that a cartel is a *grouping* of interests. While they may act in unison in those areas that serve their mutual goals, and while there usually is considerable investment interlocking, and while the trend is leading ultimately toward the creation of a single super-giant industrial and financial complex that will dominate the economic and political life of the entire planet,

---

[1] "Snake Oil From the Oil Companies," *Consumer Reports,* Feb. 1974, p. 126.

nevertheless, its component parts represent groupings within the structure, and quite often there is fierce competition between them for dominance or at least for more favorable relative position within the whole.

The largest and most powerful of these today is centered in New York City and is known as the Rockefeller group.

The Rockefeller interest in the profit potential of drugs can be traced all the way back to John D. Rockefeller's father, William Avery Rockefeller. "Big Bill," as he was known to his friends and neighbors in upstate New York, had been a wandering vendor of quack medicines made up mostly of crude oil and alcohol. He had never received any medical training, yet, professionally, he advertised himself as "Doctor William A. Rockefeller, the Celebrated Cancer Specialist" and had himself listed as a physician in the local directory. His advertising posters read: "All cases of cancer cured, unless too far gone, and they can be greatly benefited."[1]

"Doc" Rockefeller was a con artist. He cheated anyone and everyone any time he could — and boasted of it. In 1844 he was accused of horse theft. He had been suspected of bigamy. And in 1849, he was accused of raping the hired girl in the Rockefeller household. To avoid prosecution, Big Bill moved to Oswego, outside the court's jurisdiction.[2]

---

[1]John T. Flynn, *God's Gold; The Story of Rockefeller and His Times*, (Harcourt Brace and Co., N.Y., 1932), p. 53.

[2]Hoffman, *David; A Report on a Rockefeller*, *op. cit.*, p. 24.

John D. Rockefeller, in later years, recalled with pride and satisfaction, the excellent practical training he had received from his father. He said:

> He himself trained me in practical ways. He was engaged in different enterprises; he used to tell me about these things . . . .and he taught me the principles and methods of business.[1]

What were these principles and methods of business that John D. learned from his father? Biographer, John T. Flynn, in his book *God's Gold; The Story of Rockefeller and His Times*, provides the answer:

> Big Bill was fond of boasting of his own smartness and how he bested people . . . . The man had practically no moral code. He would descant on his own cunning performances for anyone's entertainment . . . . He was what was later called a "slicker," and he was fond of doing what he could to be sure his sons would be "slickers" like himself.
>
> "I cheat my boys every chance I get," he told Uncle Joe Webster. "I want to make 'em sharp. I trade with the boys and skin 'em, and I just beat 'em every time I can. I want to make 'em sharp."[2]

---

[1]Mathew Josephson, *The Robber Barons*, (Harcourt Brace and Co., N.Y., 1934), pp. 45, 46.
[2]*Op. cit.*, p. 58.

And make 'em sharp, he did, especially John D., who went on to become one of the most ruthless and most successful monopolists of all time.

Once again, we must remind ourselves that, in spite of all the current rhetoric to the contrary, monopoly is not the product of free-enterprise capitalism, but the escape *from* it. John D. Rockefeller himself had confirmed this many times in his career. One of his favorite expressions was "Competition is a sin."[1]

But there was more to it than that. John T. Flynn explains:

> His entry into business and his career after that would be, in a large measure, the story of American economic development and the war on *Laissez faire* . . . .
>
> Rockefeller was definitely convinced that the competitive system under which the world had operated was a mistake. It was a crime against order, efficiency, economy. It could be eliminated only by abolishing all rivals. His plan, therefore, took a solid form. He would bring all his rivals in with him. The strong ones he would bring in as partners. The others would come in as stockholders . . . . Those who would not come in would be crushed.[2]

---

[1]Hoffman, *Op. cit.*, p. 29.

[2]*Op. cit.*, pp. 23, 221.

The present structure of the Rockefeller empire is living proof of the success of this plan. John D., Senior, had a number of close business associates. Some originally were partners. Most were defeated rivals who had been brought into the structure. All of these men became multi-millionaires, and most of their descendents have remained closely linked with the Rockefeller family. Whether intermarriages were arranged as "unions of convenience," as were common among the ruling classes of Europe, or were the result of love, the result has been the same. The Rockefeller biological (and stockholder) strain has intermingled in an almost unbroken line through half of the nation's wealthiest sixty families and back again. Throughout it all, the aggregate is solidly controlled, economically at least, by the *one* family that constitutes the descendents of John D. Rockefeller, the First.

It is nearly impossible for an outsider to estimate the true wealth and power of the Rockefeller family today. But even a casual survey of the *visible* portion of its vast empire is enough to stagger the imagination.

The Rockefellers first established an oil monopoly in the United States in the 1870's. In 1899 this oil trust was reorganized as the Standard Oil Company of New Jersey. In 1911, as a result of a decision of the Supreme Court, Standard Oil was forced to separate into six separate companies —supposedly to break up the monopoly. This act did not, of course, accomplish its objective. The many "independent" companies that resulted continued to be owned—and in many cases even run—by the same men. None of them ever engaged in serious competition between themselves, and certainly not against Standard Oil of New Jersey, which continued to be Rockefeller's main holding company.

In the years following 1911, the Rockefellers returned to their original policy of acquiring other oil companies that, in the public eye, were "independent." Consequently, the Rockefeller family obtained either control over or substantial financial interest in such vast enterprises as Humble Oil (now called Exxon), Creole Petroleum, Texaco, Pure Oil, and others. Most of these companies control a staggering maze of subsidiaries that operate in almost every nation of the world. All-in-all, Standard Oil of New Jersey *admits* to outright control over three hundred and twenty-two companies.[1] In addition, Rockefeller established cartel links through investments in many foreign "competitors." These included Royal Dutch (Shell Oil) and a half interest in the Soviet Nobel Oil Works.

What influence the Rockefellers exert through their oil cartel, as impressive as it is, is peanuts compared to what they have accomplished in later years through the magic of international finance and investment banking.

That part of the story begins in 1891 when the First National City Bank of New York, under the presidency of James Stillman, became the main bank of the Rockefeller family. With the addition of the Rockefeller deposits, the bank became the largest in the country.

---

[1]Hoffman, *Op. cit.*, pp. 151, 152.

The Rockefellers soon became interested in banking and banking monopolies as a means of making money with even greater potential than oil monopolies. Two sons of William Rockefeller, John's brother, married daughters of James Stillman, and the Rockefeller-Stillman interlock was forged. Later, the family of John D. Rockefeller moved most of its financial interests to a bank of their own, but the descendents of William Rockefeller became, and continue to be, the majority shareholders in, and thus the owners of, the First National City Bank, which has become one of the largest financial institutions in the world. In fact, as stated in its annual report for 1953:

> Of the hundred largest non-financial corporations in the country, ninety-five have accounts with our bank. Our correspondent banking relationships are similarly wide. All of the hundred largest banks in the country outside New York City maintain accounts with us.

When the family of John D. Rockefeller left the First National City Bank, it was not because of dissatisfaction or an internal struggle for control. It was merely to absorb the competition — the hallmark of all monopoly business moves. First they established their own bank known as the Equitable Trust. Then they bought up the Chase National Bank. Meanwhile, the International Acceptance Corporation, a bank owned by Kuhn, Loeb, and Company, had merged into the Bank of the Manhattan Company. And it was this that was absorbed in 1955 by the Rockefeller's Chase National Bank resulting in the largest banking firm in the world: The Chase Manhattan.

How big is the Chase Manhattan Bank? No one on the outside really knows. We *do* know, however, that it is more like a sovereign state than a business firm. It has far more money than most nations. It has over fifty-thousand banking officers serving as ambassadors all around the world. It even employs a full-time envoy to the United Nations, for whom it serves as banker.[1]

The words "investment banks" or "investment houses" have been used several times within this discourse, and it is advisable to clarify their meaning. Before 1933, banking firms in the United States operated in two areas of activity. They handled the commercial checking accounts and deposits of individuals and corporations, an area of activity known as *commercial* banking; and they also represented clients who were buying or selling stocks and bonds in various corporate enterprises, an area of activity known as *investment* banking.

In 1933, however, in response to public alarm over the growing concentration of economic power into the hands of fewer and fewer banking dynasties, a law was passed which required commercial banks to divest themselves of all investment banking operations. The banks complied, but the result

---

[1]The U.N. always has been a pet project of the Rockefeller family. They even donated the land on which the U.N. building now stands. It's likely that they view the U.N. as the ultimate mechanism for the enforcement of monopoly power throughout the entire world, a role for which it is admirably structured.

was not what the voters had in mind. Separate investment banking firms *were* established, but they were owned by exactly the same people who also owned the commercial banks; and, as a result of the mergers that took place in the wake of this legislation, the end product was fewer firms and, thus, greater concentration of power than ever before.

For the Chase Manhattan group there was now an investment firm called the First Boston Corporation. And for the National City Group there was Harriman, Ripley, and Company and Blyth and Company. Others — such as Dominick and Dominick, and Dillon, Read, and Company — soon were to be added to the interlock as the power of the Rockefeller empire expanded. With the formation of the First Boston Corporation, for example, the powerful Mellon family threw in its lot with the Rockefeller family, and about the only substantial block that was not yet united into a single monolithic banking structure was the family of J.P. Morgan, although even they cooperated in many joint projects, such as the Federal Reserve System.[1]

With the growth of these investment banking institutions in the United States, New York has become the new focal point of world finance. Swit-

---

[1]Contrary to popular belief, the Federal Reserve System — the entity that has complete control over the creation of money in the United States — is neither owned nor run by the government. It is privately owned by the banking interests that are the subject of these passages. For more details on that aspect of monopoly — monopoly over the money system, itself — read *The Capitalist Conspiracy; An Inside View of International Banking*, by G. Edward Griffin, (American Media, Thousand Oaks, California, 1971).

zerland, in spite of the unique role it plays because of its bank secrecy and numbered accounts, cannot begin to compare with the money volume and power now centered in the United States. The American assets of any one of the multi-national corporations built around Standard Oil, ITT, Ford, or General Motors, far exceed the total assets of many nations of the world. ITT has more employees overseas than does the State Department. Standard Oil has a larger tanker fleet than the Soviet Union. IBM's research and development budget is larger than the total tax revenue of all but a handful of countries. While it is true that a great deal of foreign money does find its way into Swiss banks, there still is more money and real wealth inside the United States than in most of the rest of the world combined. Furthermore, a substantial portion of this wealth is concentrated into the hands of the financial and industrial cartelists in New York.

One percent of the population owns more than seventy percent of the nation's productive property, and ten percent own *all* of it.[1] About half of this, in turn, is held in trust by the ten leading Wall Street banks, which, in turn, are heavily influenced, if not controlled outright, by a group so small that they could be counted on the fingers of one hand. This, stated in plain English, represents the greatest and most intense concentration of wealth and power that the world has ever seen.

How did this come about? Was it the product of free-enterprise? Was it the result of providing needed goods or services at competitive prices,

---

[1]Lundberg, *The Rich and the Super Rich, op. cit.,* p. 461.

thus, capturing a larger share of the free market? Was it the consequence of mass production and distribution methods that drove down the selling price of goods to the point where they became attractive to more and more consumers? Each of these factors may have played a small part in the process, but, to whatever extent they did, it was infinitesimal compared to the larger role played by the guaranteed super profits that resulted from simply eliminating one's competition.

The apologist for cartelized industry and finance usually attempts to refute this fact by citing the profit figures for these enterprises each year. The picture they draw is modest, indeed, with an average profit of from three to seven percent. This isn't enough even to keep up with inflation, so obviously, the *finpols,* somehow are doing a lot better than that. But how?

The answer is in something known as "profits of control" — the profits that fall to those who control an enterprise. These are *not* the same as the profits paid to mere stockholders (investors of risk capital), the profits that make up the modest balance sheet so often displayed in defense of cartelized industry. The profits of control are derived from such things as advance inside information that enables one to make a killing on the stock market, extremely profitable delayed stock options, handsome fees for special services rendered, crossbreeding of high-profit contracts with affiliated companies, multi-million dollar loans at unnaturally high or low interest rates, depending on the direction of the advantage, and similar devices. All-in-all, the profits of control can run anywhere from fifty percent to many thousands of percent, depending on how small a margin of capital is required to control the total.

This is an interesting study in itself. Many people are of the opinion that it takes fifty-one percent ownership to control a corporation. Nothing could be further from the truth. While this may be true of small companies whose stock is held by a handful of people, the extremely large multi-billion dollar companies can be — and *are* — controlled by as little as five to ten percent of the total stockholders.[1]

The mechanics by which it is possible for an extreme minority to hold control — and thus the *profits* of control — of the super-giant industries are fascinating. They include all the usual tricks of business — such as proxy battles and social pressure on members of the board — plus most of the tactics of all-out war as well. They also include use of hidden allies from other countries who may own small but substantial blocks through numbered accounts in Swiss banks. But the greatest weapon of all is the powerful leverage they can obtain through their control of large blocks of stock that are held indirectly by them as part of the investment portfolios of the financial institutions they also control.

A life insurance company, for instance, is the repository of many millions of dollars that, in theory, belong to the policy-holders. Most insur-

---

[1]This is the unanimous opinion of experts in the field of high finance. See the *New York Times*, Nov. 7, 1955; also Lundberg, *op. cit.*, p. 270; also Hoffman, *op. cit.*, pp. 6, 7; and others.

ance policies are a mixture of real insurance and a savings program. The money that goes into savings typically is invested in a broad spectrum of industry, but most of it is put into the "blue chip" stocks of the largest corporations. This stock does not belong to the owners of the company; but the owners of the company — or, to be more exact, the extreme minority of owners who *control* the company — exercise the right to vote that stock just the same as if they owned it all. In this way, a minority in control of a financial institution can multiply its influence and power by a factor many hundreds of times greater than its own capital investment would suggest. This is the "magic" of investment banking, and explains why the leaders of Wall Street's great financial cartels are, historically, at the summit of the industrial empires of the United States.

The Rockefeller group has become the nation's leading practitioner of this kind of magic. In addition to the billions of dollars worth of other people's industrial stocks which it controls through the trust departments and trust companies affiliated with its commercial banking operations, in addition to the billions controlled in the same way through its investment banking firms, and in addition to the megalithic blocks of stock held in trust by the various Rockefeller foundations, it also has control over the vast stock holdings of both the Metropolitan and Equitable life insurance companies, the first and third largest in the United States. Historically, the Traveler's and Hartford insurance companies also have been within the Rockefeller orbit through such top executives as J. Doyle DeWitt and Eugene Black, both directors of Chase Manhattan Bank.

Reaching downward through this pyramid of power, the Rockefeller group has managed to place its representatives into controlling positions on the boards of a wide cross-section of industry. These include the following better known firms: Allied Chemical, American Tobacco, Anaconda, Armour and Company, ATT, Bethlehem Steel, Bulova Watch, Burlington Industries, Commercial Solvents Corporation, Continental Can, Cowles Publications, Data Control, Florida East Coast Railroad, Ford Motor, General Electric, General Foods, General Motors, Getty Oil, B.F. Goodrich, Hearst Publications, Hewlett-Packard, IBM, International Harvester, ITT, Kennecott Copper, Litton Industries, Minute Maid, National Lead, New York Central Railroad, Pan American Airways, Penn Central, Polaroid, RCA, Sears, Shell Oil, Singer, Southern Pacific Railroad, Time-Life Publications, U.S. Rubber, U.S. Steel, Virginian Railroad, Western Union, and Westinghouse—*to name just a few!*

In the specialized field of drugs and pharmaceuticals, the Rockefeller influence is substantial, if not dominant. When David Rockefeller spoke before the Investment Forum in Paris, he said that it was wise to invest in "life and risk insurance companies, business equipment companies, and companies benefitting from research into drugs."[1]

---

[1]Hoffman, *op. cit.*, p. 185.

That he has followed his own advice is a matter of record.

The Rockefeller entry into the pharmaceutical field is more concealed, however, than in most other categories of industry. The reason for this appears to be two-fold. One is the fact that, for many years before World War II, Standard Oil had a continuing cartel agreement not to enter into the broad field of chemicals except as a partner with I.G. Farben which, in turn, agreed not to compete in oil. The other is that, because of the unpopularity of Farben in this country and the need to camouflage its American holdings, Standard had concealed even its partnership interests in chemical firms behind a maze of false fronts and dummy accounts. The Chase Manhattan Bank, however, always has been the principal stock registrar for Farben-Rockefeller enterprises such as Sterling Drug, Olin Corporation, American Home Products, and General Analine and Film. When Farben's vast holdings were finally sold in 1962, the Rockefeller group was the dominant force in carrying out the transaction. One can safely assume, therefore, that, if there was any way to benefit from inside information or to place a minority into a position to reap the profits of control, the Rockefeller group did so. Consequently, it is difficult for an outsider to separate the *pure* Rockefeller control from that which is shared by I.G. Farben or its descendents. That it constitutes a major power center within the pharmaceutical industry, however, cannot be denied.

The profit potential in drugs is enormous. The very nature of the product lends itself perfectly to monopoly and cartel controls. When a person is ill or is dying, he does not question the price of a drug offered to him for relief. This is especially true if the drug is recommended by his physician and is available only through a prescription. The mystique of that procedure eliminates all competition between brands. Profits can be extremely high—not so much to the physician or the druggist—but for the firms that manufacture the drugs.

It is more than possible that this is the primary reason for the 1974 rulings requiring all but the weakest potency vitamins to be available only through a physician's prescription. Price and brand competition in vitamins simply had to be stopped. The large pharmaceutical firms supported the ruling because they knew that their existing contacts with druggists would make them the favored suppliers. This would put the smaller manufacturers out of business, leaving the field clear for the cartel. They also knew that, because prescriptions were to be required, the prices eventually could be moved upward with little chance of consumer complaint. It was merely another example of using the power of government to eliminate competition and increase costs to the consumer.

Here again is one of those road signs along the way reassuring us that we have not become lost in a maze of meaningless information that has no bearing on cancer therapy and cancer research. Although many otherwise well informed persons are totally unaware of it, cartels *do* exist. They have completely dominated the chemical industry for decades. The pharmaceutical industry, far from being exempt from this influence, has been at the center of it from the very beginning. We are travelling this long path of historical inquiry for the reason that one simply cannot evaluate the broad opposition to vitamin therapy without an awareness of these facts.

It has been observed that almost every head of state that visits the United States pays a personal visit to the head of the Rockefeller empire. In more recent years this has included visits to David Rockefeller by such personages as the Emperor of Japan and the Premier of the Soviet Union. And when Rockefeller travels to foreign lands, he always is accorded a royal welcome of the caliber usually reserved for heads of state. Yet, the American people generally do not consider the Rockefellers to be that important. As Ferdinand Lundberg observed:

> There apparently is a difference of opinion between foreign leaders . . . and the American public about the precise status of the Rockefellers. Can it be that the foreign political sharks, as they muster out the palace guard and the diplomats to greet them, are mistaken? My own view of them accords with that of the foreigners. The finpols (financial politicians) are ultra bigwigs, super-megaton bigshots, Brobdingnagian commissars of af-

> fairs. In relation to them the average one-vote citizen is a muted cipher, a noiseless nullity, an impalpable phantom, a shadow in a vacuum, a subpeasant.[1]

Perhaps the reason that Americans do not regard the Rockefellers as the "Brobdingnagian commissars" that they really are is because, like their Farben counterparts in Nazi Germany, they have wisely chosen to stay in the background. They are seldom in the news and are overshadowed by the public appearances and pronouncements of the nation's political figures. But this, too, is according to formula. The men who sit at the pinnacle of this world power prefer to leave the time-consuming and fruitless publicity-seeking to their political subordinates who, by temperament, are more suited to the task. The amount of power held by a John or a David Rockefeller may not be as great as that held for a single instant by a president of the United States. By comparison, however, the president is but a passing comet doomed to eventual oblivion.

Political figures come and go. Some are revered in the history books of their nation. Some are tried as war criminals. Others are assassinated. Most merely are cast aside when they have outlived their usefulness. But the power of the Rockefellers is handed down from generation to generation as a title of nobility and has become a living, growing, nearly immortal reality of its own.

---

[1] *Op. cit.*, p. 21.

XVII

THE CHARITY PRESCRIPTION

A preview of the drug cartel's influence over the curricula taught within the nation's medical schools; the drug-oriented training given to all medical students; the philanthropic foundation as a special creation of cartelists to avoid payment of taxes; and the use of the foundation to obtain control over educational institutions.

As we have seen, the Rockefeller group, in conjunction with the hidden hand of I.G. Farben, has become a dominant influence in the American pharmaceutical industry. One of the more obvious consequences of this reality is that one almost never finds consumer price competition in the broad and lucrative field of prescription drugs and patent medicines. The only competition generally allowed is along the basis of vague and meaningless advertising claims such as "Laboratory tests prove that Bayer is higher quality," or "Research has shown that Anacin is faster." Over the years, the major pharmaceutical houses have lived up to an agreement to stay within the narrow field of their specialty and to refrain from trying to cut into the established markets of their rivals. It is, as they say, an "orderly" industry.

One of the reasons for this, of course, is that some drugs are patented and are available only from one manufacturer. Another reason is that the prescription is made by a physician who properly is more concerned with the effectiveness of a drug than with its price. But, in addition to these, there is the fact that the drug houses bombard the market with so many new drugs each year that the physician often does not *know* how effective are the drugs he prescribes. All he knows is that he has seen them advertised in the *AMA Journal,* has been handed a "fact sheet" by a detail man representing the company which manufactures the drugs, and may have had some limited or qualified success with them on a few of his previous patients. Because he is a *practitioner,* not a *researcher,* he cannot conduct controlled experiments to determine the relative effectiveness of the new drugs as compared to the old or with similar drugs available through another drug firm. All he knows is that they seem to help some of his patients. If the first drug does not bring about the desired results, then he will issue a new prescription and try something else. The end result is that it is not unusual for a patient to end up buying and trying several drugs from several manufacturers with everybody getting a piece of the financial action.

This point was brought home quite bluntly at a conference on medical drugs sponsored in 1963 by Johns Hopkins University. One of the featured speakers was Dr. George Baehr of New York, who stated:

> As a consultant for many years to physicians in private practice, it has been my experience that many general practitioners and specialists have acquired the habit of shifting repeatedly and needlessly from one drug to another. They are usually motivated to change their prescribing habits by the persuasive propaganda of advertising literature and of visiting detail men.[1]

There is nothing about this procedure, of course, which is improper from the physician's point of view. He is doing only what he can to help his patients by making available to them what he has been told is the latest technology in the field of drugs. Remember it is not he who makes a profit from writing the prescription.

There is no questioning the fact that the doctor serves as an extremely effective salesman for a multi-billion dollar drug industry, but he is not paid for this vital service. He *has* been trained for it, however. Through the curricula within the nation's leading medical schools, students are exposed to such an extensive training in the use of drugs (and

---

[1]Omar Garrison, *The Dictocrats, op. cit.*, p. 21.

practically none in the field of nutrition) that, upon graduation, they quite naturally turn to the use of drugs as the professional treatment of choice for practically all of man's ills.

How the medical schools of the nation came to adopt these uniform curricula is the subject to which we now turn our attention.

The key to unlock this particular door of cartel intrigue is the tax-exempt foundation. The scope of this study does not permit more than a cursory review of the origins and early history of such foundations, but the salient points are these:

The Federal Reserve System, the income tax, and the tax-exempt foundations all were conceived and foisted onto the American people by the same financier-politicians whose story has been traced in the preceding pages. In fact, the Federal Reserve System was first introduced as legislation in 1913 by Senator Nelson Aldrich, and was known as the "Aldrich Plan." Aldrich was brought into the inner circle when his daughter married John D. Rockefeller, Jr. The senator's son, Winthrop Aldrich, became chairman of the Chase National Bank. Senator Aldrich was widely recognized as Rockefeller's personal representative in the Senate and, as a result, he wielded far more power and influence in Washington than any other senator of the era. One thing is certain. He would not have introduced income tax legislation if there were even the remotest chance that it would apply to such fortunes as those held by the Rockefellers, the Morgans, the Carnegies, or the Mellons.

The plan was both simple and ingenious. They would transfer the bulk of their visible assets to something called foundations. They would appoint hand-picked and loyal underlings to administer these foundations. They would require that a portion of their assets be dispersed under the appearance of charity or philanthropy. They would design most of those gifts, however, to benefit themselves, their business enterprises, or to further their political objectives. They would retain full control of their assets and use them just as freely as if they remained directly in their name. They would retain the option of terminating the foundations and reclaiming their assets at any time it would be advantageous to do so. They would completely avoid the payment of any inheritance tax upon the death of the "donor," thus insuring that the fortune remained intact and in the hands of family or corporate control in perpetuity. And they would use the supposedly charitable nature of the foundation as a means of avoiding the payment of most, if not all, of the income tax they then were advocating to be paid by everyone else.

Once again it must be noted that the "socialist" or "communist" nostrums allegedly designed to pull down the rich and elevate the poor — such as the progressive income tax[1] — always work, first, to eliminate the middle class and, ultimately, to produce just the opposite of their adver-

---

[1]The progressive income tax was specifically called for in *The Communist Manifesto*.

tised objective. That this has been true in the United States is obvious. The progressive income tax has not hurt the *finpols* one bit. Their wealth expands at an ever-increasing rate each year. The business and professional men who fall into the broad middle class, however, now are effectively blocked from rising into the selected ranks of the super-rich. With each passing decade since the enactment of the income tax, the gap widens between the top and the bottom. Again, government becomes the instrument for preventing competition and for preserving monopoly.

And make no mistake about it, it was planned that way.

Ferdinand Lundberg agrees:

> Recipients of the money must be ideologically acceptable to the donors. There is a positive record showing that, by these means, purely corporate elements are able to influence research and many university policies, particularly in the selection of personnel . . . . The foundations are staunch supporters of the physical sciences, the findings of which have many profit-making applications in the corporate sphere. . . .
>
> Whether or not these various effects were sought by the foundation creators, they are present, and the realistic observer must suppose they were what the realistic founders had in mind.[1]

[1]*The Rich and The Super Rich, op.cit.*, p. 469.

It should be noted in passing that what has been true in university research is equally true in government research. In both cases the pharmaceutical interests are able to benefit commercially from extensive drug research programs paid for wholly or in part by tax dollars. This reality was clearly demonstrated in 1972 by Dr. Frank Rauscher, director of the National Cancer Institute, when he said:

> We test about 30,000 compounds a year for anti-tumor activity in animals at the National Cancer Institute alone. Each year, for the past four or five years, an average of about three new drugs have reached the physician's bag for application to the patient.
>
> The program currently costs about 75 million dollars per year, and can be expected to generate six or seven clinically effective drugs each year. That means we're spending tax money at about the rate of 10 million dollars per drug . . . . My colleagues, Dr. Gordon Zubrod and Dr. Saul Schepartz, operate probably the nation's biggest pharmaceutical house at the National Cancer Institute.[1]

In recent years, the private physician has represented a constantly shrinking portion of the total

---

[1] "New Gains in War Against Cancer," *U.S. News and World Report*, Dec. 4, 1972, p. 41.

medical profession. As his influence wanes, he is being superseded by group clinics, state-supported institutions, and research centers. Many of these are the recipients of large grants for specific medical projects, and they become extremely sensitive to the ideological or scientific preferences of those who give the money. It's not that the donors tell them specifically what to do or what to find, it's just that the recipients know in advance that, if they stray too far outside the unstated but clearly understood objectives of those who make the grant, then that will be the last time their name is on the roll call when the free money is given out.

There is the celebrated case, for instance, of the $15,000 grant from the Carnegie Endowment for International Peace to the American Bar Association to study the United Nations Genocide Convention. When the ABA had the gall to *condemn* the convention, the Carnegie Foundation was enraged and demanded an immediate stop to the project or its money back.[1]

Another example of the influence of foundations over the world of academia is the way in which the nutrition department of Harvard has been converted into the public relations department of the General Foods Corporation. For years the head of this department at Harvard has been Professor Stare, known among health food circles as the "Cornflakes Professor." One of Professor's dubious achievements has been to defend "enriched"

---

[1] "Bar Group Accused by Carnegie Fund," *New York Times*, Oct. 15, 1950, pp. 1, 66. Also "Bar Group Denies Peace Fund Misuse," *New York Times*, Oct. 20, 1950, p. 30.

white bread and other miracle products of the processed food industry. He repeatedly dismisses as "rubbish" and "nutritional quackery" all suggestions that chemical additives to foods may not be safe or that processed supermarket foods are not just as nutritious as anything fresh from an organic garden. On one occasion he condemned Dr. Carlton Fredericks for his support of vitamin B_6 and challenged him to produce even *one* authoritative reference to support its value. Whereupon Dr. Fredericks sent Stare's own report on B_6 written years before he had come under the influence of Harvard and foundation money.[1]

Omar Garrison gives us further insight into how this influence came to be decisive:

> Perhaps it is without significance that Dr. Stare is a board member of a large can company, and that his department at Harvard has been the recipient of substantial research grants from the food industry. For example, in 1960, the Harvard president announced what he called a "momentous" gift of $1,026,000 from General Foods Corporation, to be used over a ten-year period for expansion of the nutritional laboratories of the university's school of public health, where Dr. Stare is professor of nutrition. The seductive question is: Can any scientific research remain wholly objec-

[1]Details in a lecture by Dr. Carlton Fredericks, National Health Federation Convention, Los Angeles, Jan. 16, 1972.

> tive and untainted by loyalty when it is so generously endowed by big corporations whose commercial future will be influenced by the outcome of such research?[1]

Joseph Goulden, in his authoritative study of foundations entitled *The Money Givers,* explains how foundation control has been extended to the medical profession:

> The medical profession does quiver excitedly when it hears the fast riffle of thousand dollar bills. Since Ford [through the Ford Foundation] began nationwide operations in 1950, it has spent more than a third of a billion dollars on medical schools and hospitals . . . .
>
> Foundations are popular with the medical establishment because they do so much to preserve it. A well-endowed regional foundation — Kellogg in Michigan, Moody in Texas, Lilly in Indiana — can be as influential in hospital affairs as is the state medical association, through grants for construction, operating expenses, and research.[2]

---

[1]*The Dictocrats, op. cit.,* pp. 195, 196.

[2]Goulden, *The Money Givers,* (Random House, N.Y., 1971), pp. 145, 149.

Bearing in mind that the foundations are precision tools in the hands of furthering monopolies and cartels, it follows that they would have to be used not only for expanding the wealth of those who control them but also for expanding the size and reach of government, for *total* government is the ultimate monopoly and their final goal.

This, in fact, has been the most conspicuous aspect of foundation grants since their inception. The overwhelming majority of foundation-supported projects in the social or political sciences has resulted in promoting the concept of enlarging the scope of government, supposedly as the solution to all of the problems and injustices of the nation and the world. Plush grants have gone to scholars, researchers, schools, dramatists, churches, theater groups, mass-action organizations, poets, and ivory tower think-tanks. They have been given to those who defend the Establishment, to those who are anti-Establishment, to those who claim to be in the middle, and to those who plot violent revolutions to overthrow all existing power structures. They have been bestowed upon Republicans, Democrats, ADAers, SDSers, socialists, and Communists. The apparent divergence of these groups leads the casual observer to the erroneous conclusion that the foundations are not selective or that they are promoting a kind of melting-pot democracy of ideas. But, upon closer examination, the one thing that *all* of these recipients share in common is that they promote the growth of government; and *that,* in fact, is why they have been smiled upon by the forces of monopoly.

There are a thousand examples that could be cited in support of this proposition, but let us limit ourselves only to the field of medicine which is the area of our present interest. Recent studies of socialized medicine in England and Sweden have turned up an extremely interesting fact. Because prescription drugs in these countries are "free" (paid out of taxes), the per capita use of these medications is considerably higher than in the United States. Actually, the statistics show that where an individual has no financial interest in his medical bill he tends to overuse it just to make sure that he is getting all the benefits to which he thinks he is entitled. Doctors, also, tend to write out expensive prescriptions in marginal cases of probable need just to "process" the patient through his office more quickly. The result is that, under socialized medicine, the drug manufacturers are rewarded with an automatic and maximum market saturation for their products. We can be certain that the pharmaceutical cartel that controls the medically-oriented foundations has not overlooked this fact, and we can be equally certain that the consistent history of foundation pressure for socialized medicine in the United States is no accident.

The Milbank Fund was created by Albert G. Milbank, Chairman of the Borden Company, and also the leading partner in the Wall Street law firm of Milbank, Tweed, Hope, Hadley and McCloy. Milbank was no stranger to the cartel. In fact, John J. McCloy, one of his partners, was Chairman of the Chase National Bank, trustee of the Rockefeller Foundation, chairman of the board of the Council on Foreign Relations, and a member of the Executive Committee of Squibb Pharmaceutical. The significance of the Milbank Fund is not that it has been the kindly sponsor of projects supposedly to upgrade the quality of public health, but that it was one of the first foundations to use its resources openly to promote government expansion via socialized medicine.

Richard Carter, in his devastating attack against the AMA, entitled *The Doctor Business,* recounts the story:

> During the Coolidge and Hoover administrations, organized medicine encountered little legislative difficulty. Its worst problems were those posed by the Committee on the Costs of Medical Care and the philanthropic foundations which financed the CCMC's work. The Milbank Fund was regarded as particularly virulent. Despite protests from local medical societies, it continued pilot studies in New York State which illustrated the advantages of publicly organized preventive medicine. Worse, its secretary, John A. Kingsbury, was an advocate of federal health insurance and so was its president, Albert G. Milbank. With the election of Franklin D. Roosevelt, such advocacy became formidable. It was expected that Roosevelt

would include compulsory health insurance in his Social Security laws.[1]

The entry of the Rockefeller group into the foundation arena is of paramount importance to the subject of this treatise, for no other single force has been even remotely as influential in shaping the contours of modern medicine in America. One of the first moves in that direction was made when John D. Rockefeller retained the professional services of a high-powered public relations expert by the name of Ivy Lee. When Lee was called before the Congressional Committee to Investigate Foreign Propaganda and Other Subversive Activities (this later became known as the Dies Committee, but in 1934 its chairman was the Honorable John W. McCormack of Massachusetts), he testified reluctantly that he had been retained by I.G. Farben to give professional advice to most of the top Nazi leaders, including Goebbels, the Minister of Propaganda, and Hitler himself.

Lee became famous in later years for accomplishing what seemed to be an impossible task—improving the popular image of John D. Rockefeller. He had advised the old tycoon to give away a small percentage of his great wealth each year in the form of gifts to hospitals, libraries, schools, churches, and other charities, but to do so in the most conspicuous manner possible, usually with a large building to bear his name as a continuing testimony to his generosity and benevolence.

[1]Carter, *The Doctor Business,* (Doubleday & Co., N.Y., 1958), pp. 203, 204.

To insure favorable press coverage, he advised Rockefeller to carry several rolls of shiny dimes with him at all public appearances so he could hand them out to any youngsters that might be present. It was largely through following this kind of advice that John D. Rockefeller gradually lost the old and thoroughly earned reputation for cunning and ruthlessness and became increasingly portrayed as a kind old philanthropist who loved children.

The public relations value of philanthropy, of course, was not original with Ivy Lee. Rockefeller himself had observed how the negative image of George Peabody had been converted almost overnight by conspicuous acts of public charity, and the same with his close friend Andrew Carnegie. In fact, shortly after Carnegie proclaimed his famous "Gospel of Wealth" in which he stated that men of great fortune had an obligation to further humanitarian objectives through philanthropy, Rockefeller wrote to him and said: "Be assured, your example will bear fruits."[1] Later, when the first Rockefeller general philanthropic board was created, Carnegie was made a trustee and served for eleven years. Rockefeller and Carnegie, applying the typical philosophy of industrial cartels, agreed not to compete or overlap in their philanthropic endeavors, and operated their respective foundations as though they were one; a fact which, through the years, has given each of them an economic leverage even greater than would be indicated by their separate vast resources.

---

[1]Warren Weaver, *U.S. Philanthropic Foundations; Their History, Structure, Management, and Record,* (Harper & Row, N.Y., 1967), p. 35.

The one man who probably deserves more credit than any other for advancing the profitable science of foundation philanthropy was a "modernist" minister by the name of Fred Gates. First of all, it should be noted that Gates was far more of a businessman than he was a man of God. In fact he openly acknowledged that he always had held an aversion to fundamentalist religion, and that he entered the ministry in order to promote the "social" principles which, in his view, were implied in Christ's teachings. He explained: "I wanted to side with Him and His friends against the world and His enemies. That, frankly, was the only 'conversion' I ever had."[1]

Fred Gates had attracted the attention of John D. Rockefeller as a result of his advice and efficient service to the flour magnate George A. Pillsbury. Gates had shown Pillsbury how to dispose of a portion of his estate in such a manner that, not only did he receive maximum public approval, but he also was able to capture control of extremely large sums of money from other sources as well.

This was the Gates formula: Pillsbury gave the Owatonna Baptist Academy $50,000 *on condition that the Baptist community at large would raise an equal amount*. Gates then took on the job of raising the additional funds. The end result was that $100,000 was raised in all, and it was done in such a way that the entire business community, through its own financial share in the venture, was led to identify with the "noble" project of Mr. Pillsbury.

---

[1]Nevins, *John D. Rockefeller*, (Scribner & Sons, N.Y., 1959), v. 2, p. 271.

Pillsbury put up only half, yet he obtained the same public credit and private influence over how the funds were used as he would have if he had financed the entire venture. That was getting *double* mileage out of one's philanthropy!

John D. was quick to appreciate the usefulness of such a man as Fred Gates, the creator of this concept, and soon made him a key figure in his business enterprises. Rockefeller, himself, later described Gates in these glowing terms:

> Fred Gates was a wonderful business man. His work for the American Baptist Education Society required him to travel extensively. Once, as he was going south, I asked him to look into an iron mill in which I had an interest. His report was a model of clarity!
>
> Then I asked him to make some investigation of other property in the west. I had been told this particular company was rolling in wealth. Mr. Gates' report showed that I had been deceived.
>
> Now I realized that I had met a commercial genius. I persuaded Mr. Gates to become a man of business.[1]

One of the first foundations established by Rockefeller and Gates was the General Education Board. The philosophical objective of this "philan-

[1]John K. Winkler, *John D. – A Portait in Oil* (Vanguard Press, N.Y., 1929)

thropy" was not to raise the general level of education, as many people thought at the time, but to convert the American people into a docile and manageable herd of content and uncomplaining workers for the cartel. In the very first publication of the General Education Board, Gates wrote:

> In our dreams we have limitless resources, and the people yield themselves with perfect docility to our molding hands. The present educational conventions fade from our minds, and unhampered by tradition, we work our own good will upon a grateful and responsive rural folk. We shall not try to make these people or any of their children into philosophers of mental learning or of science. We have not to raise up from among them authors, editors, poets, or men of letters. We shall not search for embryo great artists, painters, musicians, nor lawyers, doctors, preachers, politicians, statesmen of whom we have ample supply. The task we set before ourselves is very simple as well as a very beautiful one: To train these people as we find them to a perfectly ideal life just where they are. So we will organize our children into a community and teach them to do in a perfect way the things their fathers and mothers are doing in an imperfect way, in the homes, in the shop, and on the farm.[1]

---

[1] "Occasional Paper No. 1," General Education Board, 1904.

All of the biographies of John D. Rockefeller are in unanimous agreement over the fact that throughout his entire career, he harbored a virtual passion for efficiency, not only in business, but in the administration of his philanthropic funds as well. In the mind of this man, the word "efficiency" undoubtedly meant far more than merely the absence of waste. It meant expending the money in such a way as to bring about the *maximum* return to the donor.

The Gates "matching funds" formula developed for Pillsbury was refined even further for Rockefeller, and soon evolved into a set pattern in which John D. often controlled a large philanthropic venture with as little as one-fourth of the total capitalization. Scores of professional fund-raisers could be counted upon to raise the balance from the gullible public at large. But since the largest *single* contribution came from Rockefeller, he received the major public credit and was able to secure control of the *entire* fund into the hands of trustees and administrators who were entirely subservient to his will. This was the pattern that produced such profitable ventures as the Charity Organization Society, the State Charities Aid, the Greater New York Fund, and many others.

The New York Tuberculosis and Health Association was a classical example. Originally established by a group of conscientious physicians dedicated to a crusade against T.B., it soon fell captive to the financial domination of Rockefeller money. Rockefeller put in charge of the program a relatively unknown social worker by the name of Harry

Hopkins.[1] Under Hopkin's direction, the T.B. Association grew to international proportions and, by 1920, was collecting many millions of dollars each year.

Rockefeller controlled the entire operation, of course, but most of the money came from the public through contributions and the purchase of Christmas Seals. One of the great scandals of 1932 centered around the accusation made by New York City Health Commissioner Lewis I. Harris, in a letter to the *New York Times* of June 8, and by the subsequent admission of the fund's officers, "that all its money had been expended on salaries and overhead."

The philanthropy formula worked so well that it was decided to expand into other fields also. A whole spectrum of similar agencies was established to exploit the public's dread of other diseases as well. Within a few years there sprang into being such organizations as The Heart Association, The Social Hygiene Association, The Diabetes Association, The National Association for the Prevention of Blindness, The American Cancer Association, and many others.

The American Cancer Society, incidentally, was formed officially in May of 1913 at the Harvard Club in New York. In later years its basic orientation has been determined by such names appearing

---

[1]Hopkins, like so many Rockefeller proteges, moved into government work. Eventually he became WPA director, U.S. Secretary of Commerce, Lend-Lease Administrator, and close friend, confidant, and advisor to FDR. He even took up personal residency in the White House where he lived for three-and-a-half years. Later it was learned that he had been a secret member of the Communist Party.

on its board of directors as Alfred P. Sloan (General Motors), Charles D. Hilles (AT&T), Monroe Rathbone (Standard Oil), and Frederich Ecker (Metropolitan Life). The American Cancer Society holds half ownership in the patent rights to 5FU (5 flourouracil), one of the most currently popular toxic drugs now being used as "acceptable" medical treatment for cancer.[1] The drug is manufactured by the Hoffman-LaRoche Laboratories which is firmly within the IG — Rockefeller cartel orbit. Many donors to the ACS would be outraged to learn that this organization has a vested interest in the sale of drugs and a financial tie-in with the drug industry.

Rockefeller's first entry into philanthropy on a grand scale was in 1890 when, following the formula established by Gates, he pledged $600,000 to the Baptist University of Chicago on condition that the meat packers and dry goods merchants of the city also contribute a minimum of $400,000.

Biographer John T. Flynn graphically describes the reaction:

> When the news of Rockefeller's princely gift was made known, the National Baptist Education Society Convention was being held in Boston. The announcement of the gift was received with cheers . . . . When the gift was named and the actual sum of money pronounced, the audience rose and sang the Doxology. Men burst

[1]See Jones, *Nutrition Rudiments in Cancer, op. cit.*, p. 17.

> out into exclamations of praise and joy. "The man who has given this money is a godly man," chanted one leader. Another rose and exclaimed: "The coming to the front of such a princely giver! A man to lead! It is the Lord's doing. God has kept Chicago for us. I wonder at his patience."

> On the following Sabbath throughout the country, sermons of thanksgiving were preached in almost all Baptist pulpits. "When a crisis came," entoned one minister, "God had a man to meet it." "God," cried out another, "has guided us and provided a leader and a giver and so brought us out into a large place." In scores of pulpits the phrase: "Man of God!" was uttered. A writer to the *Independent* said: "No benefaction has ever flowed from a purer Christian source."[1]

[1]Flynn, *God's Gold, op. cit.*, pp. 305, 306.

XVIII

HE WHO PAYS THE PIPER

The low state of medical education in the U.S. prior to 1910; the importance of the Flexner Report in dramatizing the need for reform; the role played by the Rockefeller and Carnegie foundations in implementing the Flexner Report; and the use of foundation funding as a means of gaining control over American medical schools.

There is an old saying: "He who pays the piper calls the tune." This is one of those eternal truths that exist — and always will exist — in business, in politics, *and in education*.

We have seen how John D. Rockefeller captured the hearts of Baptist ministers with a mere $600,000 granted to Chicago University. What remains to be demonstrated is that he also captured control of the university.

Within a year after the grant, Rockefeller's personal choice, Dr. William Rainey Harper, was named president of the institution. And within two years, the teaching staff had been successfully purged of all anti-Rockefeller dissidents. A professor of economics and a professor of literature distinguished themselves by proclaiming that Mr. Rockefeller was "superior in creative genius to Shakespeare, Homer, and Dante."[1]

By comparison, another teacher, a Professor Bemis, was expelled from the staff for "incompetence" when he repeatedly criticized the action of the railroads during the Pullman strike of 1894. A few years later, after the Rockefeller family, through the "philanthropy" of John Archbald, had gained parallel influence at Syracuse University in western New York, an economics instructor by the name of John Cummons was dismissed by the Chancellor for similar reasons.

In 1953, Representative B. Carroll Reece of Tennessee received the authority of Congress to establish a special committee to investigate the power and influence of tax-exempt foundations. The committee never got very far off the ground due to mounting political pressure from multiple sources high within government itself and, eventually,Reece was forced to terminate the committee's work. During its short period of existence, however, many interesting and highly revealing facts were brought to light. Norman Dodd, who was the committee's director of research, and probably one of the country's most knowledgeable authorities on

---

[1]Josephson, *The Robber Barons, op. cit.,* p. 324.

foundations, testified during the hearings and told the committee:

> The result of the development and operation of the network in which the foundations (by their support and encouragement) have played such a significant role, seems to have provided this country with what is tantamount to a national system of education under the tight control of organizations and persons little known to the American public. . . . The curriculum in this tightly controlled scheme of education is designed to indoctrinate the American student from matriculation to the consummation of his education.[1]

Under the careful supervision of Fred Gates, John D. Rockefeller set out consciously and methodically to capture control of American education and particularly of American *medical* education. The process began in 1901 with the creation of the Rockefeller Institute for Medical Research. It included on its board such politically oriented "medical" names as Doctors L. Emmett Holt, Christian A. Herter, T. Mitchell Pruden, Hermann M. Briggs, William H. Welch, Theobald Smith, and Simon Flexner. Christian Herter was slated for bigger things, of course, and became Secretary of State under President Eisenhower. Simon Flexner also was destined for larger success. Al-

[1]As quoted by Weaver, *U.S. Philanthropic Foundations, op. cit.*, pp. 175, 176.

though his name never became as well-known as that of Herter, he and his brother, Abraham Flexner, probably influenced the lives of more people and in a more profound way than has any Secretary of State.

Abraham Flexner was on the staff of the Carnegie Foundation for the Advancement of Teaching. As mentioned previously, the Rockefeller and Carnegie foundations traditionally worked together almost as one in the furtherance of their mutual goals, and this certainly was no exception. The Flexner brothers represented the lens that brought both the Rockefeller and the Carnegie fortunes into sharp focus on the unsuspecting and thoroughly vulnerable medical profession.

Prior to 1910, the practice of medicine in the United States left a great deal to be desired. Some medical degrees could be purchased through the mail and many others could be obtained with marginal training at understaffed and inadequate medical schools. The profession was suffering from a bad public reputation and reform was in the air.

The American Medical Association had begun to take an interest in cleaning its own house. It created a Council on Medical Education for the express purpose of surveying the status of medical training throughout the country and of making specific recommendations for its improvement. But by 1908 it had run into serious difficulty as a result of committee differences and insufficient funding. It was into this void that the Rockefeller-Carnegie combine moved with brilliant strategy and perfect timing. Henry S. Pritchett, the president of the

Carnegie Foundation, approached the AMA and simply offered to take over the entire project. The minutes for the meeting of the AMA's Council on Medical Education held in New York in December of 1908 tell the story:

> At one o'clock an informal conference was held with President Pritchett and Mr. Abraham Flexner of the Carnegie Foundation. Mr. Pritchett had already expressed by correspondence the willingness of the Foundation to cooperate with the Council in investigating the medical schools. He now explained that the Foundation was to investigate all the professions: law, medicine, and theology.[1] . . .
>
> He agreed with the opinion previously expressed by the members of the Council that while the Foundation would be guided very largely by the Council's investigation, to avoid the usual claims of partiality no more mention should be made in the report of the Council than any other source of information. The report would therefore be, and have the weight of, a disinterested body, which would then be published far and wide. It would do much to develop public opinion.[2]

---

[1]This is not the subject of the present study, but the reader should not pass over the fact that exactly the same strategy for control over education was being executed in other key areas as well.

[2]Morris Fishbein, M.D., *A History of the AMA*, (W.B. Saunders Co., Philadelphia & London, 1947), pp. 987, 989.

Here was the classical "philanthropic formula" at work again. Have others pay a major portion of the bill (the AMA had already done most of the work. The total Carnegie investment was only $10,000), reap a large bonus from public opinion (Isn't it wonderful that these men are taking an interest in upgrading medical education!), and gain an opportunity to control a large and vital sphere of American life.

This is how that control came about.

The Flexner Report, as it was called, was published in 1910. As anticipated, it *was* "published far and wide," and it *did* "do much to develop public opinion." The report quite correctly pointed out the inadequacies of medical education at the time. No one could take exception with that. It also proposed a wide range of sweeping changes, most of which were entirely sound. No one could take exception with those, either. The alert researcher will note, however, the recommendations emphatically included the strengthening of courses in *pharmacology* and the addition of *research* departments at all "qualified" medical schools.

And so, the Flexner Report was above reproach and, undoubtedly, it performed a service that was much needed at the time. It is what followed in the *wake* of the report that reveals its true purpose in the total plan. Rockefeller and Carnegie began immediately to shower hundreds of millions of dollars on those better medical schools that were vulnerable to control. Those that did not conform were denied the funds and the prestige that came with those funds, and were forced out of business.

A hundred and sixty schools were in operation in 1905. By 1927, the number had dropped to eighty. True, most of those that were edged out had been sub-standard. But so were some of those that received foundation money and survived. The primary test was not their previous standing but their willingness to accept foundation influence and control.

Historian Joseph Goulden describes the process this way:

> Flexner had the ideas, Rockefeller and Carnegie had the money, and their marriage was spectacular. The Rockefeller Institute for Medical Research and the General Education Board showered money on tolerably respectable schools and on professors who expressed an interest in research.[1]

Since 1910, the foundations have "invested" over a billion dollars in the medical schools of America. Nearly half of the faculty members now receive a portion of their income from foundation "research" grants, and over sixteen percent of them are entirely funded this way. Rockefeller and Carnegie have not been the only source of these funds. Substantial influence also has been exerted by the Ford Foundation, the Kellogg Foundation, the Commonwealth Fund (a Rockefeller interlock created by Edward Harkness of Standard Oil), the Sloan Foundation, and the Macy Foundation. The

---

[1]Goulden, *The Money Givers*, *op. cit.*, p. 141.

Ford Foundation has been extremely active in the field of medical education in recent years, but none of them can compare to the Rockefellers and the Carnegies for sheer money volume and historical continuity.

Joseph C. Hinsey, in his highly authoritative paper entitled "The Role of Private Foundations in the Development of Modern Medicine," reviews the sequence of this expanding influence:

> Starting with Johns Hopkins Medical School in 1913, the General Education Board supported reorganizations which brought about full-time instruction in the clinical as well as the basic science departments of the first two years of medical education at Washington University in St. Louis, at Yale, and at Chicago. In 1923, a grant was made to the University of Iowa in the amount of $2,250,000 by the General Education Board and the Rockefeller Foundation. Similar grants in smaller amounts were made to the following state-supported medical schools: University of Colorado, University of Oregon, University of Virginia, and University of Georgia. An appropriation was made to the University of Cincinnati, an institution which received some of its support from municipal sources. Howard University and the Meharry Medical School were strengthened, the latter by some eight million dollars. The General Education Board and the Rock-

> efeller Foundation later made substantial grants to the medical schools at Harvard, Vanderbilt, Columbia, Cornell, Tulane, Western Reserve, Rochester, Duke, Emory, and the Memorial Hospital in New York affiliated with Cornell.[1]

This list, of course is not complete. It is necessary to add to it the medical schools of Northwestern, Kansas, and Rochester; each heavily endowed, either by Rockefeller money, or by the Commonwealth Fund which is closely aligned with Rockefeller interests.[2]

After Abraham Flexner completed his report, he became one of the three most influential men in American medicine. The other two were his brother, Dr. Simon Flexner of the Rockefeller Institute and Dr. William Welch of Johns Hopkins Medical School and of the Rockefeller Institute. According to Hinsey, these men, acting as "a triumvirate":

> . . . were not only involved in the awarding of grants for the Rockefeller Foundation, but they were counselors to heads of institutions, to lay board members, to members of staffs of medical schools and universities in the United States and abroad. They served as sounding boards, as stimulators of ideas and programs, as mediators in situations of difficulty.[3]

---

[1]Article reprinted in Warren Weaver's *U.S. Philanthropic Foundations, op. cit.*, pp. 264, 265.

[2]*Ibid.*, p. 268.

[3]*Ibid.*, p. 274.

The Association of American Medical Colleges has been one of the principal vehicles of foundation and cartel control over medical education in the United States and Canada. First organized in 1876, it serves the function of setting a wide range of standards for all medical schools. It determines the criteria for selecting medical students, for curriculum development, for programs of continuing medical education after graduation, and for communication within the profession as well as to the general public. The Association of American Medical Colleges, from its inception, has been funded and dominated by the Commonwealth Fund, the China Medical Board (created in 1914 as a division of the Rockefeller Foundation), the Kellogg Foundation, the Macy, Markle, Rockefeller, and Sloan foundations.[1]

By way of analogy, we may say that the foundations captured control of the apex of the pyramid of medical education when they were able to place their own people onto the boards of the various schools and into key administrative positions. The middle of the pyramid was secured by the Association of American Medical Colleges which set standards and unified the curricula. The base of the pyramid, however, was not consolidated until they finally were able to select the teachers themselves. Consequently, a major portion of foundation activity always has been directed toward what generally is called "academic medicine." Since 1913, the foundations have completely pre-empted this field. The Commonwealth Fund reports a half a million

[1]*Ibid.*, pp. 267, 268.

dollars in one year alone appropriated for this purpose, while the Rockefeller Foundation boasts of over twenty thousand fellowships and scholarships for the training of medical instructors.[1]

In *The Money Givers,* Joseph Goulden touches upon this sensitive nerve when he says:

> If the foundations chose to speak, their voice would resound with the solid clang of the cash register. Their expenditures on health and hospitals totalled more than a half-billion dollars between 1964 and 1968, according to a compilation by the American Association of Fund-Raising Counsel. But the foundations' "innovative money" goes for research, not for the production of doctors who treat human beings. Medical schools, realizing this, paint their faces with the hue desired by their customers.[2]

Echoing this same refrain, David Hopgood, writing in the *Washington Monthly,* says:

> The medical school curriculum and its entrance requirements are geared to the highly academic student who is headed for research. In the increasingly desperate struggle for admission, these academically talented students are crowding out those who want to practice medicine.[3]

---

[1]*Ibid.,* pp. 265, 266.

[2]Goulden, *The Money Givers, op. cit.,* p. 144.

[3]"The Health Professionals: Cure or Cause of the Health Crises?" *Washington Monthly,* June, 1969.

And so it has come to pass that the teaching staffs of all our medical schools are a very special breed. In the selection and training process, heavy emphasis always has been put on finding individuals who, because of temperament or special interest, have been attracted by the field of research, and especially by research in pharmacology. This has resulted in loading the staffs of our medical schools with men and women who, by preference and by training, are ideal propagators of the drug-oriented science that has come to dominate American medicine. And the irony of it is that neither they nor their students are even remotely aware that they are products of a rigid selection process geared to hidden commercial objectives. So thorough is their insulation from this fact that, even when exposed to the obvious truth, very few are capable of accepting it, for to do so would be a tremendous blow to their professional pride. Generally speaking, the deeper one is drawn into the medical profession, the more years he has been exposed to its regimens, the more difficult it is to break out of its confines. In practical terms, this simply means that your doctor probably will be the last person on your Christmas card list to accept the facts presented in this study!

Dr. David L. Edsall at one time was the Dean of the Harvard Medical School. The conditions he describes at Harvard are the same as those at every other medical school in America:

> I was, for a period, a professor of therapeutics and pharmacology, and I knew from experience that students were

> obliged then by me and by others to learn about an interminable number of drugs, many of which were valueless, many of them useless, some probably even harmful . . . . Almost all subjects must be taken at exactly the same time, and in almost exactly in the same way by all students, and the amount introduced into each course is such that few students have time or energy to explore any subject in a spirit of independent interest. A little comparison shows that there is less intellectual freedom in the medical course than in almost any other form of professional education in this country.[1]

Yes, he who pays the piper does call the tune. It may not be humanly possible for those who finance the medical schools to determine what is taught in every minute detail. But such is not necessary to achieve the cartel's desired goals. One can be sure, however, that there is *total* control over what is *not* taught, and that, under no circumstances will even one of Rockefeller's shiny dimes ever go to a medical college, to a hospital, to a teaching staff, or to a researcher that holds the unorthodox view that the best medicine is in nature. Because of its generous patron, orthodoxy always will fiddle a tune of man-made drugs. Whatever basic nutrition may be allowed into the melody will be minimal at best, and it will be played over and

---

[1]As quoted by Morris A. Bealle, *The New Drug Story,* (Columbia Publishing Co., Wash. D.C., 1958), pp. 19, 20.

over again that *natural* sources of vitamins are in no way superior to those that are man-made or synthesized. The day when orthodox medicine finally embraces the field of nutrition will be the day when the cartel behind it also has monopolized the vitamin and food product industry essential to it — not one day before.

In the meantime, while doctors are forced to spend hundreds of hours studying the names and actions of all kinds of man-made drugs, they are lucky if they receive even a portion of a single course on basic nutrition. Many have none at all. The result is that the average doctor's wife or secretary knows more about practical nutrition than he does.

Returning to the main theme, however, we find that the cartel's influence over the field of orthodox medicine is felt far beyond the medical schools. After the doctor has struggled his way through ten or twelve years of learning what the cartels have decided is best for him to learn, he then goes out into the world of medical practice and immediately is embraced by the other arm of cartel control — The American Medical Association.

So let us turn, now, to that part of this continuing story.

XIX

HE WHO CALLS THE TUNE

AMA influence over the practice of medicine in America; the means by which the leadership of the AMA keeps control away from the general membership; the extent to which the AMA is financed by the drug industry; and examples of interlock between the two.

The American Medical Association climbed into bed with the Rockefeller and Carnegie interests in 1908 for the praiseworthy purpose of upgrading American medicine. Like the young lady who compromised her virtue "just this once" to pay for a needed operation for her ailing mother, the AMA has been sharing its sheets ever since.

The impact of this organization on the average physician is probably greater than even he recognizes. First of all, the medical student cannot obtain an M.D. degree except at a school that has been accredited by the AMA. He must serve an internship only at a hospital that meets AMA standards as a teaching institution. If he decides to become a specialist, his residency must conform to AMA requirements. His license to practice is issued in accordance with state laws worked out by AMA leaders. To prove his standing as an ethical practitioner he must apply to and be accepted by his county and state societies in conformity with AMA procedures. AMA publications provide him with continuing education in the form of scientific articles, research findings, reviews and abstracts from medical books, question and answer discussions of clinical problems, evaluations of new drugs, foods, and appliances, authoritative essays, editorials, letters to the editor, and a hundred similar appeals to his intellectual understanding of the profession he practices. At the AMA's week-long convention each year, the physician is exposed to what is called "a complete post-graduate education under one roof." If he has the interest and the stamina, he can attend his choice of hundreds of lectures, exhibits, and demonstrations, watch closed-circuit color videotapes, see the latest medical films, and carry home a suitcase full of pamphlets, books, and especially free drug samples.

As Richard Carter explained in his critical work entitled *The Doctor Business:*

> On the national level, the AMA extended its authority far beyond the medical schools. As custodian of medical standards, it began determining the eligibility of hospitals to train new physicians. It gave authoritative advice on the training of nurses and technicians. It was influen-

> tial in the passage of pure food and drug legislation, exposure of unscientific remedies, and stigmatization of cultism and quackery.[1]

The AMA spends millions of dollars per year for television programs to affect public opinion, maintains one of the richest and most active lobbies in Washington, spends many millions in support of favored political candidates, is instrumental in the selection of the Commissioner of the Food and Drug Administration, and . . . well, let us just say that the AMA is a substantial force in American medicine.

Who controls the AMA? Most people would assume that the dues-paying members control their own association, but nothing could be further from the truth.

TheAMA was founded in 1847 primarily through the efforts of three men: Dr. George Simmons, Dr. J. N. McCormack, and a Dr. Reed. Simmons was really the driving force behind the organization in those early days, acting as general manager, but McCormack and Reed shared in a great deal of the association's work including legislative lobbying. Simmons is particularly interesting because he headed the AMA's drive against so-called diploma mills, yet, it is said that he had obtained his own medical degree through the mail from the Rush Medical School.

---

[1]Carter, *The Doctor Business,* (Doubleday & Co., N.Y., 1958) pp. 78, 79.

One does not have to be a good physician, of course, to run a medical association. In fact, a man with a busy personal medical practice seldom becomes involved with the leadership of the AMA simply because he doesn't have the time to spare, and, as often is the case, the temperament and dedication that are required for success in the practice of medicine are not the same as required for success in running large membership organizations. For this reason, the AMA, from its very inception, has been dominated by untypical physicians: men who enjoy the limelight and the thrill of accomplishment through medical politics. The typical physician, by comparison, is not only baffled by the intrigue and maneuvering for position behind the scenes, but wants no part of it for himself. He is more than content to leave the affairs of his association in the hands of those who enjoy the game.

The deceptive appearance of democracy is preserved through the AMA House of Delegates, which meets twice a year. Reference committees are formed for the purpose of making recommendations on the various resolutions submitted by state delegates or by the National Board of Trustees. But, following the pattern of political parties, the leadership maintains firm control over these resolutions by having the members of the reference committees appointed by the Speaker of the House, not by the delegates. The committees are firmly stacked to carry out the will of the leadership. Those occasional innocents who are appointed for protective coloration usually are bewildered and overwhelmed.

One delegate who found himself lost in the maze complained:

> It's difficult to make a sensible contribution to the work. If you're on a reference committee, all those resolutions are tossed in your lap and you can't make head or tail of the situation because you don't have time. The committee has not met before, has had no opportunity for advance study of the major issues, and is disbanded right after the convention, so the whole thing is kind of ephemeral. Your problem is solved, though, because a member of the Board of Trustees is always present at the committee meeting to "clarify" the issues for you. In the old days it used to be even worse. Until a few years ago, none of the resolutions was presented in writing. You had to sit and listen to every word, and there were times when you found yourself voting for the exact opposite of what you thought you were voting for.[1]

The president of the AMA is a mere figurehead. He has absolutely no administrative or executive duties. His primary function is to deliver talks to various groups around the country explaining the program and goals of the Association. The position primarily is an honorary one, and it is not part of the AMA's permanent leadership.

[1]*Ibid.*, pp. 73, 74.

If any members or delegates should become dissatisfied with their leadership, there is practically no way for them to make a change. In order to do so would require a concerted campaign among the other delegates to support a whole new slate of executive officers. But even that remote possibility has been effectively blocked. There is a standing rule, adopted in 1902, that reads,

> The solicitation of votes for office is not in keeping with the dignity of the medical profession, nor in harmony with the spirit of this Association, and . . . shall be considered a disqualification for election to any office in the gift of this Association.

It is through tactics like these that the AMA perpetuates dictatorial control over its members while wearing the mask of democratic response to the will of the majority.

Of course, not all physicians are blind to these facts. The AMA dictatorship was pointed out as long ago as 1922 in the December issue of the *Illinois Medical Journal,* the house organ of the Illinois Medical Society. In a scathing article entitled "The AMA Becomes An Autocracy," the journal charged that the AMA was a dictatorship organization run by one man, that it had ignored the democratic will of the membership, that it concerned itself with building a financial empire to benefit those who control it, and that it does not serve the doctors who support it with their dues and reputations.

Since 1922 the state medical journals have become financially interlocked with the *AMA Journal,* so there no longer is any possibility of publishing such harsh views. But the discontent continues. Doctors may not realize exactly who controls the AMA or why, but they increasingly are becoming aware that the organization does not represent *them*. By 1969, the AMA membership had stopped growing, and by 1970, it actually had declined. As of 1971, less than half of all physicians in the United States were paying dues.

If AMA members or delegates do not control their organization, then who does? Who constitutes this "dictatorship" to which the *Illinois Medical Journal* has referred?

The structure and operating procedures of the AMA were well conceived to put total control of that organization into the hands of the one man who occupies the chief full-time staff position. Although supposedly hired by the AMA as its employee, actually he is beyond reach of the general membership because of his inside knowledge, his ability to devote unlimited time to the task, and his powerful influence in the selection of members of the self-perpetuating Board of Trustees. But he holds even a more powerful sword than that over the head of the organization because he also is the man who is responsible for bringing in the money. The AMA could not survive on membership dues alone, and without the income secured by him, the Association would undoubtedly flounder.

The key to financial solvency for the organization has been its monthly publication, the *AMA Journal*. It was begun in 1883 by Dr. Simmons as a last ditch effort to save the infant association from bankruptcy. Its first press run was 3,500 copies and sold at a subscription rate of five dollars per year. But it was anticipated that the great bulk of the revenue would be derived from advertisers. By 1973, under the tight control of Managing Editor Dr. Morris Fishbein, it had a print order of almost 200,000 copies each month and had extended its publication list to include twelve separate journals including the layman's monthly, *Today's Health*.[1] Altogether the AMA now derives over ten million dollars per year in advertising, which is almost *half* of the Association's total income.

Who advertises in the *AMA Journal* and related publications? The lion's share is derived from the Pharmaceutical Manufacturer's Association whose members make up ninety-five percent of the American drug industry.

Morris Fishbein had become a lot more to the AMA than his title of Managing Editor would suggest. He was its chief executive and business manager. He brought in the money and he determined how it was to be spent. His investments on behalf of the Association have been extremely profitable, so the grateful membership could not, or at least dared not, complain too bitterly. One of the reasons for this investment success was that over ten million

---

[1]This magazine has been particularly vicious in its attack against vitamin B_{17} cancer therapy. See "The Pain Exploiters; The Victimizing of Desperate Cancer Patients," *Today's Health*, Nov., 1973, p. 28.

dollars of the organization's retirement fund has been put into leading drug companies.[1]

In later years, much of the executive control of the AMA has been wielded by Joe Miller, the Assistant Executive Vice President. Formerly an administrator of the government health program for Kentucky and an influential associate of the Lyndon Johnson-Bobby Baker group, Miller is viewed by many as a man who is totally devoid of any political ideology, merely playing his role for whatever personal gain or power he can derive. As such, he would be a perfect set-up for the pharmaceutical cartel with its extensive financial support of AMA programs. Either way, there is little doubt that the success of the AMA and those who direct it depends in more ways than one on the prosperity and good will of the pharmaceutical industry.

Item: In 1972 the AMA's Council on Drugs completed an exhaustive study of most of the commonly available compounds then in general use. The long awaited evaluation hit like an unexpected bomb. The Council reported that some of the most profitable drugs on pharmacy shelves were "irrational" and that they could not be recommended. And to add insult to injury, the chairman and vice-chairman of the Council stated before a Senate subcommittee that the large income derived from the various drug manufacturers had made the AMA "a captive arm and beholden to the pharmaceutical industry." The AMA responded by abolishing its

[1] "AMA Says It Owns $10 Million in Drug Shares," (UPI), *News Chronicle* (Calif.), June 27, 1973, p. 4.

Council on Drugs. The reason given was "an economy move."[1]

Item: AMA spokesman, Dr. David B. Allman, clarified one of the prime directives of his organization when he said:

> Both the medical profession and pharmacy must shoulder one major public relations objective: to tell the American people over and over that nearly all of today's drugs, especially the antibiotics, are bargains at any price.[2]

Item: While placating its member physicians with press releases and much public gesturing against government intervention in the field of medicine, the AMA has been one of the most effective forces behind the scenes to bring about just the opposite. Under the beguiling excuse of "Let us defeat *total* socialized medicine by promoting *partial* socialized medicine," it has provided the model legislation for the nation's largest single step toward total government control ever taken in this area.

The legislation is known as Public Law 92-603, passed by Congress and signed by President Nixon on October 30, 1972. It is more commonly referred to as PSRO, which stands for Professional Standards Review Organization. PSRO authorizes the Department of Health, Education and Welfare to create both a national and a series of regional

---

[1] "Crossing the Editor's Desk," *National Health Federation Bulletin*, Oct., 1973, p. 30.

[2] Carter, *The Doctor Business, op. cit.*, p. 141.

boards for the purpose of "reviewing" the professional activities of all doctors in the United States. The men on these boards are to be doctors also, but they will be selected or approved by the government; they must follow standards set down by government agencies. These government boards are authorized to compel all doctors to standardize their procedures, treatments *and prescriptions,* to conform with those federal standards. All previously confidential patient records are to be available to the government boards for inspection. Doctors who do not comply can be suspended from practice or fined up to $5,000.

At the time of its passage, PSRO applied only to those doctors and patients who were participating in the hospital medical care provision of the Social Security Act, but it was clearly understood that if these provisions were extended to more of the population — as they generally have been each year — PSRO automatically would follow.

And this entire scheme was drafted by the AMA Legal Department, submitted to Congress as part of its "Medicredit" bill, and never even approved by the AMA House of Delegates or its membership.

There are many more equally revealing items, of course, but time and space call us back to our point of departure. It is undeniable that the foundations and the financial-industrial forces behind them have performed a great service in helping to elevate the American medical profession above the relatively low level of prestige and technical competence it endured in 1910. It is probable, however, that the profession, in time, would have done so by itself, and it is certain that it would have been far better off if it had. The price it has paid for listening to the siren call of money has been too high. It has allowed itself to be lured onto the reef of a new medieval dogmatism in medicine — a dogmatism that forces all practitioners into a compliance with holy pronouncements of scientific truth — a dogmatism that has closed the door on the greatest scientific advance of the Twentieth Century.

XX

THE PROTECTION RACKET

Cartel agents in the federal government; the CFR examined as a parallel structure for cartel control over U.S. foreign policy; cartel influence within the FDA; examples of FDA scientific ineptitude; and the growth of FDA's administrative power.

In 1970, Dr. Herbert Ley made a statement that, coming from a lesser source, easily could be dismissed as the rantings of an uninformed malcontent. Considering that Dr. Ley is a former Commissioner of the Food and Drug Administration, however, his words cannot be brushed aside so lightly. He said:

> The thing that bugs me is that the people think the FDA is protecting them. It isn't. What the FDA is doing and what the public *thinks* it's doing are as different as night and day.[1]

[1]*San Francisco Chronicle*, Jan. 2, 1970, as quoted in *Autopsy On The A.M.A.*, (Student Research Facility, Berkeley, 1970), p. 42.

What *is* the FDA doing? As will be shown by the material that follows, the FDA is "doing" three things:

> First, it is providing a means whereby key individuals on its payroll are able to obtain both power and wealth through granting special favors to certain politically influential groups that are subject to its regulations. This activity is similar to the "protection racket" of organized crime: for a price, one can induce FDA administrators to provide "protection" from the FDA itself.
>
> Secondly, as a result of this political favoritism, the FDA has become a primary factor in that formula whereby cartel-oriented companies in the food and drug industry are able to use the police powers of government to harass or destroy their free-market competitors.
>
> And thirdly, the FDA occasionally does some genuine public good with whatever energies it has left over after serving the vested political and commercial interest of its first two activities.

A brief backward glance at the total landscape will help us to appreciate more fully the present extent of cartel influence, not only in the FDA, but at all levels of the federal government, for it is an historical fact that the centers of political power long have been the easy target of cartel penetration and control.

Previously we have outlined the degree to which it succeeded in placing its friends and agents into such areas of government as the office of the Alien Property Custodian, the Attorney-General's office, the State Department and the White House itself. In addition to the list of names formerly mentioned, however, there also must be included such government dignitaries as Secretary of State Dean Rusk (head of the Rockefeller Foundation, as was John Foster Dulles); Secretary of the Treasury Douglas Dillon (a member of the board of the Chase Manhattan Bank); Director of the U.S. International Bank for Reconstruction and Development, Eugene Black (Second Vice-President and Director of Chase Manhattan); President of the U.N. World Bank, John J. McCloy (Chairman of the Board of Chase Manhattan, and trustee of the Rockefeller Foundation, and Chairman of the Executive Committee for Squibb Pharmaceutical);[1] Senator Nelson Aldrich (whose daughter married John D. Rockefeller, Jr., and whose son, Winthrop, became Chairman of the Chase National Bank and Ambassador to Great Britain); President Nixon and Attorney-General John Mitchell (Rockefeller Wall Street attorneys for such drug firms as Warner-Lambert); and many

[1]McCloy had been Assistant Secretary of War from April 1941 to November 1945. As High Commissioner in West Germany after the war, he was instrumental in making Konrad Adenauer, his brother-in-law, Chancellor of West Germany. He also was Chairman of the Board of the Ford Foundation and chief U.S. disarmament negotiator.

others far too numerous to mention by name. But the list of men who are or were in key positions within the Rockefeller group reads like a "Who's Who in Government."

The extent of hidden Rockefeller influence within the federal government can be approximated by noting that David Rockefeller is Chairman of the Council on Foreign Relations and that the CFR is sustained financially through grants from the Rockefeller foundations, the Carnegie fund and similarly interlocked tax-exempt foundations.

The CFR is semi-secret in its operation. It shuns publicity and members are sworn not to disclose to the public the proceedings of its conferences and briefings. It has a formal membership of approximately sixteen hundred elite personalities.

In *Harper's* magazine for July, 1958, there is an article entitled "School for Statesmen," written by CFR member Joseph Kraft. Boasting that membership in this obscure organization had become the magic key that opens the door of appointments to high government posts, Kraft explained that, even then, CFR membership included:

> . . . the President, the Secretary of State, the Chairman of the Atomic Energy Commission, the Director of the Central Intelligence Agency, the Board chairmen of three of the country's five largest industrial corporations, two of the four richest insurance companies, and two of the three biggest banks, plus the senior partners of two of the three leading Wall

> Street law firms, the publishers of the two biggest news magazines and of the country's most influential newspaper, and the presidents of the Big Three in both universities and foundations, as well as a score of other college presidents and a scattering of top scientists and journalists.

Rockefeller's CFR, from behind the scenes, has dominated this nation for decades. CFR members include top executives and journalists for the *New York Times,* the *Washington Post,* the *Chicago Daily News,* the *Christian Science Monitor, Harper's, Look, Time, Life, Newsweek, U.S. News and World Report,* the *Encyclopedia Britannica,* CBS, NBC, MGM, the Motion Picture Association of America; they include directors of the Ford Foundation, the Rockefeller Foundation, the Carnegie Endowment Fund, the Kettering Foundation and the Sloan Kettering Institute for Cancer Research; they include Presidents Hoover, Eisenhower, Johnson, and Nixon;[1] Secretaries of State Stettinius, Acheson, Dulles, Herter, Rusk, and Kissinger; a fantastic percentage of the President's Cabinet, Under-Secretaries, the Fed-

[1]According to Dan Smoot's excellent study of the CFR entitled *The Invisible Government,* President Kennedy also had been a member. The basis for this claim is a personal letter from the president in which it is said that he claimed membership. I have not seen this letter, however, and the CFR staff, in a letter to me dated June 11, 1971, stated flatly: "the facts of the matter are that President Kennedy was invited to join the Council but, insofar as our records indicate, never accepted that invitation either formally or informally through the payment of membership dues." In view of this, I felt it was best to omit President Kennedy's name from the list, which is impressive enough without it.

eral Reserve Board, Ambassadors to other countries, Supreme Court Justices, and presidential advisors. Over one hundred CFR members were appointed to key government posts under the Nixon administration alone. And remember, the entire organization has only sixteen hundred members. Yes, as Joseph Kraft boasted in his "School for Statesmen" article in *Harper's,* this organization, dominated by Rockefeller as chairman of the board, and by Rockefeller's economic dependents at all levels of control, has indeed become the unofficial training camp and personnel placement agency for practically all positions within the federal government — especially those that relate to U.S. foreign policy and world government. The average person has never heard of the CFR, yet it is a major part of the unseen government of the United States.[1]

The other part, of course, is more concerned with domestic affairs than foreign affairs and reaches into every branch of the federal government. The FDA, which we now will examine in detail, is merely one example of the success of that penetration and control. What will be shown as true with the FDA could be duplicated in every other agency as well.

Let us begin by acknowledging that which is obvious. The FDA could not have achieved nor maintained the public confidence it now enjoys if it did not occasionally do some real good. The record on this point is quite clear. The FDA has nipped

---

[1]For more information about the CFR, read *The Capitalist Conspiracy* by G. Edward Griffin (American Media, Thousand Oaks, Calif., 1971); also, *The Invisible Government* by Dan Smoot (Western Islands, Belmont, Mass., 1962).

many a medical racket in the bud and has clamped down on numerous firms that had been guilty of unsanitary processing, of selling putrid or contaminated food and of distributing adulterated or misbranded drugs. In this it deserves to be commended for its diligence. As we shall see, however, this showcase aspect of the FDA record pales by comparison to its other record of ineptitude and outright corruption.

In March of 1972, after repeated inquiries from concerned Congressmen, the FDA made public its official cleanliness standards as applied to the food processing industry. To everyone's horror it was learned that the FDA allows approximately one rodent pellet per pint of wheat, ten fly eggs per eight and a half ounce can of fruit juice, and fifty insect fragments or two rodent hairs for three and a half ounces of peanut butter.[1]

For years, the FDA defended the use of the hormone Diethylstilbestrol (DES) as an artificial fattening agent for cattle. Then, after the evidence became too overwhelming to ignore, it was finally banned because even trace amounts of this substance as residue in the meat was shown to be a possible factor in inducing cancer in those humans who consumed it.[2] But the same week that it banned DES from the cattle to make sure that even trace amounts could not find their way into human consumption, it gave its approval to the "morning-

---

[1]*Consumer Reports,* March, 1973, p. 152.

[2]Incidentally, DES is an artificial female sex hormone. The logic for the higher incidence of cancer is implicit in the important role played by estrogen in the trophoblastic thesis of cancer. Here is just one more grain of evidence added to the mountain.

after contraceptive" — a pill containing a full fifty milligrams of the drug and to be taken daily for five days. As one cattleman commented bitterly: "It turns out that a woman would have to eat 262 tons of beef liver to get the same amount of DES as the FDA makes legal for the next-morning medication."[1]

Although the subject is not yet totally free from its share of controversy, it is now widely recognized, both in and out of the medical profession, that there is a definite relationship between heart attacks and high cholesterol diets. With each passing year, the clinical evidence to support this view continues to grow. But evidence does not daunt the king's soothsayers at the FDA whose official position on cholesterol, even as late as 1965, was this:

> Any claim, direct or implied, in the labeling of fats or oils . . . that they prevent or mitigate or cure diseases of the heart or arteries, is false or misleading, and constitutes misbranding within the meaning of the Federal Food, Drug and Cosmetic Act.[2]

There are approximately 2,500 chemical additives currently being used by the food industry for the purpose of flavoring, coloring, preserving, and generally altering the characteristics of its pro-

---

[1] "On Science," by David O. Woodbury, *Review of the News,* June 13, 1973, p. 27.

[2] Hearings Before the Senate Subcommittee on Administrative Practices and Procedures, 1965, Part 2.

ducts. The safety factor on most of these has not been determined — or even investigated — by the FDA.[1] As in the case of DES, the evidence is strong that many of them are harmful, particularly if consumed over a prolonged period of time. The FDA response to this situation is extremely interesting. Instead of rushing into battle to "protect the people," as it has done in the case of those "dangerous" health foods and vitamins, it warmly embraces and defends the cartel food processors and chemical firms that otherwise might be damaged by loss of markets.

The following statements, taken directly from official FDA "Fact Sheets,"[2] tell the story with no need of further comment:

> In general, there is little difference between fresh and processed foods. Modern processing methods retain most vitamin and mineral values . . . .

> Nutrition Research has shown that a diet containing white bread made with enriched flour has nearly the same value as one containing whole grain bread . . . .

> Chemical fertilizers are not poisoning our soil. Modern fertilizers are needed to produce enough food for our population . . . .

---

[1] "Food Additives," *Scientific American,* March, 1972, p. 20.

[2] Fact Sheets for July, 1971 and CSS-F11 for Nov. 1971.

> When pesticides on food crops leave a residue, FDA and the Environmental Protection Agency (EPA) make sure the amount will be safe for consumers . . . .[1]

> Vitamins are specific chemical compounds, and the human body can use them equally well whether they are synthesized by a chemist or by nature .

In November of 1971, the FDA issued a "Fact Sheet" on the subject of "quackery." It says:

> The term "quackery" encompasses both people and products . . . . Broadly speaking, quackery is misinformation about health.

If the preceeding hogwash about DES, cholesterol and the glories of processed foods, chemical fertilizers, pesticides, and synthetic vitamins is not "misinformation about health," then there is *nothing* that could be so labeled!

The *Oxford Universal Dictionary* defines a quack as "one who professes knowledge concerning subjects of which he is ignorant." By either definition, FDA spokesmen are the biggest quacks the world has ever seen, and it's about time that the American people began to recognize them as such.

---

[1]The reader is reminded that the chemical fertilizer and pesticide industries are, like the drug industry, but subsidiaries of the larger cartelized chemical and petroleum industries.

There is an important distinction between a quack and a charlatan. A quack may be presumed an honest man who truly *thinks* he is helping his patients. A charlatan, on the other hand, is fully aware of the inadequacy of both his knowledge and his treatment. A man, therefore, can be a quack, or both a quack *and* a charlatan.

Unfortunately, there is a lot more than mere quackery within the FDA.

In 1960, during the much publicized investigation of the drug industry conducted by the Senate, it was revealed that many top FDA officials had been receiving extra-curricular financial "incentives" from some of the very companies they were supposed to regulate. For example, Dr. Henry Welch, director of the FDA Antibiotic Division, had been paid $287,000 in kick-backs (he called them "honorariums") that were derived from a percentage of drug advertising secured for leading medical journals. His superiors were fully aware of this conflict of interest but did nothing to terminate it. It was only after the fact was made public and caused embarrassment to the administration that Welch was asked to resign.

In 1940, an incident occurred that, had it been widely publicized, perhaps would have shocked the nation into realizing that the FDA was not protecting the people, but was protecting the cartelists instead. It was at that time that Winthrop Chemical was under fire for shipping 400,000 tablets labelled as "Sulfathiazole," which were found later to contain five grains of Luminal each. One or two grains of Luminal puts people to sleep. Five grains puts some of them to sleep *permanently*. These tablets are known to have killed seventeen victims in various parts of the country. Winthrop Chemical failed to notify the public immediately of the fatally poisonous character of the pills. Instead, the company, with the aid and approval of the A.M.A. Council on Pharmacy and Chemistry of the American Medical Association, continued to push the sale of the Sulfathiazole pills, thus increasing the number of fatalities. The FDA was sympathetic toward Winthrop Chemical and extremely helpful. Exercising their bureaucratic powers, Dr. Klumpp, head of the FDA drug division, and his superior, FDA Commissioner Campbell, refrained from prosecuting for the deaths. They helped to hush up the matter and merely revoked Winthrop's license to ship Sulfathiazole for three months, after the market had been glutted with the product. The suspension of shipment for three months was an utterly meaningless gesture. Commenting on this revolting episode, Ambruster adds:

> Dr. Klumpp, by this time, had moved onward and upward. He had accepted a position awarded him by Dr. Fishbein and became Director of the A.M.A. division on food and drugs and secretary of its Council on Pharmacy and Chemistry (the same council that had "accepted" Winthrop's Sulfathiazole and approved its advertising). And Dr. Klumpp kept moving. Not long thereafter, Edward S.

> Rogers, chairman of the Board of Sterling Products, announced that Dr. Klumpp had been elected president of Winthrop.[1]

Some years later, an antibiotic drug by the name of Chloramphenicol was manufactured and distributed by Parke-Davis and Company. Shortly after its release, reports began to appear in the medical literature to the effect that Chloramphenicol was responsible for blood toxicity and leukopenia (reduction of the white blood cells), and that it had caused several deaths from aplastic anemia.

The man who was director of the FDA's Bureau of Medicine at that time — and the man who could have ordered Parke-Davis to withdraw this drug from the market — was Dr. Joseph F. Sadusk. Instead of clamping down on Parke-Davis, however, Sadusk used his official position to *prevent* the drug from being recalled, and even ruled against requiring a precautionary label.

Finally, in 1969, after the drug had earned a substantial profit for its producer, and after it had been replaced by a newer product, Parke-Davis was allowed to get off the hook merely by sending a letter to all physicians stating that chloramphenicol was no longer the drug of choice for any of the infections it originally had been designed to cure.

Soon afterward, Dr. Sadusk left the FDA, supposedly to work at his alma mater, Johns Hopkins University. But, within the year, the pay-off

[1] Ambruster, *Treason's Peace, op. cit.*, p. 213.

was complete: He became vice-president of Parke-Davis and Company.

Dr. Sadusk's successor was Dr. Joseph M. Pisani who shortly resigned to work for The Proprietary Association, the trade association that represents the manufacturers of non-prescription drugs — a major part of the very industry Dr. Pisani had "regulated."

Dr. Pisani was replaced by Dr. Robert J. Robinson, whose stay was even shorter than that of his predecessor. He became a top executive at Hoffman-La Roche, a leading manufacturer of prescription drugs.

Omar Garrison, in his splendidly researched book, *The Dictocrats*, continues the list:

> Dr. Howard Cohn, former head of FDA's medical evaluation, who made a profitable transition from the agency to Ciba Pharmaceutical Company;
>
> Dr. Harold Anderson, chief of FDA's division of anti-infective drugs, who terminated his government employment to take a position with Winthrop Laboratories;
>
> Morris Yakowitz, who felt that a job with Smith, Kline and French Laboratories would offer greater personal rewards than his post as head of case supervision for FDA; and

> Allen E. .Rayfield, former director of Regulatory Compliance, who chucked his enforcement duties (including electronic spying) to become a consultant to Richardson-Merrell, Inc.[1]

In 1964, under pressure from Congress, the FDA released a list of its officials who, during the preceding five years, had left the agency for employment in industry. Out of the eight hundred and thirteen names appearing on that list, eighty-three — better than ten percent — had taken positions with companies they previously regulated. Many of these people, of course, were from the very top FDA echelons of management — men who were charged with making decisions and issuing directives. Not only that, while these men were with the FDA, they had access to extensive information regarding the research and processes of all companies. When they went to work for *one* of those companies, therefore, there is no reason why they couldn't have taken that information with them which, quite obviously, could put the firm that hired them at a tremendous advantage over its competitors.

Here, again, we find the classic pattern of government bureaucratic power being used, not for the protection of the people as is its excuse for being, but for the aggrandizement of individuals holding that power and for the elimination of honest competition in the market place. The voters

[1]*Op. cit.*, pp. 70, 71.

approve one extension of government power after another always in the naive expectation that, somehow, they will benefit. But, in the end, they inevitably find themselves merely supporting a larger bureaucracy through increased taxes, paying higher prices for their consumer goods and losing one more chunk of personal freedom.

There are almost no exceptions to this rule, as will be obvious if one but reflects for a moment on the results of government entry into such areas of economic activity as prices and wages, energy conservation, environmental protection, health care and so on.

As the Frenchman, Frederic Bastiat, observed well over a hundred years ago, once government is allowed to expand beyond its prime role of protecting the lives, liberty and property of its citizens; once it invades the market place and attempts to redistribute the nation's wealth or resources, inevitably it falls into the hands of those who will use it for "legalized plunder." There is no better way to describe the governments of the world today—and the government of the United States is no exception.

The FDA was added to the ever-lengthening list of government regulatory agencies in 1906, largely as a result of the crusading efforts of a government chemist by the name of Harvey Washington Wiley. Spurred on largely by the organized dairy industry which wanted the government to pass laws which would hinder competition from non-dairy substitutes, Wiley became nationally famous through his books and speeches against "fraud and poison" in our food. Pioneering the pattern that was followed many years later by Ralph Nader, Wiley succeeded in drumming up tremendous support from both the public and in Congress for government regulation and "protection." The result was the Pure Food and Drug Act of 1906 which created the FDA and gave it wide powers over the food and drug industries. Wiley became its first director.

The first major revision of the Food and Drug Act came in 1938 as a result of a fatal blunder made by the chief chemist at the S.E. Massengill Company of Tennessee. The previous year, one hundred and seven people — mostly children — had died from ingesting an anti-biotic substance known as "Elixir of Sulfanilamide." The chemist had tested the compound for appearance, flavor and fragrance, but had not tested it for safety.

The attendant publicity resulted in public acceptance of increased powers to the FDA requiring all drug manufacturers to test each new compound for safety and to submit the results of those tests to the agency for approval prior to marketing. The FDA also was empowered to remove from the market any existing substance it believed to be unsafe.

From a strictly theoretical point of view, the first part of this law was beyond reproach, but the second part was a colossal mistake. It is logical to require a food or drug manufacturer to take reasonable steps to insure the safety of his product. It is also logical to require him to place appropriate warnings on his product labels where there is a possibility that its improper use could result in harm. But to give a government agency the power to prohibit the marketing of a substance because it feels it is unsafe — this was the crack in the dike that eventually destroyed the barrier against the rushing floodwaters of favoritism and corruption. After all, *most* drugs could be removed from the shelves on the truthful assertion that they are unsafe; and, as we have seen, the process by which some are removed and others allowed to remain is not always a scientific one.

As *Science* magazine reported:

> The FDA is not a happy place for scientists to work . . . . Several researchers showed the students [who were gathering data on the FDA] atrocity logs in which they kept detailed accounts of assaults on their scientific integrity . . . . The most common complaint was that the FDA "constantly interferes" with medium and long-range research projects, at least partly from fear that the results will embarrass the agency. The students also criticized the FDA for retaliating against scientists who disagree with its position.[1]

Granting the government the power to suppress products because of allegedly being "unsafe" was bad enough. But it was nothing compared to the

---

[1] "Nader's Raiders on the FDA: Science and Scientists 'Misused' " *Science*, April 17, 1970, pp. 349-352.

fiasco that was enshrined into law as the Kefauver-Harris amendments to the Food and Drug Act on October 10, 1962. Following in the wake of the publicity given to the deformed babies born to European mothers who had taken the drug thalidomide, the new law gave the FDA the power to eliminate any drug product that it claimed was *ineffective* as well!

The thalidomide scare, of course, had absolutely no bearing on the new law. First of all, thalidomide was not being used in the United States. And secondly, the birth defects were not caused by a lack of the drug's "effectiveness," but lack of adequate testing to determine "safety" and long-range side effects.[1]

It is almost impossible to prove that any particular drug is effective. What will work for one may not work for another. The test of effectiveness often is a subjective evaluation on the part of the user. Effectiveness can be determined only by the patient either alone or with consultation with his physician. Putting such power into the hands of political appointees with their almost unbroken record of corruption throughout the years is sheer madness. And, as we shall see in a following chapter, it is precisely this aspect of the "protection racket" that has prevented Laetrile from being

---

[1]Incidentally, thalidomide has since been shown to be highly effective in the treatment of leprosy patients and has been credited with saving many lives. But, because of government restrictions on its manufacture and use, many leprosy patients are being denied the drug which, to them, could mean the difference between life and death. See "Thalidomide Combats Leprosy," (AP), *Boston Globe*, June 29, 1969, p. 50. Also, "Horror Drug Thalidomide Now Used to Save Lives of Leprosy Patients," *National Enquirer,* Nov. 25, 1973, p. 50.

available in the United States and, thus, has been responsible for the needless suffering and death of millions.

Perhaps it should be mentioned just for the record — although it should be obvious without saying — that by far most of the employees of the FDA are honest and conscientious citizens who are not participants in fraud, corruption, or favoritism. Most of these people, however, are at the lower echelons and have practically no voice in the policies of the agency they serve. But the higher one climbs within the structure, the greater become the temptations, and the very highest positions of all are reserved for those who have demonstrated their talents, not in the field of science where truth is king, but in the field of politics where truth, often as not, is chained in the deepest dungeon as a dangerous enemy to the throne.

The result of concentrated government power, however, is almost as deadly when wielded by honest men as it is in the hands of those who are dishonest. This point was brought home quite convincingly by Lynn Kinsky and Robert Poole in an analysis prepared by them for *Reason* magazine. Discussing the impossibility of determining drug "effectiveness *vs.* ineffectiveness" for populations as a whole, they wrote:

> The uppermost concern of the bureaucratic mind is rules and procedures expressed in countless official forms and paperwork. The inference, in the FDA's case, is that if the bureaucrat does not know how to ensure that a drug is "effec-

> tive," the next best thing is to require such a mountain of paperwork that the bureaucrat is "covered" at every possible turn. As a result, since the FDA began requiring "effectiveness" documentation, the length of time it takes to get a New Drug Application processed has tripled. Preparing the monumental paperwork adds millions of dollars to a drug firm's research budget — which has the effect of discouraging smaller (perhaps more innovative) firms from even attempting to get new drugs approved.[1]

It bears repeating that the FDA could not long maintain public confidence if it did not occasionally go after a few genuine villains. Generally speaking, however, these culprits turn out to be individuals or relatively small-time operators. The industrial giants often are guilty of the same offenses, but the FDA extends to them an unofficial favored status. One of the reasons for this double standard is that the larger companies have the financial resources to challenge the FDA's actions in the courts, a procedure that often reveals the shabbiness of the agency's work, thus damaging its public image. Since the FDA is especially interested in the favorable publicity resulting from its efforts to "protect the people," it quite naturally prefers to pick on the little guy who cannot afford to fight back.

---

[1]"The Impact of FDA Regulations on Drug Research in America Today," by Lynn Kinsky and Robert Poole, *Reason,* Vol. 2, No. 9, reprint, pp. 9, 10.

In 1962, for example, the FDA, in cooperation with state health officials, seized a supply of safflower oil capsules in a small Detroit store on the basis that they were being used to promote the book, *Calories Don't Count,* by Herman Taller, M.D. It is widely accepted today that, indeed, in a dietary program, calories do *not* count for many people nearly as much as do the carbohydrates. But, in 1962, the FDA had declared that this book should not be read by the American people, and especially that safflower oil capsules could not be sold in any way that connected them with the theme of the book. This, in their great wisdom, was declared as false labeling.

Following standard procedure, the FDA tipped off the local news media that a seizure was about to take place, and, as a result, when the officials arrived on the scene, members of the press were on hand to fully document and photograph the great raid. Needless to say, the public was both impressed and grateful to learn that their FDA was on the job "protecting" them from such unscrupulous merchants of fraud.

The main point, however, is that the city's largest department store also had been displaying the books and capsules. But, prior to the raid on the smaller store, the FDA had called the officials of the larger store, advised them of the pending seizure, and suggested that they could avoid embarrassing publicity if they would merely remove the offending merchandise quietly and voluntarily. The agency had correctly reasoned that it could accomplish its goal better by picking on the little guy and avoiding a confrontation with a firm that had the resources to fight back.

Sometimes the failure to treat the big operators with the same harshness as the small is due, not to the fact that they are large, but because they are "in." They are part of the cartel establishment. For example, during the 1970 hearings before the House Subcommittee on Intergovernmental Relations, it was revealed that a small journal was forced by the FDA to publish a retraction of certain statements contained in an advertisement for an oral contraceptive. But the large and prestigious *New England Journal of Medicine* which carried the same ad was not required to publish any retraction at all. When asked about this discrepancy, FDA Commissioner Charles Edwards replied that the larger magazine "didn't really mean to offend."[1]

This is not to say, of course, that the FDA never tackles a larger firm, for occasionally it does. But, when it does, you can be sure that the cards are stacked against the defendant. Regardless of one's financial resources, unless he is part of the international *finpol* interlock, he cannot hope to match the unlimited resources of the federal government. Private citizens must hire attorneys. The government has buildings full of attorneys on the tax payroll just waiting to justify their salaries. It matters not in the least to the FDA how long the litigation drags on, for the delays, postponements, and continuations actually are part of its strategy to bankrupt the defendant with astronomical legal expenses.

---

[1] "Who Blocks Testing of Anti-Cancer Agent?," *Alameda Times Star* (Calif.), Aug. 3, 1970.

In the court proceedings against Dr. Andrew Ivy, for example, the trial lasted for almost ten months. Testimony of 288 witnesses filled 11,900 pages of transcript—enough to make a stack seven feet high. It is estimated that the FDA spent between three and five million dollars of the taxpayers' money. There is no way that the average citizen can hope to match that kind of legal offensive.

On top of this financial handicap, the defendant must face the fact that there are very few judges or juries who will have the courage to decide a case against the FDA, whose attorneys are adept at planting in their minds that if they should do so, and if they are wrong, they will be personally responsible for thousands of deaths. Under this kind of intimidation, a judge or jury is almost always inclined to conclude that they will leave the scientific questions up to the scientific experts (the FDA!), and that they will concern themselves strictly with the questions of law.

However, even in those cases where the court's verdict is favorable to the defendant, he often must face the wrath of FDA officials who then make it a point to harass him and, hopefully, to initiate additional law suits.

Commenting on this aspect of the protection racket, Omar Garrison writes:

> During the course of a legal battle which appeared to be going against the government, a ranking FDA official told the defense attorney: "If this case plays out, we

> will just work up another lawsuit, you know."

> It was not an idle threat. There is documented evidence to show that, in case after case, a respondent exonerated by the court has emerged from the ordeal (often exhausted and bankrupt) only to be faced with a second or even third indictment . . . . The dictocrats seem to reason that sooner or later a defendant will exhaust his financial resources and lose the will to defend himself when he realizes that he is pitted against the limitless potential of the national government.[1]

The limitless potential of the national government includes a lot more than a battery of tax-supported lawyers. Once an individual has incurred the wrath of the FDA, he can expect to find himself the target of harassment from other agencies of the federal government as well. Probably first at his door will be the man from IRS to scrutinize his tax records with a determination to find *something* wrong. If the defendant sells a product, the Federal Trade Commission will take a highly personal interest in his operations. If he has programs on radio or television, the stations that carry his message will be contacted by the Federal Communications Commission and reminded that such programing is not in the best public interest. The man from OSHA

[1]Omar Garrison, *The Dictocrats, op. cit.*, pp. 153, 156.

(Occupational Safety and Health Administration) surely will want to examine his facilities for possible (inevitable) violations of obscure safety and health codes. The Fair Employment Practices Commission may suddenly discover unacceptable employment or hiring practices. If he is a physician, he can look forward to closer attention from PSRO (Professional Standards Review Organization) to evaluate his judgment in the care of his patients. As a last result, he may even find himself the object of Post Office action resulting in the denial of such a basic business necessity as the delivery of mail. And superimposed upon all these actions there has been the constant and conscious effort of the FDA to secure maximum exposure in the mass communications media for the dual purpose of perpetuating its own image of "protecting the people" while at the same time destroying the reputations and businesses of those it has singled out for attack. The advance notice to the press corps of a planned raid or arrest thus becomes an essential part of the FDA's strategy. Even if the defendant eventually is exonerated in court, he will be viewed by the general public as criminally suspect because of the lingering impact of the dramatic news stories and pictures of his arrest. The economic damage done to the defendant as a result of this carefully contrived publicity often is far greater than any fine or penalty that could be imposed in court.

Lest this sweeping indictment sound too harsh or exaggerated, let us turn our attention next to specific examples and actual cases.

XXI

THE ARSENAL OF COMPLIANCE

Specific examples of government harassment of the organic nutrition and vitamin industry; the important role played by the mass communications media in discrediting Laetrile in the public mind; and a comparison of the cost of typical Laetrile therapy with that of orthodox cancer treatments.

As touched upon briefly in the preceding chapter, one of the principal weapons in the FDA's arsenal of compliance is the press release and the pre-arranged news coverage of raids and arrests. Trial by manipulated public opinion can be of far more consequence than trial by jury. The defendant, even if innocent of the charges against him — or, more likely, even if guilty of the charges *per se* but innocent of any real wrong-doing — will forever carry the stigma of suspected guilt in the eyes of the public.

Basically, this is the rationale behind the "cyanide scare" publicity given to Laetrile and apricot kernels. The honest scientific verdict is that these substances are as safe as almost any edible thing can be. Yet, the public knows only that they have been labeled as "dangerous" and that those who promote their use are not to be trusted.

The mass communications media has been all too willing to cooperate in this venture. The reason is not that the major news outlets are firmly in the hands of the same international *finpols* who dominate the federal government — true though that may be[1] —it merely is due to the fact that newsmen, like everyone else, do not like to work more than they have to and, consequently, are inclined to accept ready-made stories with a minimum of independent research — plus the fact that most of them have never had any reason to question the expertise or the integrity of FDA spokesmen. In other words, like the rest of the population at large, most newsmen have a lot yet to learn about the inherent qualities of big government. The result of this reality is that the press and the electronics media have, for all practical purposes, become the propaganda arms of the FDA.

To illustrate this point, there is an inexhaustible supply of slanted or biased news stories, of which the following examples are typical.

Mrs. Mary Whelchel had operated a boarding house on the American side of the Mexican boundary near San Diego for the use of cancer patients under the care of Dr. Contreras. To her it was far more of a mercy mission than it was a commercial

[1]See the discussion of the CFR in the previous chapter. Also note that the Hearst empire has been in the Rockefeller orbit since 1932 when it was saved from financial collapse by a $25,000,000 loan from the Chase National Bank.

enterprise. Yet, in February of 1971, she was arrested and thrown in jail because she had provided Laetrile for her boarders.

Shortly after her release, Mrs. Whelchel wrote an open letter for publication in the *Cancer News Journal.* Here, in her own words, is what happened:

> Dear Friends,
>
> Most of you will know by the time this letter reaches you that on Feb. 25, 1971 at 12:30 p.m., Charles Duggie (California Food and Drug Officer), Fred Vogt (San Diego D.A. Office), Frances Holway (San Diego police matron), and John McDonald (Imperial Beach Police) came to my home and arrested me for "selling, giving away and distributing" Laetrile as a CURE for cancer.
>
> I was also accused of spreading "propaganda" to people to get them to go to Mexican doctors instead of their medical advisors in the States. . . . I was told they had papers to "search and seize" and that I was under arrest. They proceeded to go through my house like a tornado. Everything was removed from my files, desk and shelves, including checks, personal letters, receipts and books. One word covers it — EVERYTHING!
>
> Finally, at 4:00 p.m. I was taken to the county jail to be booked and

mugged. . . . I was put in the "drunk tank," and there I stayed. . . .

As I sat in that horrible jail and looked around at the four barren walls, and the drunks, prostitutes, dope addicts — plus it had no windows, and mattresses were thrown helter-skelter on the floor — I had time to reflect over the past eight years. At first I asked myself: "How and why did I get here?" I was panic stricken! For a person who has never broken the law, outside of a traffic ticket or two, in a lifetime — here I was in jail!

It is terribly frightening. You are cut completely off from civilization it seems. No way to contact a soul! Other than the call to my sons, I had no way of knowing if anything was being done to get me out. I was not allowed to talk to anyone but the inmates. Most of them were too drunk or high to understand a word. As time passed (there are no clocks) and no word came from the outside, I felt like the forgotten man; in my case, the forgotten woman!

I believe in Laetrile wholeheartedly. I believe with all my heart that it is the answer to the control of cancer. After living twenty-four hours a day for eight years with cancer patients, how could there be a single doubt? I came up with my answer. Yes, it has been worth every minute of it, and regardless of how the

> trial comes out, I want to say now, for the record, I would do the same thing, the very same thing all over again.[1]

For comparison, let us see how this incident was treated in the press. All across the country, newspapers picked up the story as it first had been planted in *The New York Times*. Headlines screamed: CANCER CLINIC RING SEIZED IN CALIFORNIA. The public was led to believe that the FDA had launched a daring raid on one of the most dangerous and despicable criminals of the Twentieth Century smuggling "illicit drugs" into the country and preying upon innocent, helpless, and desperate cancer victims.

It said:

> California food and drug agents moved this week to break up what they described as an "underground railroad" that has been transporting cancer victims into Mexico for treatment with a drug that is banned in the United States and Canada.
>
> Charges of criminal conspiracy and fraud were lodged against Mrs. Mary C. Whelchel whose boarding house has been a haven for cancer patients from all parts of the United States en route to Mexico for treatment with the so-called wonder drug. . . .

---

[1] *Cancer News Journal,* Jan./Apr., 1971, p. 14.

> The Mexican authorities are also looking into the operation of the cancer clinics.[1]

"CLINIC RING," indeed!

Most local police departments are pushovers for the FDA quacks. They often accept FDA pronouncements at face value. Consequently, they usually can be counted on to cooperate fully in any investigation or arrest. Sometimes, a police investigator, without realizing that he has been deceived by FDA propaganda, concludes that Laetrile "smugglers" are really no different from dope pushers dealing in heroin. When such lawmen are interviewed by the press, they become extremely quotable and helpful to the FDA.

The following news article from the *Seattle Post-Intelligence* is a classic example:

> Bellevue — At least five Washington residents including two doctors have been linked with sales of an illegal anti-cancer drug known as Laetrile, a result of a month long investigation by Bellevue police, the P-I has learned.
>
> Detectives conducting the probe yesterday said they may have only scratched the surface of a drug sales operation covering several states and Mexico. . . .
>
> Two motives appear to exist for those advocating Laetrile, according to Belle-

---

[1] "Cancer Clinic Ring Seized in California," New York Times Service, *The Arizona Republic,* Feb. 28, 1971, p. 24-A.

> vue detective Bill Ellis, heading the investigation. "Some of those involved may believe that the drug actually works to cure or halt the progress of cancer," Ellis said.
>
> "But we can't rule out the profit motive," he added.
>
> "There is a lot of money to be made selling this drug."...
>
> "Every indication is that patients are required to stay on the drug for life," Ellis said. "This makes an ideal situation for a bunco artist, preying on desperate people who feel they have nothing to lose."
>
> Police also are concerned that those touting Laetrile for the profit motive may find it just as lucrative and as simple to import other drugs including heroin.
>
> "If a person can successfully smuggle one illegal drug into the U.S. in substantial quantities, what is to prevent them from diversifying," Ellis posed.[1]

The heavy hand of FDA propaganda is evident in this "news" story, and it is likely that neither detective Ellis nor the reporter are even remotely aware that they had become victimized by *real* bunco artists of the first order.

---

[1] "Five Linked to Sale of Illegal Cancer Drug," Dec. 21, 1972, pp. 1, 5.

Aside from the completely ludicrous and dishonest innuendo about Laetrile advocates "possibly" smuggling heroin (there never has been a single shred of evidence to justify this suspicion), one of the favorite FDA lines is that those who distribute Laetrile are making exorbitant profits. As a matter of fact, the California Department of Public Health, in its publication *The Cancer Law*, claimed that essentially the same material could be purchased substantially cheaper under the commercial name of Amygdalin, and the American Cancer Society has even gone to such ludicrous extremes as to say that Laetrile used in an injection actually costs only ten to fifteen cents.[1]

Let us examine the facts.

First of all, the average cost of one gram of injectible Laetrile in 1974 was approximately three dollars, which makes it just about the cheapest injectible in the doctor's office.

Perhaps the biggest factor influencing the price of Laetrile, however, is that the government has made it illegal to use as an anti-cancer agent. This has forced its source of supply into a black market operation which, because of its need for secrecy and the ever-present possibility of arrest, fines, or imprisonment, always inflates the price of any commodity in order to cover the extra expenses of smuggling and to compensate the suppliers for their risk. If the government would remove its legal restraints, Laetrile could be manufactured and sold in the United States by mass production and distribu-

[1]ACS quoted in "Cancer Relief or Quackery?" *Washington Post*, May 26, 1974, pp. C1, C4.

tion techniques which, in a very short time, probably would bring its price down to less than one-third of its present level.

And speaking of exorbitant costs and profits, why doesn't the FDA concern itself over these matters within the field of *orthodox* medicine?

In an article in the *San Francisco Chronicle* entitled "Beware the Quick Cancer Cure," Dr. Ralph Weilerstein of the California FDA's Advisory Council expressed shock and concern over the fact that a typical thirty day Laetrile treatment in Mexico may cost a patient between one thousand and two thousand dollars. First of all, these figures were grossly exaggerated. As *Time* magazine reported in 1971:

> Contreras' claims for Laetrile are as modest as his fees. The doctor charges only $10 for a first visit, $7 for subsequent visits. $3 for a gram of the drug.[1]

According to Dr. Contreras, his total medical charges seldom have exceeded seven hundred to a thousand dollars. Most of his patients are from out of the country, however, and so they also must pay for lodging, meals, and transportation. The total expense *may* run as high as two thousand dollars, but it is unfair to imply that it is all going into the doctor's pocket as pure profit.

If Dr. Weilerstein wants to compare apples with apples, let him explain why it is that a terminal cancer patient undergoing *orthodox* therapy in the

[1] "Debate Over Laetrile," *Time*, April 12, 1971.

United States will spend, on the average, thirteen thousand dollars on surgery, radiology, chemotherapy, hospitalization, or a combination of them all. May we suggest that, if the FDA really wants to get into areas where it can express shock and concern, this is virgin territory long awaiting exploration.

Needless to say, establishment newspapers and magazines have been reliable and unquestioning outlets for FDA propaganda. So, too, have the major networks and most of the local radio and TV stations. A perfect example was NBC's "First Tuesday" program broadcast on March 2, 1971. To the average viewer who knew none of the background, this program undoubtedly appeared to be an objective documentary. Mr. Ed Delaney, the program's host, indeed, did have filmed interviews of people representing both sides of the controversy. But, as is so often the case, the opinion of the viewer actually was predetermined by careful selection and film editing of who was allowed to say what, and in what sequence.

There are hundreds of cancer patients seeking the services of Dr. Contreras' clinic every day. They come from all age groups, all walks of life, and from all educational backgrounds. Yet, NBC interviewed only those patients who were relatively inarticulate or who would appear to be ignorant, confused, and desperate. None of them were allowed to tell of any help they might have received from Laetrile, so the resulting impression was that no one actually had benefited.

Then came the lengthy "rebuttal" — highly organized and polished interviews with Dr. Jesse Steinfeld, the Surgeon General of the United States, Dr. Charles Edwards, head of the FDA, and other "highly respectable" establishment physicians. The overwhelming conclusion was that "Laetrile may sound fine in theory, but it just doesn't work!"

The Laetrile advocates who had trustingly cooperated with NBC in the preparation of the program were stunned. They had been led to believe that they would be given a fair hearing before the court of public opinion but, from the very beginning, they never even had a chance.

Under the label of "public service broadcasting," the nation's TV stations have put anti-nutrition propaganda films on the air literally thousands of times and at no charge to their sponsors. The AMA's film called *Medicine Man*, for example, portrays health lecturers as pitch men and crooks, and cleverly instructs the viewer how to spot their "techniques." What the film actually does, however, is to lump all health lecturers into one bag — the good and the bad together, and to make blanket statements and observations that obviously are true when applied to the bad but that are false when applied to the good. The result is that the viewer tends to become programmed to react negatively against *all* of them, and because he is looking for "Techniques" rather than "substance," he thus is effectively conditioned to reject the responsible health lecturer along with the irresponsible. To him *all* health lecturers are charlatans because they all use some of the same "techniques" as those used in the film. It does not occur to him that most of the same or similar techniques are used by *all* lecturers on *all* subjects — particularly those who are lecturing *against* health lecturers!

Another propaganda film with a similar approach was produced by the American Cancer Society and is called *Journey Into Darkness*. Featuring guest star Robert Ryan as the host, the film is a masterpiece of scripting and acting. Weaving several stories into one, it portrays the mental torture experienced by several cancer victims as they grapple with the decision of whether they should take the advice of their wise and kindly doctor and pursue *proven* orthodox treatments with a very high chance of recovery, or should they allow their fears and doubts to overcome their judgment and seek the *unproven* and suspect treatments of a medically untrained quack who promises miracle cures but whose only real interest is in how much money the patient can afford to pay. In the end, some make the "right" choice and resolve to follow the guidance of their doctor. Others make the "wrong" choice and begin their long and tragic *journey into darkness*.

To the uninformed, this film undoubtedly is extremely convincing. Because they know that cancer quackery *does* exist, they are misled into accepting that anything not approved by the ACS automatically falls into that category. They do not stop to realize that the people they watched on the screen were merely actors, that the story was not real, or that the script was written in conformity to the propaganda objectives of the FDA. Nevertheless, this film has been shown as a "public service" on hundreds of TV stations and in thousands of classrooms, service clubs, fraternal, charity, and civic organizations, producing a profound impact on public opinion. So convincing is the message that countless viewers who later contract cancer will not even *listen* to the Laetrile story — even though their physician has told them there no longer is any hope under orthodox treatment.

As a sidelight, it is both interesting and ironic to note that actor Robert Ryan, star of *Journey Into Darkness,* fell victim of his own propaganda. He died of cancer in July of 1973 after undergoing extensive cobalt therapy. His wife, Jessica, died of cancer one year previously.

While the press release, the manipulated news story, and the one-sided use of radio and TV constitute some of the most frequently used weapons in the FDA's "arsenal of compliance," there are many others that are even more effective and deadly. Generally they are reserved for those tough customers who cannot or will not be stopped by mere public opinion. One of these is the destruction of an individual's credit rating. It is standard practice for the FDA to write or phone Dun & Bradstreet to advise them of one's "difficulty with the government." A notice to Better Business Bureau also is customary.

The next escalatory step of harassment is to stop the publication or distribution of all printed matter, including books and pamphlets. The book,

One Answer to Cancer, written by Dr. William Kelly, was legally blocked because it advocated diet rather than orthodox therapy. The court ruled that distribution of the book would constitute a clear and present danger to the general public and that the government's duty to protect the health and welfare of its citizens supersedes the doctor's constitutional right of free speech. Since Dr. Kelly was a dentist rather than an M.D., he also was accused of "practicing medicine without a license."

In fact, this is a favorite FDA ploy. Many health writers and lecturers have been arrested on just such an excuse. If a man prescribes a change in diet as a means of eliminating simple headache, he is practicing medicine without a license. If he suggests that you take vitamin C or bioflavonoids for a cold, he is practicing medicine without a license. If he recommends iron or fruit or natural roughage for bowel regularity, he is practicing medicine without a license. If he suggests that natural substances to be found in nature's foods can be an effective control for cancer, he *certainly* is practicing medicine without a license. But let a major drug firm hire a ham actor to go on TV and proclaim to the millions that Bayer is good for headache, that Vicks is good for a cold, that Exlax is good for regularity, or that orthodox medicine can cure 60% of all cancers, and never will one FDA eyebrow be raised.

In order to avoid the appearance of being "book burners," FDA officials have claimed that they are censuring books, not because of the ideas they advocate but because the books actually are being used as sophisticated "labels" for products.

They may not have any jurisdiction over *ideas*, but they do have total control over *products*. So, if the author, publisher, distributor, or seller of the book also should happen to have a product to sell that in any way is explained or promoted in the book — which is only logical for them to do — then the book *and* the product are seized by the FDA because of false or deceptive *labeling*.

Denied access to the printed page, many nutrition-oriented writers take to the lecture hall. Here, too, they are stopped. They can be arrested either for practicing medicine without a license or — especially if they have a product to sell — false labeling.

One such case was that of Mr. Bruce Butt, an elderly gentleman who was arrested for showing a pro-Laetrile film in Carlisle, Pennsylvania. Two and a half years later, all charges against Mr. Butt were dismissed in court but not until he had been forced to suffer gigantic legal fees, and after the publicity had thoroughly branded him in the public mind as a "health food nut," a "crackpot," and a "cancer quack."

If the object of FDA harassment is still alive and kicking after all of this, then there is yet one more weapon in the government's arsenal of compliance that surely will drop him in his tracks: Cut off his mail! The Post Office, after all, is just another branch of the same federal machinery, and it will honor, without question, any FDA administrative or court ruling to the effect that a publication or product is "not in the public interest." On the basis of this glib phrase, at least six unorthodox health books and their advertising have been banned from the mail. The Cardiac Society, for example, had earned FDA displeasure by selling vitamin E as a means of raising funds to carry on its work to educate the public about the relationship between vitamin E and a healthy heart. Incoming mail to the organization's headquarters was intercepted by the Post Office and returned to the sender marked "fraudulent!"

Charles C. Johnson, Jr. , Administrator of the Environmental Health Service, the agency which, for a while, supervised the activities of the FDA, has summed up very well the present attitude of government officials when he said: "We have a variety of tools in our arsenal of compliance."[1]

The phrase "arsenal of compliance" tells us a great deal about the mentality of the hardened bureaucrat and, as we have seen, it is a perfect description of what the average citizen now must face when he challenges the government that he has so blandly — perhaps even approvingly — watched grow over the years. In the name of "protecting the people" — in the field of nutrition as in all other fields of human interest and activity — it rapidly is becoming the greatest single threatening force *from* which the people now need protecting.

---

[1]Garrison, *The Dictocrats, op. cit.*, p. 50.

XXII

THE DOUBLE STANDARD

An analysis of the FDA's double standard in which harmless non-drug materials such as organic vitamins and food supplements are burdened with restrictions and regulations in excess of those applied to many toxic and dangerous drugs; special consideration of FDA attitudes toward aspirin, apricot kernels, Aprikern, bitter almonds, fluoridated water, and marijuana.

The FDA's unrelenting war on organic vitamins, food supplements, and non-drug medicines is well known. Much of the agency's time and resources are spent each year warning the public about the dangers that lurk in the nutritional approach to health. When it comes to the broad category of drugs, however, there is, by comparison, a marked lack of concern. In fact, quite to the contrary, there is a gently implied admonition: "Don't be concerned about harm from drugs. Take whatever we have approved and relax. You're in safe hands."

For example, in July of 1971 the FDA issued a "Fact Sheet" on the subject of drug side effects. Under the heading: "Should People Fear Drugs Because of Possible Side Effects?" we find this answer:

> Drugs should be respected rather than feared. A physician's decision to use a drug is a considered one. It is *his* decision that it is better to treat a disease with a certain drug than leave it untreated, and that there is greater danger in not using the drug.[1]

The comment regarding the supremacy of the physician's decision, of course, is to be taken with a rather large grain of salt. It is an excellent philosophy but, as any physician who has tried to use Laetrile or other vitamin therapy will tell you, it simply is not true. And now, with increasing government regulation of what a doctor may or may not prescribe for individual patients (through such federal agencies as PSRO), it is evident that the government wants physicians to become merely robots who are trained to administer only approved "Federal treatment number 9714-32" in response to "Federal group diagnosis number 7482-91." But the statement "Drugs should be respected rather than feared" is a totally honest reflection of FDA philosophy and, when compared to its paranoia

[1]Fact Sheet CSS-D2 (FDA) 72-3001.

over organic vitamins, it offers a convenient vantage point from which to observe the operation of its double standard.

Congressman Craig Hosmer, outspoken critic of the FDA's one-sided attack on the organic nutrition and vitamin industry, has said:

> I have been informed that there never has been an accidental death due to vitamin overdosage, but it is said one person dies every three days from taking lethal doses of aspirin . . . . But, despite the fact that Americans buy twenty million pounds of aspirin a year, FDA has never publicly considered any kind of regulation or warning on labels. Instead, the agency has spent its time and millions of the taxpayer's dollars establishing arbitrary daily dosages for harmless vitamins and minerals.[1]

Congressman Hosmer has hit the bull's eye. The danger to public health does not lie in organic food supplements or vitamins sold in health food stores. It lies in the vast inventories of toxic man-made drugs. Nothing recommended by a health lecturer ever produced such tragedies as thalidomide babies. The records show that as many as five percent of all hospital admissions now are the result of adverse reactions to legally acquired

---

[1]Garrison, *The Dictocrats, op. cit.*, p. 217.

prescription drugs.[1] It has been estimated that no less than one and a half million people are sent to the hospital each year as a result of orthodox drugs —which means that these legally acquired materials are injuring hundreds of times more people than all the illegally acquired psychedelic drugs put together. And, after a patient is admitted to the hospital for reasons other than drug reactions, his chances of falling victim of drug sickness more than doubles. Drug sickness *in* the hospital now strikes well over three and a half million patients each year.[2]

As long ago as 1960, it was acknowledged that at least forty new diseases or syndromes had been attributed to drugs used in therapy,[3] and the number has grown impressively since then.

The situation with non-prescription over-the-counter drugs is almost as bad. Aspirin—first produced by Bayer of I.G. Farben—is a classic example. Americans have been "sold" on aspirin to the tune of over twenty million pounds per year. That's approximately sixteen billion tablets, or an average of eighty tablets per person, each year!

Aspirin, of course, is a drug. It is completely man-made. It is widely recognized as dangerous if taken in excessive doses—especially for children. Overdoses can result not only from a single large ingestion but also from continuous use which pro-

---

[1] "Important Prescribing Information from FDA Commissioner Charles C. Edwards, M.D.," U.S. Department of Health, Education and Welfare, 1971.

[2] Martin Gross, *The Doctors,* (Random House, N.Y., 1966).

[3] President Kennedy's Consumers' Protection Message of March 15, 1962.

duces accumulative effects. Every year, there are at least ninety deaths in the United States from overdoses of aspirin.[1]

Ninety deaths *each year* is no small matter. Yet, the FDA does nothing except to require each aspirin label to state the recommended safe dosage plus the admonition: "or as recommended by your physician." The important point, however, is not that the FDA should do *more*, but that it applies a glaringly unfair double standard against natural food and vitamin products. In November of 1973, for example, it stopped the production and distribution of a product known as Aprikern. Aprikern is the trade name given to apricot kernels that have been ground, cold pressed to remove the fatty oils, and encapsulated. The process retains the nitriloside or vitamin B_{17} content, increases the potency concentration by approximately 20%, reduces the caloric content, and increases the resistance to rancidity. Aprikern, therefore, had become extremely popular among those who were knowledgeable of the vitamin B_{17} story.

Based upon obscure "studies" allegedly conducted at the University of Arizona School of Pharmacology, the FDA announced that Aprikern contained "a poison which would kill both adults and children."[2]

Note that the FDA did not say that Aprikern actually *had* killed any adults or children—as aspirin does every week—but that it *could* do so. Note

---

[1] FDA Fact Sheet, July 1971, (FDA) 72-3002.

[2] "These Two Health Foods 'Dangerous'," (UPI) *News Chronicle*, Nov. 28, 1973, p. 11.

also that, during the court case that resulted from the legal action instituted by the FDA against the manufacturer, the scientists from the University of Arizona who had conducted the toxicity experiments on rats which supposedly proved that Aprikern was dangerous, testified that the results of their tests were inconclusive and that they would not stand behind the interpretation widely publicized by the FDA.

Undaunted, the FDA *continued* to press its case stating that it was conducting tests of its own and that these surely would "prove" that Aprikern is dangerous.[1]

William Dixon, chief of Arizona's Consumer Protection Division which worked jointly with the FDA in the initial action against Aprikern, told newsmen:

> We could wait six months for the FDA tests, but if some kid died from eating this stuff, I wouldn't want our office to be responsible.[2]

From this, may we assume that Mr. Dixon's office *is* responsible for deaths from aspirin overdose? Or are we to suspect that all of this pretended concern for the public welfare is just so much eye wash to conceal an unconscionable double standard whereby agencies of government are being

---

[1]And it is possible that they will — even if they have to hit those helpless rats over the head with a hammer to produce the desired results!

[2]"Suit Labels Health Food as Harmful," *Phoenix Gazette*, Nov. 28, 1973

used on behalf of the drug cartel to harass and destroy competition from the non-drug health industry? We may ponder what Mr. Dixon's concern would be if "some kid," or some adult, for that matter, dies from *not* "eating this stuff."

Leaving no stone unturned, Arizona's Health Commissioner, Dr. Louis Kassuth, went so far as to issue a public warning that, even though whole apricots would not be affected by the government embargo, their pits should not be cracked open and, above all, *the kernels must not be eaten.*[1]

Ah, it is so comforting to have such wise and beneficent political experts watching over us and protecting us from our own folly. How wretched we would be without them. How reassuring it is to pick up a copy of a government publication entitled *Requirements of the United States Food, Drug, and Cosmetic Act,* and read:

> Because of their toxicity, bitter almonds may not be marketed in the United States for unrestricted use. Shipments of sweet almonds [which do *not* contain vitamin B_{17}] may not contain more than five percent of bitter almonds. Almond paste and pastes made from other kernels should contain less than twenty-five parts per million of hydrocyanic acid (HCN) naturally occurring in the kernels.[2]

---

[1]"Apricot Pits Hit by Ban," *Phoenix Gazette,* Nov. 29, 1973, p. B-1.

[2]That's only one four-hundreths of one percent. FDA Publication No. 2, June, 1970, p. 26.

Needless to say, there is not a single over-the-counter drug on the market today that could pass toxicity restrictions even remotely as severe as these. The law does not protect us. It is a weapon *against* us.

In a letter to this author dated December 26, 1971, Dr. Ernst T. Krebs, Jr. anticipated the FDA's action against Aprikern by over two years when he explained:

> The full awareness of the significance of vitamin B_{17} (nitriloside) is now registering in the minds of our bureaucrats and those whom they serve. The attitude is becoming obvious even to us that these people feel vitamin B_{17} is too good and too valuable for the Indians. Just as in the past when valuable minerals or oil were discovered on Indian lands, government bureaucracy would move the Indians away to "better land," so attempts are being made now to move all innovators and pioneers on vitamin B_{17} away from the development—through the invocation of one legal ruse or another—until it "cools," and then allow monopoly supporting the involved bureaucracy to preempt the field . . . .
>
> Please keep in mind that the potential or waiting market for Aprikern is at least as great as that for all the other vitamins, including C. Today, bureaucracy can make or break a billion dollar market within a few days with merely a few pro-

> nouncements or edicts. A Surgeon-General bought just like fresh beef (but not as intrinsically valuable), can say "yes" or "no" on phosphate or non-phosphate detergents on evening TV. He reads his lines as they are given to him, and the markets move accordingly. Despite a few twists and turns for window trimming, monopoly is almost always sustained in this game.

The FDA perpetually informs the public that "nutritional quackery" is big business with huge profits. But it remains strangely silent about the really big business and the super profits of the drug industry. FDA spokesmen speak with great concern about a supposed five hundred million dollars spent each year on vitamins and food supplements. Even if that figure is accurate, which is unlikely, it is minuscule compare to the staggering annual expenditure of four *billion,* three hundred *million* dollars spent on prescription drugs plus another one *billion,* eight hundred million for drugs sold over the counter.[1] The absence of FDA "public concern" over this sector of its responsibility is highly revealing.

The FDA acknowledges that it has received reports of "excessive promotional activity by some representatives of pharmaceutical manufacturers" — meaning that not all "detail men" from the drug firms are totally honest in the description of their company's product. Nevertheless, it completely

[1]Gross, *The Doctors, op. cit.*

ignores this area of inquiry and devotes a major portion of its resources and manpower to wiretapping, bugging, and following health lecturers in an attempt to catch them making a claim that, even though it may be true, comes into conflict with an FDA ruling. At a time when the FDA is pleading inadequacy of tax funds to properly enforce sanitation standards within the processed food industry, or safety standards within the drug industry, it boasts about expanding its operations against such public enemies as the purveyors of wheat germ, rose hips, honey, and apricot kernels.

Another example of the FDA's double standard is its attitude toward sodium fluoride, the substance that is added to the water supplies of over four thousand communities in the United States on the supposition that fluoridated water somehow helps to reduce cavities. It is interesting to note, however, that the original 1939 studies by Dr. H. Trendley Dean that led to this speculation, specifically warned that those communities with low rates of tooth decay had in their natural drinking water, not only unusually high levels of fluoride, but also much more calcium as well. The report then stated that: ". . . . the possibility that the composition of the water in other respects [than fluoride] may also be a factor should not be overlooked."[1]

It *was* overlooked, however, and remains so today. In truth, there is little hard evidence that

---

[1]Dean, "Domestic Health and Dental Caries," *Public Health Report*, May, 1939, 54:862-888.

fluorides actually do what is claimed for them, and much evidence to the contrary. In fact, during the original investigation by Dr. Dean, he reported that, in 1938, in Pueblo, Colorado, thirty-seven percent of the people were caries-free with 0.6 parts per million of fluoride in the water. Yet, in East Moline, Illinois, with a whopping 1.5 ppm of fluoride — almost three times as much — only eleven percent of the population were found without caries. We note, also, that the city of Washington, D.C., which has had a fluoridated water supply for twenty years, now has the highest dentist-to-population ratio in the entire nation. Instead of having fewer cavities than citizens of non-fluoridated communities, Washingtonians have almost a third *more!*[1]

But that is not really the important point. Even if sodium fluoride *did* reduce cavities as its promoters claim, the fact is that this chemical is extremely toxic even in small quantities. So much so, in fact, that drug companies are required to warn consumers that the presence in pills of as little as one milligram of this substance can cause illness in some persons.

Extensive studies in Antigo, Wisconsin, Grand Rapids, Michigan, and Newburgh, New York, all showed that within months of adopting fluoridation of the water supply, the death rate from heart disease in these cities nearly doubled and leveled out at almost twice the national average. Likewise, in the Philadelphia Zoo there was a sharp

[1]Garrison, *The Dictocrats, op. cit.,* pp. 229, 230.

increase in animal and bird deaths that coincided with the introduction of fluoridated water.[1]

Dr. Paul H. Phillips, a University of Chicago biochemist who has spent twenty-nine years in research on fluoride toxicity, has pointed out that sodium fluoride, even when taken in extremely minute quantities, accumulates and builds up in the skeletal parts of the body. Symptoms of chronic fluoride poisoning may not appear for many years, and when they do, they can be very hard to diagnose. They can manifest themselves in many forms such as vascular calcification, disorders of the kidneys, bowels, skin, stomach, thyroid, and nervous system, and may be responsible for headaches, vomiting, mongolism, mouth ulcers, pains in the joints, and loss of appetite.

Dr. Simon A. Beisler, chief of Urology at New York's Roosevelt Hospital, has said:

> I just don't feel this thing has been researched the way it should have been. Fluoride in water can reach every organ in the body and there are indications that it can be harmful over a long period of time.[2]

Aluminum companies, as a result of their manufacturing process, give off tremendous quantities of fluoride compounds as waste products. Much of this goes into the air and eventually finds its way

---

[1]See news release dated August 1972 and "Is Fluorine Pollution Damaging Hearts," by K.A. Baird, M.D., (Citizen Action Program, 608 Gowan Rd., Antigo, Wisc., 54409).

[2]Garrison, *op. cit.*, pp. 228-230.

back to earth where it becomes noxious to both man and animal. Breathing the fumes is bad enough but once it is absorbed into edible plants, it is converted into such organic compounds as fluoracetate or fluorcitrate which are at least five hundred times more poisonous than the inorganic salt. This means that vegetables and fruits which have been irrigated by fluoridated water supplies could become potential killers.[1]

As would be expected, aluminum companies habitually are the objects of successful damage suits. In 1946 a plant in Troutdale, Oregon, was sued by a local citizen who proved that the health of his family had been damaged by fluoride fumes. In 1950 a Washington plant was ordered by a Tacoma court to pay damages to a rancher whose cattle had been poisoned by eating fluoride contaminated grass. In June, 1958, Blount County, Tennessee farmers were awarded indemnity for fluoride damage to cattle and crops.[2]

Europe also has had its fluoride problems. The "death fogs" of 1930 were finally attributed to acute fluoride intoxication. In a similar 1940 disaster in Donora, Pennsylvania, fluoride concentrations in the blood of victims were found to be twelve to twenty-five times higher than in the blood of unaffected persons.[3]

---

[1]K.A. Baird, M.D., *op. cit.*, p. 4.

[2]"Industry's Fluoride Problem," by Lee Hardy, *National Health Federation Bulletin*, Oct. 1973, p. 20.

[3]See K. Roholm, *"The Fog Disaster in the Meuse Valley, 1930," Journal of Industrial Hygiene Toxicology*, 1937, 19:126-136. Also Philip Stadtler, "Fluorine Gases in Atmosphere Blamed for Death," *Chemical and Engineering News*, 1948, 26:3962.

The November 13, 1972, issue of the *Journal of the American Medical Association* published the results of a Mayo Clinic investigation into two cases of fluoride poisoning that occurred after drinking water that was fluoridated to the extent of 2.6 parts per million in one case and only 1.7 ppm in the other. These concentrations are highly significant because many artificially fluoridated water supplies are maintained at *one* ppm! One can only wonder how many cases of mild fluoride poisoning go unreported or are attributed to some other cause.

"We're not exactly sure what the problem is," says the doctor, "but it's probably some kind of viral infection. Take these pills four times a day for a week and, if they don't do the job, we'll try something else. Tricky things, those viruses."

It is interesting to note that, while one community after another in the United States rushes to fluoridate its water supply, many European countries are moving in the opposite direction. West Germany banned fluoridation on January 4, 1971. Sweden did so on November 18, 1971. And the highest court of the Netherlands declared fluoridation illegal on June 22, 1973. As the National Health Federation asked pointedly: "Do these countries know something we don't or refuse to accept?"[1]

If fluorides were not used in water supplies of the nation, they probably would be discarded as a *waste* byproduct with little other commercial use

[1]NHF Anti-fluoride Petition, March, 1974.

except in aerosol sprays, drugs, rat poison, and certain brands of toothpaste. It is significant, therefore, that while the FDA has waged relentless war against harmless vitamins, apricot kernels, and Laetrile, it has endorsed the wide-spread and *compulsory* consumption of sodium fluoride in every glass of water we drink.

As noted in a previous chapter, the FDA has steadfastly refused to allow even the testing of Laetrile because of so-called "deficiencies" in the mountains of paperwork required for IND (Investigation of New Drug). It has stated that Laetrile's *safety* has not been sufficiently established to warrant its use on human beings. Aside from the fact that Laetrile's safety record is *well*-documented, and that all the currently FDA approved drugs are notoriously *un*safe, this action is even more unpalatable when compared to the favorable treatment given to new drugs marketed by some of the large drug companies. In 1970, for example, the Searle Pharmaceutical Company received FDA approval to market an estrogen oral contraceptive within just one week after application. Testimony before the House Subcommittee on Intergovernmental Relations, however, revealed that the data submitted was British (it is normal FDA policy to insist on American data), and that the British data itself clearly stated that it concerned effectiveness only, *not* safety.

When Congressman Fountain asked FDA Commissioner Dr. Charles C. Edwards what was the primary reason behind his agency's favorable handling of Searle's application, he replied that it was "public safety." When asked to explain how public safety was involved in this decision, Edwards blurted out that it is "not our policy to jeopardize the financial interests of the pharmaceutical companies."[1]

Serc is another drug that has received FDA favorable treatment. First marketed in 1966 by Unimed, Inc., it was offered to the public for use in treating Meniere's Syndrome, a complication of the inner ear leading to dizziness and loss of balance. To make a long story short, there was substantial evidence that Serc actually made the symptoms of Meniere's Syndrome worse in many patients. In spite of repeated complaints from the medical profession and even from Congress, the FDA refused to require Unimed to cease marketing the drug — even though it officially admitted that the data submitted on behalf of Serc was "defective," "inadequate," and contained "untrue statements of material facts." Acknowledging that further studies were needed, the FDA defended its decision to allow Serc on the market by saying: "The studies could not be financed unless marketing of the drug was permitted to continue."[2] In other words, Unimed was given permission to continue to sell a drug already found to be ineffective while consumers were put in the position of financing the research that, hopefully, would prove that it had some value after all. What a contrast to the FDA's unyielding

---

[1] "Who Blocks Testing of Anti-Cancer Agent?" *Alameda Times Star* (Calif.), Aug. 3, 1970.

[2] *Consumers Reports,* March, 1973, pp. 155-156.

opposition to Laetrile and the nutritional products of nature.

As Senator William Proxmire phrased it:

> The FDA and much, but not all, of the orthodox medical profession are actively hostile against the manufacture, sale and distribution of vitamins and minerals as food or food supplements. They are out to get the health food industry and to drive the health food stores out of business. And they are trying to do this out of active hostility and prejudice.[1]

The subject of psychedelic drugs constitutes perhaps the final madness in the FDA's insane asylum of double standards. Omar Garrison recalls the story:

> Americans reacted with a sense of shock, followed by nationwide cries of indignation, when FDA Commissioner James L. Goddard told an audience of university students that he would not object to his daughter smoking marijuana any more than if she drank a cocktail . . . .
>
> Even the normally permissive *Time* magazine clucked with mild disapproval, noting that Goddard's opinion "was particularly surprising because the FDA di-

[1]As quoted in *National Health Federation Bulletin,* April 1974, cover.

> rector has been so strict in demanding that drug companies show clear proof on the efficacy and safety of their products before he allows them on the market. There is still almost no research, however, into what marijuana does — and does not do — to the human mind and body, and no scientific evidence that proves or disproves that it is better or worse than alcohol.[1]

A short time prior to this, Dr. Goddard had expressed great concern over the extent to which Americans were consuming unneeded vitamin pills, and called for tighter restrictions on the formulation and sale of these harmless commodities. He had supported FDA rulings and penalties calling for up to thirty years in prison for those who advocate the use of harmless herbs and food supplements for the alleviation of metabolic disease. Now he had given his blessings to *cannabis sativa* which, regardless of all else that might be said about it, is *far* from harmless.

For instance, on May 20, 1974, Dr. Hardin B. Jones, professor of medical physics and physiology at the University of California and Assistant Director of the University Donner Laboratories in Berkeley, appeared before the Senate Internal Security Subcommittee and testified:

> As an expert in human radiation effects [it is my observation that damage] . . . even in those who use cannabis "moderately"

---

[1]*Ibid.*, pp. 175, 176.

> is roughly the same type and degree of damage as in persons surviving atom bombing with a heavy level of radiation exposure, approximately 150 roentgens. The implications are the same. . . . Reports of the Department of Health, Education and Welfare are inadequate scientifically, do not touch accurately on the principal matters needing clarification, and, in many instances, are likely to lead the public to believe that science has proven marijuana harmless.[1]

This, then, is the double standard of the FDA. We can buy aspirin and a hundred other drugs of questionable safety by the barrelful. We can buy alcoholic beverages by the case and tobacco products by the carload. In over four thousand communities we are *forced* to drink sodium fluoride. Yet, at the same time, the FDA literally has been burying organic food supplements and vitamins under a mountain of red tape, restrictions, and harassment.

When a woman takes the life of her unborn child on the theory that she may do what she wishes with *her own* body, she receives the sanction of the Federal Supreme Court. But if she purchases Laetrile in an attempt to *save* a life — either her child's or her own — she has participated in a criminal act.

This double standard is an outrageous insult to the intelligence of the American people.

---

[1](AP) "Marijuana Smoking Poisonous, M.D. Says," *Boston Herald American,* May 21, 1974, pg. 2.

XXIII

TO WALK THE HIGHEST WIRE

The means by which doctors are intimidated against the use of Laetrile; the Sloan-Kettering investigation of Laetrile as a case history of capitulation; and the courageous stand of Dr. John Richardson against the FDA.

Undoubtedly the FDA would be pleased if it could prevent all public utterances in favor of drugless medicine or organic nutrition but, because of constitutional guarantees of freedom of speech to which it still must at least pay lip service, it has had to settle, for the time being, for allowing people to *talk* all they want, so long as they cannot distribute the vitamin or food *materials* about which they speak. People may advocate vitamin B_{17} from the rooftop, but if the consumer cannot actually put his hands on apricot kernels, Aprikern, Laetrile, or some other product containing this substance, then no real harm is done to the *status quo*. Consequently, the FDA has devoted a major part of its enforcement energies to the task of harassing or destroying those who produce, distribute, or actually administer vitamin B_{17} for the prevention or the control of cancer.

Doctors are particularly singled out for strong action for the obvious reason that, if too many of them were allowed to use vitamin therapy without being chastised by professional and public agencies, other doctors might be tempted to explore for themselves, and it could well result in opening the floodgates of medical acceptance in *spite* of FDA and AMA pronouncements and decrees. Each doctor that dares to resist, therefore, must be brutally and publically destroyed as a gruesome example, seen and understood by all other doctors, as what they, too, can expect if they should be foolish enough to follow suit.

This point was made abundantly clear during the trial of Mr. Harvey Howard of Sylmar, California, who was prosecuted for selling Laetrile tablets to cancer victims. One of the witnesses for the state was Dr. Ralph Weilerstein of the California Department of Public Health. During cross-examination, Dr. Weilerstein was asked if he knew of any "reputable" doctors who prescribed Laetrile. Weilerstein answered: "So far as I know, any doctor who has prescribed Laetrile in California since 1963 has been successfully prosecuted."[1]

So there we have it. Every doctor who has prescribed Laetrile has been prosecuted. Any doctor who is prosecuted cannot be "reputable." Therefore, no "reputable" doctor ever has prescribed Laetrile!

---

[1] "Sylmar Man Faces Trial on Cancer Quack Count," *L.A. Times*, Van Nuys section, Sept. 15, 1972.

The dilemma facing a doctor, then, is this. Shall he follow his Hippocratic oath and his sense of moral obligation to do that which he honestly believes is best for his patient, or shall he abide by the bureaucratic rules laid down by politican-doctors on behalf of vested commercial and political interest? Human nature being what it is, some will follow the higher law. Many will not.

Dr. Ernst T. Krebs, Jr., himself a veteran of repeated legal battles with the FDA, in a letter dated March 9, 1971, warned physician John Richardson, M.D., what would be in store for him if he publicly became identified with Laetrile. Commenting upon a proposed magazine article about Laetrile to be written by Dr. Richardson, Dr. Krebs said:

> It is only fair to emphasize, however, that once a physician has embarked upon such a path he is given no way to escape his printed words. These can have a devastatingly destructive effect upon his professional status, upon his wife and family, even upon his personal safety.
>
> At a lecture at Sheraton-West in Los Angeles last Thursday, a sincere and obviously intense woman (whom I had previously met) arose during the question and answer period. "I was a physician in the U.S.S.R., but I left for what I believed was a free country. But now I am told by the County [Medical] Society

> that, if I dare use Laetrile, they will get me and my license. I want to follow your work. What should I do?"
>
> I replied, "You have a great responsibility as a doctor in a society in which there is a great shortage of physicians. Forget Laetrile and do your very best where you are, and in doing this you may be much more effective than joining a battle for which you possibly are not prepared. Trained in dialectical materialism as you were, you may smile at this. It is possible that the Lord has not touched your shoulder for service on this front. I know only that He has touched mine."

The reference to the possibility of danger to Dr. Richardson's personal safety was not made lightly or without justification. Elsewhere in this same letter Dr. Krebs explained:

> As my secretary will tell you, since she was with me, five hours after presenting a rather effective lecture on cancer before an audience of about four hundred in Los Angeles, the windshield was shot out of my car on the road back to San Francisco. The next night the glass window in the tail gate was shot out (three hundred miles removed from the first shooting). The police said, "Maybe someone is trying to tell you something."

> We do not want to dwell on the matter of physical violence, but the late Arthur T. Harris, M.D., was threatened by two men with assassination if he continued to use Laetrile. Since that time we have decentralized the work so that, if any two of us are shot out of the saddle, it will have only a slightly negative effect on the program.

It takes a certain type of man to stand up against pressures and threats of this kind. There are many who talk a good line about courage and standing on principle, but, when the chips are down and the Establishment begins to play dirty, there are relatively few who will persevere.

Dr. Krebs is one of those men. Even as a student doing post-graduate work at the university, he had been a strong advocate of the trophoblastic thesis of cancer and had become conspicuous for his experimental work with vitamin B_{17}. In a letter to the author dated September 23, 1973, Dr. Krebs described the pressures that were brought to bear on him as a result:

> I was assured by my academic mentors that if I refused to obey, conform, and be controlled — be a member of the Club — I would pass into oblivion. I would be denied academic recognition, degrees, jobs, institutions, etc. My answer in the vernacular was for them to stuff the entire business because we still had enough

> freedom in this country for me to go out to establish my own research foundation — The John Beard Memorial Foundation — under the despised doctrine of free enterprise.

There is no better illustration of the effectiveness of such intimidation on the profession at large than what transpired in 1973 at the Sloan-Kettering Institute for Cancer Research. On November first, at an international cancer conference held in Baden-Baden, Germany, representatives of Sloan-Kettering formally announced the results of their first series of tests with Laetrile. Although those tests had been made only on laboratory mice, the results were so encouraging that plans already had been formulated for testing on humans. The first step in these plans was, in the words of the researchers themselves, an "assessment of the tremendous use of Amygdalin-Laetrile in Germany, Italy, Mexico, and other countries."

The experiments on mice were conducted by Dr. Kanematsu Sigiura over a nine month period beginning on September 12, 1972. The summary of his findings was issued on June 13, 1973, and stated:

> The results clearly show that Amygdalin significantly inhibits the appearance of lung metastasis in mice bearing spontaneous mammary tumors and increases significantly the inhibition of the growth of the primary tumors . . . . Laetrile also seemed to prevent slightly the appear-

> ance of new tumors . . . . The improvement of health and appearance of the treated animals in comparison to controls is always a common observation. . . . Some preliminary data about Swiss Webster mice is shown in Table II. A total of five mice were used. As seen, three of these mice which had small mammary tumors and were treated as usual with amygdalin showed tumor regression and, in two of these, tumors could no longer be detected. . . . Dr. Sigiura has never observed complete regression of these tumors in all his cosmic experience with other chemotherapeutic agents.[1]

The reader is advised to go back and read that last section again for, as we shall see, just a few months later, spokesmen for Sloan Kettering were flatly denying that there was any evidence whatsoever that Laetrile had any value.

About a month *prior* to the public announcement at Baden-Baden of Dr. Sigiura's "cosmic" findings, this author wrote a short article entitled "A Scenario — Just for the Record." Published in October of 1973, it said:

> Sloan-Kettering is, of course, the epitome of the orthodox Medical Establishment. With untold millions of dollars

[1]"A Summary of the Effect of Amygdalin Upon Spontaneous Mammary Tumors in Mice," Sloan-Kettering report, June 13, 1973.

channelled through its facilities in the "War on Cancer," it would be embarrassing, to say the least, merely to end up serving the function of *confirming* what a handful of independent researchers, without a penny of tax money to support them, have been saying *for over twenty years*. A triumph by free enterprise of such magnitude simply must not be acknowledged by the Establishment which is so deeply committed to government subsidies, government programs, and government control.

Consequently, it is predictable that most of those in science and medicine who now are dependent on government directly or indirectly for support — and that includes Sloan-Kettering — now will struggle to find ways to (1) get on board the Laetrile train; (2) do so in such a way as to save face in spite of their incredible past error, and (3) prevent those who have pioneered Laetrile from receiving the primary credit.

While it always is dangerous to speculate about the future in *precise* terms, nevertheless, it seems probable that the Establishment scenario will be as follows:

LAETRILE IS NOT LAETRILE. Increasingly, the name Laetrile will be replaced by Amygdalin. Great attention will be given to the different kinds and sources of this substance.[1]

The final product may even be combined with another substance which, supposedly, will increase the beneficial effect of the Amygdalin. The name of the final substance will not be Laetrile.

TRIUMPH OF MAN OVER NATURE. In order to vindicate the scientific expense, the final product must appear to be a *man*-made substance. If any recognition at all is given to the *natural* mechanisms, it will be only in passing to the really "important" reactions effected by the man-made concoction. We will be told that it was nature that gave us cancer in the first place, and that man, as a result of his infinite intellect and industry, has in fact improved upon nature. Those who developed and pioneered Laetrile will be mentioned only as early researchers who had stumbled across a small part of the total answer.

GOVERNMENT VINDICATED. Perhaps the most important objective of

---

[1]It should be noted that, in a strictly scientific sense, there *are* minor differences in the molecular arrangements of Laetrile and amygdalin compounds. Nevertheless, the word Laetrile is properly used to denote those *special* compounds that have been developed for cancer therapy, and not to refer to them as such is to cloud the basic issue in the public mind.

Establishment Medicine is to preserve or bolster the sagging image of government. Government direction, control, and ultimately government monopoly in the field of medicine must be sold to the American people at all costs. Consequently, we most likely will be told over and over again how a cure for cancer — that most dread disease — has, at last, been found as a result of the federal government's "War on Cancer." We will be told that the task was much too large to be undertaken by private research; that only government could have done it, not in the name of profit, but in the name of all mankind. In fact, it may develop that the credit will be given to an international effort carried on jointly between *several* governments (most likely the United States and the Soviet Union acting through the World Health Organization of the U.N.) and, thus, be used as a means of generating increased public support of, not just government, but *international* government, as well.

PROFIT. It long has been the policy of large world-wide industries to operate in such a way as to reduce competition between them so as to realize the greatest possible level of profits . . . . The chemical and pharmaceutical industries are well-known to have been consistent par-

> ticipants in restraint-of-trade and cartel agreements.

After describing the Standard Oil agreement with I.G. Farben on the hydrogenation process referred to in a previous chapter, the article continued:

> As it was with the hydrogenation process, so it is with Laetrile. For two decades Laetrile has been viewed as competition which must be eliminated. But now that it is obvious it cannot be eliminated, the move is to "obtain therefrom such benefits as we can, and assure the distribution of the products in question through our existing marketing facilities."
>
> We can look forward to the prospects of having Laetrile mass-produced either under the name Amygdalin or in conjunction with some man-made compound under an entirely different name, and then distributed through existing channels of prescription drugs. There will be little or no price competition in such distribution and, although the actual price will not seem unreasonable considering the benefits derived, there will be an overly ample profit margin to the manufacturers. Above all, however, it will

> not be regarded as a nutritional factor or as a vitamin, and, thus, the general prestige and sales market for drugs will not be endangered. The present drive of Establishment Medicine against vitamins consequently can continue without hindrance.
>
> All of this is part of the anticipated scenario which begins with the tests of Sloan-Kettering. Will it turn out this way? Of course, only time will tell. Perhaps even this prediction, if read by enough people, could set into motion a series of events that would cause it *not* to come to pass. As a matter of fact, that is the very reason the prediction is being made. It is axiomatic that deception cannot be successful if the person to be deceived is warned in advance. By making it clear beforehand what is expected, it is this author's hope either to thwart the deceivers altogether, or at least to force them to seek an alternate course which either will be less harmful or more obvious.[1]

Little was it realized when these words were published just how prophetically accurate they would become. Many of the predictions, of course, still remain to be tested by future events, but none of them have yet been proven wrong, and the gen-

[1]Committee for Freedom of Choice newsletter, Oct. 1973.

eral theme underlying the specifics has been borne out in a most dramatic way.

This author was informed by a reliable source close to Sloan-Kettering that the publication of "A Scenario" had caused a great deal of concern among the top officials there. It had complicated their task which was already difficult in view of strong pressures "from above" to drop the entire Laetrile investigation. It was suggested that a "softer" approach would make it easier for established researchers to "move in our direction," and that a continuation of the "hard line" could only delay the ultimate acceptance of Laetrile. It was suggested that Dr. Lloyd Old, in charge of the research project at Sloan-Kettering, really was firmly convinced of the trophoblastic thesis and was most anxious to help, but that all this hard-line talk about vested interests, cartels, and political corruption was making his superiors — and *their* superiors — increasingly touchy about the whole matter.

If true, this was an incredible admission. Here was a group of professional researchers charged with the grave responsibility of finding a means to stop the annual cancer slaughter. The lives of millions literally hang on the outcome of their work. Yet, they were saying that bad public relations or the loss of prestige in the public mind could well force them to abandon or bury a research project which, by their own admission, was extremely promising!

Researchers — even those on the staffs of such prestigious institutions as Sloan-Kettering — must eat. Once they break the discipline of the Establishment, there are few places that will hire them. So they follow orders and keep quiet.

Three months later, on January 10, 1974, Dr. Robert Good, the president of Sloan-Kettering, announced flatly that the extensive evidence produced by its previous tests now simply did not exist and even went so far as to describe his own organization's formal presentation at Baden-Baden and its official statements given to the press at that time as a "premature leak" of information. Dr. Good said:

> At this moment there is no evidence that Laetrile has any effect on cancer. . . . A premature leak last fall of test information from the laboratory had given thousands of cancer victims false hope that Laetrile might work.[1]

As stated in "The Scenario:"

> By making it clear beforehand, what is expected, it is this author's hope either to thwart the deceivers altogether, or at least to force them to seek an alternate course which either will be less harmful or more obvious.

---

[1] "News in Brief; The Nation," *L.A. Times*, Jan. 10, 1974, Part I, p. 2.

It is the considered opinion of many that for Sloan-Kettering to reject the project completely is both less harmful *and* more obvious than for it to proceed along the lines of the scenario for, in this way, the road is still open ahead to a real solution to cancer *without* the further concentration of economic and political power.

At the time of this writing sources inside Sloan Kettering have said that a third round of clinical trials with Laetrile has been just as promising — if not more so — than the first. We are told that those in charge of the project are hesitant to discuss the matter publicly until the entire series of tests is complete, and that they are hoping to announce the effectiveness of Laetrile just as soon as they have enough data to satisfy all the skeptics. This, of course, sounds like a reasonable course of action, but we will not hold our breath waiting — especially since those tests could well be stretched out over many months or even years. Let us hope that those inside Sloan Kettering will be successful in resisting the pressures from above, but we must be pardoned for postponing our celebrations until completion of the deed.

There are those who feel that, aside from the question of profits and power, it makes little difference who receives the credit for solving the cancer problem as long as it *is* solved and people are no longer dying. But it *does* make a difference. It makes a *big* difference if the people, organizations, and philosophies given the credit are, in truth, the very ones that were responsible for its hindrance. It *does* make a difference if those who earn the honorary degrees and medical prizes are the ones who, by their ignorance, arrogance, or subservience, held back the truth for over two decades. And it makes a *substantial* difference if those who claim the privilege of political leadership do so as the result of policies which have caused so much suffering and death among their fellow citizens that it can be classfied only as mass-murder. The difference it makes, in other words, is that *the future must not be entrusted to those who have betrayed the past.*

The Sloan-Kettering episode was merely another confirmation of the fact that there are relatively few within the medical profession who are able to stand up against the crushing pressures for conformity. Returning again to Dr. Kreb's letter of counsel to Dr. Richardson, Krebs wrote:

> Cancer is where the action is. The innocents who touch Laetrile experience a traumatic syndrome unparalleled in American life. This is why we so strongly counsel many fine and dedicated doctors to refrain. Of course, every society always has a few who cannot live fully without walking the highest wire in the tent.

Dr. Richardson appreciated this caution from his friend who had already walked the wire, but he had been to the top of the tent himself and there was no turning back once he had become convinced through his own clinical experience that nutritional therapy actually worked.

John Richardson was no stranger to unpopular causes. As a long-time member of The John Birch Society, he already had sampled the bitter taste of attacks in the Establishment press and the predictable public scorn that always is generated by such attacks. He knew that, while most people usually will agree that "you can't believe a thing you read in the papers," nevertheless, they *do* believe without question almost everything that is printed. Also, the Birch Society long had been trying to tell the American people that there was little difference between Communism, Fascism, Nazism, Socialism, New Dealism, or any other kind of "ism" that is based upon the concept of big government. It had advanced the argument that the only solution to most of the world's problems today lay in the reduction of the size and power of government. In so doing, it had taken aim at the very mainspring of the cartel's mechanism for profit and power. If this mainspring of big government were to be disabled, the machinery of every petty dictator and despot also would be brought to a halt. Individuals or organizations may be allowed to oppose lesser parts of the mechanism such as "Communist subversion," or "corruption in public office," or "tax loopholes," or even "deficit spending." But let an organization draw a bead on the prime mover behind all of these manifestations — the concept of big government itself — and it will know the wrath of the cartel *finpols,* the Communists, the neo-Nazis, the petty bureaucrats, and all other would-be dictators of the American Republic. Each of these may fight the other for relative rank and wealth within what they believe will be a world government of unlimited power, but they all close ranks against the common enemy who has the audacity to advocate — *and to work for* — a reduction in the size and power of government.

Consequently, Dr. Richardson not only was used to the scorn of many of his fellow citizens who slavishly but unwittingly follow the lead of the opinion molders in the mass press, but he also was sufficiently informed about the dual nature of monopoly and totalitarian government to readily understand the true nature of the broad forces arrayed against him. While others in the Laetrile movement tried to "enlighten" the FDA to its error in hopes that it would change its position, he knew that they totally were wasting their time. While others circulated petitions requesting the FDA to grant permission for the further testing of Laetrile, he said: "Get the FDA out of it altogether." While others were stunned at the blatantly unfair treatment given to them by the TV directors of NBC, he was surprised only that it wasn't worse. And while others instruct their attorneys to find some legal technicality to avoid a full confrontation with the law, Dr. Richardson has sought ways to test the constitutionality of the law itself and is determined to take the issue, not only to the Supreme Court of the federal government but to the ultimate Supreme Court of the land — The Court of Public Opinion.

Dr. Richardson was arrested on June 2, 1972, for violating the California FDA's "anti-quackery" law — which means that he was charged with using Laetrile in the treatment of cancer. Armed officials burst into his office and, in the presence of patients (as well as news photographers whom the FDA had tipped off to cover the arrest), they handcuffed him and his two nurses and hauled them off to jail like dangerous criminals. The office was ransacked and every bit of Dr. Richardson's personal files and correspondence was seized. Patients desperately in need of medical treatment were sent home. One child with advanced cancer of the leg died shortly afterward. And it is not impossible that the death could have been prevented if it had not been for the delays and the psychological trauma resulting from the arrest.

Dr. Richardson's legal battle for medical freedom was long and costly. In May of 1974, after two years of litigation and two trials — both of which resulted in hung juries — the judge advised the food and drug authorities that they had failed to prove their case and that, consequently, all charges against Dr. Richardson were being dismissed.

The excellent point made during the trials by defense attorney George Kell was that vitamin B_{17} was used by Dr. Richardson, not for the treatment of the lump or bump that orthodox medicine *calls* cancer, but for a general metabolic deficiency condition which *causes* the lump or bump. The tumors are the *symptom* of the disease, not the disease itself.

This is an important scientific and legal point, but it is much too narrow to be of major significance to the overall problem. It may be that, as a result of this case, American doctors will be able to use Laetrile if they drop the word *cancer* from their vocabulary, but it is anticipated that the FDA will not let it rest there. It is both possible and likely that new administrative rulings or definitions will be forthcoming to close the door on medical freedom once again.

It is obvious, therefore, that, regardless of the success of this particular case, the major battles are yet to come. There must be many similar court and legislative victories before the ultimate constitutional goal is achieved. And if these battles are to be fought, they must be led by men such as Ernst Krebs and John Richardson — men who do not shirk from the danger or the controversy. Let us hope that there will be many like them who are not afraid to step forward and to walk the highest wire.

XXIV

A QUESTION OF MOTIVES

Conclusions regarding the specific motives that have led various groups into opposition to vitamin therapy; particular perspective given to the role played by desire for world government; a review of the "limited" vs. "total" conspiracy theories; and an appraisal of grass-roots backlash as a force for potential change.

"Who are they, John? Why would anyone want to hold back a cure for cancer?"

It was skepticism and curiosity behind this question addressed to Dr. John Richardson that led this author into what turned out to be a two-and-a-half year research and writing project. This lengthy tome is the result of that effort, and well over half of its pages have been devoted to an attempt to answer that key question of motives. It is time, now, to draw this information together into specific conclusions.

First of all, as emphasized many times during the course of this study, the overwhelming majority of those in the medical, pharmaceutical, research, and fund-raising industries are deeply conscientious individuals dedicated to their work. It is their firm conviction that what they are doing, as channeled within the confines of "the system," is in the best interest of mankind. This is particularly true of the typical physician who has received little training in organic nutrition, has never heard of the trophoblastic thesis of cancer, never has had a chance to use Laetrile, never has read a favorable review of vitamin therapy in accepted medical journals, and never has had any reason to question the reliability of the foundation and tax-supported "experts" who claim to have done the research. The very worst that can be said about these men and women is that they are biased against vitamin therapy.

But bias is universal. It probably is true that there never has been a truly unbiased man. We all are biased in favor of those things we believe to be true. It is a myth that, somehow, scientists are less biased than artists, businessmen, or politicians. They may be expert at *pretending* objectivity, for that is the expected image of their profession, but they are just as closed-minded on just as many topics as the rest of us — no more, no less. Their bias against vitamin therapy is, under the circumstances, both natural and understandable. It may be deplorable, but it certainly is not sinister.

Moving down the scale of motives, we come next to what might be called "careerism." The careerist is not a bad guy either, but he does suffer from a strong vested interest which often gets in the way of objectivity. It was described aptly by columnist Charles McCabe:

> You might be wondering if the personnel of the American Cancer Society, of cancer research foundations, and other sainted organizations, are *truly* interested in a cure for cancer. Or whether they would like the problem which supports them to continue to exist. You might even grow so base as to believe that there is a certain personality type which is deeply attracted to exploitable causes. They might be called the true blue careerists. I recently had this type defined for me with admirable succinctness:
>
> "The crucial concept is that of a careerist, an individual who converts a public problem into a personal career and rescues himself from obscurity, penury, or desperation. These men work with a dedication that may appear to be selfless so long as the problem is insoluble.
>
> "Should proposals for change in public policy or the normal evolution of our culture threaten resolution of the mess, it becomes apparent that they have a vested interest in maintaining the magnitude and emotional load of the problem . . . ."

> This strange and dangerous kind of reformer has always been with us. The type has gained a truly formidable acceptance in our time. These are the guys who know the answers for problems which do not, at the moment, have any convenient answers. They resist like hell the approach of any real answer which might threaten their holy selflessness.[1]

It is natural for the careerist to gravitate into such apparently humanitarian organizations as the American Cancer Society. Not only does this provide him with the aura of status among his approving friends, but it also provides some pretty nice employment in a low pressure field devoid of competition or of the economic necessity to show either a profit or even tangible results. In fact, it is the very *lack* of results that adds stature to his position and importance to his work. In this cushy atmosphere, the careerist leisurely dreams up endless schemes for raising funds. Sailors line up on the deck of an aircraft carrier to be photographed from the air as they spell out "Fight Cancer." Public buildings everywhere display posters bearing the slogan "Fight Cancer With a Check-up *and a Check.*" Housewives are recruited to hold rummage sales and to go from door to door raising funds. Athletes are urged to participate in special sporting events. Employees are pressured to authorize payroll de-

---

[1]"The Fearless Spectator," *San Francisco Chronicle*, Sept. 27, 1971, p. 35.

ductions. Service clubs are persuaded to sponsor information booths, carnivals, and movie-mobiles. And relatives of deceased cancer victims are encouraged to have obituaries state "the family prefers contributions to the American Cancer Society."

In this way, the careerist is able to enlist the services of over two million volunteers each year who, in turn, collect about one hundred million dollars. Of this amount, only about one-fourth goes into actual research. *None* of it goes into the investigation of possible nutritional factors. Once *that* door is opened, of course, the final solution to the cancer problem will walk right into those plush offices, stand on the deep pile carpet, and announce in no mistaken terms that the American Cancer Society, and those who work for it, are no longer needed. And, thus, will be fulfilled the promise contained in this official ACS statement:

> The American Cancer Society is an emergency organization, a temporary organization, seeking in its independent Crusade to obtain enough dollars to wage an unrelenting fight against cancer.[1]

Perhaps that was a freudian slip, but notice that it did not say that the objective was to *defeat* cancer, but merely to *fight* cancer. Unless cancer is *defeated,* the fight could go on *forever*. The American Cancer Society has been an "emergency organization, a temporary organization" since 1913!

[1] "American Cancer Society, Inc." ACS booklet, undated, p. 17.

The tracks of the careerist are evident everywhere. It is obvious that careerism has been an important factor in the opposition to vitamin therapy—not just in the field of cancer, but in multiple sclerosis, muscular dystrophy, and other noninfectious diseases as well. It is equally certain, however, that this opposition has not been the result of conscious, premeditated malice. Rather, it has been the product of the subconscious need which characterizes the careerist personality. We are still dealing with men and women who basically are innocent of evil intent.

As we move down the scale of motives into the next category, however, the shading begins clearly to take on the hue of grey. The category is profit.

Profit, *per se,* is neither good nor bad. It depends on the circumstances under which it is earned. Profit is merely another word for "pay." It is the compensation received by an individual in return for risking his savings or for investing his time in a business venture. Profits, therefore, like other forms of pay, are good *if* they are earned in such a way that no one is coerced or cheated. So long as there is complete freedom of choice to buy or not to buy, or to buy from another source, and so long as all voluntary agreements between buyer and seller, lender and borrower, are fulfilled honestly, then the profits that result are fair—regardless of their size. But if any party to the transaction is coerced into terms or prices he would not otherwise accept, or if his options to take his business elsewhere have been limited by conspiracy or any other forces outside of free market competition, then the profits that result, no matter how small, are unfair because they have been garnered wholly or partly by force or deceit. It makes little difference if these acts are imposed by government, trade associations, labor unions, cartels, or organized crime syndicates.

Obtaining money through coercion or deception is the essence of theft. And it is *this* kind of profit that now shows up on our scale.

It long has been the policy of multi-national companies to operate in such a way as to reduce competition between themselves for the purpose of limiting consumer options, pushing prices above the natural level dictated by supply and demand, and, thus, realizing an artificially high level of profits. Such arrangements between companies are called restraint-of-trade agreements. The chemical and pharmaceutical industries are well-known to have been both the pioneers of and the leading participants in cartel restraint-of-trade. Much of the vicious and totally dishonest opposition to non-drug therapy in cancer can be understood only with this fact in mind.

The reality of price-fixing in the field of drugs shows itself in many ways. One of them is that some drugs manufactured in the United States are sold much cheaper if they are destined for other countries. To lower the prices in America, even though the drugs are produced there, would violate price-support agreements. As pointed out by Senator Gaylord Nelson, Chairman of the Senate Small

Business Subcommittee on Monopoly:

> Yes, many American drug companies sell drugs to domestic wholesalers at different prices, depending on where the drug is to be used. If the domestic wholesaler states that the drug will be shipped overseas, his price may well be fifty percent lower. It would be hard to find a more glaring case of price discrimination against the American consumer than this one.[1]

Artificially inflated prices are not the only byproduct of cartel agreements. Scarcity of product selection, *or no product at all,* sometimes can be much worse. We are not speaking here of limiting the number of manufacturers for a particular product within a particular territory—although that is bad enough—but of holding a product off the market completely so as to more fully exploit an existing product that may be more profitable. This appears to have been the rationale behind the Standard Oil-Shell decision to de-emphasize its hydrogenation process whereby it can make high-grade gasoline from low-grade coal (an interesting thought-for-the-day during contemporary periods of so-called "energy crisis").

In the field of medicine, it was this same artificial manipulation of markets that led to the unconscionable delay in the use of sulfa. Richard

---

[1] "Ask Them Yourself," *Family Weekly, News Chronicle,* Oct. 7, 1973, p. 1.

Sasuly comments:

> I.G. Farben sometimes held back new products or methods. The sulfa drugs are a case in point. . . . There were American cartel partners of the I.G. who were willing to rest on what looked like assured markets and therefore held back new developments . . . .
>
> I.G. had been holding back from the public of the whole world a great life-saver because it wanted a product which it could patent and hold exclusively . . . . It is difficult and painful to try to estimate the number of lives which might have been saved if sulfanilamide had not been buried in the laboratories of a vast monopoly which had been trying to pick its own most profitable time for granting new medicines to the public.[1]

The super-profits of the drug and research industry are, needless to say, greatly enhanced by the rising toll of cancer. A substantial portion of the income for these industries now is channeled through the federal government and winds up in the pockets of politically favored individuals and institutions. With the federal cancer budget now running over one and a half billion dollars a year, the potential for corruption is enormous.

---

[1]Sasuly, *I.G. Farben, op. cit.,* pp. 134, 135, 32.

"Who needs the primitive old fashioned form of graft in government," asks Dr. Krebs, "when a division of HEW can aseptically award Hoffman-LaRoche with a $1,250,000 contract for 5-FU 'clinical investigation' of this drug when, without patent protection, the same amount of the chemical could be produced for about $17,000?"[1]

With the subject of graft and political corruption, we now have arrived at a fourth and still lower stratum of motives, a stratum that must not be overlooked if we are to understand and cope with those forces acting against freedom of choice in cancer therapy. It is a fact of life that there are those with political ambitions who will seize upon any excuse for the expansion of their influence and power over others. The cancer crisis is tailor-made for their objectives. While they may have had no part in creating that crisis, nevertheless their professed interest in solving it is largely a sham and a ploy to win approval of the voters and to further secure themselves in the seat of governmental power.

As government becomes more onerous and oppressive to the people, it needs public relations tidbits to reassure and mollify the restless citizen. If a resented dictatorship could successfully hold off public knowledge of vitamin B_{17} until after it has funded billions for research in a much ballyhooed "war on cancer," and if the final solution to the cancer problem can be sold to the people as a "victory" in that war, then the masses could be further

[1]Letter to the author dated Dec. 26, 1972.

conditioned to accept government as the logical agent in the field of medicine and even might be persuaded to view their dictatorship with worshipping eyes of trust and gratitude. "Big brother may be harsh," they will say, "but he is *good!*"

There is much to be learned in this regard by observing the pattern of Hitler's rise to power. Encouraged by the cartels in the background, the German parliament had expanded Bismarck's initial plan of government medical care until it had become a dominant aspect of everyday life in pre-Nazi Germany. Matthew Lynch and Stanley Raphael, in their scholarly study, *Medicine and the State,* tell us:

> Although it is difficult to estimate with any precision how great a role this [socialist] network played in assisting the Nazi rise to power, there can be little doubt that it was a considerable one. The administration of social insurance reached into every corner of the country, and at least 70 per cent of its personnel belonged to the ADGB [German General Trade Union Congress] which was taken over by the Nazis. The whole social insurance structure, and its sickness division in particular, was a natural, ready-made network for the spread of Nazi influence and control.[1]

[1]Lynch and Raphael, *Medicine and the State,* (originally published 1963 by Charles C. Thomas. Reprinted by Association of American Physicians and Surgeons, Oak Brook, Ill., 1973), p. 34.

Socialized medicine's value to the success of Nazism also was recognized by the Canadian parliament's committee on health insurance. In a special report issued in March of that year, the committee stated bluntly:

> During the early years of Hitler's regime, the government's medical programme was looked upon by many observers as one of the greatest props of the totalitarian state.[1]

Following in the footsteps of Bismarck and Hitler, American political leaders for years have been competing with each other to see which one can push the nation faster and deeper into a government health care program. Not one prominent voice in Washington ever has been raised in favor of actually *reducing* present levels of government involvement. Consequently, year after year, we move closer and closer to a system of medicine advocated and practiced by all totalitarian regimes.

In spite of continuing political pressures from above, the American people have been slow to embrace government medicine, especially since they have been able to see the disastrous consequences of similar programs in other countries. But their resistance has been weakened tremendously by the rapidly rising costs of medical care, *most of which can be attributed directly to the fantastic*

[1]Report of the Advisory Committee on Health Insurance, March 16, 1943, (King's Printer, Ottawa), p. 108.

costs of orthodox cancer therapy. In other words, if an inexpensive control for cancer were to be made available today, the nation's medical bill would be so drastically reduced that tomorrow there would be little steam left in the boiler for government intervention in this vital field. The politician and the bureaucrat may speak with concern over the rising costs of medical care, but secretly they are delighted because this provides them with a *cause celebre,* a justification for their expansionist proposals.

The Honorable John G. Schmitz, former Congressman from California, in a special report to his constituents dated October 27, 1971, offered this analysis:

> Very early in this year's Congressional session, Senator Edward Kennedy introduced with enormous fanfare a bill (S. 34) grandiloquently entitled "The Conquest of Cancer Act." Its formula for conquering cancer was very simple, if a bit shopworn: set up a new Federal bureau with lots of money.
>
> Assuming—quite correctly, as it turned out—that opposition to the "Conquest of Cancer Act" would promptly be labelled as tantamount to being in favor of cancer, President Nixon got in line with his own "Conquest of Cancer Act," differing in no essential respect from Senator Kennedy's bill but carrying a different

> number (S. 1828). This bill passed the Senate by the lopsided vote of 70 to 1.
>
> The "railroad" was on, and the American Cancer Society, in full page advertisements in the *New York Times* and the two major Washington papers, had the unmitigated gall to state that "objections to the bill have come mainly from people who do not have expert cancer knowledge." My files bulge with statements from some of the outstanding scientists, physicians, and cancer researchers in the United States opposing the Kennedy-Nixon grandstand play, including one signed by no less than four Nobel prize winners in medicine . . . .
>
> Another sprawling bureaucracy is not going to find either cause or cure any faster. More likely, it will actually hamper the search for them by "locking in" the present preconceptions and biases of researchers specializing strictly in this field.

The quantity of tax dollars squandered on blind alley cancer research projects is staggering. Americans will tolerate any absurdity, it seems, so long as it is promoted as an attempt to resolve some popular "crisis." The "crisis" in Vietnam, the "crisis" in the Middle-East, the ecology "crisis," the energy "crisis," the population "crisis"—the list is limited only by the creative imagination of the manipulators and the naive gullibility of the manipulated. Each crisis is built up in the public mind as a prelude to their willing acceptance of still further encroachment upon their liberties.

In August of 1973, President Nixon announced a *five year plan* in the battle against cancer. Reminiscent of the classical Soviet approach to such problems, this really was an announcement that the "crisis" had become institutionalized. It was a guarantee that the goals would *not* be achieved. Each failure will result in revised goals, greatly expanded bureaucracy, and another five year plan.

The federal budget for the cancer "crisis" now is over half a *billion* dollars a year and is steadily climbing. As Congressman Schmitz observed, "The railroad is on," and it is a gravy train in the grand political tradition.

Government control over scientific research almost never produces usable results, except in the field of destructive weapons and related hardware such as rockets. The reason is that this is the only field in which government has a *primary* interest. It is a question of instinct for self-survival and governments, like living creatures, have this instinct. In fact, it is the *only* government instinct that can be relied upon with any degree of certainty, and it will be activated just as readily against its own citizens as it will against those of a rival government—which is why there are such things as revolutions.

Those who feel that government should direct non-military scientific projects, such as the quest for cancer control, would do well to ponder the significance of a report in the *Los Angeles Times* of

December 6, 1972. After describing at some length the massive undertaking of an international cancer research program (the IARC) — a joint venture of the governments of the United States, the Soviet Union, France, Britain, West Germany, Italy, the Netherlands, Belgium, Australia, and Japan—the article stated that the agency had recently acquired massive headquarters in a six million dollar building in Lyon, France. And then it explained:

> Now, seven years after its founding, and two weeks after moving into a new fourteen story headquarters building in Lyon, the agency feels it has come to terms with its own personality.[1]

Incredible as it may seem, after seven years of research, after the expenditure of untold millions of tax dollars from eleven countries, and after taking occupancy of a six million dollar, fourteen story building, all that this government project can show for results is the exciting discovery that "it has come to terms with its own personality."

Such are the predictable fruits of all government growths in the orchard of non-military science.

The steel ring of government control perceptively tightens around our necks. We are told what foods we may or may not eat, what vitamins we may purchase and in what potency or combinations, what medical treatments we may seek, whom we

[1] "Cancer Control Inquiry Reaches Around World," *L.A. Times*, Dec. 6, 1972, p. A-2.

may hire, what we must pay, what prices we may charge, to whom we must sell, where our children must go to school, what they must learn, and soon we are to be told what physician to see and what drugs to take. Each of these insults to our individuality has been inspired by a series of national or international "crises." The end result is that there now is a crisis much more serious and real than all the others put together. It is a crisis of personal freedom.

The people of the United States, as well as those in every other country in the world, step-by-step are traveling the road to bondage. They are following the pied piper of big government playing the beguiling tunes of security, brotherhood, and equality. At the end of that road lies the cage of a world totalitarian regime deceptively decorated for now as an international democratic forum where men of good will can come together in the cause of peace.

It is no secret that the U.N. is the special creation of the same international groupings that comprise the world's hidden cartel structure. The role played in the United States by the Rockefeller grouping and the Council on Foreign Relations has been chronicled in a previous chapter and need not be repeated. It should be recognized, however, that, for over three decades, the *only* consistent and firmly pursued foreign policy objective of the State Department (staffed almost exclusively by members of the CFR) has been to hasten the strengthening of the U.N. into a true world government and to bring about the subordination to it of all nations-

—including the United States. On the assumption that sovereignty among nations is the cause of war, the Grand Design of U.S. foreign policy is to eliminate all such sovereignty by transferring control of the entire world's military might—especially nuclear weapons—into the hands of U.N. politicians. Under the slogan of *disarmament for peace*, therefore, the wheels now are in motion to create a world political entity entirely in the hands of the international *finpols* who created it. With ultimate control over all nuclear weapons, that super-state will be so powerful that no man or no disarmed nation-state could resist its edicts.[1]

It is impossible to understand U.S. foreign policy without this background knowledge. Everything done by present leaders of the United States conforms to this goal of world government. *Everything!* Before it would be possible to merge the United States with the rest of the nations of the world, it would be necessary to bring their economies and standards of living into line. That means massive foreign aid to the less developed nations to bring them *up* and all kinds of wasteful spending, exhausting wars, and shortage-creating restrictions to bring the United States *down*.

The subject of foreign policy *is* relevant to the politics of cancer. Just as it was learned years after

---

[1]For a more detailed analysis of this question, the reader is referred to three previous works by the author: *The Fearful Master – A Second Look at the United Nations*, *The Grand Design – An Overview of U.S. Foreign Policy*, and *The Capitalist Conspiracy – An Inside View of International Banking*. All three publications may be ordered from American Media, P.O. Box 4646, Westlake Village, Calif. 91359.

the fact that the American space program was deliberately held back at the highest decision levels in Washington so as to give the Soviets the international prestige of putting up the first artificial satellite (which brought their scientific and military credibility *up* in the eyes of the world and provided further justification for American disarmament concessions), it also is quite possible that the same motivation is partially responsible for holding back public awareness of a control for cancer. It is now quite obvious that American political leaders are extremely anxious to have the cure for cancer come from another country or at least as a result of international efforts. Once again, we find that their primary concern is to make sure that the ultimate victory will be achieved in such a way as not to enhance the prestige or position of the United States but to further the concept of internationalism and the goal of world government.

In January, 1972, former presidential candidate Hubert Humphrey put it this way:

> There is rich precedent for making the U.N. our forum. We used it to get the treaty that prohibits putting weapons in outer space. And the one that does the same for the seabed. Now we hope to get an international agreement on the environment there. Why not also for the global war on cancer? Should diplomats be the only ones to talk in the U.N. about war, arms control, and peace treaties? Why can't doctors talk there, too, about

> ways of enlisting all mankind in advancing scientific medicine?[1]

An article from UPI dated February 1, 1972, reported that President Nixon had ordered his top cancer officials to work closely with other nations, particularly the Soviet Union and the Peoples Republic of China. The article stated: "Nixon stressed that he wanted the anti-cancer campaign to be an international effort."[2]

In September of that same year, President Nixon addressed the National Cancer Conference at the Biltmore Hotel in Los Angeles. During his speech, he stressed that cancer research was one of the main forces through which peoples of the world can "work for peace." The concept of "peace," of course, usually is offered as a political synonym for world government and the U.N. Nixon explained:

> Perhaps the fight against cancer can help to teach the world that, despite immense differences between cultures and values and political systems, nations must work together to meet their common needs. Like drug abuse, like hijacking, like terrorism, cancer is an international

---

[1] "We Must Pool the World's Anti-Cancer Resources," Hubert H. Humphrey, *Family Weekly,* Jan. 23, 1972, p. 14.

[2] "World Cancer Battle Waged," UPI, *The Daily Review,* Hayward, Calif., Feb. 1, 1972.

> menace. We must confront it with an international alliance.[1]

At the risk of becoming redundant, it should be stated once again that big government is the necessary ally of monopoly, and *world* government is the goal of the cartelists and *finpols* who have been the quiet, seemingly philanthropic sponsors and promoters of the U.N. from its very inception. The fact that the majority of Americans are unaware of this fact or that *they* are sincere in their hopes for international peace and brotherhood does not alter the grim reality one bit. Everything the cartels and multi-national companies do is in furtherance of one or both of their two objectives: the creation of greater wealth for those who control them and the coalescing of all political power into fewer and fewer hands with the apex of that power converging into world government—and with themselves firmly in control from behind the scenes.

Anthony Sampson in his book *The Sovereign State of ITT*, touched upon this phenomenon when he wrote:

> That multinational companies need a more effective control is accepted by many of their own employees. But who can control them? The conventional remedy is for the nations to organize themselves into greater units, and eventually

---

[1]"Cancer War A Force for Peace—Nixon," *L.A. Herald Examiner*, Sept. 28, 1972, p. 1.

> into some kind of world government, in order to limit the abuses; the multinational enterprises would thus stimulate world society through a contained process of conflict.[1]

Charles Levinson, secretary-general of the International Federation of Chemical and General Workers' Union in Geneva, has learned about the cartel from years of first hand knowledge and confrontation, and he tells it like it is. This is how he told it to the *Wall Street Journal* as published on June 17, 1974:

> Geneva — When the United Nations held hearings here late last year on the problems posed by multinational companies, officials assumed that one of the star witnesses would be trade unionist Charles Levinson.
>
> After all, they reasoned, he is a prolific author on the topic, passionately eager to challenge the multinationals and articulately at home in the spotlight. Besides, he lives just up the hill from the Palais des Nations hearing room.
>
> But Mr. Levinson declined the invitation to testify — for reasons that went something like this: "One, I'm not a clown.

[1]*Op. cit.*, pp. 304, 305.

Two, I'm not a member of the Atlantic Council. Three, I don't fornicate with the foundations."

Instead of seeking truth, Mr. Levinson says, the UN officials wanted "clowns" to perform in a forum carefully contrived to make the UN look alive while giving the multinationals a protective coat of whitewash. In Mr. Levinson's view, the UN and such prestigious private groups as the Washington-based Atlantic Council and the Rockefeller Foundation are all parts of an international elite that manages much of the world's business, finance, politics, and even wars, to its own advantage. . . .

Does that mean Mr. Levinson is out to destroy the multi-nationals? "No, no, no, absolutely not," he says. "You cannot be against multinationals as such. It isn't possible." There is "no possibility of a modern enterprise functioning in today's world" unless it attains a global scale, he says.

Nor does his avowed socialism mean he would like to see all the giants nationalized someday. "I am no longer in support of the collectivization of the means of production according to classical Marxist concept," he states. In fact, he adds, "I am afraid of extensive nationalization. "It would only concentrate more power in the hands of authoritarian right-wing regimes . . . while in eastern Europe state ownership has meant "merely replacing one group of elitists with another."

What Mr. Levinson does want goes beyond ordinary bread-and-butter unionism to what he depicts as a last chance to preserve a measure of human freedom against a capitalist-Communist conspiracy. . . .

As things look from his austere office in a luxury building, companies are "authoritarian" and increasingly interlocked. "Look at that chart on the wall," Mr. Levinson says with a gesture. The pale-blue paper bears the names of the world's 50 largest chemical companies, listed both horizontally and vertically with black dots to show the joint ventures they have with one another. "I stopped doing them," he says. "That thing would have become black." Among the major petroleum companies, "I counted 2,000 joint ventures" before stopping, he says, and he estimates that they probably have 10,000. Before long, he predicts, all modern industries will be "completely controlled and dominated by a handful of

> multinational companies, all interlinked, all joint-ventured, all financially integrated in the same banking consortia." . . .
>
> To a large extent, he says, the power is "centered within David Rockefeller's operation." This sphere encompasses, he charges, not only the Chase Manhattan Bank, which Mr. Rockefeller chairs, but also the big oil companies, Secretary of State Henry Kissinger and many corporations that Mr. Levinson sees as linked through foundations in two ways: The corporations' executives run the foundations, and the foundations own shares of the corporations.[1]

Many people have been so sheltered from the hard economic and political realities of the world that they find it almost impossible to believe that such worthy endeavors as world peace or cancer research have been twisted and degraded to serve the selfish motives of a few. The thought of malicious conspiracy hiding behind the smiling mask of humanitarianism is repugnant to their minds and alien to their experience. Europeans tend to be more alert to this possibility for their political history is so filled with conspiracies that they look upon them more as the rule than as the exception. Americans, however, have not had this historical

---

[1] "How One Man Helps Unions Match Wits With Multinationals," by Richard F. Janssen, *Wall Street Journal,* June 17, 1974.

experience, and the average citizen is vulnerable because of it. Judging all others by his own standards, he cannot believe that there are men who would sacrifice the lives of others for the advancement of their own positions. Perhaps in *other* countries, yes, but not in America. It is as though the casting of his personal ballot somehow has sanctified his candidates and made them incapable of selfish motives or foul deeds. Consequently, many people instinctively back away from any thought of there being a conscious direction behind the opposition to Laetrile and prefer to believe that all is ignorance and bureaucratic bungling.

It is possible, of course, to view the long history of harassment as just that. But exactly the same argument is offered as an excuse in all the other problem areas of society. We are told that inflation, for instance, is not consciously planned; it just happens because of ignorance and bureaucratic bungling. Price controls and rationing are not planned either; they are merely the unfortunate consequences of ignorance and bureaucratic bungling. The growing rolls of welfare recipients are not planned; they merely are the result of fallacious idealism and bureaucratic bungling. Rising crime is not planned by anyone but is just the result of short-sighted judicial philosophy and bureaucratic bungling. Gasoline shortages and the energy crisis are not the result of conspiracy but of an unforeseen Middle-East conflict and bureaucratic bungling.

The exhaustion of the nation's reserves in continual no-win wars is not the result of design but merely a lack of clear foreign policy objectives and bureaucratic bungling. The ever-increasing rules, regulations, subsidies, and restraints connected with every phase of our lives—none of this is planned, you understand; it is just the accidental outcome of ignorance at all levels of society and, of course, bureaucratic bungling.

It might be possible to accept that any one, or two, or even a *dozen* of these tragedies are not planned, but when all the pieces are fitted together like a giant jig-saw puzzle, an obvious pattern emerges that is obscured when looking only at one or two pieces at a time. The design is so clear, so uniform, and so universal that it defies all rationality to think that its existence is mere coincidence. The pattern, simply stated, is this: In every one of these problem areas, the only tangible and consistent product of all effort and expenditures is the growth of government control over its citizens. Furthermore, the very people who stand to benefit most from this trend, either financially or politically, always are in the forefront of the effort to convince others that such growth of government is both necessary and desirable. And thirdly, these recipients of power are not ignorant, either of historical perspective or of current realities. From *their* point of view, they are *not* bungling the job.

Let us acknowledge that it is not at all necessary for political or industrial leaders to consciously choose the suffering and death of millions in order for that to be the result of their schemes.

A man may pursue his business with such intensity and singlemindedness that both his family and health suffer greatly. In the end, he may lose his wife and even his life, but that was not his goal.

Likewise, men of finance and politics do not have to sit down together in one giant cabal and decide to hold back Laetrile or vitamin therapy, and it is certain that they do not consciously seek to commit genocide by thwarting a line of research that they *know* will lead to life-saving discoveries. Most of what has happened in this field is the blind result of forces and policies previously set in motion in the quest of other economic and political goals. Their organizations and institutions react reflexively against any obstacle to drug profits. The result is a scientific quagmire which now is claiming millions of lives each year. The fact that, occasionally, one of them also is drawn into that quagmire—as for instance when Winthrop Rockefeller died of cancer in 1973—is small consolation indeed.

The fact that some of the top financial and political leaders of the world *have* died of cancer is strong evidence to support the conclusion that much of the opposition to Laetrile in the past has been more a result of general rather than specific conflicts of interest. It is important to understand, therefore, that many of those who, for financial or political reasons, have opposed the development of Laetrile have not done so with any desire to cause suffering and death. Their single, all-consuming drive has been to expand their financial and political power. And *anything* that gets in the way must be destroyed.

Laetrile got in the way. First the nutritional concept upon which it rests is anathema to the multi-billion dollar drug industry. Second, the fact that it is a product of free-enterprise was an affront to the bureaucracy of big government. Third, the final solution to the cancer problem surely will terminate the gigantic cancer research industry, most of the radio-therapy industry, and much of the surgery now being performed. Loss of revenue in these fields will be catastrophic to thousands of professional fund-raisers, researchers, and technicians. And fourth, the elimination of cancer from the national medical bill will reduce the average cost of medical care each year so drastically that much of the current political pressure for socialized medicine will evaporate into thin air. Yes, Laetrile definitely got in the way.

These reflections lead inexorably to the conclusion that, while there may not be a *specific* conspiracy to hold back a control for cancer, there definitely is a *general* conspiracy which produces those results just the same. Ferdinand Lundberg, in his *The Rich and the Super-Rich,* approached the subject this way:

> Actually, the results at both the top and the bottom are contrived. They are the outcome of pertinacious planning . . . . In any event, overeager members of the financial elite have been caught and convicted in American courts of many literal subconspiracies, so that even in the narrow juristic sense many of them stand forth individually as certified simon-pure conspirators. Consequently, even if there

> is not a single all-embracing conspiracy in juristic terms, it is a fact that there are and have been hundreds of adjudicated single conspiracies. The conspiracy theory, then, has a little more to it than honors-bound academics concede.[1]

Dr. Ernst T. Krebs, Jr., writing to Dr. John Richardson in 1971, stated:

> The view of the "limited conspiracy" is something with which we all can live. This holds that government has unwittingly been used as a tool in behalf of powerful special interests. Those of us who live with the view of the "limited conspiracy" treat it as something as real as the air we breathe . . . .
>
> When you witness our so-called leaders in Washington no longer even making a pretense at moral behavior but accepting the insults of truth with indifference, one finds the conspiratorial theory quite plausible. It would seem that only men who are acting on orders under a plan would continue to flaunt their corrupt practices before the world. Such men can have no real concern or interest in the welfare of their country, which they openly degrade . . . .[2]

---

[1]*Op. cit.*, pp. 21, 327.

[2]Letters dated March 9 and August 3, 1971.

To better understand the *limited* or *specific* conspiracy in the field of cancer, let us imagine a tall cylinder. The cylinder represents a conglomerate of interests, some competing, some overlapping, some in a state of change. *All* of them, however, are bound together by the mutual desire to enhance personal wealth and power by using the force of government to eliminate competition. There are many strata within that cylinder. In fact, almost every level of human activity is represented: banking, commerce, industry, medicine, education, law, politics, to name just a few. What we have done in this study is merely to examine one slice out of that cylinder. We have reached into the broad stratum of medicine and removed only one thin cross-section marked *cancer*. Unfortunately, what we have exposed there can be duplicated at *any* level if only we could spare the time to look.

The reality, therefore, is that there is both a specific or limited conspiracy *and* a general or all-encompassing one. In the field of cancer, as in all other fields, the primary conscious motives of those who conspire are not to create suffering, slavery, or death, but to further their own wealth and power. None but a very few of the most ruthless at the top ever stop to consider the ultimate consequences of their acts. Most are swept along by the momentum of their own institutions. They either go along and are rewarded or they drop away and are crushed.

Thus, the conspiracy becomes as a living, self-propagating organism. Parasitically, it grows and feeds upon those who are not part of it. It saps our freedoms and the fruits of our labor through the sucking tentacles of government. It must be stopped before it completely exhausts and destroys its host.

What possible force can be strong enough to break the fatal grip? Is there anything that can rip away this parasite before it is too late?

There is. It is the invincible force of public opinion. Even dictatorships tremble at its spectre for, once aroused and rallied behind valiant leadership, there is no political or military power on earth that can match it.

Already one can feel a growing backlash at the grass roots level. With thousands of cancer victims as living testimony to the effectiveness of vitamin B_{17}, with hundreds of thousands discovering on their own the value of organic nutrition in direct contradiction to the FDA-AMA position, with Billie Sol Estes and Watergate-type scandals leading millions to realize that they neither can believe nor trust their political leaders, we are coming rapidly to a point of open resistance to government which could make the Boston Tea Party look like child's play.

There are still a few, of course, who, in spite of everything, continue to reassure themselves that totalitarian government could never be imposed on the American people. With each new edict and each new loss of personal liberty, they respond cheerfully. "Don't worry. It can't happen here."

To which Dr. Krebs replies:

> IT CAN HAPPEN HERE. In the U.S.S.R. people are prevented from

> fleeing the country because their masters tell them they are not fit to choose the political system under which they are to live. The choice must be made for them . . . . In the U.S.A. cancer victims are prevented from fleeing for their lives for Laetrile in foreign countries because their government tells these people they are not fit to decide such matters for themselves . . . .
>
> Those who feed the refugees from the U.S.S.R. are prosecuted . . . . Those who feed the cancer refugees from the U.S.A. with admittedly harmless accessory food (vitamin B_{17}) are similarly prosecuted and persecuted.
>
> IT IS HAPPENING HERE. Tyranny knows no boundaries. Unopposed, it flourishes malignantly. How great it would be if even a very small society of patriotic American physicians, banding together, could invoke the Nuremberg principles of defying government in its evil or murderous ends and defiantly use Laetrile.[1]

The mood of rebellion is in the air. Increasingly, men and women who never dreamed of breaking the law are responding to the principles of Nuremberg. They are being driven to choose be-

[1]Open Letter on occasion of arrest of Mrs. Mary C. Whelchel, Feb. 28, 1971.

tween loyalty to the system or loyalty to conscience. In some cases they must even choose between the law or life itself. Many are coming to realize that the system which commanded their loyalty in the past is no longer a reality. It is a hollow shell, a democratic facade thinly veiling the stark structure of dictatorship. When they pledge allegiance to the United States of America and to the Republic for which it *stood,* they do so in sadness as one bids a last requiem farewell at the funeral of a departed loved one.

This is the mood and character of that grassroots public opinion that can and *will* break the grip of the conspiracy. It already is too late to be otherwise. We have come to the last depot stop where men who value their scientific credentials or their personal honor must either get on board or miss the train altogether, because that train is going to keep its schedule with history—with them or without them.

XXV

A WORLD WITHOUT CANCER

Areas of need for future research with B_{17}; how the Laetrile controversy differs from cancer therapy controversies of the past; an analogy between biological and political cancer; and a future projection of how both can be conquered together.

Considering the lack of beneficial results obtained by orthodox medicine, it has been said that voodoo witchcraft would be just as effective — and perhaps even more so — for at least then the patient would be spared the deadly side effects of radiation and chemical poisoning. Just as we are amused today at the primitive medical practices of history, future generations surely will look back at our own era and cringe at the senseless cutting, burning, and poisoning that now passes for medical science.

The advocates of vitamin B_{17} are the first to admit that there is yet much to learn about the natural mechanisms involved in the cause and control of cancer and that there is need for continued caution and understatement. For one thing, there is a growing suspicion among experienced clinicians that B_{17} *in foods* is more effective than in the currently processed and concentrated forms. They would prefer their patients to obtain it in this natural state except for the fact that it is next to impossible to ingest sufficient quantities that way to be therapeutically effective in the treatment of advanced cancer. When the patient needs massive doses quickly, the physician has only one recourse, and that is to administer B_{17} in the highly concentrated, purified, and injectable form. But in the process it is possible that other trace substances associated with B_{17} as it occurs in the natural state may have been eliminated — substances which either act against cancer themselves, or which may serve as catalysts causing either the B_{17} to function more efficiently or stimulating still other mechanisms of the body into action. Just as it is believed by some that organic vitamins obtained from real foods are superior to man-made or synthetic vitamins because of the trace substances found in one but not in the other, so, too, there is a growing respect for B_{17} in the *natural* state.[1] At any rate, even though the basic truths have been unlocked, there is still much to learn, and Laetrile advocates humbly admit the need for continued research.

There have been many other medical controversies centered around cancer therapy.

---

[1]Regardless of what people may believe in this respect, recent FDA rulings, if they are allowed to stand, will make it illegal for anyone to claim or even imply that vitamin supplements derived from organic sources are superior to those that are synthesized. In fact, they will even forbid the manufacturer to identify the source on his label. Thus, truth in packaging is declared illegal by the FDA!

Perhaps the best publicized of these was Dr. Andrew Ivy's chemical formula known as Krebiozen. The Laetrile controversy is substantially different from most of the others, however, in that the formula has not been kept a secret. Its chemical composition and its action have been openly described and willingly shared with all who express an interest. There are no enforceable patents on its manufacture and, consequently, no profits to its discoverer. Dr. Krebs has stated that he has no proprietary interest in Laetrile of any kind, has never received payment for the formula, and has never refused to share his technical knowledge with anyone who desired to manufacture it. His standard reply to all such inquiries is: "Laetrile is the property of all mankind."

A significant aspect of the Laetrile controversy, therefore, is that the proponents have nothing to gain, while the detractors have much to lose. Admittedly, as long as Laetrile is forced by the FDA into a black market operation, those who manufacture and distribute it can be expected to derive substantial profits. These profits, however, merely will reflect the necessary and fair price paid by those who are not willing to run the risk of imprisonment to those who are. After public opinion forces the legalization of Laetrile, the price, of course, will plummet. After that, there will be a transition period of a few years in which vitamin B_{17} will be manufactured in various concentrated forms in order to treat existing cancer victims. This, too, will be a source of income, but, in the absence of government restrictions favoring any one or two manufacturers, others will be attracted into the field and the resulting honest competition can be expected to bring the cost of injectible B_{17} even lower — perhaps to less than one-tenth of present levels. The cost of low concentrate tablets for routine daily use probably will drop to about the same as that of any other vitamin, perhaps even lower.

The most encouraging part of all, however, is that, even if government were to succeed in totally stopping the supply of Laetrile, we still could obtain all the vitamin B_{17} we need to maintain normal health, and we could do so quite legally by selecting the appropriate food. It is abundant in the seeds of apricots, peaches, plums, nectarines, cherries, berries, and apples. It is found in lima beans, bean sprouts, millet, and many other foods. It may take a little effort to obtain it, but no government action — short of imprisonment itself — can stop us from doing so.

Once the story of vitamin B_{17} is widely known, once ground nitriloside-bearing seeds are used on our foods as a routine seasoning, then the battle against cancer finally will be won. In the wake of that battle, of course, there will be many pitiful casualties, men and women who learned the truth too late. Some, mercifully, may be brought back from the edge of the grave for an uncertain time, but they will bear the disfiguring scars of their wounds from surgery and radiation. They may be relieved from pain, but no amount of B_{17} can repair their bodies or return them to total health. Others more fortunate, who were treated sooner and who escaped the butchery of orthodox therapy, will return to a fully normal and productive life completely fulfilling their expected span of years. In all such cases, however, substantial maintenance doses will be required to prevent the body's metabolic barrier from breaking once again at the weak spot of its old rupture.

In time, of course, the generation so affected will die off, and, with it, the last vestiges of the Twentieth Century's greatest medical catastrophe will disappear into the history books.

But what of the *other* cancer? The malignancy that is spreading through the body-politic and destroying its substance, what of that? Are we to save our health only so that we and our children can become more productive serfs?

There are many parallels that can be drawn between cancer and totalitarianism. Government, for example, is much the same as trophoblast. Like its counterpart in our bodies, government is both normal and necessary. No civilization could come to birth without it. It is a vital part of the life cycle.

Government, however, just like the trophoblast, must be held in check to prevent it from growing, feeding upon, and ultimately destroying its host — the civilization itself. In a literal sense, every dead civilization of the past either has been killed quickly by infection from foreign sources — the military force of conquerors — or has died the slow, horrible death of cancer, as the internal trophoblast of government grew to monstrous proportions and gradually consumed all there was. In the end, the civilization and the cancerous government were buried together in a common grave.

In biological terms, the trophoblast cell is held in check by the *intrinsic* action of the pancreatic enzymes and by the *extrinsic* action of vitamin B_{17}. If either is deficient, the body is in danger. If both are weak, the trophoblast will grow and tragedy is certain. In terms of society, government is held in check by the *intrinsic* action of constitutional safeguards such as the division of political powers and other built-in checks and balances. It is restrained also by the *extrinsic* action of public awareness and vigilance over elected officials. If either is deficient, the civilization is in danger. If both are weak, government will grow and the civilization will die.

The analogy is devastating. It is obvious that both our intrinsic and extrinsic defenses are in bad repair, if functioning at all. Supreme Court decisions one-by-one have toppled the constitutional restraints against federal centralism, and the public now appears to stand mesmerized before the dazzling crystal pendant of collectivism swinging from the fingers of Big Brother. And the totalitarian trophoblast is running wild.

Can our civilization be saved? Or has the cancer progressed too far? That, of course, is the urgent question asked by *every* cancer victim. And the answer is the same: "We won't know until we try."

In all honesty, the prospects do not look good. The disease is far advanced and, as of right now, there is little chance of an immediate halt to the progress. Our only course of attack is to begin to build up the natural defenses as rapidly as possible, particularly the extrinsic factor of public awareness and vigilance over elected officials. The intrinsic task of rebuilding constitutional safeguards will take a little longer but will follow as a secondary consequence of our efforts in the primary field.

What we must do, therefore, is to manufacture the vitamin of an aroused public opinion and inject it as rapidly and in as large doses as possible, into the body-politic. The heaviest doses should be injected directly into the tumor itself. Let the federal government — particularly the FDA — feel the powerful surge of this substance. It will be like selective poison to the malignant cell.

Specifically, the FDA must be cut back to size. There is absolutely no logic in granting our servant government the power to tell us what medicines or foods we may use. The *only* legitimate function of government in this field is to police labeling and packaging to insure that the public is correctly informed on what it buys. If the substance is dangerous, then it should be labelled as such but not withheld. In other words, give the people the facts and let them decide for themselves. Ninety-nine percent of the present function of the FDA should be abolished!

After the tumor has begun to wither at the primary site of the FDA, our vitamin of public opinion then must be injected into the bloodstream of Congress and allowed to circulate freely into every other agency and bureau of government as well. Each and every one of them is just as riddled with the malignancy of despotism as is the FDA, and each and every one of them needs to be brought back under control.

Yes, with sufficient effort and sacrifice, the patient *can* be saved. Whether or not our humane civilization and our freedoms can be *fully* restored is, of course, another matter. They probably cannot. The cancer of collectivism already is too far advanced and the damage is too great to permit a full recovery. For one thing, our people have lost the spirit of independence and self-discipline that are prerequisites for such recovery. They have grown soft and dependent upon their government subsidies, welfare payments, retirement benefits, unemployment compensation, tax-supported loans, price-supports, minimum wage laws, health care, government schools, public transportation, food stamps, and federal housing. Realistically speaking, it is too much to expect that they will voluntarily give up any of these things even if they know that, in the long run, it will be better for the system *and* for them. They still will not do it.

Conditions in America today were clearly seen almost two hundred years ago by the French philosopher, de Tocqueville. Viewing the seeds of centralism sown into our infant government even then, de Tocqueville predicted that the proud and defiant American would, in time, come to view government intervention in his daily life, not as acts of "despotism" which would drive him to another rebellion, but as "benefits" bestowed by a kind and paternalistic state. Describing the effect of such a system upon any people who embrace it, he wrote:

> The will of man is not shattered, but softened, bent and guided. Men are seldom forced by it to act, but they are constantly restrained from acting. Such a power does not destroy . . . but it compresses, enervates, extinguishes and stupefies a people, till each nation is reduced to nothing better than a flock of timid and industrious animals, of which the government is the shepherd.[1]

With the reading of these lines from out of the past, one is forcibly reminded of the words of Fred Gates, guiding spirit of Rockefeller's tax-exempt foundations: "In our dreams we have limitless resources, and the people yield themselves with perfect docility to our molding hands."

The cancer of collectivism can be halted, but the damage it has already done cannot be repaired. Our civilization can be restored to a high degree of political health and vigor. Nevertheless we will have to live with our wounds and our scars.

But that is not so bad as it may seem at first. Like any cancer patient, we come eventually to the realization that it could be a lot worse. Instead of bemoaning the fact that we may never regain the total vigor of our past, we can rejoice over the opportunity to retain life at all. Considering the alternative of a lifeless existence in the dull, collective monotone of Orwell's *1984,* we should thank God for this opportunity to salvage as much of our freedoms as we still have. Instead of giving up in

---

[1]As quoted by Garrison, *The Dictocrats, op. cit.,* p. 306.

despair and surrendering our bodies and our minds to the ravages of a progressive and painful end, we should leap at the chance —*any* chance — to isolate the ugly tumor of totalitarianism and rebuild what we can of our natural defenses against its spread. Any other course is unconscionable and stupid.

Let us, therefore, get down to specifics. All the rhetoric in the world is useless unless it is coupled with a tangible and realistic plan of action. Let us close this study by outlining at least the main features of that plan.

First of all, as mentioned previously, the FDA should be knocked down to size. Perhaps it should be abolished altogether. If its function were merely to guarantee honest labeling and packaging, there is no reason why some other agency such as that in charge of standards, weights, and measures couldn't handle the job.

Would this result in a new wave of drug tragedies, another crop of thalidomide babies? Of course not. Let us suppose that the FDA had only the power to require the label and literature of thalidomide to state that "this drug is dangerous for use by women during periods of potential pregnancy and may result in deformed infants." Thalidomide is available only through the prescription of a licensed physician. No physician would prescribe such a drug without first considering this warning, and it is likely that he would not prescribe it to any woman of child-bearing age. But the decision would be his *based upon full knowledge of the facts,* which is the way it should be. Thalidomide received a great deal of publicity, but it is no different than hundreds of other dangerous drugs that may be obtained only through a prescription. If one is banned, they all should be banned. The FDA, however, does not need the power to ban these drugs in order to protect our health. Honest labeling is more than adequate.

Nicholas von Hoffman, commentator for the Washington Post, confirmed this point when he wrote:

> It would be very hard to show that the FDA's power to ban or regulate the sale of a compound has worked to protect the public. Even in a celebrated case like thalidamide, what was important was warning pregnant women they'd jeopardize their babies if they took it. The power to insist on proper labeling so doctor and patients are adequately warned about the properties of drugs is what's decisive.
>
> But the power to forbid something's use, to stop research, why should the government have such power? To protect us? But we're not wards of the state, we're citizens.[1]

[1] "And if it Works . . . .," *The Washington Post,* June 4, 1971.

Nor is Mr. von Hoffman alone. Milton Friedman, of *Newsweek* magazine, agrees:

> The 1962 amendments to the Food, Drug, and Cosmetic Act should be repealed. They are doing vastly more harm than good. To comply with them, FDA officials must condemn innocent people to death. In the present climate of opinion, this conclusion will seem shocking to most of you — better to attack motherhood or even apple pie. Shocking it is — but that does not keep it from also being correct. Indeed, further studies may well justify the even more shocking conclusion that the FDA itself should be abolished.[1]

Abolish the FDA? But who would enforce standards of sanitation in preparation of food and drugs? Good grief! Since when do free men need government to tell them how to be clean? To start off, the FDA's performance in that field has been far from a paragon of excellence. But more important, any manufacturer in his right mind would naturally seek the highest possible sanitation standards if for no other reason than to avoid lawsuits from customers. One can be sure also that inspectors from companies that underwrite the manufacturer's product liability insurance have more than a casual interest in their client's stan-

---

[1] "Frustrating Drug Advancement," *Newsweek*, Jan. 8, 1973.

dards of sanitation. Since violation of the underwriter's standards can result in higher premiums or in cancellation of the insurance, the manufacturer would be a fool to ignore them. At any rate, local health agencies are more than adequate for the job of maintaining sanitation standards. Federal inspectors are no more intelligent or wise than state, county, or city inspectors, and there is no need for such wasteful duplication.

Contamination and adulteration of food and drug products are bound to happen from time to time, of course. But they also happen under the present system of FDA guardianship. The truth is that the FDA serves no reasonable or necessary function in this field and should be withdrawn from it completely.

It is time to stop this nonsense about humbly petitioning the FDA to grant us permission to test Laetrile, to sell apricot kernels, to take high-potency vitamins, or to do any of a hundred other *specific* things which it prohibits. Asking the FDA to approve these is like asking the wolf to okay the lunch in Little Red Riding Hood's basket. It is time we realized that the FDA has no business in this field at all. We must stop asking meekly for permission and throw the rascal out on his ear!

How is this to be accomplished? Returning again to the trophoblast analogy, our first task is to manufacture and inject the extrinsic factor which is the vitamin of public opinion. The intrinsic factor will be the re-building of legislative, judicial, and constitutional safeguards. Within this category, our most immediate work is in the courts. We must provide legal defense for those physicians and distributors who have the courage to risk their reputations and their livelihoods (to say nothing of a jail sentence) by standing against the bureaucracy. Of necessity, however, the legal battles fought on their behalf initially must be on narrow grounds and defensive in nature. The primary thrust of most of these cases will be merely to prove that the use of vitamin B_{17} does not in fact violate the law.

The objective here is not to change the law, (for laws are not changed in court) but merely to keep the defendant out of jail. Even if these cases are successful, however, they do not really solve the problem, for the FDA is still fully operable and free to rewrite its rulings, to tighten them up so as to override the court's decision. Sooner or later, the doctor or the distributor will be under arrest again.

Obviously, the law must be changed. At the very least, that means legislation specifically to remove the FDA from jurisdiction over vitamins, or a lawsuit on behalf of cancer victims challenging the constitutionality of the infringement upon their rights. Both lines of attack must be launched.

The ultimate contest, however, will be fought on the larger battleground of whether the government should have *any* power over our food, medicine, or health. It will be only around this question that the many issues will lose their fuzzy edges and a chance for a real victory will become possible. In order to abolish the FDA, or at least to restrict its operation to truth in labeling and packaging, we will need either legislation passed through Congress or a constitutional amendment. We should pursue *both*.

The possibility of a constitutional revision is not as extreme as it may sound. In fact, Dr. Benjamin Rush of Philadelphia, a signer of the Declaration of Independence, a member of the Continental Congress, Surgeon-General of Washington's armies, and probably the foremost American physician of his day, had urged his colleagues to include "medical liberty" in the First Amendment at the time it was drafted. He wrote:

> Unless we put medical freedom into the Constitution, the time will come when medicine will organize into an undercover dictatorship. . . . To restrict the art of healing to one class of men and deny equal privileges to others will constitute the Bastille of medical science. All such laws are un-American and despotic . . . and have no place in a republic . . . . The Constitution of this Republic should make special provision for medical freedom as well as religious freedom.[1]

It is a startling fact that there are more human beings alive right now than the sum total of all those born from the beginning of time to the beginning of this century. If we fail to heed Dr. Rush's advice; if we fail to realize that medical freedom is just as important as the other freedoms guaranteed by the Bill of Rights; then, before this century is over, more human beings will have died of cancer than

---

[1]As quoted by Bealle, *The New Drug Story, op. cit.,* p. 188, and by Dr. Dean Burk in *The Cancer News Journal,* May/June, 1973, p. 4.

the total of all men who have ever lived on this earth prior to that time. And this will happen in a century during which the solution was *known* and written in the scientific record.

In the days ahead the controversy over medical freedom will intensify. Let it come. The reputations of honest men will be tarnished by the FDA, and respectable business ventures will be ruined. So be it. Innocent men will be tried before corrupt or frightened judges and thrown in prison. It is maddening but it cannot be helped, for the battle is not of our choosing. Our only alternative is to resist or not to resist — to fight back with all we have or to surrender and perish. Yes, the battle is grim, but the stakes are high. We must not be intimidated by the strength of the opposition, and, above all, we must not fail. *Someone* simply has to stand up against the bureaucracy. And we are the ones who must do it!

You and your family now may become secure from the threat of cancer. But, in most cases, that is only because someone else has taken the time to bring these facts to your attention. Can you do less for others?

Join with us in this gigantic undertaking. Make this your personal crusade. Dedicate yourself to *freedom of choice,* not just in cancer therapy, but in all spheres of human activity. Once we get the government off our backs, then all things become possible. The biological and political trophoblasts will be conquered together and man, at last, will inherit the bountiful world of health and freedom that is his birthright — a *world without cancer.*

APPENDIX

SUGGESTED MECHANISMS OF ACTION OF VITAMIN B_{17}

*Charles Gurchot, Ph.D.**

Oral doses of vitamin B_{17} seem not to be much affected by the action of the acid medium of the stomach, but pass into the intestine where the substance is acted upon by bacterial enzymes.

In the intestine the enzyme complex Emulsin containing the enzymes β-glucosidase, Benzocyanase, and others, degrades the Amygdalin into four components: Hydrocyanic acid, Benzaldehyde, Prunasin, and Mandelonitrile, which are absorbed into the lymph and portal circulations.

Cyanide is converted to thiocyanate probably in the blood circulation, and certainly in the liver by the enzyme rhodanese in the presence of sulfur-bearing compounds. The circulating thiocyanate exerts certain physiological effects on blood pressure and thyroid action, and is not excreted rapidly. (In the absence of the enzyme or sulfur, the cyanide may form cyano-hemoglobin.)

In cancer patients some thiocyanate finds its way to the site of the cancer lesion.

The benzaldehyde formed in the intestine

*Reprinted with permission from *Physician's Handbook of Vitamin B_{17} Therapy*, (Science Press International, Sausalito, Calif., 1973).

probably has no important function, but in the circulation forms benzoic acid and is excreted as benzaldehyde hippurate.

Prunasin (the mono-glucoside of Mandelonitrile) can circulate in the body and reach the malignant lesion, and as such hydrolyse to liberate hydrocyanic acid, benzaldehyde, and one glucose molecule.

Prunasin may also be changed in the liver to Mandelonitrile glucuronoside. This conversion to the glucuronoside may take place in two different ways: 1) by combining with glucuronic acid, which would remove one sugar molecule; 2) by oxidation of the terminal alcohol group of the prunasin glucose molecule.

The mandelonitrile is absorbed from the intestine, going directly to the liver where it is converted by the detoxification mechanism of joining it to glucuronic acid. It may then be excreted as the glucuronide or find its way to the site of a malignant lesion.

Glucosidic enzymes at the lesion may hydrolyse prunasin into its components cyanide, benzaldehyde, and a glucose molecule, to interfere with tissue respiration. In the process of enzyme hydrolysis pure mandelonitrile, as an intermediate step, may be released.

Mandelonitrile of itself may undergo spontaneous hydrolysis to HCN and benzaldehyde or enzymatic decomposition by benzocyanase present in the emulsin complex.

Mandelonitrile glucuronide may be hydrolysed

at the tumor site by β-glucuronidase to yield HCN, benzaldehyde and glucuronic acid.

Benzaldehyde released through these processes at the site of the malignant lesion may be reduced to benzyl alcohol, and combine with the thiocyanate to form benzo thiocyanate. This compound is further reduced to a thio-alcohol, benzo mercaptain, and hydrocyanic acid. In this manner HCN reappears and may continue to do so in a cyclic manner until the intracellular conditions that permit the reaction involved in the cycle are no longer operative.

These phenomena would explain the synergistic effect of benzaldehyde and cyanide in depressing the metabolism of mouse tumor slices in the Warburg apparatus.

In the absence of rhodanese the cyanide probably exerts its lethal effects on cell respiration, which is relatively small in cancer cells, by interference with the cytochrome oxidase enzymes.

Cyanide, either as such, or as mandelonitrile, may combine with glucose to form cyanoglucose, which, on hydrolysis forms a glucuronide heptose analogous to gluconic acid, which would be excreted, or dehydrogenated to heptose, which also would be excreted. The conditions for this transformation exist in cancer tissue and would constitute anti-gluconeogenesis.

SICKLE CELL ANEMIA AND THE METABOLITES OF VITAMIN B_{17}

*By Robert G. Houston**

Summary

The rarity and mildness of sickle cell anemia in black parts of Africa and the West Indies as compared with those in the U.S. is associated with a prevalence of thiocyanate yielding foods in native tropical diets, and parallels a divergence in the incidence of both neoplastic and rheumatoid diseases. Cyanate, an inhibitor of sickling, develops from the oxidation of thiocyanate, which is formed from vitamin B_{17}, or nitrilosides (beta-cyanogenetic glucosides), in food plants. Clinical use of cyanate and of thiocyanate has ameliorated sickle cell anemia at dosage levels derivable from African diets. It is proposed that the disease represents an unrelieved nutritional dependency on thiocyanate and nitrilosides in those genetically affected.

Introduction

Many chronic anemias were proved to be nutritional deficiency conditions. Involvement of nutritional factors in sickle cell anemia has precedent

---

*Reprinted with permission of the author, 115 E. 86th Street, New York, N.Y. 10028

in reports[1-3] that this genetic disease is associated with a high folic acid requirement. Recent reports that cyanate inhibits sickling[4-12] may imply, as proposed by Krebs[13], a specific dietary basis. The purpose of this study is to examine a reciprocal correlation between the occurrence of sickle cell anemia and the thiocyanate yield of African and American diets, which suggests the hypothesis that sickle cell anemia may be a genetically determined nutritional anemia involving dependence on cyanate precursors.

Cyanate, thiocyanate and sickling

Cerami, Manning and Gillette have shown that cyanate irreversibly inhibits the sickling of red blood cells *in vitro*[4,5] and extends the life span of treated sickle cells to near normal range *in vivo*[6,7]. On a scientific basis established by the work of Pauling, Ingram, Murayama and Nalbandian, they found that cyanate permanently binds with the distinctive amino-terminal valine residues of hemoglobin S resulting in a protein with functional properties more like those of normal hemoglobin A[5]. Others have confirmed its antisickling effects[8,9].

Clinical trial of cyanate used orally on sickle cell anemia patients was reported by Gillette *et al.*[10-12] at Rockefeller University as finding definite hematological improvement and decrease in the hemolytic anemia, without serious adverse side effect. It was noted however that since the cells inhibited from sickling will eventually be replaced, "this therapy would have to be continued for the life of the patient"[11].

Life-long dependence on an exogenous chemical factor for health would characterize a nutritional dependency, were the factor or its precursors obtainable from the natural diet. For cyanate, this is in fact the case.

Cyanate is formed as a product of the oxidation of thiocyanate [14-16], which is catalyzed in the erythrocyte by hemoglobin[17]. Hence, thiocyanate may also be expected to produce clinical benefit in sickle cell anemia.

Indeed, in 1932 Torrance and Schnabel[18] discovered that thiocyanate (Potassium Sulphocyanate) promptly and entirely relieved the anemic sickle cell crisis after all else had failed. Incredibly this remarkable finding, 40 years in advance of current research, was subsequently neglected. The fact that the daily dosage of thiocyanate used (500 mg.) was less than half the daily dosage of sodium cyanate (1000-1200 mg.) used by Gillette *et al.*[11] suggests that thiocyanate has at least a similar degree of efficacy in the disease as cyanate.

The direct power of thiocyanate ion to prevent sickling has been proposed by Pauling [19] on the basis that it rivals urea as a hydrogen bond breaking agent, and thus shares the rationale for urea therapy[20] in preventing sickle cell crises.

Dietary derivation of thiocyanate

It is known that the thiocyanate ion is physiologically present in mammalian fluids [21], and that it is derivable from the beta-cyanogenetic glucosides in food plants[22]. Widespread in the vegetable kingdom, these were termed nitrilosides and designated vitamin B_{17} by Krebs[23] in light of various reported physiological functions[24,25], including clinically observed hematopoietic effects[26,27].

Nitrilosides, which are considered in themselves nontoxic[22-24,28,29], form thiocyanate upon their hydrolysis in the body, through the action with sulfur of the enzyme rhodanese[30] which is found in all normal body tissues[31]. A similar enzymatic conversion can occur in plants, with a sometimes substantial development of preformed thiocyanates[32].

Clinical administration of the nitriloside amygdalin thus fosters a rise in thiocyanate in the body fluids[33,34]. Thiocyanate levels many times that of controls have been found in the serum of animals feeding on nitrilosidic grasses[35]. High plasma levels of thiocyanate are produced in rats[36] and in humans[37-39] by cassava, a tropical food plant rich in both nitriloside and thiocyanate[40]. Wide fluctuations in the thiocyanate metabolic pool result from such influences[22].

Will regularly occurring high blood levels of cyanate and thiocyanate from dietary precursors irreversibly inhibit the sickling of red blood cells and thereby prevent the general manifestation of sickle cell anemia? If so, we should expect rare or mild occurrence of the disease in susceptible populations on thiocyanate-yielding diets, and its full homozygous occurrence and morbidity only in populations whose diets are devoid of significant thiocyanate sources. Further, we should expect some correlation between dietary dosages and those found clinically useful.

Thiocyanate yield of African and U.S. diets

Food production figures[41] indicate that 80% of the tropical African diet may consist of thiocyanate-yielding foods. The main staples of sub-Sahara Africa are cassava, yams (*Dioscorea* sp.), and sorghum and millet grains [41]. Nitrilosidic beans are also eaten.

Sorghum and millet contain (up to 0.5%) the nitriloside dhurrin, and cassava is a comparable, though variable, source of the nitriloside linamarin (phaseolunatin)[22]. Both nitrilosides can produce an amount of thiocyanate equivalent to 1/5th their weight, or twice their HCN component[24].

In addition, linamarin yields acetone and dhurrin yields an isomer of salicylic acid[23], which may be acetylated by, for example, acetic acid formed from the reaction of HCN with hydrochloric acid in the stomach[32]. This signifies additional antisickling potential in view of a report[42] that acetylsalicylic acid, or aspirin, can increase the oxygen affinity of sickle cell hemoglobin *in vitro* to a level at which sickling is generally inhibited, and retards the formation of prostaglandin which induces sickling.

The common practice of prolonged soaking and fermentation of cassava considerably dissipates its nitriloside content, although this may be compensated in part by the addition of sugar in some preparations which, with enzymes and aldehydes of the plant, can cause free HCN to disappear with the formation of glucocyanohydrin[40]. Some cyanogenetic glucoside may survive all methods of preparation[43], but highest levels would occur in dry, unfermented, bitter varieties of cassava which are eaten in some rural areas[37,43,44].

Traces of HCN in cassava, arising from the premature catabolism of linamarin in the bruised plant, would be detoxified in the body to both thiocyanate and cyanate[45]. The safety of the intact nitriloside *per se* consists in the functional preponderance in the body of the NCH-detoxifying enzyme rhodanese over the hydrolyzing enzyme beta-glycosidase[27,30].

In addition, cassava in many forms may be a rich source of preformed thiocyanate. Oke[32,40] in Nigeria reports that compared with a thiocyanate range in other vegetables of 0.4-4.1 mg%, a figure of 60.0 mg% was obtained for 'gari,' a traditional native food made by fermentation of cassava, and 70.0-80.0 mg% for cassava flour, also, 50.0-60.0 mg% for yam flour, which too is widely used in Africa. With its additional 60% water content, a 200 g yam may contain 40 mg of thiocyanate.

One kilogram of such foodstuffs per day[41,36,44] could thus provide the native African with up to a gram of thiocyanate. This is the oral dosage level found successful in sickle cell anemia in the Rockefeller University clinical trial of cyanate[11], and is twice the dosage of thiocyanate successfully used to resolve sickle cell crises by Torrance and Schnabel[18].

In comparison, the American diet lacks significant nitriloside sources[24]. It also appears to lack substantial sources of preformed thiocyanate. Yams might be an exception; however, these are only occasionally eaten. Among common vegetables the highest thiocyanate levels are found in the cabbage family (*Brassica*): 0.7-10.2 mg per 100 g of fresh material; while milk may provide 2-8 mg per quart[46]. It is reasonable to assume that the American black, even if he ate half a pound of cabbage a day and could drink a quart of milk, would generally not obtain more than 25 mg of thiocyanate from his daily diet, or about 1/40th the estimated maximum African intake.

The American black population may thus be regarded as controls for an African population undergoing continuous cyanate treatment, in an immense natural experiment. What were the associated results?

Sickle cell anemia in the U.S., Africa and the West Indies

Raper[47] concluded that while sickle cell anemia occurs in 1 in about 50 sicklers in the U.S., its incidence is less than 1 in 1000 sicklers in Africa. The clinical impression is not only that sickle cell anemia is rare in Africa compared with America, but also that morbid features of the disease are probably less common in Africa. This is in spite of the fact that, probably due to natural selection for the malaria resistance conferred by the gene[48], the incidence of sickle cell trait over tropical Africa is nearly three times as high as in U.S. blacks.

Sickle cell trait, the relatively benign heterozygous condition, occurs in up to 10% of the 22 million blacks in the U.S., of whom sickle cell anemia affects nearly 50,000[49], an incidence fully compatible with the mathematically predictable genetic occurrence of the homozygous condition[50] in which the gene is double-dominant.

By contrast, in Africa sickle cell trait affects up to 25% of a susceptible population of nearly 300 million blacks[51]. There is a parabolic relationship between trait incidence and homozygosity: if the trait is 9% there occur 0.2% homozygotes, but if the trait is 25% there occur 1.6%, or 8 times as many homozygotes[52]. The African population represents, therefore, the birth of several million homozygotes from the union of trait carriers.

Yet in the entire quarter century of 1925-1950, less than 100 cases of sickle cell anemia had been recorded in Africa for all ages[47]. Not a single case was recorded in Nigeria until 1952[53].

Neel[54], noting the paucity of case reports of this disease from Africa, has questioned whether the results of homozygosity for the gene were the same in Africa as in the U.S. Yet he found in the U.S. no apparent correlation between such results and the amount of Caucasian admixture.

The evidence thus suggests the existence in Africa of an inhibiting environmental factor on the clinical manifestation of the disease. An unknown "protective factor" was in fact postulated to account for the rarity of sickle cell anemia in South and East Africa[55]. In this regard it is significant that the homozygous sickle cell condition, which is the genetic basis for the anemia, has been reported occurring in an asymptomatic form in African adults[56-59]. This would make general detection difficult indeed, and indicates the involvement of some non-genetic factor.

Motulsky[50], recognizing the very low prevalence of sickle cell anemia in underdeveloped areas of Africa, attributes this to the death of most patients in early infancy. From his experience in Uganda, Lehmann[56] doubted this view on the grounds that "even if they had died in early infancy, it would have been such a 'slaughter of the innocents' that it could not have escaped our attention."

In severely malnourished areas of the central Congo it was reported that the majority of sickle cell homozygotes succumb before the age of two[48,52], a finding some geneticists quickly generalized. But in Rhodesia the average onset of the disease is not until the age of nearly six, a year later than in the better fed U.S., and its clinical appearance is both infrequent and relatively mild[60]. The Rhodesian patients demonstrated greater resistance to malaria than normal individuals or those with sickle cell trait. A factor moderating the severity of sickle cell disease thus seems to occur in infancy beyond the age of 6 months, before which the infant is protected by fetal hemoglobin[61].

In Rhodesia, Uganda, and East Africa, millet porridge, rich in nitriloside, is the standard weaning food, commencing at age 6 months[62]. In West Africa, the weaning food is cornmeal porridge, starting later[62]. Thomas[63] in West Africa reports that almost 40% of the infants receive no milk or fish up to the age of two years, and that in some regions cassava and yams are seldom given to infants. Thus they may lack the postulated protection of dietary sources of thiocyanate, and lack also the sulfur-containing amino acids, which are involved in its formation and conservation[32]. This may explain the occurrence of sickle cell anemia in infants in some areas of West Africa[64], and its mitigation and rarity in later age groups[58,65,66], when the normal cassava, yam and millet dietary pattern is in effect.

As is well-known, sickle cell anemia is relatively benign in the West Indies[67]. Those with the homozygous condition are found living to elderly ages in Jamaica, and often deny ever having experienced serious crises. The Jamaican diet is rich in folic acid[67], and here too cassava and yams are staples[68].

Electrophoretic evidence

Although overall infant mortality, affecting all genotypes, is much higher in Africa than in the U.S., conventional electrophoretic analyses of blood specimens of infant and adult populations indicate that the African sickle cell homozygotes have the same 20-35% survival to adulthood as to the American homozygotes[48,69]. Since the gene is more frequent, this means there must be many more of them as a proportion of the adult population than in America, yet the clinical disease is much rarer in African adults[47]. New evidence suggests that the electrophoretic method on which such survival estimates are based may have considerably underestimated the situation in Africa, and accords with the observations of Konotey-Ahulu[70] in Ghana that the survival of the sickle cell homozygote may be a major factor explaining the high incidence of the gene in Africa.

Cyanate is capable of increasing the electrophoretic mobility of hemoglobin S, by conferring extra negative charges to the molecules[71]. Electrophoretic analysis of hemoglobin S treated by cyanate and a precursor shows an additional fraction with the faster mobility of hemoglobin A[72]. Hence, dietary availability of cyanate precursors may have masked many adult African sickle cell homozygotes (Hb SS) as heterozygotes (Hb AS or a variant) in electrophoretic studies.

Indirect evidence for such masking would include the mysterious increase, in excess of comparative viability, of 'heterozygotes' in later African age groups on electrophoresis, which parallels the per cent decrease of sickle homozygotes in such studies[69], and the virtually total absence of both clinical sickle cell anemia and the electrophoretic Hb SS patterns in all ages in rural tribes of Uganda showing the highest trait frequencies (40%), where the homozygote incidence for the gene must be 20 times that of blacks in the U.S.[66,73].

Wells and Itano[74] speculated that diet may influence variations observed in the electrophoretic patterns of sickle cell disease. It is pertinent that such rural tribes and older Africans would be more likely to adhere to native diets rich in cyanate precursors, using less processed, bitter forms of cassava higher in nitriloside, than would younger and more urbanized Africans[37,43,44].

Cancer in African and American blacks

One of the great epidemiological mysteries of Africa is the rarity and decrease of cancer in later age groups[75-77], quite contrary to the experience in the U.S. where cancer incidence increases with advancing age and cancer mortality is 18% higher in blacks than in whites[78].

The standardized, age-adjusted cancer rate of Uganda is one third that of blacks in the U.S.[76]. Surprisingly, from age 45 to 75 when spontaneous cancer shows its enormous increase, rising in American black women from an annual incidence of 543 to 1170 per 100,000, it decreases in rural Ugandan women from 223 to 41 per 100,000 — less than 1/20th the American rate (pre-1960 figures)[76]. Similarly, the elderly population of Ibadon, Nigeria has 1/10th the cancer rate of blacks of the same age in New York[77]. As Davies *et al.*[76] have observed, this phenomenon is of great significance to cancer research, for it indicates that there is not a necessary association between cancer and the biological effect of aging.

In this connection Schweitzer[79] has written that for several decades his hospital at Lamberene in Gabon did not see a single case of cancer among the cassava-eating native tribes, and he believed its subsequent occurrence to be due to the substitution of European canned and refined foods. Ohsawa[80] observed at Lamberene that cassava (manioc) comprised 80-90% of the original native diet, and that the wild manioc was eaten, the rest of the diet consisting of bitter green bananas and wild herbs, with little meat.

The rarity of cancer in these groups with relatively high nitriloside diets is of interest in view of the reported demonstrations of nitriloside as an anti-cancer agent[23,81] in cell culture[28,82], animals[83,84], and human patients[26,27,33,34,82], and as a dietary correlate in cancer-free animal and human populations[24,33].

Rheumatoid disease in Africa and the U.S.

Krebs[23], who related nitriloside deficiency to the etiology of neoplasia, has proposed that the alleviation of rheumatoid disease by salicylates may have a preventive, nutritional counterpart in the derivability of such compounds from the metabolism of dietary nitrilosides (vitamin B_{17}).

Whereas rheumatoid disease afflicts over ten million individuals in the U.S., incapacitating one million, very few cases have been reported among the larger population of tropical Africa, a rarity which has defied explanation[85]. Significantly, a salicylic acid isomer is nutritionally available from the nitriloside dhurrin in millet and sorghum grains[23], which are staples in West Africa and throughout tropical Africa[41,63]. This may account for the extreme rarity of acute rheumatism in the Gold Coast[86] and the uncommon occurrence of rheumatoid arthritis and osteoarthritis throughout the African tropics[87]. It may also contribute to the alleviation of sickle cell anemia in these areas, in view of laboratory[42] and clinical[88] evidence for a beneficial effect of aspirin in sickle cell disease, although aspirin has often failed to relieve the pain of sickle cell crisis[86].

Implications

The formation of several promising antisickling agents — cyanate, thiocyanate, and aspirin-related compounds — as metabolic products of vitamin B_{17} (nitriloside) amplifies the probability that it is the root protective factor for carriers of the sickle cell gene, homozygotes and also heterozygotes, who may be affected in stress conditions[51]. Subsidiary mechanisms of action are thus to be expected. For example, the formation of methemoglobin in the generation of cyanate from thiocyanate which occurs in the red blood cell[17] may reduce the concentration of hemoglobin capable of sickling within the cell. Clinical induction of methemoglobin for this purpose was found to inhibit sickling and prolong red cell survival, although the inducing agents used had unacceptable properties[89].

Since clinical and dietary dosages are comparable, clinical amelioration of sickle cell anemia by cyanate[10-12] and by thiocyanate[18] must logically represent protective effects of thiocyanate-yielding native diets in parts of Africa and the West Indies where the disease is generally rare or mild. Its full homozygous occurrence in blacks in the U.S., where the diet yields little thiocyanate, may represent therefore an unrelieved nutritional dependency on cyanate precursors, in association with which sickle cell genes must have evolved in their ancestral tropical habitat. It follows that sickle cell anemia may constitute a genetically determined nutritional deficiency disease, involving a dependency on thiocyanate and its precursors, the nitrilosides.

This hypothesis would predict clinical value of

nitriloside (Laetrile) and thiocyanate-yielding diets in the treatment of sickle cell anemia.

The association in Africa between rarity of neoplastic and rheumatoid diseases and elevated levels of dietary nitrilosides suggests, in light of the therapeutic applications of the vitamin and its metabolites, the potential usefulness of nitriloside-containing foods or supplements to block the age-associated increase of spontaneous cancer and rheumatoid disease, as well as the occurrence of sickle cell anemia, in other populations.

REFERENCES FOR HOUSTON ARTICLE

[1]Pierce, L. F., Rath, C.F. "Evidence for folic acid deficiency in the genesis of anemic sickle cell crisis." *Blood,* 1962, *20,* 19.

[2]Lindenbaum, J. "Folic acid deficiency in sickle cell anemia." *New Engl. J. Med.,* 1963, *269,* 875.

[3]Watson-Williams, E.J. "Role of folic acid in the treatment of sickle cell disease," *in* Abnormal Haemoglobins in Africa (edited by J. Jonxis); p. 435. Davis, Philadelphia, 1965.

[4]Cerami, A., Manning, J. M. "Potassium cyanate as an inhibitor of the sickling of erythrocytes in vitro." *Proc. natn. Acad. Sci. U.S.A., 1971, 68,* 1180.

[5]Manning, J. M., Cerami, A., Gillette, P. N., deFuria, F.G., Miller, D. R. "Chemical and biological aspects of the inhibition of red blood cell sickling by cyanate." *Adv. exp. Med. Biol.,* 1972, *28,* 253.

[6]Gillette, P. N., Manning, J. M., Cerami A. "Increased survival of sickle cell erythrocytes after treatment in vitro with sodium cyanate." *Proc. natn. Acad. Sci. U.S.A., 1971, 68,* 2791.

[7]Cerami, A. "Cyanate as an inhibitor of red-cell sickling." *New Engl. J. Med., 1972, 287,* 807.

[8]May, A., Bellingham, A. J., Huehna, E. R. "Effects of cyanate on sickling." *Lancet,* 1972, *i,* 658.

[9]Segal, G. B., Feig, S. A., Metzer, W. C., McCaffrey, R. P. "Effects of urea and cyanate on sickling in vitro." *New Engl. J. Med., 1972, 287,* 59.

[10]Gillette , P. N., Peterson, C. M., Manning, J. M., Cerai, A. "Decrease in the hemolytic anemia of sickle cell disease after administration of sodium cyanate." *J. clin. Inv.,* 1972, *51,* 36a.

[11]Gillette, P. N., Peterson, C. M., Manning, J. M., Cerami, A. "Preliminary clinical trials with cyanate." *Adv. exp. Med. Biol.,* 1972, *28,* 261.

[12]Cerami, A., Manning, J. M., Gillettep, P. N., de Furia, F., Miller, D. Gradiano, J. H., Peterson, C. M. "Effect of cyanate on red blood cell sickling." *Fed. Proc.,* 1973, *32,* 1668.

[13]Krebs, E. T., Jr. Personal communications, 1972.

[14]Wilson, I. R., Harris, G. M. "Oxidation of thiocyanate ion by hydrogen peroxide. 1. The pH-independent reaction," *J. Am. chem. Soc.,* 1960, *82,* 4515.

[15]Oram, J. D., Reiter, B. "The inhibition of streptococci by lactoperoxidase, thiocyanate, and hydrogen peroxide." *Biochem. J.,* 1966, *100,* 382.

[16]Chung. J., Wood, J. L. "Oxidation of thiocyanate to cyanide and sulfate by the lactopersoxidase-hydrogen peroxide system." *Arch. Biochem. Biophys.,* 1970, *141, 73.*

[17]Chung, J., Wood, J. L. "Oxidation of thiocyanate to cyanide catalyzed by hemoglobin." *J. biol. Chem.,* 1971, *246,* 555.

[18]Torrance, E. G., Schnabel, T. G. "Potassium Sulphocyanate: a note on its use for the painful crises in sickle cell anemia." *Ann. intern. Med.,* 1932, *6,* 782.

[19]Pauling, L. Personal Communication, 1973.

[20]Nalbandian, R. M., Murayama, M. Sickle Cell Hemoglobin: Molecule to Man; p. 133. Little, Brown, Boston, 1973.

[21]Funderburk, C. F., Van Middlesworth, L. "Effect of thiocyanate concentration on thiocyanate distribution and excretion." *Proc. Soc. exp. Biol. Med.,* 1971, *136,* 149.

[22]Montgomery, R. D. "Cyanogens," *in* Toxic Constituents of Plant Foodstuffs (edited by K. Liener): p. 143. Academic Press, New York, 1969.

[23]Krebs, E. T., Jr. "The nitrilosides (vitamin B_{17}): their nature, occurrence, and metabolic significance. Antineoplastic vitamin B_{17}." *J. appl. Nutr.,* 1970, *22,* 75.

[24]Krebs, E. T., Jr. "The nitrilosides in plants and animals: nutritional and therapeutic implications," *in* The Laetriles — Nitrilosides — in the Prevention and Control of Cancer; p. 1. McNaughton Foundation, Montreal, 1967.

[25]De Long, E. W. "Neglected natural plant factors: the beta-cyanogenetic glucosides. Intestinal flora and the role of the *B*-cyanogenetic glucosides." *J. appl. Nutr.*, 1955, *8,* 343, 356.

[26]Morrone, J. A. "Chemotherapy of inoperable cancer: preliminary report of 10 cases treated with Laetrile." *Exp. Med. Surg.*, 1962, *20,* 299.

[27]Krebs, E. T., Jr., Bouziane, N. R. "Nitrilosides (Laetriles): their rational and clinical utilization in human cancer," *in* The Laetriles — Nitrilosides — in the Prevention and Control of Cancer; p. 49. McNaughton Foundation, Montreal, 1967.

[28]Burk, C., McNaughton, A. R. L., von Ardenne, M. "Hyperthermy of cancer cells with amygdalin-glucosidase and synergistic action of derived cyanide and benzaldehyde." *Minerva Chirurgica,* 1969, *24,* 1144.

[29]Dispensatory of the United States (1960 edition); p. 44.

[30]. Sumner, J. B., Somers, F. G. Chemistry and Methods of Enzymes; p. 98. Academic Press, New York, 1947.

[31]Rosenthal, O. "Distribution of rhodanese." *Fed. Proc.*, 1948, *7,* 181.

[32]Oke, O. L. "The role of hydrocyanic acid in nutrition." *World Rev. Nutr. Diet.*, 1969, *11,* 170.

[33]Nieper, H. A. "Problems of early cancer diagnosis and therapy: 1. Nitrilosides, particularly amygdalin, in cancer prophylaxis and therapy." *Agressologie,* 1970, *11,* 1.

[34]Navarro, M. D. "Laetrile therapy in cancer." *Philippine J. Cancer,* 1962, *4,* 204.

[35]Flux, D. S., Butler, G. W., Johnson, J. M., Glenday, A. C., Peterson, G. B. "Goitrogenic effects of white clover." *New Zealand J. Sci. Tech.*, 1956, *38,* 88.

[36]Osuntokun, B. O. "Cassava diet and cyanide metabolism in rats." *Brit. J. Nutr.*, 1970, *24,* 797.

[37]Monekosso, G. L., Wilson, J. "Plasma thiocyanate and vitamin B_{12} metabolism in Nigerian patients with neurological diseases." *Lancet,* 1966, *i,* 1062.

[38]Delange, F., Ermans, A. M. "Role of a dietary goitrogen in the etiology of endemic goiter on Idjwi Island." *Am. J. clin. Nutr.*, 1971, *24,* 1354.

[39]Osuntokun, B. O., Durowoju, J. E., McFarlane, H., Wilson, J. "Plasma amino-acids in the Nigerian Ataxic Neuropathy." *Brit. med. J.*, 1968, *3,* 647.

[40]Oke, O. L. "Cassava as food in Nigeria." *World Rev. Nutr. Diet.*, 1968, *9,* 227.

[41]Oke, O. L. "A nutrition policy for Nigeria." *World Rev. Nutr. Diet.*, 1972, *14,* 1.

[42]Klotz, I. M., Tam, J. W. O. "Acetylation of sickle cell hemoglobin by aspirin." *Proc. natn. Acad. Sci. U.S.A.*, 1973, *70,* 1313.

[43]Ekpechi, O. L., Dimitriadou, A., Fraser, R. "Goitrogenic activity of cassava (a staple Nigerian food)." Nature, 1966, *2,* 1138.

[44]Osuntokun, B. O. "An ataxic neuropathy in Nigeria." *Brain,* 1968, *91,* 215.

[45]Williams, R. T. Detoxification Mechanisms; p. 391. Wiley, New York, 1959.

[46]Van Etten, C. H. "Goitrogens," *in* Toxic Constituents of Plant Foodstuffs" (edited by I. Liener); pp. 117, 121. Academic Press, New York, 1969.

[47]Raper, A. B. "Sickle-cell disease in Africa and America: a comparison." *J. trop. Med. Hyg.*, 1950, *53,* 49.

[48]Neel, J. V. "Genetics of human hemoglobin differences." *Ann. hum. Genet.*, 1956, *21,* 1.

[49]Scott, R. B. "Health care priority and sickle cell anemia." J.A.M.A., 1970, *214,* 731.

[50]Motulsky, A. G. "Frequency of sickling disorders in U.S. Blacks." *New Engl. J. Med.*, 1973, *288,* 31.

[51]Bernstein, R. E. "Mass screens for sickle cell disease." *J.A.M.A.*, 1973, *223,* 438.

[52]Lambotte, C. "Sickle-cell anemia," *in* Disease of Children in the Subtropics and Tropics (edited by D. B. Jelliffe); p. 531. Arnold, London, 1970.

[53]Jelliffe, D. B. "Sickle-cell disease." *Trans. Roy. Soc. trop. Med. Hyg.*, 1952, *46*, 169.

[54]Neel, J. V. "Data pertaining to the population dynamics of sickle cell disease." *Am. J. hum. Genet.*, 1953, *5*, 154.

[55]Song, J. Pathology of Sickle Cell Disease, p. 95. Thomas, Springfield, Ill., 1971.

[56]Edington, G. M., Lehmann, H. "Expression of the sickle-cell gene in Africa," *Brit. med. J.*, 1955, *1*, 1308.

[57]Jacob, G. F. "A study of the survival rate of cases of sickle-cell anemia." *Brit. med. J.*, 1957, *1*, 738.

[58]Konotey-Ahulu, F. I. D., Ringelhann, B. "Sickle-cell anemia, sickle-cell thalassaemia, sickle-cell haemoglobin C thalassaemia in one Ghanaian family." *Brit. med. J.*, 1969, *1*, 607.

[59]Watson-Williams, E. J., Weatherall, D. J. "The laboratory characterization of human haemoglobin variants," *in* Abnormal Haemoglobins in Africa (edited by J. Jonxis); p. 99. Davis, Philadelphia, 1965.

[60]Bell, R. M. S., Gelfand, M. "Sickle cell disease in Rhodesia." *J. trop. Med. Hyg.*, 1971, *74*, 148.

[61]Song, J. Pathology of Sickle Cell Disease, p. 37. Thomas, Springfield, Ill., 1971.

[62]Swaminathan, M. "The nutrition and feeding of infants and preschool children in the developing countries." *World Rev. Nutr. Diet.*, 1968, *9*, 85.

[63]Thomas, H. M. "Some aspects of food and nutrition in Sierra Leone." *World Rev. Nutr. Diet.*, 1972, *14*, 48.

[64]Mabayoje, J. O. "Sickle-cell anaemia." *Brit. med. J.*, 1956, *1*, 194.

[65]Lehmann, H. "Sickle-cell anaemia." *Brit. med. J.*, 1953, *2*, 1217.

[66]Lehmann, H. "Sickle-cell anaemia and sickle-cell trait as homo- and heterozygous gene-combinations." *Nature*, 1951, *167*, 931.

[67]Serjeant, G. R., Richards, R., Barbor, P. R. H., Milner, P. F., "Relatively benign sickle-cell anaemia in 60 patients over 30 in the West Indies." *Brit. med. J.*, 1968, *3,* 86.

[68]Montgomery, R. D., Cruikshank, E. K., Robertson, W. B., McMenemey, W. H. "Clinical and pathological observations on Jamaican neuropathy." *Brain,* 1964, *87,* 27.

[69]Allison, A. C. "Notes on sickle-cell polymorphism." *Ann. hum. Genet.,* 1954, *19,* 39.

[70]Konotey-Ahulu, F. I. D. "Maintenance of high sickling rate in Africa — role of polygamy." *J. trop. Med. Hyg.,* 1970, *73,* 19.

[71]Pacheco, J., Melvin, M., Gabuzda, T. "Carbamylation of individual globin subunits by 14C-cyanate." *Clin. Res.,* 1972, *20,* 471.

[72]Kraus, L. M., Rasad, A., Kraus, A. P. "Carbamyl phosphate modification of hemoglobin S structure resulting in altered sickling." *Adv. exp. Med. Biol.,* 1972, *28,* 253.

[73]Lehmann, H., Raper, A. B. "Maintenance of high sickling rate in an African community." *Brit. med. J.,* 1956, *2,* 333.

[74]Wells, I. C., Itano, H. A. "Ratio of sickle-cell anemia hemoglobin to normal hemoglobin in sicklemics." *J. biol. Chem.,* 1051, *188,* 65.

[75]Edington, G. M., Gilles, H. M. Pathology in the Tropics; p. 580. Arnold, London, 1969.

[76]Davies, J. N. P., Wilson, B. A., Knowelden, J. "Cancer incidence of the African population of Kyadondo (Uganda)." *Lancet,* 1962, *2,* 328.

[77]Edington, G. M., Hendrickse, M. "Incidence and frequency of lymphoreticular tumors in Ibadan and the Western State of Nigeria." *J. natl. Cancer Inst.,* 1973, *50,* 1623.

[78]Fontaine, S. A., Henschke, U. K., Leffall, L. D., Jr., et al. "Comparison of the cancer deaths in the black and white U.S.A. population from 1949 to 1967." *Med. Ann. D.C.,* 1972, *41,* 293.

[79]Schweitzer, A. "How the white man's diet affects natives of Africa," *in* A Cancer Therapy (by M. Gerson); pp. 158-159. Dura Books, New York, 1958.

[80]Ohsawa, G. Cancer and the Philosophy of the Far East; pp. 8-10. Swan House, Binghamton, N.Y., 1971.

[81]Reitnaur, P.G. "Amygdalic acid glycoside in cancer research and cancer therapy." *Arzneim. Forsch.*, 1972, *22,* 1347.

[82]Rossi, B., Guidetti, E., Dekkers, C. "Clinical trial of chemotherapeutic treatment of advanced cancers with 1-mandelonitrile-beta-diglucoside," *in* The Laetriles — Nitrilosides — in the Prevention and Control of Cancer; p. 81. McNaughton Foundation, Montreal, 1967.

[83]McNaughton Foundation FDA — Investigative New Drug Application 6734, Amygdalin (Laetrile), 1970; pp. 247-248, 00080-00093.

[84]Burk, D. Unpublished observations, June, 1973.

[85]Felsenfeld. O. Synopsis of Clinical Tropical Medicine; p. 26. Mosby, St. Louis, 1965.

[86]Edington, G. M. "Sickle-cell diseases in the Accra district of the Gold Coast." *Brit. med. J.*, 1953, *2,* 957.

[87]Edington, G. M., Gilles, H. M. Pathology in the Tropics; p. 595. Arnold, London, 1969.

[88]Ndugwa, C. M., Kanyike, F. B. "Analysis of patients attending sickle cell anaemia clinic, New Mulago Hospital, 1970;-1971." *East African med. J.*, 1973, *50,* 189.

[89]Beutler, E. "The effect of methemoglobin formation in sickle cell disease." *J. clin. Invest.*, 1961, *40,* 1856.

INDEX